CONTRIBUTORS

Samuel H. Barondes

Herman Buschke

Diana Deutsch

M. S. Gazzaniga

Paul E. Gold

Robert L. Isaacson

Marcel Kinsbourne

Neal E. A. Kroll

James L. McGaugh

R. K. Nakamura

Allen M. Schneider

Larry R. Squire

Gordon Stanley

Saul Sternberg

Wayne A. Wickelgren

Frank Wood

SHORT-TERM MEMORY

SHORT-TERM MEMORY

Edited by

DIANA DEUTSCH
J. ANTHONY DEUTSCH
Department of Psychology
University of California, San Diego
La Jolla, California

ACADEMIC PRESS   *New York   San Francisco   London   1975*

A Subsidiary of Harcourt Brace Jovanovich, Publishers

ACADEMIC PRESS, INC.
111 Fifth Avenue, New York, New York 10003

United Kingdom Edition published by
ACADEMIC PRESS, INC. (LONDON) LTD.
24/28 Oval Road, London NW1

Library of Congress Cataloging in Publication Data

Deutsch, Diana.
        Short-term memory.

        Includes bibliographies and index.
        1.   Memory.   I.   Deutsch, J. Anthony, (date)   joint
author.   II.   Title.   [DNLM: 1.   Memory, Short-term.
WL102 D483s]
BF371.D47   153.1'22   74-31323
ISBN 0–12–213350–1

CONTENTS

Chapter 14.   A Single-Trace, Two-Process View of Memory
Storage Processes
Paul E. Gold and James L. McGaugh

Chapter 15.   Protein-Synthesis Dependent and Protein-Synthesis
Independent Memory Storage Processes
Samuel H. Barondes

LIST OF CONTRIBUTORS

Numbers in parentheses indicate the pages on which the authors' contributions begin.

SAMUEL H. BARONDES (379), *Department of Psychiatry, University of California, San Diego, La Jolla, California*

HERMAN BUSCHKE (73), *The Saul R. Korey Department of Neurology, Albert Einstein College of Medicine, Bronx, New York*

DIANA DEUTSCH (107), *Department of Psychology, University of California, San Diego, La Jolla, California*

M. S. GAZZANIGA (293), *Department of Psychology, State University of New York at Stony Brook, Stony Brook, New York*

PAUL E. GOLD (355), *Department of Psychobiology, School of Biological Sciences, University of California, Irvine, Irvine, California*

ROBERT L. ISAACSON (313), *Department of Psychology, University of Florida, Gainesville, Florida*

MARCEL KINSBOURNE (257), *Hospital for Sick Children, Toronto; Department of Paediatrics, University of Toronto; Department of Psychology, University of Waterloo, Waterloo, Ontario, Canada*

NEAL E. A. KROLL (153), *Department of Psychology, University of California, Davis, Davis, California*

JAMES L. McGAUGH (355), *Department of Psychobiology, School of Biological Sciences, University of California, Irvine, Irvine, California*

R. K. NAKAMURA (293), *Department of Psychology, State University of New York at Stony Brook, Stony Brook, New York*

ALLEN M. SCHNEIDER (339), *Department of Psychology, Swarthmore College, Swarthmore, Pennsylvania*

LARRY R. SQUIRE (1), *Department of Psychiatry, University of California, San Diego, La Jolla, California*

GORDON STANLEY (181), *Department of Psychology, University of Melbourne, Melbourne, Australia*

SAUL STERNBERG (195), *Bell Laboratories, Murray Hill, New Jersey*

WAYNE A. WICKELGREN (41,65,233), *Department of Psychology, University of Oregon, Eugene, Oregon*

FRANK WOOD (257), *Department of Psychology, Wake Forest University; Section on Neuropsychology, Bowman Gray School of Medicine, Wake Forest University, Winston-Salem, North Carolina*

PREFACE

Much of the literature in experimental and physiological psychology is devoted to short-term memory. Like many useful terms introduced into science, its meaning was originally vague—a hope that patient work would transform a nebulous, barely perceptible shadow into a substantial, tangible entity. Sometimes such hopes are fulfilled and the dimly apprehended concept crystallizes to become refined and sharp. At other times, the nebulosity dissolves on investigation and rejoins the void. As some concepts crystallize and others dissolve, science progresses. Such progress is largely brought about by a collocation of the diverse uses of a particular concept. Such a collocation facilitates evaluation of a concept. For instance, the idea of short-term memory has been used in human experimental psychology, clinical, and physiological psychology. The use of a similar term in these fields implies an identity of meaning. Whether such an identity exists can be clarified to the various users only by having them compare their own use of the term with others' use of it. Such a comparison is greatly facilitated and sharpened if the various examples of usage are brought together. This volume is an attempt to sharpen the process of conceptual evolution by providing the scientist and the student with a selection of views and uses of the notion of short-term memory. Our purpose is not to provide a unitary view or a ready-made answer but to put a body of evidence in readily accessible form in front of the jury of our fellow workers.

SHORT-TERM MEMORY

CHAPTER

1

SHORT-TERM MEMORY AS A BIOLOGICAL ENTITY[1]

LARRY R. SQUIRE

[1] This work was supported by a grant from the A. P. Sloan Foundation and by NIMH Grant MH18282 to S. H. Barondes.

1

I. INTRODUCTION

Theories of learning commonly distinguish between short-term and long-term memory. For example, behavioral evidence based on studies of human learning indicates that shortly after learning, memory has different characteristics than at a later period of time (Norman, 1970; Spence & Bower, 1968). In terms of the biological substrate of memory, such evidence is consistent with quite a range of possibilities. On the one hand, memory might depend on distinct physiological mechanisms at different times after learning that are isomorphic to the behaviorally inferred processes. On the other hand, this behavioral evidence might also be explained by supposing that the learning experience initiates a single biological process that develops quantitatively with time and affects behavior differently as it grows. A variety of experimental strategies have been used to explore these possibilities, the most prominent of which have been studies of normal and experimentally disturbed memory in animals and cellular neurophysiological studies of learning in invertebrates. Although much of this evidence is inconclusive, the results of these studies taken together constitute strong evidence that memory depends on separate biological processes at different times after training. In the following pages, this work will be reviewed.

The distinction between short-term and long-term memory originates in the intuitions of William James (1890) and in consolidation theory (Müller & Pilzecker, 1900). James postulated the existence of so-called primary and secondary memories on introspective grounds, reasoning that holding memory in consciousness for a few moments after an event seemed distinct from calling memory back into consciousness some time later. Consolidation theory held that after an event is registered, a period of time is required for the development of memory. During the consolidation period, memory is tentative and disruptible. When consolidation is completed, memory is established in some kind of stable form. From these ideas grew the more specific hypothesis that memory during the consolidation period might be based on a short-term physiological process distinctly different from the process operating after the consolidation period is complete (Hebb, 1949; Hilgard & Marquis, 1940).

II. RETROGRADE AMNESIA

Evidence interpreted as supporting the notion that two fundamentally distinct information storage mechanisms might exist came initially from studies in which attempts were made to disrupt memory in trained animals. Manipulations designed to interrupt organized electrical activity in the nervous system, like electroconvulsive shock (ECS) or anoxia, disrupted memory only when treatment was administered soon after training (see Glickman, 1961). Treatments at progressively longer intervals after training exerted progressively less disruptive effect. Moreover, well-learned habits were quite invulnerable to such manipulations. For example, insertion of conductors or insulators into the visual cortex did not disturb the performance of previously acquired visual discriminations (Sperry & Miner, 1955; Sperry, Miner, & Myers, 1955), and cerebral ischemia in dogs did not impair the performance of a delayed response task (Nielsen, Zimmerman, & Colliver, 1963). The finding that memory becomes progressively less vulnerable to disruption following training has subsequently been well documented in man (Barbizet, 1970; Russell & Nathan, 1946) and in experimental animals (McGaugh & Herz, 1972). These observations seem to support the consolidation hypothesis and the related idea that memory during the consolidation period might depend on a specialized process.

The duration of this hypothetically distinct time period for consolidation has been difficult to estimate. For rats learning one-trial passive avoidance tasks, some investigators demonstrated with ECS a steep gradient of retrograde amnesia lasting about 10 sec (Chorover & Schiller, 1965; Quartermain, Paolino, & Miller, 1965). Brief gradients of retrograde amnesia have also been observed in human patients experiencing petit mal epilepsy (Geller & Geller, 1970). At the outset, however, it was difficult to reconcile brief retrograde amnesia with the retrograde amnesia gradients up to 6 hr reported for mice given ECS (Kopp, Bohdanecky, & Jarvik, 1966). Long gradients could be obtained even when rats and mice were tested under the same experimental conditions (Schneider, Kapp, Aron, & Jarvik, 1969). It became increasingly clear that a fixed duration for consolidation might not be demonstrable. Estimates varied as a function of species (Schneider *et al.,* 1969), age (Thompson, 1957), task (Herz, 1969), and amnesic agent (Bohdanecky, Kopp, & Jarvik, 1967).

It has been suggested that some of the disagreement concerning the

temporal characteristics of retrograde amnesia may reflect differences in
the effectiveness of the amnesic treatment (Cherkin, 1969; Gold, Macri,
& McGaugh, 1973). For example, increasing the intensity of electroconvulsive shock increased the length of the retrograde amnesia gradient up
to about 4 hr (Gold *et al.,* 1973). These findings indicate that the threshold
for disruption of memory by ECS continues to increase for at least 4 hr
following a learning trial. How long beyond 4 hr the amnesic threshold might continue to increase was not determined. Longer gradients have
been obtained, however, with other amnesic agents. Bitemporal injections
of puromycin (Flexner, Flexner, & Stellar, 1963) or actinomycin-D
(Squire & Barondes, 1970) disrupt one-day-old memory but not seven-
day-old memory. Cholinergic drugs also affect seven-day-old memories
differently than one-day-old memories (Deutsch, 1971). Thus, there is
evidence that memory is changing for several days after training.

If the length of retrograde amnesia gradients does in fact reflect the
duration of a short-term memory fixation process, then one might expect
that, with time, memory should become invulnerable to these kinds of
treatments. Yet, recent evidence indicates that even 20-year-old memories
can be disturbed (Squire, 1974a; 1974b). Psychiatric patients receiving a
series of electroconvulsive treatments for depression were given a questionnaire designed after Warrington's test (Warrington & Silberstein, 1970)
for remote public events. High school and college students did poorly on
the questions, indicating that one must have lived through the years in
question in order to do well on the test. Patients filled out the questionnaire after their first or shortly after their fifth electroconvulsive treatment. The results indicated that memory for events occurring 20 years ago
can be disrupted by five treatments in the absence of changes in intelligence test scores. If consolidation is interpreted to apply only to some
short-lived memory fixation process, then it follows from these data that
memory loss cannot always be taken to indicate incomplete consolidation.
These results, then, do not support the notion that susceptibility to amnesia
reflects an incomplete consolidation process. Instead, the results suggest
that amnesic agents can produce a state of disturbed recall. Recall difficulty could reflect neural "noise" (Weiskrantz, 1966) or could result from
direct impairment of the neural substrate for memories that are weakly
represented in the nervous system.

Although the results of these sorts of experiments have not permitted
an estimate of the time period during which a specialized short-term memory process might operate or even convincingly demonstrated that such a
process exists, they do place constraints on the physiological mechanisms
that could be involved in the development of memory. Specifically, several

experiments indicate that memory cannot depend on sustained neuronal activity for more than a few seconds after training. Consider, for example, that hypothermia in hamsters was not amnesic itself but prolonged the period during which ECS produced amnesia (Gerard, 1955). Also, two ECS treatments 1 hr apart were more disruptive than either one alone (Mah, Albert, & Jamieson, 1972). Finally, a short period of spreading depression or fluorothyl administration was less disruptive than a long one (Albert, 1966a; Cherkin, 1969). These findings indicate that amnesic treatments often interfere with memory by apparently slowing down the formation of memory rather than by stopping it altogether. Yet, if memory depended exclusively on organized electrical activity during the period after training, it is difficult to see why a short period of spreading depression, for example, which causes massive neuronal discharges, should not disrupt memory as much as a longer period of depression. The fact that no known amnesic agent acts in an all-or-none fashion during the hours after training is strong evidence that memory does not depend exclusively on patterned neuronal activity during this period. It appears more likely that beyond a few seconds after training, some other process is operating in addition to or instead of patterned activity.

These suggestions are also supported by recent experiments in which a period of cerebral ischemia was initiated 20 sec after single daily classical conditioning trials in goats (Baldwin & Soltysik, 1965, 1966). This procedure resulted in a period of isoelectric EEG at cortical and subcortical sites beginning 45–65 sec after each trial and lasting about 1.5 min. An isoelectric EEG usually indicates a dramatic loss of neuronal spike activity (Baumgartner, Creutzfeldt, & Jung, 1961). Animals subjected to this procedure acquired both cardiac and somatic components of the response at the same rate as control animals. These findings constitute strong evidence that memory cannot depend exclusively on sustained neuronal activity for more than a few seconds after a learning trial.

More specific conclusions about the biological nature of the events leading to memory storage cannot be drawn from these sorts of experiments. Electroconvulsive shock, for example, has many effects in addition to disrupting cerebral electrical activity (Cotman, Banker, Zornetzer, & McGaugh, 1971; Essman, 1972). Moreover, the amnesic effects of ECS are correlated with the extent to which the ECS disrupts cortical theta activity (Landfield, McGaugh, & Tusa, 1972). It is an interesting possibility that ECS might exert its amnesic effect, not by interfering directly with electrically (or chemically) coded neural interactions, but by interfering with a specialized neural system that must be operative for memory to become stable.

In summary, the phenomenon of retrograde amnesia is interesting primarily because it indicates that memory changes after learning. It has not been useful as an argument for the existence of a distinct short-term memory mechanism. It was originally hoped that the duration of the consolidation period might correspond to the lifetime of a specialized information storage mechanism. However, the retrograde amnesia data are equally consistent with the idea that a unitary process develops after training, grows stronger with time, and continues to develop for at least several days after training and perhaps longer. It remains possible, and even likely, that some specialized short-term process might exist for a short time after training. But, since the disruptive agents now available may have multiple effects, it is difficult to know whether an amnesic agent is disrupting one or several mechanisms, and it is corespondingly difficult to make statements about what kinds of biological processes are being disrupted.

III. ABNORMALLY RAPID FORGETTING

Under certain circumstances, memory may decay at an abnormally rapid rate. Rapid forgetting is the hallmark of human memory pathology (Barbizet, 1970) and has also been observed in experimental animals in a number of situations. This phenomenon has been interesting because of the possibility that rapid forgetting following training might reflect the decay of a specialized short-term memory process. Moreover, if amnesic treatment prevents the development of lasting memory, the time required for forgetting could reflect the lifetime of this putative short-term memory process. Early evidence on this point was consistent with the existence of a short-term process having a lifetime of 3–6 hr. When formation of lasting memory was blocked by cathodal polarization (Albert, 1966b), protein synthesis inhibition (Barondes & Cohen, 1967), or ECS (Geller & Jarvik, 1968), forgetting occurred 3 to 6 hr after training.

However, the time required for forgetting to occur is sometimes shorter (Andry & Luttges, 1972; McGaugh & Landfield, 1970; Watts & Mark, 1971) and sometimes longer (Agranoff, 1970) than 3–6 hr (see Table 1-1). Thus, forgetting curves exhibit the same sort of variability as retrograde amnesia gradients. In both cases, it is clear that no single temporal parameter will fit the data from different experimental situations.

It is possible, however, that the time required for forgetting to occur might be constant within one experimental situation, and it is interesting to investigate the specific shape of the forgetting curve in a single species

TABLE 1-1

Time of Appearance of Amnesia after Training[a]

Appearance of amnesia after training	Species	Nature of amnesic treatment and time treatment was given relative to training[b]	Reference
Seconds– minutes	Man	Hippocampal surgery before testing	Milner, 1966
90 min	Chick	CXM 5 min before	Watts & Mark, 1971
2–3 hr	Mouse	CXM 30 min before	Andry & Luttges, 1972
3–6 hr	Mouse	AXM 5 min before	Barondes & Cohen, 1968
3–5 hr	Rat	Cathodal polarization 5 min before	Albert, 1966b
3–6 hr	Mouse	ECS 20 sec after	Geller & Jarvik, 1968
6–12 hr	Fish	KCl immediately after	Davis & Klinger, 1969
1–3 days	Fish	AXM immediately after	Agranoff, 1970
2 weeks	Mouse	CXM 30 min before	Flood *et al.*, 1972
<1 hr	Mouse	ECS 8 sec after	
1–24 hr	Mouse	ECS 20 sec after	McGaugh & Landfield, 1970
1–3 hr	Mouse	CXM 30 min before 15 trials	
6–12 hr	Mouse	CXM 30 min before 21 trials	Squire & Barondes, 1972b
1–24 days		ECS immediately after, 70 mA	Hughes, Barrett, & Ray, 1970a
24–42 days	Rat	ECS immediately after, 40 mA	

[a] In each case, separate groups of animals were tested for retention at different times after training. The time required for amnesia to develop after training has sometimes been taken as the lifetime of a putative short-term memory process.

[b] CXM = cycloheximide. AXM = acetoxycycloheximide. ECS = electroconvulsive shock; KCl = potassium chloride.

and task. If forgetting occurred at a constant rate following disruption while the effectiveness of the amnesic agent were varied, this would argue for the existence of a separate short-term memory process having a fixed lifetime (Fig. 1-1a). Alternatively, if short-term memory had a variable lifetime (or if forgetting were not related to the properties of a short-term process), then forgetting might occur at different rates when the effectiveness of the amnesic agent were varied (Fig. 1-1b).

These alternatives have been tested by giving mice 21 or 27 trials of discrimination training during a period of extensive inhibition of cerebral protein synthesis (Squire & Barondes, 1972b). Following 21 training trials, memory decayed rapidly and was undetectable 3 hr later. Following 27 trials, memory decayed more slowly. Considerable memory was still in evidence 6 hr after training, and 12 hr were required for amnesia to develop.

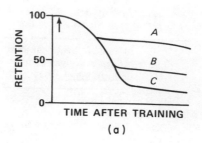

(a)

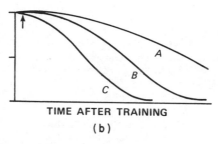

TIME AFTER TRAINING

(b)

Fig. 1-1. Hypothetical forgetting curves depicting the time course of development of amnesia after treatment. In each case, amnesic treatment is given shortly after training (arrow), at one of three levels of effectiveness (A, B, C). (a) If decay of memory after treatment reflects the diminution of a residual short-term memory process having a fixed lifetime, then for three levels of increasing amnesic effectiveness (A, B, C), memory would be expected to decay at a constant rate, but to reach different asymptotes. In the figure, the asymptotic level of performance in each case indicates the strength of long-term memory that survives treatment. (b) If decay of memory reflects either the diminution of a residual short-term memory process having a variable lifetime or the varying strength of an impaired long-term memory process, then for three levels of increasing amnesic effectiveness (A, B, C) memory should decay at a variable rate to the same asymptote. The available evidence indicates that memory decays at a variable rate when amnesic effectiveness is varied.

The same result has been obtained in a different way by varying the intensity of ECS or the interval between training and ECS. Under these circumstances, memory decay proceeds at slower rates as the interval between training and ECS increases or as ECS intensity decreases (Hughes, Barrett, & Ray, 1970a, 1970b; McGaugh & Landfield, 1970). These results, taken together, indicate that rapid loss of memory after training cannot reflect the decay of a specialized, short-term memory having a *fixed* lifetime. Instead, memory decays at a variable rate depending on the effectiveness of the amnesic agent.

It remains possible that a short-term memory process could account for decay if this process is assumed to have a lifetime that varies as a function of the severity of the amnesic treatment or the level of training. Although such an interpretation is possible in those experiments in which decay varies over a period of a few hours or less (Andry & Luttges, 1972; Watts & Mark, 1971; McGaugh & Landfield, 1970; Squire & Barondes, 1972b), it seems awkward to postulate a short-term memory process that can last as long as days or even weeks, as required by those experiments in which decay time can vary across this time scale (Agranoff, 1970; Flood, Rosenzweig, Bennett, & Orme, 1972; Hughes, Barrett, & Ray, 1970a, 1970b).

These considerations have led to an alternative explanation for rapid decay of memory (Squire & Barondes, 1972a, 1972b). Whereas forgetting that occurs during the hours after training could reflect exclusively the decay of a short-term memory process, it might in addition reflect the decay of a weakly established "permanent" memory system. According to this view, some of the physiological changes that normally underlie enduring memory may partially survive amnesic treatment. In the case of protein synthesis inhibition, for example, some changes of the type that subserve permanent memory may be established at the time of training by the slight capacity for cerebral protein synthesis that survives inhibition. A weakly established memory of this type may be imperfectly maintained and could decay abnormally rapidly. Clearly, an abnormal rate of memory loss need not imply a qualitatively distinct, short-term memory process.

Although the times required for decay of memory in animals following amnesic treatment have not provided strong evidence for the existence of a specialized short-term memory process, one reported case of extraordinarily rapid forgetting in man is illuminating in this regard. Following bilateral excision of hippocampal gyrus, uncus, amygdala, and anterior hippocampus for relief of intractable seizures (Scoville & Milner, 1957), this individual (H.M.) exhibited a profound anterograde amnesia characterized by difficulty in holding onto new information for more than a few minutes (Milner, 1966). If rehearsal were made difficult or prevented, information could rarely be retained for more than a minute (Milner, 1966; Wickelgren, 1968). Yet H.M. suffered no discernible personality change, scored considerably above average on a standard intelligence test, and had a normal immediate memory span. It is difficult to explain the facts of this case adequately without recourse to two separate memory processes. One of the most compelling experiments was an extension of the usual digit span test (Drachman & Arbit, 1966). In this test, the digit span was determined, and then subjects attempted progressively longer lists of digits. When an error was made, the same list was presented again and again until the list was repeated back correctly. Under these conditions, normal subjects were able to extend their digit span up to 20 digits, requiring fewer than 15 trials to succeed at any list length. The patient H.M. began with a digit span of 6, within the normal range, but was unable to extend his digit span by a single digit even after 25 repetitions of the same list. These results strongly suggest that the neural mechanisms required for registering and repeating back short lists of digits are distinctively different from the mechanisms involved in remembering longer lists.

In summary, whereas the evidence for separate memory mechanisms in animals remains inconclusive, studies in man have provided compelling evidence that a specialized neural process may exist for a few seconds (or minutes) after learning and that medial temporal structures are specifically involved at this time in the memory storage process.

IV. SHORT-LIVED HABITS AS EVIDENCE FOR SHORT-TERM MEMORY

If it were possible to demonstrate a habit or a class of habits that can be retained for only a limited period of time, one might argue that such habits could be mediated by a specially developed short-term memory process. However, for many forms of behavioral modification that are retained for brief periods of time, it has often been possible to extend the retention interval considerably under appropriate conditions. For example, behavioral habituation of gill and siphon withdrawal in the marine mollusk *Aplysia* normally endures for only a few minutes (Pinsker, Kupfermann, Castellucci, & Kandel, 1970). However, appropriately spaced training procedures produced habituation that lasted for more than a week (Carew, Pinsker, & Kandel, 1972). Thus there is no reason to argue on the basis of the behavioral evidence that a special process underlies retention for the first few minutes after training. Of course, cellular neurophysiological studies (see Kandel & Spencer, 1968, and Section XI of this chapter) may reveal differences in physical substrates of memory at different times after training despite these behavioral considerations.

Even in certain delayed-response and delayed-alternation tasks in which primates have difficulty holding information for more than a minute or two (Jacobsen & Nissen, 1937), a biologically distinct memory process is not needed to account for rapid decay of memory. First, the duration of memory depends on the conditions of training—in other one-trial delay tasks, animals may remember the location of reward for an hour or even a day (Alpern & Marriott, 1972; Baldwin & Soltysik, 1969; Beritashvili, 1971). Second, at least one kind of putative short-term holding process can be directly ruled out. Memory during the delay period cannot be based exclusively on sustained neural activity because a period of cerebral ischemia and concomitant isoelectric EEG initiated during the delay period has no effect on delayed response performance (Baldwin & Soltysik, 1969).

In summary, the fact that some memories fade in a few seconds, minutes, or hours after learning provides no evidence for or against the assertion that the duration of a memory may reflect what type of physiological process is initiated following training. One can suppose just as easily that the duration of memory might be determined, quantitatively, by the strength or extensiveness of one type of physiological process that is initiated at the time of training.

V. BIPHASIC RETENTION FUNCTIONS

Several workers have reported dips in the performance of normal untreated animals during retention tests at specific times after training (see Table 1-2). Dips in performance occurred between one minute and one

TABLE 1-2
Time of Performance Dip after Training[a]

Time of dip after training	Species	Task[b]	Reference
1 hr	Rat	AA	Kamin, 1963
1 hr	Cuttlefish	PA	Messenger, 1971
1 hr and 8 hr	Octopus	PA	Sanders & Barlow, 1971
2 min	Mouse	PA	Irwin et al., 1968
3-5 min	Chick	PA	Cherkin, 1971
30 min	Mouse	PA	Zerbolio, 1969
1 min	Goldfish	PA	Riege & Cherkin, 1972

[a] In each case, separate groups of normal, untreated animals were tested for retention at different times after training. Dips in performance after training have sometimes been interpreted as transition points between separate memory processes.

[b] AA = active avoidance. PA = passive avoidance.

hour after training. Some of these results have been interpreted to reflect transition points between short-term and long-term memory processes. However, all of these tasks used shock or other punishment in the training. Except for one study (Kamin, 1963), all of the tasks were of the passive-avoidance type, in which an animal must withhold a dominant response to avoid an aversive stimulus. In the passive-avoidance task, normal memory is inferred from high response latencies. Since these sorts of tasks are sensitive to the activity and arousal state of the animal, it is always difficult to be sure that the observed effects reflect direct changes in the substrate for memory rather than time-dependent changes in emotionality or activity. The argument from these data to specialized short-term memory processes seems unjustified unless the results can be extended to an appetitively motivated choice situation, in which activity and arousal should interact minimally with the response under study.

Cholinesterase inhibitors exert amnesia in rats 7 days after training, but not one day after training (Deutsch, 1971). In addition, under some training conditions, partial amnesia is produced when a cholinesterase inhibitor is given 30 min after training. This biphasic response has been interpreted to be the result of a cholinesterase-induced depolarization block in the central nervous system, which occurs either because an unusually large amount of transmitter substance is released or because the sensitivity of the post synaptic receptor is unusually high (Deutsch, 1971). Accordingly, it has been suggested that one or both of these conditions exists immediately after training, disappears sometime after 30 min, and then develops again several days after training. The implication that only central cholinergic synapses are involved in this effect must be viewed cautiously, however, since cholinesterase-induced amnesia was readily reversed by methylscopolamine (Squire, Glick, & Goldfarb, 1971), a cholinergic blocking agent that crosses the blood–brain barrier with difficulty. Yet, whatever the physiological basis of the effect, a U-shaped curve representing susceptibility to amnesia as a function of training-retention interval is of great interest. It is unlikely that amnesia results from a simple emotionality change because, at a time when rats would have been amnesic for the original habit, they acquired the reversal of this habit faster than normal control (Deutsch & Rocklin, 1972). Moreover, all these results have been obtained in discrimination tasks, so changes in activity should minimally affect the response measure. A strikingly similar U-shaped effect has been demonstrated when multiple ECS treatments were given at different times after training (Wiener, 1970). Treatments at 30 min or at 7 days after training produced amnesia, but treatments at 1 or 3 days after training were ineffective. Taken together, these results strongly suggest that a distinct memory process exists for a short period of time after training. As the first process decays, a more permanent storage process develops.

VI. ONTOGENY OF MEMORY

If biologically distinct memory processes exist, they might have different developmental time courses. Neonatal rats can be taught a simple escape response during the first days of life (Misanin, Nagy, Keiser, & Bowen, 1971). Seven-day-old and 9-day-old animals acquire this habit at the same rate. In 7-day-old rats, retention of the habit was observed at 1 hr after training but not after 6 or 24 hr. Nine-day-old rats remembered for at least 4 days (Nagy, Misanin, Newman, Olsen, & Hinderlith, 1972). It is not possible to attribute this marked increase in retentive capacity to any gross feature of development. Many neurophysiological and biochemical changes are occurring in the neonatal rat brain during this period (Himwich, 1962). Formation of synaptic junctions in the rat brain can be detected during this time (Woodward, Hoffer, Siggins, & Bloom, 1971), but the rapid phase of synapse formation, at least in the molecular layer of cortex, does not begin until the third week of life (Aghajanian & Bloom, 1967).

These behavioral results are of interest because they suggest that the capacity for enduring memory may emerge rapidly. Although a parametric study on this point has not yet been made, it is possible that a 6-hr memory capacity could emerge simultaneously with a 4-day memory capacity. Such a sudden increase in retentive capacity might best be explained by the appearance at this time of a specialized neural process that permits enduring plastic changes in the nervous system. Such a result would be unlikely to reflect a sudden, quantitative leap in the capacity of an already operative process.

VII. ANATOMICAL SUBSTRATES OF MEMORY

Several attempts have been made to prove the existence of a specialized short-term memory process by referring short-term memory and long-term memory to separate anatomical regions. In one such case, bitemporal injections of puromycin were given at different times after training a shock-escape, spatial-discrimination task (Flexner, Flexner, & Stellar, 1963). Mice injected 1 day after training were amnesic during a later test session, but mice injected 7 days after training were not affected. Amnesia could be induced 7 days after training, however, by injecting the drug at temporal, frontal, and ventricular sites. These results were interpreted to indicate that memory was initially localized subcortically but subsequently spread to occupy wide areas of the brain. A similar hypothesis involving a shift in the locus of memory from subcortex to cortex during the minutes following training was adopted by Paolino and Levy (1971). In their study, rats trained in a one-trial, passive-avoidance task became amnesic when cortical spreading depression was initiated 16 min after training, but not when it was initiated immediately after training.

However, the hypothesis that subcortical structures *participate* in memory-storage processes for some particular interval after training does not mean that recently acquired information actually *resides* in these structures. A simpler view is that memory is stationary and distributed over a large number of sites in the brain, and that for some critical period after training subcortical structures are specifically required for strengthening the distributed memory-trace system.

VIII. SERIAL OR PARALLEL MEMORY PROCESSES

If separate short-term and long-term memory processes exist, they could conceivably be arranged in series or in parallel. A series arrangement would imply that some physiological changes are required for the initiation or development of subsequent ones. A parallel arrangement would imply that a set of physiological changes are initiated and developed independently of other sets and that neither is necessary for the normal development of the other. If memory processes were arranged in parallel, it might be possible to impair short-term memory but to allow long-term memory to develop normally. Such a result would constitute strong evidence for the existence of distinct memory processes. Some recent results that have been interpreted as supporting a parallel arrangement of memory processes will now be considered in detail.

Rats learned a simple avoidance task on Day 1 during unilateral spreading depression of one hemisphere (Albert, 1966b). No retention was observed on Day 3, when unilateral spreading depression was initiated on the opposite hemisphere, unless a single "transfer" trial without depression was interposed on Day 2. These results have generally been taken as evidence for interhemispheric transfer of information, and consequent "one-trial learning" by the hemisphere which was depressed during training. Other interpretations have been suggested (Schneider, 1967), but several arguments (Squire & Liss, 1968) and more recent experiments (Mayes & Cowey, 1973; Nadel, 1971; Nadel & Burešová, 1968) favor a memory interpretation of this phenomenon. In the experiments to be described, all disruptive agents were applied to the hemisphere that "learned" during the "transfer" trial.

Cathodal polarization initiated 5 min after learning produced rapid forgetting in 3–6 hr, yet these amnesic effects could be reversed up to 11 hr after learning by initiating a period of anodal polarization. On the basis of these results, two parallel memory mechanisms were postulated—one with a lifetime of 3–6 hr responsible for temporary recall during the consolidation period, and a second with a lifetime of at least 11 hr serving as a template for long-term retention.

These results can be interpreted more simply, however, by supposing that a single process develops gradually after learning. One can further suppose that, following cathodal polarization, this process decays to a point where it is below the threshold for recall but is not completely gone. By 11 hr after learning, this process has further weakened, but it can still be revived by anodal polarization. This interpretation does not require the existence of two separate memory processes. It requires only the reasonable assumption that the absence of behavioral evidence for memory need not imply that none of the physiological correlates of memory remain in the brain.

Other evidence interpreted in favor of parallel memories was that spreading depression initiated soon after learning interfered with immediate recall but did not prevent the formation of memory, as memory could be recovered later by anodal polarization. These data can be explained in the same way by supposing that a single process develops after learning. Following spreading depression, this process is below the threshold for recall but not entirely obliterated. Later on, it can be revived by a period of anodal polarization.

Electrical brain stimulation has also been used to interfere with memory. Rats received a foot shock contingent on a well-learned bar-pressing response and 4 sec later received stimulation to medial reticular formation (MRF) or hippocampus (Kesner & Connor, 1972). The MRF group failed to exhibit normal response suppression when tested 1 min later but exhibited normal suppression 24 hr later. The hippocampal group was opposite, remembering normally at 1 min but not at 24 hr. These results were interpreted to indicate that MRF stimulation interfered with a short-term memory process that is arranged in parallel with a long-term process. Accordingly, short-term retention was blocked by MRF stimulation, but long-term retention emerged normally. Although these results are consistent with the existence of two parallel memory processes, they cannot strongly support such a hypothesis. Specifically, a temporary loss of memory need not imply that a short-term memory process has been lost, as seems to be required by such an hypothesis. Moreover, recovery of memory need not imply that another, parallel memory process has developed. Other simpler explanations can account for temporary memory loss just as well. First, a viable memory process might not be available for a time because of neural "noise." In this case, recovery of memory might occur immediately, once the aftereffects of the amnesic treatment have worn away. Second, only the later stages of a serially organized information storage process might have been impaired. In this case, recovery might occur gradually, reflecting the time required for an operative storage process to be reestablished. For example, inhibition of protein synthesis during training produces amnesia that is spontaneously reversible under some circumstances (Quartermain & McEwen, 1970; Serota, 1971; Squire & Barondes, 1972b). If synthesis of m-RNA and protein are required for formation of new memory (see Squire & Barondes, 1972a), then recovery of memory could reflect the fact that m-RNA, synthesized during training, begins to synthesize protein again after inhibition has worn off (Flexner, Flexner, & Roberts, 1966; Barondes & Squire, 1972b).

In summary, the available evidence for parallel short-term and long-term memory processes is unconvincing. The experimental data can be adequately explained by supposing that a learning experience generates single or multiple physiological processes that develop in series according to a specific timetable.

Most of the evidence reviewed in this and preceding sections can be satisfactorily explained by a unitary process. However, some of the evidence seems to favor the idea that memory is distinctly different at different times after learning and that short-term and long-term memory may depend on distinct biological processes. Specifically, the following observations make the best case: (1) the amnesic syndrome following bilateral, medial temporal lesions (Milner, 1966, Section III) and (2) U-shaped curves of amnesic susceptibility (Deutsch, 1971, Section V).

Differences between short-term and long-term memory processes could exist at the level of the single neuron or might be realized only at higher levels of nervous integration. For example, at the neuronal level, two types of plastic changes might occur to alter interneuronal communication, each type at a particular time after training. Alternatively, at a higher level of analysis, the development of one type of plastic change at synapses might be influenced at specific times after training by organized input from other brain regions. In the following sections, more specific physiological hypotheses will be developed. The available evidence indicates that a variety of mechanisms are available to regulate synaptic connectivity at the neuronal level and suggests that different types of plastic changes at synapses may underlie memory at different times after training.

IX. MACROMOLECULAR SYNTHESIS

When inhibition of cerebral protein synthesis is initiated in mice just before or shortly after a training experience, mice do not retain the experience for more than a few hours (Barondes & Cohen, 1968). This finding and an accumulating body of other evidence has suggested that the synthesis of brain protein during or shortly after training is required for the formation of permanent memory (Squire & Barondes, 1972a; Barondes & Squire, 1972a). However, a definitive conclusion is difficult to obtain with these methods because the drugs used in these studies may have other pharmacological effects besides inhibition of protein synthesis.

In addition, it could be argued that inhibition produces amnesia by inactivating a rapidly turning-over, constitutive, regulatory protein involved in the development of memory rather than by blocking synthesis of inducible protein. The fact that amnesia develops in mice when the inhibitor is introduced 5 min before training but not when it is introduced 30 min after training (Barondes & Cohen, 1968) would require this hypothetical constitutive protein to have a turnover time of a few minutes. Although brain proteins on the average have half-lives of several days (Lajtha, 1964), examples of rapidly turning-over regulatory proteins do exist, e.g., in the response of adrenal cells to ACTH (Garren, Ney, & Davis, 1965).

Since protein synthesis is important in cellular regulatory mechanisms (Jacob & Monod, 1961), it would be surprising if it were not involved in memory in some way. The idea that proteins are involved does not require that memory must be stored by synthesis of new and unique molecules that represent specific kinds of information (Ungar, 1970) or by alterations in the metabolic efficiency of whole neurons (Pfaff, 1969). Instead, it is possible that synthesis of one or a few protein molecules is a critical event for altering synaptic relationships (Barondes, 1965). This event could be extremely subtle in terms of the biochemical machinery of an entire neuron. The proteins whose synthesis might be involved in altering neuronal relationships could be of several types: (1) enzymes that regulate the synthesis or destruction of neurotransmitters, (2) receptor molecules on the postsynaptic neuron, (3) structural proteins, or (4) proteins that regulate, directly or indirectly, a specific synaptic event that alters synaptic efficacy. Whichever type of protein is involved in memory storage, proteins synthesized during training presumably could be involved in the expression of memory only after some time interval. It has been estimated in mammalian cells that about 100 msec is required for the addition of one amino acid to a polypeptide chain (Hunt, Hunter, &

Munro, 1969). By this calculation, assembly time for proteins having $10^2–10^3$ amino acids (and molecular weights of 10,000–100,000) would range from $10^1–10^2$ sec. Second, a period of time might be required for transport of newly synthesized proteins to nerve endings, where they would be in a position to influence synaptic interactions. If one takes the rate of fast axoplasmic flow in central neurons to be about 40 mm/day (McEwen & Grafstein, 1968), then one can calculate that this process could conceivably occur in short interneurons in less than 5 min. The presence of ribosomes in dendrites (Bodian, 1965) might permit an even shorter lag between the synthesis of proteins and a consequent influence on the synaptic region. It also remains possible that some special class of protein might be synthesized at the nerve ending (Ramirez, Levitan, & Mushynski, 1972), but imperfections in subcellular fractionation techniques have made it difficult to confirm or deny this possibility with any certainty. Given all these considerations, it seems reasonable to suppose that at least one minute would be required between training and the time when proteins synthesized during training could affect synaptic activity. If synthesis

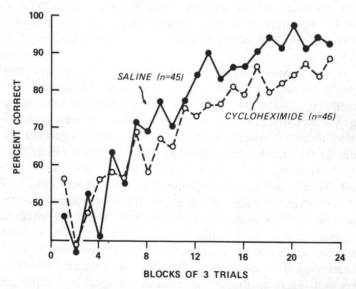

Fig. 1-2. Mice were given prolonged training in a discrimination task shortly after administration of saline or cycloheximide (120 mg/kg), a potent reversible inhibitor of protein synthesis. Mice given saline or cycloheximide are indistinguishable during the first 15–25 trials, but thereafter the mice given cycloheximide lose ground to the saline controls. The divergence in the learning curves occurs about ten minutes after the beginning of training. The results cannot be explained by known side effects of cycloheximide (from Squire & Barondes, 1973).

of protein for information storage requires prior synthesis of new m-RNA (see Squire & Barondes, 1972a), this interval would be even longer. Recent behavioral evidence is consistent with the idea that newly synthesized proteins may be required within a few minutes after the beginning of training for full expression of memory. Mice given prolonged training during inhibition of protein synthesis exhibited normal learning for 10-min (15–25) trials but then lost ground to normal mice, as Fig. 1-2 shows (Squire & Barondes, 1973; Squire, Smith, & Barondes, 1973).

These findings have considerable bearing on presumed distinctions between short-term and long-term memory. It has been pointed out that much of the available behavioral evidence can be accounted for by a single type of plastic change that alters synaptic connectivity as a result of training and that develops with time. However, the suggestion that development of memory depends on protein synthesis necessarily requires some other process, independent of protein synthesis, to exist in order to maintain information while synthesis of protein is under way. The next section considers possible candidates for this process.

X. CANDIDATES FOR SHORT-TERM MEMORY MECHANISMS

Several short-lasting, plastic properties of nerve cells and tissue have been identified. Sherrington (1906) was among the first to appreciate the important observation that nervous activity often outlasts a stimulus. Later, the existence of reverberatory, self-reexciting neural circuits was postulated, specifically to meet the need for a physiological mechanism that could maintain activity for a few seconds after a stimulus. Although developed originally to explain reflex afterdischarges (Forbes, 1929), it was recognized that such a mechanism might also be involved in other phenomena. In the following years, the concept was extended to encompass spontaneous movement (Kubie, 1930), facilitation (Lorente de Nó, 1935), and finally short-term memory (Hebb, 1949; Hilgard & Marquis, 1940). There is no direct evidence, however, that reverberatory activity actually occurs in the nervous system, let alone that it is the basis for temporary information storage. Moreover, activity in closed loops seems specifically ruled out in certain transient, plastic phenomena. Afterdischarges in an isolated cortical slab following electrical stimulation may persist for 30 min, although as long as 20 sec may pass with no sign of neural activity (Burns, 1954). In the intact rat, a period of increased firing in cortex following anodal polarization survives a period of cooling or spreading depression, which would be expected to disrupt reverberatory activity (Gartside, 1968).

In contrast, several other existing phenomena have been suggested as candidates for short-term storage mechanisms, and these have been analyzed in some detail.

A. Post-Tetanic Potentiation

Following high-frequency stimulation of preganglionic fibers or of a monosynaptic spinal-reflex pathway, the response of the next neuron is potentiated for several minutes (see Hughes, 1958). The duration of potentiation may be extended to an hour or more with long periods of tetanization (Spencer & Wigdor, 1965). The potentiated response has been shown to be specific to the activated synapse. Other afferents to a cell are not potentiated when one afferent is tetanized, and the postsynaptic neuron itself is not potentiated when it is stimulated antidromically (Larrabee & Bronk, 1947). In the peripheral nervous system, at least, post-tetanic potentiation depends on a presynaptic change in amount of transmitter released and does not appear to involve a change in postsynaptic receptor sensitivity. After tetany of cat sciatic nerve, the sensitivity of muscle to acetylcholine is not altered (Hutter, 1952). Furthermore, potentiation can be demonstrated at neuromuscular junction in the presence of high Mg^{2+} concentration, which prevents release of a transmitter (Del Castillo & Katz, 1954).

B. Post-Tetanic Depression and Low-Frequency Depression

Many synaptic pathways respond to high-frequency or low-frequency stimulation by a decrease in responsiveness. At neuromuscular junction of crayfish, stimulation at high frequencies or at frequencies as low as one per minute produces progressive diminution of synaptic response (Bruner & Kennedy, 1970). In *Aplysia,* decrements may last for many minutes (Bruner & Tauc, 1966). In the presence of high Mg^{2+} concentration, which interferes with transmitter release, crayfish neuromuscular junction exhibited a normal decrementing response to repeated stimulation in spite of a markedly lower initial junctional potential (Bruner & Kennedy, 1970). Thus, low-frequency depression probably also depends on a presynaptic reduction in release of excitatory transmitter. In the crayfish, the possibility that a build-up of inhibition is involved can be directly ruled out by demonstrating a normal decrementing response in a surgically isolated excitatory axon (Bruner & Kehoe, 1970).

C. Heterosynaptic Facilitation

A short-term plastic change involving two inputs has been demonstrated in central synapses of *Aplysia* (Kandel & Tauc, 1965). Priming stimulation to one input can facilitate the response of a cell to test stimulation of a second input for 30 min or more. This effect occurs in the absence of conductance changes in the postsynaptic cell. Although a postsynaptic change in receptor sensitivity cannot be ruled out, heterosynaptic facilitation is believed to depend on a presynaptic mechanism, whereby terminals of an axon responding to the priming stimulation impinge presynaptically on an axon responding to the test stimulation (Kandel & Tauc, 1965; Carew, Castellucci, & Kandel, 1971). The development of heterosynaptic facilitation is not accompanied by any changes in input resistance of the postsynaptic cell (Carew et al., 1971). Moreover, heterosynaptic facilitation can be distinguished from post-tetanic potentiation because they are affected differently by cooling and ion substitution (Tauc & Epstein, 1967).

It is interesting to note the operational similarity between heterosynaptic facilitation and pseudoconditioning. Repeated presentation of conditioned and unconditioned stimuli, according to a schedule that in *Aplysia* can produce heterosynaptic facilitation, produces changes in unit activity in rat brain (Gerbrandt, Skrebitsky, Burešová, & Bureš, 1968; Olds, Disterhoft, Segal, Kornblith, & Hirsch, 1972). Reports that classical conditioning procedures may elicit unit responses distinct from those elicited by pseudoconditioning procedures (Olds et al., 1972) cannot yet be analyzed in cellular terms. Even in simpler neural systems it is not clear what mechanism in addition to heterosynaptic facilitation might account for reported differences between paired (classical) and unpaired (pseudoconditioning) procedures (Von Baumgarten & Djahenparwar, 1967).

D. Presynaptic Inhibition

Presynaptic inhibition at vertebrate and invertebrate synapses is usually quite short-lasting (see Eccles, 1964). However, a related heterosynaptic depression has been demonstrated in *Aplysia,* which may last nearly an hour (Tauc, 1965). On the basis of several experiments, it has been concluded that heterosynaptic depression is presynaptic in origin and that it probably resembles heterosynaptic facilitation in terms of the neural connections that are involved (Tauc, 1965).

E. Differential Repolarization Rates

When isolated mammalian cerebral cortex is stimulated repetitively with an electrical stimulus, a series of afterbursts that may persist for an hour is initiated (Burns, 1954, 1958). These afterdischarges have been interpreted as being caused by slower repolarization time of the dendritic component of neurons as compared to the somatic component. Multiple responses of cells in cat lateral geniculate to a single stimulus can persist for 20 msec and seem to be correlated with the course of repolarization in dendrites (Tasaki, Polley, & Orrego, 1954), but the role of this mechanism in longer-lasting aftereffects of stimulation is unknown.

F. Summary

This brief summary has identified a number of mechanisms that have the potential to alter synaptic connectivity for several minutes after a stimulus. Until recently, the idea that any of these mechanisms might have a role in short-term information storage was only speculation. Although parallels between certain behavioral phenomena and these neural events had been noted (Bruner & Tauc, 1966; Kandel & Tauc, 1965), meaningful correlations between whole behavior and cellular events could not be made until the cellular neurophysiological correlates of a behavioral event had been worked out. This has recently been accomplished for the gill-withdrawal response in *Aplysia* (Kupfermann & Kandel, 1969). Using this system, it has now been possible to analyze the neuronal mechanisms underlying habituation and dishabituation of this response. The results of these studies, which will now be reviewed, suggest that low-frequency depression and heterosynaptic facilitation are responsible for behavioral habituation and dishabituation, respectively (Castellucci, Kupfermann, Pinsker, & Kandel, 1970).

It is easy to object to this reductionistic strategy by arguing that in higher animals memory will eventually prove to be organized differently or to depend on different principles than in invertebrates. Indeed, there can be no question that some important features of primate or mammalian memory will not be exhibited by lower forms. However, the fact that, at some level of description, higher and lower forms may be markedly divergent need not discourage efforts to seek principles in these lower forms that might be quite general. For example, just as many properties of neural morphology and transmitter biochemistry are quite similar in invertebrate and vertebrate nervous systems, so might some of the biological facts about plasticity in invertebrates be applicable to higher animals. It is also possible that a reductionistic approach will be useful in the generation of hypotheses about information storage that are expressed in more global, structural terms, much in the same way that cellular studies of feature detectors (Hubel & Wiesel, 1962; Lettvin, Maturana, McCulloch, & Pitts, 1961) have influenced general theories of visual perception (Sutherland, 1968). Since there is considerable disagreement about the behavioral criteria for memory (Bullock, 1966), it seems premature to rule on the potential usefulness of any particular example of plasticity. In fact, one might consider instead the possibility that behaviors found in lower forms are evolutionary predecessors of more complex behavior and that these behaviors exhibit principles that will prove fundamental to the behavior of more highly evolved animals. Finally, as Kandel and Spencer (1968) have forcibly pointed out, the reductionistic approach has a methodological advantage as well: many cellular hypotheses about the basis of memory can be specifically tested. In contrast, more globally stated hypotheses are much less amenable to experimental investigation in the present technology.

XI. CELLULAR ANALYSIS OF HABITUATION: A MODEL SHORT-TERM PROCESS

Habituation of the gill-withdrawal response of *Aplysia* occurs when a brief jet of water is repeatedly applied to the siphon or mantle shelf (Pinsker *et al.,* 1970). The response remains habituated for several minutes in the absence of further stimulation and can be dishabituated by a water jet to the neck region. In these and several other respects, habituation in *Aplysia* resembles the habituation that has been found in vertebrates (Thompson & Spencer, 1966). It has been possible to analyze the cellular basis of habituation and dishabituation in *Aplysia* by studying the phenomenon in a progressively reduced neural system (Castellucci *et al.,* 1970). Repeated stimulation of skin or siphon nerve, in a manner that produces habituation in the intact animal, produced a decrement in responsiveness of a major motoneuron (L7) involved in the behavioral response. This decrement was accompanied by a progressive decrease in polysynaptic excitatory potential. A progressive build-up of inhibition in excitatory interneurons or in parallel afferent inhibitory fibers did not seem to be involved in the habituated response since this decrement could also be demonstrated in an apparently monosynaptic pathway from a sensory neuron of the skin to L7. The conclusion that inhibition is not involved agrees with the finding that picrotoxin or strychnine, which abolishes several forms of inhibition, did not affect habituation of spinal reflexes in cat

(Thompson & Spencer, 1966). These findings strongly suggest that habituation in *Aplysia* is due to a change in efficacy of excitatory synaptic transmission, resulting from either a decrease in transmitter release or a decrease in sensitivity of postsynaptic membrane. A presynaptic change seems likely, since other known transient changes in synaptic efficacy seem to depend on presynaptic events. It has been suggested that behavioral habituation depends on the phenomenon of low-frequency depression (Castellucci *et al.*, 1970), whereby low-frequency stimulation of a presynaptic element results in reduced transmitter release (Del Castillo & Katz (1954). The decremented response in *Aplysia* is somewhat longer-lasting than at neuromuscular junction of vertebrates or invertebrates. This difference could reflect characteristics of central versus peripheral synapses or could mean that additional mechanisms are operating in the case of habituation in *Aplysia*.

Dishabituation in *Aplysia* appears to be a special case of heterosynaptic facilitation, originally described in *Aplysia* in purely electrophysiological terms (Kandel & Tauc, 1965). The two phenomena are operationally identical. Dishabituation of the unitary, presumably monosynaptic, postsynaptic potential could be obtained by stimulation of skin or another sensory neuron. Post-tetanic potentiation could be ruled out as a mechanism for this effect, since facilitation of the habituated response occurred in the absence of altered activity in the sensory neuron of the habituated pathway (Castellucci *et al.*, 1970).

The presumed role of protein synthesis in the development of enduring memory has been discussed earlier in this chapter (Section IX), as has the need for short-term processes that could operate while macromolecular synthesis is occurring. If low-frequency depression or heterosynaptic facilitation is to be the basis for a rapidly developing and transient memory process, then one should expect that these phenomena would develop independently of protein synthesis. This possibility has now been tested. During prolonged, extensive inhibition of protein synthesis in *Aplysia,* post-tetanic potentiation and the neuronal correlates of habituation and dishabituation developed normally and persisted for normal lengths of time (Schwartz, Castellucci, & Kandel, 1971). Thus, these plastic changes proceed independently of protein synthesis and could conceivably function as temporary storage mechanisms while a more permanent storage mechanism is developing.

It has recently been shown that the use of spaced training procedures can produce habituation that will persist for 3 weeks (Carew *et al.,* 1972). As a result, cellular studies of long-term modifications in behavior can now be undertaken. Whether or not long-term habituation in *Aplysia* is affected by protein-synthesis inhibition is not yet known. In the mouse, long-term habituation of behavioral activity was not affected by cycloheximide (Squire, Geller, & Jarvik, 1970), but these results do not fully exclude a requirement for protein synthesis. The direct effects of cycloheximide on activity (Segal, Squire, & Barondes, 1971; Squire *et al.*, 1970) dictated that the drug be administered after the habituation session, and initiation of protein-synthesis inhibition after, rather than before, training exerts a relatively weak amnesic effect (Barondes & Cohen, 1968).

In summary, cellular analysis of transient plastic events in simple neural systems and pharmacological studies of learning in rodents suggest that distinct memory storage processes might exist. The evidence is consistent with the existence of a short-lasting process that is presynaptic and that does not depend on protein synthesis, and a more stable, longer-lasting process that depends on *de novo* protein synthesis for its development.

XII. A PROPOSED ORGANIZATION OF SHORT-TERM AND LONG-TERM MEMORY PROCESSES

In the preceding section, some general suggestions have been made about the kinds of physiological mechanisms that might underlie short-term and long-term memory. These ideas have important implications for structural models of memory that are stated in more global, "systems" terms, since any model of memory based on these physiological mechanisms will be constrained in certain ways. For example, such a model must allow for a minute or two between training and the development of long-term memory, since this amount of time must pass before a mechanism dependent on macromolecular synthesis could be operative (Section IX). Similarly, such model should allow that short-term memory might endure for several minutes after training, since the candidates for short-term memory discussed earlier (Sections X, XI) can survive for this period in the absence of macromolecular synthesis. An arrangement of memory processes that incorporates these ideas is proposed in Fig. 1-3. The global organization of this model and its physiological underpinnings will now be considered in detail. The discussion will consider, in turn, (1) the short-term process, (2) the transition from the short-term to the long-term process, (3) the long-term process, and (4) the phenomenon of retrograde amnesia.

A. The Short-Term Process

Short-term memory is presumed to last for varying periods after training as a function of training conditions and post-training events. The

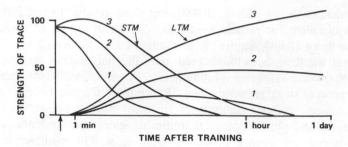

Fig. 1-3. A model depicting a possible relationship between short-term and long-term memory processes (STM, LTM) at three different levels of training. The short-term process presumably develops within milliseconds. It is presumed to initiate long-term changes that require a minute or two to develop. As long as it endures, the short-term process continues to stimulate the development of long-term memory. Thus, the longer the short-term process persists, (1, 2, or 3), the stronger and more durable will be the long-term process (1, 2, or 3). The short-term process itself is presumed to support a high level of retention for only a minute or two after training. Thereafter, the short-term process declines and the long-term process develops. The long-term process may sometimes continue to develop for days after training and perhaps longer (e.g. trace 3). When amnesic treatment is given after training (arrow) the resulting long-term process will be imperfect and short-lived (e.g. trace 1), whether treatment disorganizes the short-term or the incipient long-term process.

longer the short-term process persists, the stronger the resulting long-term process will be. It has been suggested previously that the short-term process may serve only to prime the long-term process and may endure for only a few seconds (Weiskrantz, 1966). By the present view, an interval of a few seconds is the minimal duration of the short-term process and not sufficient for the development of normal long-term memory. The suggestion that the short-term process normally lasts longer than a few seconds is based on several electrophysiological and behavioral considerations. First, calculated times for protein synthesis, which is believed to be required for long-term memory (Barondes & Squire, 1972a; Squire & Barondes, 1972a), suggest that a minute or two must pass before a process dependent on protein synthesis could be operative (Section IX). Second, in central synapses of *Aplysia,* the neuronal correlates of habituation may be detectable for up to an hour (Bruner & Tauc, 1966). Since inhibition of protein synthesis does not affect short-lasting habituation (Schwartz, *et al.,* 1971), the persistence of detectable memory during this interval presumably depends on mechanisms other than those that are believed to subserve long-term memory (Section XI). Third, the duration of short-term memory for up to an hour is consistent with the work of Deutsch (1971), indicating a U-shaped retrograde amnesic gradient. The first early phase of amnesic susceptibility persists for at least 30 min after training (Section V). Finally, this view of short-term memory is supported by the finding that the capacity for 1-hr retention may appear at an earlier time postnatally than the capacity for 6-hr to 4-day retention (Nagy *et al.*, 1972; Section VI). All these considerations are consistent with the existence of a process that can sometimes last many minutes rather than only a few seconds.

The survival of short-term memory for minutes to an hour after training is presumed to require an appropriate level of training and the absence of interfering input during the period after training. Although the patient H.M. may retain information for several minutes when rehearsal is permitted, when rehearsal is prevented he forgets what he has just learned in a few seconds (Milner, 1966; Wickelgren, 1968). Normal human subjects may also forget rapidly during the seconds after a learning trial when the opportunity for rehearsal is prevented (Peterson & Peterson, 1959). In this sense, the duration of the short-term process is presumed to be shortened by interference. The nature of reinforcement might also influence the duration or the effectiveness of the short-term process, as proposed by Landauer (1969).

Although the short-term process is postulated to survive under some circumstances for as long as an hour after training, it appears likely that the long-term process begins to develop rather rapidly. Thus, memory is presumed to depend exclusively on the short-term process for only a few minutes after training. Performance should be impaired beyond this interval if the long-term process does not develop (Fig. 1-3). At least two kinds of evidence are consistent with this view. First, inhibition of protein synthesis impairs expression of memory within minutes after the beginning of training (Squire & Barondes, 1973; Squire, Smith, & Barondes, 1973), suggesting that information depends partially on a protein-synthesis-dependent information-storage process by this time (Section IX). Second, in patients with bilateral temporal lobe damage, amnesia may develop within minutes after training even when rehearsal is permitted (Milner, 1966), suggesting that a more stable process has failed to develop (Section III).

On the basis of present evidence, it is suggested that short-term memory may depend on a phenomenon like post-tetanic potentiation or low-frequency depression, involving presynaptic alterations in the amount of transmitter released (Section XI). It is of interest that a high concentration of Mg^{2+}, which blocks synaptic activity by preventing transmitter release, does not affect the development of either post-tetanic potentiation (Del Castillo & Katz, 1954) or low-frequency depression (Bruner & Kennedy, 1970). These results suggest that synaptic activity may not be re-

quired for the maintenance of the short-term process. Thus, in the present
view, short-term storage of information need not depend on continuous
circulation of nerve impulses in an arrangement of reverberating pathways
(Hebb, 1949). Instead, transient alterations could occur in the electrophysiological properties of individual neural elements, but sustained activity *between* these elements would not be necessary for the integrity of
the process.

B. The Transition from a Short-Term Process to a Long-Term Process

The short-term process is presumed to be arranged serially with the
long-term process (Fig. 1-3). The short-term process can lead to long-
lasting changes in synaptic efficacy, requiring synthesis of new macromolecules. These changes are presumed to involve either a stable presynaptic
change in the characteristics of transmitter release or a change in the sensitivity of the postsynaptic receptor. In addition, it is possible that transition from short-term to long-term memory requires organized inputs from
other regions of the nervous system. For example, in man, the hippocampal
complex appears to be required for the development of lasting memory
(Drachman & Arbit, 1966; Milner, 1966).

Whatever the mechanism of transition from short-term to long-term
memory, the same synapse is presumed to be capable of participating in
both processes. In the case of habituation of gill withdrawal in *Aplysia,*
for example, it is known that cell L7, a major motoneuron involved in the
gill-withdrawal response, exhibits a transient reduced excitatory postsynaptic potential (EPSP) as a result of the habituating stimulus (Castellucci
et al., 1970). If this response is to remain habituated for weeks (Carew
et al., 1972), then this same motoneuron should continue to exhibit altered properties. In this sense, both short-term and long-term changes in
synaptic efficacy can occur at the same site. Of course, long-term memory
for the response could require many additional neural elements. Whereas
a monosynaptic pathway to L7 can exhibit short-term plastic properties
(Castellucci *et al.,* 1970), it is not yet known whether the monosynaptic
pathway is also capable of long-term plastic modification. Further work
with simple nervous systems can be expected to define more precisely the
minimal system capable of long-term modification.

C. The Long-Term Process

It is sometimes supposed that once the long-term memory process develops, it will persist at a given level of strength for a long period of time.

According to this idea, when amnesic treatment is given at some interval after training, memory would not be expected to decay to zero, but to decay to an asymptote representing the strength of long-term memory that has developed up to that time (McGaugh & Dawson, 1971). However, experimental support for this idea is lacking (Section III). For example, when three different intensities of ECS were given at a constant interval after training, memory decayed at different rates and eventually reached the same asymptote (Hughes, Barrett, & Ray, 1970a). It therefore seems reasonable to suppose that the duration of the long-term process is variable (Fig. 1-3). The duration of long-term memory could be variable even if it is mediated by a stable biochemical change. For example, a small change in synaptic efficacy mediated by protein synthesis might be imperfectly maintained, and its effect on behavior could be rapidly diminished as a result of interfering activity in the same pathways.

The present model also supposes that the long-term process continues to develop after the short-term process has abated. This feature of the model is required in order to account for the relative invulnerability of 7-day- versus 1-day-old memory (Section I). Several kinds of mechanisms might be involved (Barondes & Squire, 1972b). Perhaps repeated input into a modified, plastic synapse continues to initiate the events which produced the modification originally. In addition, it is possible that long-term stability of memory could involve the appearance of new neural elements, such as have been reported to result from a prolonged, enriched environment (Volkmar & Greenough, 1972) or from brain lesions (Lynch, Mosko, Parks, & Cotman, 1973).

Presently available evidence offers no basis for choosing between the presynaptic or postsynaptic region as the site of long-term change. A number of presumably postsynaptic biochemical events have been found to result from electrical (Wilson & Berry, 1972) or pharmocological (Cedar & Schwartz, 1972) stimulation, but the relevance of these events to plasticity is not at all clear at present.

It seems likely that the cellular mechanisms underlying long-term changes in synaptic efficacy will prove not to be specific to the memory process. Other long-lasting neural events such as denervation hypersensitivity (Emmelin, 1961; Trendelenburg, 1963) may provide useful information about information storage mechanisms and might be analogous to memory in certain ways, as suggested by Sharpless (1964). Other useful parallels might be found in the effects of chronic drug treatment (Mandell, Segal, Kuczenski, & Knapp, 1972), in long-lasting examples of potentiation following electrical stimulation (Lomó, 1966), or in the phenomenon of drug tolerance, which can last for long periods of time and may require protein synthesis for its development (Way, Loh, & Shen, 1968).

Following the development of long-term alterations in a set of neurons, altered activity of the individual members of the set would be expected to contribute in a probabilistic fashion to the behavior of the whole set. In complex networks, therefore, information can probably be meaningfully related only to the behavior of a population of neurons rather than to the behavior of the individual elements (John, 1972). On the other hand, in instances where whole behavior of an animal can be related to the output of a few identified cells, and where the synaptic inputs to these cells turn out to be plastic, it should be possible to relate information to changes at specific synaptic sites (Kandel, Castellucci, Pinsker, & Kupfermann, 1970).

D. Retrograde Amnesia

According to the proposed scheme, an interval of at least a minute or two is required between training and the time when long-term memory develops to a sufficient strength to influence behavior (Fig. 1-3). If memory indeed depends on a short-term process of the type proposed, it might be thought that memory should be equally susceptible to disruption throughout this interval. Yet, the available evidence clearly indicates that gradients of retrograde amnesia may be quite steep; i.e., memory is more susceptible to ECS given 1 sec after training than to ECS given 5 sec after training (Chorover & Schiller, 1965; Quartermain et al., 1965). Steep gradients of retrograde amnesia have usually been explained by supposing that long-term memory develops perceptibly during the seconds after training (McGaugh & Dawson, 1971; Weiskrantz, 1966). However, one can also account for steep gradients of retrograde amnesia in the present formulation if the long-term process does not appear for a minute or two after training. It need only be assumed that, so long as it is operative, the ECS-sensitive, short-term process initiates the first steps in a series of events that eventually leads to long-term memory. By this view, when the short-term process is disrupted by ECS, some long-term memory will still develop, and its strength will be a function of how long the short-term process endured before it is disrupted. Disruption of long-established memory by ECS (Squire, 1974a; 1974b) cannot be explained by the characteristics of short-term memory processes but might result from neural "noise" (Weiskrantz, 1966), which temporarily makes long-term memory inaccessible.

There is an alternative account of brief retrograde amnesic gradients that does not require that the amnesic treatment disrupt critical events involved in memory storage. Indeed, some of the cellular events involved in both short-term and long-term memory may not be susceptible to ECS, so that memory might continue to develop after treatment. In this case, amnesia could result from the neuronal aftereffects of amnesic treatment being read into storage along with the informationally significant signal. Events occurring close together in time are often related to each other, and it is therefore adaptive that the coding processes of temporally contiguous events should influence each other. Accordingly, the neural aftereffects produced by ECS given one second after learning may introduce noise into the memory-coding process that was initiated by the immediately prior learning trial. Electroconvulsive shock at later times would be less disruptive because the neural aftereffects of ECS and the acquired information are processed more separately. By this view, any manipulation or event that has distinct neural aftereffects might be expected to have amnesic effects. Perhaps this notion could account for the finding that certain kinds of "natural" treatments can be amnesic. For example, the presentation of a nude photograph in the middle of a serial learning test produced retrograde amnesia for two items and anterograde amnesia for six items (Ellis, Detterman, Runcie, McCarver, & Craig, 1971). Whether amnesic treatments disrupt memory by disrupting the storage process as such or by adding noise to the storage process cannot be determined by the present evidence. A clearer answer to this question will become available when the critical biological events leading to storage of information are known and the effects of disruptive manipulations on these events are understood.

This discussion is relevant to the current controversy concerning whether amnesia involves a deficit in consolidation or retrieval (Miller & Springer, 1973). The issue will be considerably clarified when some of the biological processes involved in memory storage have been identified. It will probably be very difficult to settle this matter by argument from indirect evidence. For example, the mere fact that memory recovers at some time following amnesic treatment is not sufficient grounds to argue that the defect was in retrieval (Miller & Springer, 1973). Memory might sometimes recover because early stages of a serially organized storage process survive treatment. If this process continues to operate, the later stages of the storage process might be reestablished (Section VIII).

XIII. CONCLUSION

Although the model under discussion is consistent with a sizable body of behavioral, pharmacological, and neurophysiological data, it remains largely speculative because the evidence on which it is based is, for the most part, indirect. It is hoped, nevertheless, that it serves as a useful summary for the current evidence and that it might suggest some decisive experiments. As the focus for future investigations is directed increasingly toward well-characterized neural systems, the description of memory should acquire greater precision.

Two types of evidence have been reviewed. The first type has involved the behavior of whole animals and is quite indirect. These studies have provided little information about what the physical substrate of plastic changes in the nervous system might be. Nevertheless, these studies have provided some indirect evidence suggesting that memory is organized differently soon after learning rather than later after learning. The evidence is consistent with the existence of a first process that is operative for up to one hour after training and another, more stable process that is operative within a minute or two after training. In addition, a number of possibilities can be ruled out by the available evidence. One example is the idea that the short-term process has a fixed lifetime of several hours (Section III).

A second smaller body of evidence speaks to the question of what the physical basis of information storage at different times after learning might actually be. In *Aplysia*, short-lasting habituation has many of the characteristics of a known electrophysiological event, low-frequency depression (Kandel *et al.*, 1970), which has been described in the peripheral nervous system. Short-lasting habituation also occurs normally in spite of prolonged, extensive inhibition of protein synthesis (Schwartz *et al.*, 1971). By contrast, long-term modification of behavior in the rat (Daniels, 1971), mouse (Squire & Barondes, 1972a), chick (Mark & Watts, 1971), and goldfish (Agranoff, 1970) is markedly impaired by inhibition of protein synthesis. These findings are consistent with the operation of two distinct information-holding processes, one lasting for minutes and dependent on presynaptic alterations in the electrophysiological properties of neurons, and a second one that requires protein synthesis.

Current notions about memory have benefited from a dual approach, which endeavors on the one hand to provide a structural description of behavioral phenomena, and on the other hand to determine their biological bases. The structural approach attempts to provide a general description of behavioral events and underlying hypothetical processes. The biological approach attempts to identify the cellular correlates of behavioral events and processes. Even when the structural approach falls short of providing a definitive statement about the organization of hypothetical processes, it describes phenomena that a biological theory must explain. Questions about memory can be couched in either behavioral or cellular terms, but one might expect that the most complete and satisfying answers to such questions will be obtained by a dual experimental approach that encompasses both levels of inquiry.

REFERENCES

Aghajanian, G. K., & Bloom, F. D. The formation of synaptic junctions in developing rat brain: A quantitative electron microscopic study. *Brain Research,* 1967, **6,** 716–727.

Agranoff, B. W. Recent studies on the stages of memory formation in the goldfish. In W. L. Byrne (Ed.), *Molecular approaches to learning and memory.* New York: Academic Press, 1970.

Albert, D. J. The effects of spreading depression on the consolidation of learning. *Neuropsychologia,* 1966, **4,** 49–64. (a)

Albert, D. J. The effects of polarizing currents on the consolidation of learning. *Neuropsychologia,* 1966, **4,** 65–77. (b)

Alpern, H. P., & Marriott, J. G. A direct measure of short-term memory in mice utilizing a successive reversal learning set. *Behavioral Biology,* 1972, **7,** 723–732.

Andry, D. K., & Luttges, M. W. Memory traces: Experimental separation by cycloheximide and electroconvulsive shock. *Science,* 1972, **178,** 518–520.

Baldwin, B. A., & Soltysik, S. S. Acquisition of classical conditioned defensive responses in goats subjected to cerebral ischaemia. *Nature,* 1965, **206,** 1011–1013.

Baldwin, B. A., & Soltysik, S. S. The effects of cerebral ischaemia, resulting in loss of EEG, on the acquisition of conditioned reflexes in goats. *Brain Research,* 1966, **2,** 71–84.

Baldwin, B. A., & Soltysik, S. S. The effect of cerebral ischaemia or intracarotid injection of methohexitone on short-term memory in goats. *Brain Research,* 1969, **16,** 105–120.

Barbizet, J. *Human memory and its pathology.* San Francisco: Freeman, 1970.

Barondes, S. H. The relationship of biological regulatory mechanisms to learning and memory. *Nature,* 1965, **205,** 18–21.

Barondes, S. H., & Cohen, H. D. Delayed and sustained effects of acetoxycycloheximide on memory in mice. *Proceedings of the National Academy of Sciences, U.S.A.,* 1967, **58,** 157–164.

Barondes, S. H., & Cohen H. D. Memory impairment after subcutaneous injection of acetoxycycloheximide. *Science,* 1968, **160,** 556–557.

Barondes, S. H., & Squire, L. R. Time and the biology of memory. In G. Tindall (Ed.), *Clinical neurosurgery.* Baltimore: Waverly Press, 1972. (a)

Barondes, S. H., & Squire, L. R. Slow biological processes in memory storage and "recovery" of memory. In J. McGaugh (Ed.), *Brain, chemistry, and behavior.* New York: Plenum, 1972. (b)

Baumgartner, G., Creutzfeldt, D., & Jung, R. Microphysiology of cortical neurons in acute anoxia and in retinal ischaemia. In H. Gastaut & J. S. Meyer (Eds.), *Cerebral anoxia and the EEG.* Springfield, Illinois: Thomas, 1961.

Beritashvili, I. S. *Vertebrate memory.* New York: Plenum Press, 1971.

Bodian, D. A suggestive relationship of nerve cell RNA with specific synaptic sites. *Proceedings of the National Academy of Sciences, U.S.A.,* 1965, **53**, 418–425.

Bohdanecky, Z., Kopp, R., & Jarvik, M. E. Comparison of ECS and fluorothyl-induced retrograde amnesia. *Psychopharmacologia,* 1968, **12**, 91–95.

Bruner, J., & Kehoe, J. Long-term decrement in the efficacy of synaptic transmission in molluscs and crustaceans. In G. Horn & R. A. Hinde (Eds.), *Short-term changes in neural activity and behaviour.* Cambridge: University Press, 1970.

Bruner, J., & Kennedy, D. Habituation: Occurrence at a neuromuscular junction. *Science,* 1970, **169**, 92–94.

Bruner, J., & Tauc, L. Habituation at the synaptic level in *Aplysia. Nature,* 1966, **210**, 37–39.

Bullock, T. E. Single systems for the study of learning mechanisms. *Neurosciences Research Progress Bulletin,* 1966, **4**, 105–233.

Burns, B. D. The production of after-bursts in isolated unanaesthetized cerebral cortex. *Journal of Physiology,* 1954, **125**, 427–446.

Burns, B. D. *The mammalian cerebral cortex.* London: Arnold, 1958.

Carew, T. J., Castellucci, V. F., & Kandel, E. R. An analysis of dishabituation and sensitization of the gill-withdrawal reflex in *Aplysia. International Journal of Neuroscience,* 1971, **2**, 79–98.

Carew, T. J., Pinsker, H. M., & Kandel, E. R. Long-term habituation of a defensive withdrawal reflex in *Aplysia. Science,* 1972, **175**, 451–454.

Castellucci, V., Kupfermann, I., Pinsker, H., & Kandel, E. R. Neuronal mechanisms of habituation and dishabituation of the gill-withdrawal reflex in *Aplysia. Science,* 1970, **167**, 1745–1748.

Cedar, H., & Schwartz, J. H. Cyclic adenosine monophosphate in the nervous system of *Aplysia californica.* II. Effect of serotonin and dopamine. *Journal of General Physiology,* 1972, **60**, 570–587.

Cherkin, A. Kinetics of memory consolidation: Role of amnesic treatment parameters. *Proceedings of the National Academy of Sciences, U.S.A.,* 1969, **63**, 1094–1101.

Cherkin, A. Biphasic time course of performance after one-trial avoidance training in the chick. *Communications in Behavioral Biology,* 1971, **5**, 379–381.

Chorover, S. L., & Schiller, P. H. Short-term retrograde amnesia in rats. *Journal of Comparative and Physiological Psychology,* 1965, **59**, 73–78.

Cotman, C. W., Banker, G., Zornetzer, S. F., & McGaugh, J. L. Electroshock effects on brain protein synthesis: Relation to brain seizures and retrograde amnesia. *Science,* 1971, **173**, 454–456.

Daniels, D. Acquisition, storage, and recall of memory for brightness discrimination by rats following intracerebral infusion of acetoxycycloheximide. *Journal of Comparative and Physiological Psychology,* 1971, **76**, 110–118.

Davis, R. E., & Klinger, P. D. Environmental control of amnesic effects of various agents in goldfish. *Physiology and Behavior,* 1969, **4**, 269–271.

Del Castillo, J., & Katz, B. Statistical factors involved in neuromuscular facilitation and depression. *Journal of Physiology,* 1954, **124**, 574–585.

Deutsch, J. A. The cholinergic synapse an dthe site of memory. *Science,* 1971, **174**, 788–794.

Deutsch, J. A., & Rocklin, K. Anticholinesterase amnesia as a function of massed or spaced retest. *Journal of Comparative Physiology and Psychology,* 1972, **81**, 64–68.

Drachman, D. A., & Arbit, J. Memory and the hippocampal complex. II. Is memory a multiple process? *Archives of Neurology,* 1966, **15**, 52–61.

Eccles, J. C. *The physiology of synapses.* New York: Academic Press, 1964.

Ellis, N. R., Detterman, D. K., Runcie, D., McCarver, R. B., & Craig, E. M. Amnesic effects in short-term memory. *Journal of Experimental Psychology*, 1971, **89**, 357–361.

Emmelin, N. Supersensitivity following "pharmacological denervation." *Pharmacology Reviews*, 1961, **13**, 17–38.

Essman, W. B. Neurochemical changes in ECS and ECT. *Seminars in Psychiatry*, 1972, **4**, 67–79.

Flexner, J. B., Flexner, L. B., & Stellar, E. Memory in mice as affected by intracerebral puromycin. *Science*, 1963, **141**, 57–59.

Flexner, L. B., Flexner, J. B., & Roberts, R. B. Stages of memory in mice treated with acetoxycycloheximide before or immediately after learning. *Proceedings of the National Academy of Sciences, U.S.A.*, 1966, **56**, 730–735.

Flood, J. L., Rosenzweig, M. R., Bennett, E. C., & Orme, A. E. Influence of training strength on amnesia induced by pretraining injections of cycloheximide. *Physiology and Behavior*, 1972, **9**, 589–600.

Forbes, A. The mechanism of reaction. In C. Murchison (Ed.), *The foundations of experimental psychology*. Worcester, Massachusetts: Clark University Press, 1929.

Garren, L. D., Ney, R. L., & Davis, W. W. Studies on the role of protein synthesis in the regulation of corticosterone production by adrenocorticotropic hormone *in vivo. Proceedings of the National Academy of Sciences, U.S.A.*, 1965, **53**, 1443–1450.

Gartside, I. B. Mechanisms of sustained increases of firing rate of neurons in the rat cerebral cortex after polarization: Reverberating circuits or modification of synaptic conductance. *Nature*, 1968, **220**, 383–384.

Geller, A., & Jarvik, M. E. The time relations of ECS induced amnesia. *Psychonomic Science*, 1968, **12**, 169–170.

Geller, M., & Geller, A. Brief amnestic effects of spike-wave discharges. *Neurology*, 1970, **20**, 1089–1095.

Gerard, R. W. Biological roots of psychiatry. *Science*, 1955, **122**, 225–230.

Gerbrandt, L. K., Skrebitsky, V. G., Burešová, O., & Bureš, J. Plastic changes in unit activity induced by tactile stimuli followed by electrical stimulation of single hippocampal and reticular neurons. *Neuropsychologia*, 1968, **6**, 3–10.

Glickman, S. E. Perseverative neural processes and consolidation of the memory trace. *Psychological Bulletin*, 1961, **58**, 218–233.

Gold, P. E., Macri, J., & McGaugh, J. L. Retrograde amnesic gradients: Effects of direct cortical stimulation. *Science*, 1973, **179**, 1343–1345.

Hebb, D. O. *The organization of behavior*. New York: Wiley, 1949.

Herz, M. J. Interference with one-trial appetitive and aversive learning by ether and ECS. *Journal of Neurobiology*, 1969, **1**, 111–112.

Hilgard, E. R., & Marquis, D. G. *Conditioning and learning*. New York: Appleton-Century-Crofts, 1940.

Himwich, W. A. Biochemical and neurophysiological development of the brain in the neonatal period. *International Review of Neurobiology*, 1962, **4**, 117–158

Hubel, D. H., & Wiesel, T. H. Receptive fields, binocular interaction, and functional architecture in the cat's visual cortex. *Journal of Physiology*, 1962, **160**, 106–154.

Hughes, J. R. Post-tetanic potentiation. *Physiological Review*, 1958, **38**, 91–113.

Hughes, R. A., Barrett, R. J., & Ray, O. S. Retrograde amnesia in rats increases as a function of ECS-test interval and ECS intensity. *Physiology and Behavior*, 1970, **5**, 27–30. (a)

Hughes, R. A., Barrett, R. J., & Ray, O. S. Training to test interval as a determinant of a temporally graded ECS-produced response decrement in rats. *Journal of Comparative and Physiological Psychology*, 1970, **71**, 318–324. (b)

Hunt, T., Hunter, T., & Munro, A. Control of hemoglobin synthesis: Rate of translation of the messenger RNA for the A and B chains. *Journal of Molecular Biology*, 1969, **43**, 123–133.

Hutter, O. F. Post-tetanic restoration of neuromuscular transmission blocked by D-tubocurarine. *Journal of Physiology*, 1952, **118**, 216–227.

Irwin, S., Banuazizi, A., Kalsner, S., & Curtis, A. One-trial learning in the mouse. *Psychopharmacologia*, 1968, **12**, 286–302.

Jacob, F., & Monod, J. Genetic regulatory mechanisms in the synthesis of proteins. *Journal of Molecular Biology*, 1961, **3**, 318–356.

Jacobsen, C. F., & Nissen, H. W. Studies of cerebral function in primates. IV. The effects of frontal lobe lesions on the delayed alternation hbit in monkeys. *Journal of Comparative Psychology*, 1937, **23**, 101–112.

James, W. *Principles of psychology*, Vol. 1. New York: Dover, 1890.

John, E. R. Switchboard versus statistical theories of learning and memory. *Science*, 1972, **177**, 850–864.

Kamin, L. Retention of an incompletely learned avoidance response. *Journal of Comparative and Physiological Psychology*, 1963, **56**, 713–718.

Kandel, E. R., Castellucci, V., Pinsker, H., & Kupfermann, I. The role of synaptic plasticity in the short-term modification of behavior. In G. Horn & R. A. Hinde (Eds.), *Short-term changes in neural activity and behaviour*. Cambridge: University Press, 1970.

Kandel, E. R., & Spencer, W. A. Cellular neurophysiological approaches in the study of learning. *Physiological Review*, 1968, **48**, 65–134.

Kandel, E. R., & Tauc, L. Mechanism of heterosynaptic facilitation in the giant cell of the abdominal ganglion of *Aplysia depilans*. *Journal of Physiology*, 1965, **181**, 28–47.

Kesner, R. P., & Connor, H. S. Independence of short- and long-term memory: A neural system analysis. *Science*, 1972, **176**, 432–434.

Kopp, R., Bohdanecky, Z., & Jarvik, M. E. Long temporal gradient of retrograde amnesia for a well-discriminated stimulus. *Science*, 1966, **153**, 1547–1549.

Kubie, L. S. A theoretical application to some neurological problems of the properties of excitation waves which move in closed circuits. *Brain*, 1930, **53**, 166–177.

Kupfermann, I., & Kandel, E. R. Neural controls of a behavioral response mediated by the abdominal ganglion of *Aplysia*. *Science*, 1969, **164**, 847–850.

Lajtha, A. Protein metabolism in the nervous system. *International Review of Neurobiology*, 1964, **6**, 2–98.

Landauer, T. K. Reinforcement as consolidation. *Psychological Review*, 1969, **76**, 82–96.

Landfield, P. W., McGaugh, J. L., & Tusa, R. J. Theta rhythm: A temporal correlate of memory storage processes in the rat. *Science*, 1972, **175**, 87–89.

Larrabee, M. G., & Bronk, D. W. Prolonged facilitation of synaptic excitation in sympathetic ganglia. *Journal of Neurophysiology*, 1947, **10**, 139–154.

Lettvin, J. Y., Maturana, H. R., McCulloch, W. S., & Pitts, W. H. Two remarks on the visual system of the frog. In W. A. Rosenblith (Ed.), *Sensory Communication*, Cambridge: M.I.T. Press, 1961.

Lomó, T. Frequency potentiation of excitatory synaptic activity in the dentate area of the hippocampal formation. *Acta Physiologica Scandinavica*, 1966, Suppl. 277, 128.

Lorente de Nó, R. Facilitation of motoneurons. *American Journal of Physiology*, 1935, **113**, 505–523.

Lynch, G. S., Mosko, S., Parks, T., & Cotman, C. W. Relocation and hyperdevelopment of the dentate gyrus commissural system after entorhinal lesions in immature rats. *Brain Research,* 1973, **50,** 174–178.

Mah, C. J., Albert, D. J., & Jamieson, J. L. Memory storage: Evidence that consolidation continues following electroconvulsive shock. *Physiology and Behavior,* 1972, **8,** 283–286.

Mandell, A. J., Segal, D. S., Kuczenski, R. T., & Knapp, S. Some macromolecular mechanisms in CNS neurotransmitter pharmacology and their psychobiological organization. In J. McGaugh (Ed.), *The chemistry of mood, motivation, and memory.* New York: Plenum Press, 1972.

Mark, R. F., & Watts, M. E. Drug inhibition of memory formation in chickens. I. Long-term memory. *Proceedings of the Royal Society of London: B,* 1971, **178,** 439–454.

Mayes, A. R., & Cowey, A. The interhemispheric transfer of avoidance learning: An examination of the stimulus control hypothesis. *Behavioral Biology,* **8,** 193–205.

McEwen, B. S., & Grafstein, B. Fast and slow components in axonal transport of protein. *Journal of Cellular Biology,* 1968, **37,** 494–508.

McGaugh, J. L., & Dawson, R. G. Modification of memory storage processes. *Behavioral Science,* 1971, **16,** 45–63.

McGaugh, J. L., & Herz, M. J. (Eds.) *Memory consolidation.* San Francisco: Albion, 1972.

McGaugh, J. L., & Landfield, P. W. Delayed development of amnesia following electroconvulsive shock. *Physiology and Behavior,* 1970, **5,** 1109–1113.

Messenger, J. B. Two-stage recovery of a response in *Sepia. Nature,* 1971, **232,** 202–203.

Milner, B. Amnesia following operation on the temporal lobes. In C. W. M. Whitty, & O. L. Zangwill (Eds.), *Amnesia.* London: Butterworths, 1966.

Miller, R. R., & Springer, A. D. Amnesia, consolidation, and retrieval. *Psychological Review,* 1973, **80,** 69–79.

Misanin, J. R., Nagy, M., Keiser, E. F., & Bowen, W. Emergence of long-term memory in the neonatal rat. *Journal of Comparative and Physiological Psychology,* 1971, **77,** 188–199.

Müller, G. E., & Pilzecker, A. Experimentelle Beitrage zur Lehre vom Gedachtniss *Zeitschrift Für Psychologie,* 1900, **1,** 1–300.

Nadel, L. Interhemispheric transfer: Monocular input and varied sensory conditions. *Physiology and Behavior,* 1971, **6,** 655–661.

Nadel, L., & Burešová, O. Monocular input and the reversible split-brain. *Nature,* 1968, **220,** 914–915.

Nagy, M. Z., Misanin, J. R., Newman, J. A., Olsen, P. L., & Hinderlith, C. F. Ontogeny of memory in the neonatal mouse. *Journal of Comparative and Physiological Psychology,* 1972, **81,** 380–393.

Nielsen, H. C., Zimmerman, J. M., & Colliver, J. C. Effect of complete arrest of cerebral circulation on learing and retention in dogs. *Journal of Comparative and Physiological Psychology,* 1963, **56,** 974–978.

Norman, D. A. (Ed.) *Models of human memory.* New York: Academic Press, 1970.

Olds, J., Disterhoft, J. F., Segal, M., Kornblith, C. L., & Hirsch, R. Learning centers of rat brain mapped by measuring latencies of conditioned unit responses. *Journal of Neurophysiology,* 1972, **35,** 202–219.

Paolino, R. M., & Levy, H. M. Amnesia produced by spreading depression and ECS: Evidence for time dependent memory trace localization. *Science,* 1971, **172,** 746–748.

Peterson, L. R., & Peterson, M. J. Short-term retention of individual verbal items. *Journal of Experimental Psychology*, 1959, **58**, 193–198.

Pfaff, D. W. Parsimonious biological models of memory and reinforcement. *Psychological Review*, 1969, **76**, 70–81.

Pinsker, H., Kupfermann, I., Castellucci, V., & Kandel, E. R. Habituation and dishabituation of the gill-withdrawal reflex in *Aplysia*. *Science*, 1970, **167**, 1740–1742.

Quartermain, D., & McEwen, B. S. Temporal characteristics of amnesia induced by protein synthesis inhibitor: Determination by shock level. *Nature*, 1970, **228**, 677–678.

Quartermain, D., Paolino, R. M., & Miller, N. E. A brief temporal gradient of retrograde amnesia independent of situational change. *Science*, 1965, **149**, 1116–1118.

Ramirez, G., Levitan, I. B., & Mushynski, W. B. Highly purified synaptosomal membranes from rat brain. *Journal of Biological Chemistry*, 1972, **247**, 5382–5390.

Riege, W. H., & Cherkin, A. One-trial learning in goldfish: Temperature dependence. *Behavioral Biology*, 1972, **7**, 255–263.

Russell, W. R., & Nathan, P. W. Traumatic amnesia. *Brain*, 1946, **69**, 280–300.

Sanders, G. D., & Barlow, J. J. Variations in retention performance during long-term memory formation. *Nature*, 1971, **232**, 203–204.

Schneider, A. M. Control of memory by spreading cortical depression: A case for stimulus control. *Psychological Review*, 1967, **74**, 201–215.

Schneider, A. M., Kapp, B., Aron, C., & Jarvik, M. E. Retroactive effects of transcorneal and transpinnate ECS on step-through latencies of mice and rats. *Journal of Comparative and Physiological Psychology*, 1969, **69**, 506–509.

Schwartz, J. H., Castellucci, V. F., & Kandel, E. R. The functioning of identified neurons and synapses in the absence of protein synthesis. *Journal of Neurophysiology*, 1971, **34**, 939–953.

Scoville, W. B., & Milner, B. Loss of recent memory after bilateral hippocampal lesions. *Journal of Neurological and Neurosurgical Psychiatry*, 1957, **20**, 11–21.

Segal, D. S., Squire, L. R., & Barondes, S. H. Cycloheximide: Its effects on activity are dissociable from its effects on memory. *Science*, 1971, **172**, 82–84.

Serota, R. G. Acetoxycycloheximide and transient amnesia in the rat. *Proceedings of the National Academy of Sciences, U.S.A.*, 1971, **68**, 1249–1250.

Sharpless, S. Reorganization of function in the nervous system: Use and disuse. *Annual Review of Physiology*, 1964, **26**, 352–388.

Sherrington, C. S. *The integrative action of the nervous system*. New Haven, Connecticut: Yale University Press, 1906.

Spence, K. W., & Bower, G. H. (Eds.) *Advances in the psychology of learning and motivation research and theory*, Vol. 3. New York: Academic Press, 1968.

Spencer, W. A., & Wigdor, R. Ultra-late PTP of monosynaptic reflex responses in rat. *Physiologist*, 1965, **8**, 278.

Sperry, R. W., & Miner, N. Pattern perception following insertion of mica plates into visual cortex. *Journal of Comparative and Physiological Psychology*, 1955, **48**, 463–469.

Sperry, R. W., Miner, N., & Myers, R. E. Visual pattern perception following subglial slicing and tantalum wire implantations in the visual cortex. *Journal of Comparative and Physiological Psychology*, 1955, **48**, 50–58.

Squire, L. R. Amnesia for remote events following electroconvulsive therapy. *Behavioral Biology*, 1974a, **12**, 119–125.

Squire, L. R. A stable impairment in remote memory following electroconvulsive therapy. *Neuropsychologia*, 1974, in press. (b)

Squire, L. R., & Barondes, S. H. Actinomycin-D: Effects on memory at different times after training. *Nature,* 1970, **225,** 649–650.

Squire, L. R., & Barondes, S. H. Inhibitors of RNA or protein synthesis and memory. In J. Gaito (Ed.), *Macromolecules and behavior,* 2nd ed. New York: Appleton-Century-Crofts, 1972. (a)

Squire, L. R., & Barondes, S. H. Variable decay of memory and its recovery in cycloheximide-treated mice. *Proceedings of the National Academy of Sciences, U.S.A.,* 1972, **69,** 1416–1420. (b)

Squire, L. R., & Barondes, S. H. Memory impairment during prolonged training in mice given inhibitors of protein synthesis. *Brain Research,* 1973, **56,** 215–225, *in press.*

Squire, L. R., Geller, A., & Jarvik, M. E. Habituation and activity as affected by cycloheximide. *Communications in Behavioral Biology,* 1970, **5,** 249–254.

Squire, L. R., Glick, S. D., & Goldfarb, J. Relearning at different times after training as affected by centrally and peripherally acting cholinergic drugs in the mouse. *Journal of Comparative and Physiological Psychology,* 1971, **74,** 41–45.

Squire, L. R., & Liss, P. H. Memory as affected by cortical spreading depression: A critique of stimulus control. *Psychological Review,* 1968, **75,** 347–352.

Squire, L. R., Smith, G. A., & Barondes, S. H. Cycloheximide can affect memory within minutes after the beginning of training. *Nature,* 1973, **242,** 201–202.

Sutherland, N. S. Outlines of a theory of visual pattern recognition in animals and man. *Proceedings of the Royal Society of London: B,* 1968, **171,** 297–317.

Tasaki, I., Polley, E. H., & Orrego, F. Action potential from individual elements in cat geniculate and striate cortex. *Journal of Neurophysiology,* 1954, **17,** 454–474.

Tauc, L. Presynaptic inhibition in the abdominal ganglion of *Aplysia. Journal of Physiology,* 1965, **181,** 282–307.

Tauc, L., & Epstein, R. Heterosynaptic facilitation as a distinct mechanism in *Aplysia. Nature,* 1967, **214,** 724–725.

Thompson, R. The effect of ECS on retention in young and adult rats. *Journal of Comparative and Physiological Psychology,* 1957, **50,** 397–400.

Thompson, R. F., & Spencer, W. A. Habituation: A model phenomenon for study of neural substrates of behavior. *Psychological Review,* 1966, **73,** 16–43.

Trendelenburg, V. Supersensitivity and subsensitivity to sympathomimetic amines. *Pharmacological Reviews,* 1963, **15,** 225–276.

Ungar, G. Roles of proteins and peptides in learning and memory. In G. Ungar (Ed.), *Molecular mechanisms in memory and learning.* New York: Plenum Press, 1970.

Volkmar, F. R., & Greenough, W. T. Rearing complexity affects branching of dendrites in the visual cortex of the rat. *Science,* 1972, **176,** 1445–1447.

Von Baumgarten, B. J., & Djahenparwar, B. Time course of repetitive heterosynaptic facilitation in *Aplysia Californica. Brain Research,* 1967, **4,** 295–297.

Warrington, E., & Silberstein, M. A questionnaire technique for investigating very long-term memory. *Quarterly Journal of Experimental Psychology,* 1970, **22,** 508–512.

Watts, M. E., & Mark, R. F. Drug inhibition of memory formation in chickens. II. Short-term memory. *Proceedings of the Royal Society of London: B.,* 1971, **178,** 455–464.

Way, E. L., Loh, H. H., & Shen, F. Morphine tolerance, physical dependence, and synthesis of brain 5-hydroxytryptamine. *Science,* 1968, **162,** 1290–1292.

Weiskrantz, L. Experimental studies of amnesia. In C. W. M. Whitty, & O. L. Zang-will (Eds.), *Amnesia*. London: Butterworths, 1966.

Wiener, N. I. Electroconvulsive shock induced impairment and enchantment of a learned escape response. *Physiology and Behavior*, 1970, **5**, 971–974.

Wilson, D. L., & Berry, R. W. The effect of synaptic stimulation on RNA and protein metabolism in the R2 soma of *Aplysia*. *Journal of Neurobiology*, 1972, **3**, 369–379.

Wickelgren, W. A. Sparing of short-term memory in an amnesic patient: Implications for strength theory of memory. *Neuropsychologia*, 1968, **6**, 235–244.

Woodward, D. J., Hoffer, B. J., Siggins, G. R., & Bloom, F. E. The development of synaptic junctions, synaptic activation, and responsiveness to neurotransmitter substances in rat cerebellar purkinje cells. *Brain Research*, 1971, **34**, 73–97.

Zerbolio, D. J. Memory storage: The first post-trial hour. *Psychonomic Science*, 1969, **15**, 57–58.

CHAPTER

2

THE LONG AND THE SHORT OF MEMORY[1]

WAYNE A. WICKELGREN

[1] This research was supported by Grant MH 17958 from the National Institute of Mental Health, U.S. Public Health Service.

One of the most frequently considered theoretical questions in memory research over the last 15 years has been whether it is useful to distinguish between short-term and long-term memory traces (primary and secondary memory). Do human beings have one or two (or more) dynamically different memory traces mediating performance at retention intervals ranging from several seconds to several years? The present article considers this theoretical question. Consideration of this question is limited primarily to verbal memory because that is where the relevant evidence exists. Sensory memories (persistence of vision or audition, adaptation, etc.) are ignored.

Specifically, this article is concerned with the validity of distinguishing between some kind of short-term memory with a time constant on the order of seconds (the "short trace") from some type of longer-term memory that may last from tens of seconds to years (the "long trace"). There is no evidence at present to justify splitting long-term memory into components such as intermediate- versus long-term memory. The physiological evidence for this distinction is not at all convincing (see review by Deutsch, 1969), and the psychological evidence presented by Wickelgren (1969) has been better accounted for by a single long trace with increasing resistance to forgetting (Wickelgren, 1972b).

Throughout this article, the terms "short-term and long-term retention" will represent the methodological distinction between memory tested at short delays (usually less than 10 seconds) versus long delays (tens of seconds to years). The terms "short and long traces" will represent an assumed theoretical distinction between two dynamically different memory traces.

The present article is organized into three sections: The first section discusses some general concepts that are important for making distinctions between memory traces. The second section considers a large variety of irrelevant evidence for distinguishing between short and long traces, evidence which is irrelevant either because it can be interpreted within a single-trace theory or because it can be interpreted by assuming dynamically identical traces in two different coding modalities (e.g., phonetic versus semantic modalities). The third section considers relevant dynamic evidence for distinguishing between short and long traces.

I. CONCEPTUAL BACKGROUND

Although there are three lines of relatively convincing evidence favoring a distinction between short and long traces (primary and secondary memory), it is a sad fact that the vast majority of all of the cited evidence is worthless for making the distinction between short and long traces. There are various reasons why different pieces of evidence are worthless, but there are two recurrent conceptual errors. First, coding differences are often confused with dynamic differences. Second, differences in decay rate are considered to establish differences in trace dynamics. These conceptual errors are discussed in this section.

If the subject learns two word-word paired associates, say A-B and C-D, one would say that two different memory traces were established: one trace for the A-B association and one trace for the C-D association. If anyone doubted that these were two different memory traces, it could be demonstrated that they were different by showing that $C-E_i$ interpolated learning caused more interference with the C-D association than with the A-B association and vice versa for interpolated $A-E_i$ interpolated learning. The fact that different manipulations affect the two traces differently does not argue that the two traces are dynamically different. That is to say, this evidence does not establish that the laws of forgetting are different for the two memory traces. In fact, in this case, undoubtedly the two traces would be considered to be stored in the same coding modality as well as having the same dynamic laws of forgetting.

Now let us consider a slightly less obvious case where memory for a picture is compared with memory for an abstract (not easily visualizable) word-word paired associate. In this case, one presumes that not only are the two traces logically different, but they are stored in what we might consider to be two different coding modalities (visual versus verbal). It is beyond the scope of this article to consider what observations and manipulations are relevant for demonstrating differences in coding modalities.

However, any such demonstrations of a modality difference, by themselves, prove nothing regarding the question of whether the two traces are dynamically different. Two traces coded in different modalities may have the same dynamic laws of forgetting, as we assume hold for two traces which are simply logically different (A-B versus C-D) but are stored in the same coding modality. To demonstrate that there are two dynamically different types of memory traces, the short trace and the long trace, it is necessary to show that any alleged differences in forgetting for two types of memory traces can only be explained by assuming a dynamic difference, not simply a coding difference.

The second conceptual error very frequently made in this area is that differences in forgetting rate (decay rate) alone are evidence for distinguishing short and long traces. Under many conditions, memory appears to undergo an initial period of rapid forgetting followed by a long period of relatively slower forgetting. From this fact alone, some investigators have concluded in favor of two memory traces: the short trace characterized by rapid forgetting and the long trace characterized by slow forgetting. Fallacies in this line of reasoning have been discussed previously by Gruneberg (1970), and the present discussion is largely a restatement of Gruneberg's arguments.

There are two basic fallacies involved in the superficial use of differences in forgetting rate to distinguish two dynamically different memory traces. First, rapid forgetting occurring immediately after learning does not, in and of itself, require the assumption of two memory traces. Ever since Jost's second law was formulated in the late 1800s (see Hovland, 1951), it has been established by virtually every relevant study that the forgetting rate for long-term retention decreases with increasing delay, no matter what dependent measure of memory is used. A recent quantitative study of this phenomenon by Wickelgren (1972b) also found that forgetting rate is continuously decreasing with increasing retention interval from delays of tens of seconds up to delays of over two years. Thus, from the mere *qualitative* finding of decreasing decay rate with increasing retention interval, one cannot argue for a distinction between short and long memory traces, since the long trace itself very likely demonstrates this qualitative phenomena.

Only if one could show that retention functions which fit at long retention intervals cannot be extrapolated to fit the results for short retention intervals (under 10 sec) would there be evidence of the existence of a short trace distinct from the long trace. There have been careful quantitative analyses attempting to demonstrate the necessity for assuming two memory traces (e.g., Atkinson & Crothers, 1964; Waugh & Norman, 1965; Wickelgren, 1969). However, none of these quantitative studies assumed a long trace that was rapidly decreasing in its decay rate over the first 10 sec. Furthermore, there are many options for extrapolation of the long trace into the first 10 sec that are consistent with the form of the retention function for long delays, and it is quite possible that one of these options would provide a good fit of the single-trace theory to the data at short retention intervals. I know this is true in some cases where I previously thought only a dual-trace theory would fit. At present, it is not clear what conclusions can be drawn regarding the number of traces operating at short retention intervals under conditions where there is some long-term retention.

The second defect in the rapid forgetting argument is that, even if one could show that two memory traces with different decay rates are required in order to fit retention functions across a variety of situations, the two traces might differ in decay rate merely because they came from different coding modalities. The physiological character of the trace and the underlying psychological laws of forgetting in both cases might be identical.

For example, verbal memory traces may include a rapidly decaying phonetic component and a more slowly decaying semantic component. It is known that the forgetting rate for long-term retention (presumably the long trace) is greater the greater the similarity of interpolated to original material (even by a recognition measure—see Wickelgren, 1972b, for a review). Thus, the phonetic trace will have a much higher average similarity between original and interpolated material than will the semantic trace. Both traces might be subject to the same factors producing forgetting in precisely the same way, with the only difference being due to the similarity between original and interpolated material. Thus, even vast differences in decay rate for two traces do not necessarily imply dynamic differences. Precisely this point has been made by Gruneberg (1970).

II. IRRELEVANT EVIDENCE

A. Associative versus Nonassociative Structure of Memory

Two basic types of memory structures have been proposed as models for human memory: associative and nonassociative. In an associative memory, each concept has a relatively unique internal representative and these internal representatives have different degrees of association to each other depending upon how frequently they have been contiguously activated in the past. By contrast, in a nonassociative memory, there is an ordered set of locations (boxes, registers, cells, etc.) into which the internal representative of any concept can be coded, and sequences of concepts are stored in order in this ordered set of locations. A tape recorder is a good example of a nonassociative memory. As each successive sound occurs, a pattern representing that sound is impressed on a successive portion of the magnetic recording tape.

Human long-term verbal memory has long been regarded as being associative, though psychologists have rarely attempted to state a precise definition of associative memory, let alone give systematic consideration to evidence relevant to the issue. Elsewhere, Wickelgren (1972a) has given a relatively precise definition of an associative memory and discussed several lines of evidence for the proposition that long-term verbal memory is associative.

During the revival of interest in short-term memory in the late 1950s and early 1960s, many short-term memory researchers implicitly or explicitly assumed that short-term retention was from a nonassociative memory ("buffer" storage). If this were true and if long-term retention were from an associative memory, then clearly there would be two traces with fundamentally different coding properties. Such a fundamental difference in coding would virtually prohibit the possibility that the two traces could have identical dynamics.

However, there never was any evidence for the nonassociative character of verbal short-term memory, and Wickelgren (1965a, 1965b, 1965c, 1966, 1967b, 1972a) performed a series of studies to demonstrate that short-term memory is also associative. Thus, there is no support here for a dual-trace theory.

B. Phonetic versus Semantic Coding

At one point, it was conjectured that short-term verbal retention was from a phonetic modality while long-term verbal retention was from a semantic modality. It is now quite clear that verbal short-term retention can include an encoding of both phonetic and semantic features, and that verbal long-term retention can include an encoding of both phonetic and semantic features. The earlier hypothesis was always absurd on the face of it, since understanding spoken speech requires that the meaning of words be available within hundreds of msec following presentation, and speech recognition and articulation require long-term memory for the phonetic constituents of words. Furthermore, considerable formal experimental evidence now exists for the proposition that both phonetic and semantic memories are potentially available at both short and long retention intervals (see Shulman, 1971, for a thorough review; see also Gruneberg, Colwill, Winfrow, & Woods, 1970; Gruneberg & Sykes, 1969; Shulman, 1970, 1972).

When subjects read words rapidly without getting the meaning, only the phonetic trace may be formed. When long retention intervals are filled with interpolated verbal activity, only the semantic trace may be available (the phonetic trace having been completely destroyed or made irretrievable by interference from the interpolated material). However, both phonetic and semantic traces can be present at both short and long retention intervals.

At this point, it is appropriate to raise the question of what this all has to do with the issue under discussion, namely, distinguishing two dynamically different types of traces.

The question of the existence of two coding modalities for verbal material is largely orthogonal to the question of the existence of two dynamically different traces. The independent character of these two theoretical issues is easy to demonstrate. It might be that there is only one dynamic type of memory trace in the phonetic coding modality, and the same type of trace also operates in the semantic modality. Alternatively, there may be only one dynamic type of trace in the phonetic modality, but it may have different dynamic properties from the single memory trace operative in the semantic modality. Still another alternative is that either or both of the phonetic and semantic coding modalities has both short and long traces operative. This could produce a short and long phonetic trace and a short and long semantic trace. At present, there is no evidence to indicate which of these possibilities obtains. Thus, there is no support here for distinguishing two dynamically different memory traces.

C. Two-Component Retention Functions and the Recency Effect

Both free recall and probe recall paradigms exhibit substantial recency effects: The terminal item in a list is recalled with a probability near unity and correct recall decreases rapidly the farther an item is from the end of the list. In the middle or initial portions of a list, the proportion correct is still above chance but declines at a far slower rate as a function of further increases in the retention interval. For long lists, there appears to be a nearly asymptotic level of recall over the middle of the list with a small primacy effect (to be ignored in the present discussion) and a large recency effect. Recall from the more slowly decaying (or asymptotic) section of the serial position curves is viewed to be based on the long trace (secondary memory) and recall from the recency section to be based either on the short trace (primary memory) alone or on a combination of both short and long traces.

This argument for distinguishing short and long traces is defective on at least two different counts. First, as discussed in the Conceptual Background section, the fact that the memory trace appears to be decaying more rapidly initially after learning and then more slowly does not, in and of itself, require the assumption of two memory traces. Long-term retention, by itself, demonstrates this phenomenon and the strength-resistance theory of Wickelgren (1972b, 1974) accounts for the continuously declining decay rate with a single trace. Second, even if one showed that the retention function which fit at long retention intervals could not be extrapolated to fit at short retention intervals, one still would not have proved the necessity of assuming two dynamically different memory traces. The two traces could be a phonetic and a semantic trace, different in coding properties and in decay rate, but not necessarily in basic dynamic properties.

In the free-recall studies, where the middle positions of the list appear to form an asymptote, it might be argued that one had to assume two traces because one trace decayed and the other did not decay at all. However, one knows from other studies that long traces must be assumed to be decaying, albeit at a rate sufficiently slow to show little difference over retention intervals from 20 to 40 sec.

In addition, the free-recall paradigm does not control order of recall and rehearsal strategies adequately to permit using the exact shape of the serial position function to infer anything about the number of traces and their dynamic properties. For example, Rundus, Loftus, and Atkinson (1970) have demonstrated that the frequency of rehearsal declines monotonically from the beginning to the end of the list in a free-recall study. Given this fact, it is perfectly reasonable to interpret the "asymptotic" middle section of free-recall serial position curves to be reflecting an approximately even trade-off between degree of learning and length of retention interval. With important uncontrolled factors such as amount of rehearsal and amount of prior output (retrieval) interference, it is rather ridiculous to try to conclude anything about the dynamics of memory from free recall.

D. Differential Effects on the Serial Position Curve

A principal strategy in attempting to verify the distinction between short and long traces has been to determine whether variables can be found that affect only the terminal section of the serial position curve or only the initial and medial sections. If a variable affects only the terminal section, it is presumed to be affecting only the short trace. If a variable affects only the initial and medial sections or if the variable has a "constant" effect across all serial positions, then the variable is presumed to be affecting only the long trace.

Across the entire gamut of such studies, there appears to be some flexibility with respect to whether the "subtraction method" is applied under the assumption that a variable affecting the long trace will show up uniformly at all serial positions or whether the subtraction method is not applied under the assumption that the long trace only appears in the initial and medial positions. One might object to this flexibility. However, since none of these studies provides any evidence that is definitive in demonstrating the distinction between short and long traces for a variety of other reasons, it is not necessary to quibble about whether or not to apply the subtraction method or what theoretically motivated subtraction method to use.

1. Interpolated Interference

A variety of studies have now demonstrated that requiring subjects to count backwards, pronounce words, or engage in a variety of other interpolated interfering activities following presentation of a list depresses the terminal section of the serial position curve and has a relatively small effect on the nonterminal sections. This effect has been found most frequently in free recall (Bartz & Salehi, 1970; Glanzer & Cunitz, 1966; Glanzer, Gianutsos, & Dubin, 1969; Glanzer & Schwartz, 1971; Postman & Phillips, 1965; Raymond, 1969), but similar effects have also been found in probe recall with paired associates (Rundus, 1970). If it were possible to argue that there was indeed *no* effect of interpolated material on the nonterminal section of the serial position curve, then this evidence might be taken as a definitive demonstration of the existence of two dynamically different memory traces. However, studies typically demonstrate some, albeit smaller, decremental effect of interpolated interference on the initial and medial sections of the serial position curve in conjunction with the greater effect on the terminal section. Furthermore, it is well known from other studies that long-term retention is decreased by retroactive interference, so whether or not the effect is observed in these studies, or is statistically significant, is a matter of no consequence. As Gruneberg (1970) has pointed out, nonterminal items have already gone through their period of steepest decline due to the interference from subsequent list items. So with a single trace theory, one expects to see a much larger effect of the postlist task on terminal than on nonterminal items. Thus, this evidence is worthless for distinguishing between short and long traces.

2. Order of Recall

Studies by Deese (1957), Murdock (1963), Raffel (1936), and Tulving and Arbuckle (1963, 1966) show that forcing subjects to recall the early items of a list first greatly reduces the recall of terminal items but has little effect on nonterminal items. This effect is the output interference analogue of the effects of an interpolated interfering task. Precisely the same arguments apply regarding its lack of definitiveness for the single- versus dual-trace issue.

3. Long-Delayed Recall and Recognition

Although items in terminal positions are recalled with the highest probability in immediate free recall, Craik (1970) demonstrated that terminal items actually had lower "final" recall (after a sequence of 10 free-recall lists) than did items in either initial or medial positions. These results have been essentially replicated for a three-week delayed recognition test by Rundus et al. (1970), though the delayed recognition of terminal items was not substantially worse than that of medial list items. These results were viewed as somewhat surprising in that terminal items were retrieved with highest probability in immediate recall, but nevertheless had a lower probability of final recall at the end of the entire session. The dual-trace interpretation was that terminal items were recalled well on the basis of the short trace (primary memory) even though they had lower degree of long trace acquisition. Craik interpreted the results "to pose a serious problem for one-process models [p. 148]."

Once again, the conclusion is unwarranted. According to a single trace theory, the terminal items could have a lower degree of acquisition but be recalled better immediately after the end of a list because of their shorter retention interval. By the end of the session, the relative difference in retention intervals for terminal versus nonterminal items is negligible, and the final recall reflects only the initial difference in degree of acquisition (largely due to greater rehearsal of initial items according to Rundus et al., 1970). The single trace explanation of these results is completely straightforward, and this phenomenon gives no support whatsoever for two traces.

4. Repetition versus Imagery Instructions

Smith, Barresi, and Gross (1971) demonstrated that instructing subjects to repeatedly pronounce (rehearse) paired associates produced superior probed recall for the terminal pairs of the list, but inferior performance for nonterminal pairs, by comparison to imagery instructions. This result was taken to indicate that imagery improved the long trace (secondary memory) more than repetition, but that repetition benefited the short traces (primary memory) more than imagery. This experiment probably does demonstrate the existence of two memory traces with different coding properties, namely, a visual trace and a verbal phonetic trace, with the visual trace having the slower decay rate under the conditions of this experiment. However, for reasons mentioned in the Conceptual Background section, there is no reason on the basis of this study to conclude that the dynamic properties of these two traces are different. For all we know on the basis of this study, the phonetic trace mediating superior performance for the repetition group at the terminal positions may be a long-term phonetic trace that is rapidly interfered with by presentation of subsequent pairs.

5. Presentation Rate

By contrast to the relatively small number of variables that are alleged to affect only the terminal section of the serial position curve, rate of presentation is but one of many variables alleged to affect primarily initial and medial sections of serial position curves. Glanzer and Cunitz (1966), Murdock (1962), and Raymond (1969) have all found that a slower rate of presentation of items facilitates free recall of items from initial and medial sections of a list while having no effect whatsoever on the recall of terminal items. This, it is alleged, supports the distinction between short and long traces, since the hypothesized two traces appear to be affected differently by the independent variable of presentation rate. The conclusion is completely unwarranted.

In the first place, it must be noted that varying presentation rate in this design confounds two important variables, namely, study time for each item and the retention interval (measured in time). Thus, it is pertinent to ask how each of these two more basic variables is affecting the terminal versus the nonterminal sections of the serial position curve. When study time has been manipulated independently of retention interval, increased study time is known to have a beneficial effect at all retention intervals (Hellyer, 1962; Peterson & Peterson, 1959; Wickelgren, 1969; Wickelgren & Norman, 1971). According to a dual-trace analysis of these studies, increased study time must be presumed to be increasing the level of acquisition of both short and long traces. Thus, it would be absurd to believe that study time is having a qualitatively different effect on the hypothesized two-component traces in the free-recall studies. What is presumably happening in the confounded free-recall studies is that the increased delay for slower presentation rates is approximately compensating for the beneficial effects of increased study time for the terminal items but failing to compensate for the nonterminal items. This could be because there are two memory traces and the beneficial effects of increased study time are substantially greater for the long trace than for the short trace. However, the rate of decay of long traces is known to decrease with increasing delay. Thus, the effects of increased delay for the terminal items ought to be substantially greater than for the nonterminal items, assuming the single-trace theory. The point is that qualitative analyses cannot decide the issue. Only a thorough quantitative analysis that is unavailable at present could perhaps make a case for the dual-trace theory.

In the second place, since these presentation-rate effects are for free recall, there is always the possibility that the results are due to a confounding with rehearsal strategies or order of recall. For example, at slower presentation rates, subjects may report nonterminal items earlier and surely do rehearse nonterminal items more than at faster presentation rates. Such possible and probable confoundings completely vitiate this phenomenon as evidence for two separate memory traces.

6. Modality Effects

The initial Murdock (1966) article showed a superiority at terminal positions for auditory presentation and a crossover demonstrating superiority at initial positions for visual presentation using a probed paired-associate design. However, further studies by Murdock (1967, 1968, 1969) have obtained a variety of results including consistent superiority for auditory presentation at all positions, superiority for auditory presentation at terminal positions turning into no difference at initial positions, and even greater superiority for auditory presentation at initial positions than at terminal positions. Although the overall tendency is for a greater superiority of auditory presentation at terminal positions, the findings are not completely consistent in demonstrating a differential effect of this variable on retention at longer versus shorter retention intervals. However, even if the most extreme effect, namely, a crossover with auditory versus visual presentation, could be consistently obtained, it would not imply two dynamically different memory traces. Just as with the crossover in the Smith et al. (1971) study of imagery versus repetition instructions, the results might be due to the presence of phonetic versus visual traces with essentially equivalent dynamics (though different rates of decay under the experimental conditions). Even for materials assumed to be processed in the same modality, decay rate varies with the similarity of interpolated learning to original learning (Wickelgren, 1972b). Thus, it is not possible to argue that a difference in decay rate, in and of itself, implies a difference in basic trace dynamics, since these different decay rates may simply reflect differences in the similarity of interpolated to original material in different modalities of storage.

7. Familiarity

Raymond (1969) and Sumby (1963) have shown that free recall of high frequency words is superior to low frequency words for nonterminal items, but only marginally superior for terminal items. Along the same line, Raymond demonstrated a significantly greater free recall of words over trigrams for nonterminal positions, but an insignificant superiority of words over trigrams for terminal positions after the subtraction method had been used. Since the difference appears to be quantitative, not qualitative, an established quantitative theory regarding trace dynamics is required in order to argue for two traces. Furthermore, these studies use free recall for which the results may be confounded by differences in rehearsal strategies and order of report. Finally, even if it could be established that there were two traces involved, the two traces might differ only in their coding properties and not in their dynamic properties. Specifically, familiarity might influence the degree of acquisition in the semantic modality more than in the phonetic modality, but the storage dynamics of both traces could follow the same laws.

8. List Length

In free recall, Murdock (1962) and Postman and Phillips (1965) have found that increased list length decreases the probability of correct recall at nonterminal positions but not at terminal positions. Comparing the effects of list length as a function of serial position is a rather difficult thing to do, since it is not clear what positions should be compared. Because there are both substantial primacy and recency effects in free recall, it is reasonable to equate either starting from the end of the list or starting from the beginning of the list. If one equates positions starting from the end of a list, the recall probabilities for terminal items are not very different for different list lengths, but at some point earlier in the list, the shorter list lengths lie above the longer list lengths in recall probability.

Within a single-trace theory, this effect may simply be attributed to the greater opportunity for rehearsal that earlier items have on the list as compared to later items and need imply nothing whatsoever concerning the presence of two versus one memory trace. Equating from the end means that greater list length implies a greater number of prior items at each position being compared. It is reasonable to assume both a priori and on the evidence of Rundus and Atkinson (1970) that the more prior list items, the fewer later rehearsals an item receives. Thus, it will be remembered less well. However, this effect should be small to nonexistent for terminal items since they have few to no subsequent opportunities for rehearsal prior to recall.

The fact that in longer list lengths (20 items or more) there appears to be an approximately asymptotic section of the serial position curve in the middle of the list, does not make this comparison any more relevant to the issue of one versus two memory traces. All that the approximately asymptotic middle section means is that a combination of rehearsal strategies, initial acquisition differences, order of report, and differential retention interval is approximately balancing for these serial positions. Since list length affects the degree of primacy, rehearsal strategies, and possibly order of report for this asymptotic section on the curve, it would not be surprising if the various variables should balance out at a higher level for shorter list lengths, even if only a single memory trace were present. Interpretation of these free-recall data is so complex that at present absolutely nothing can be concluded from them with respect to the single- versus dual-trace issue.

9. Concurrent Task Load

Murdock (1965) and Silverstein and Glanzer (1971) showed that requiring subjects to perform a concurrent task (card sorting and number addition) during presentation of a list lowers recall of the nonterminal items in the list. The more difficult the concurrent task, the greater the effect. This effect is absent or possibly reversed at terminal positions. Once again, the differential effect of this variable on the terminal versus nonterminal sections of the serial position curve is not useful evidence for distinguishing two memory traces. There could well be only a single memory trace with subjects adopting different rehearsal strategies under the different conditions, namely, rehearsing initial and medial items more frequently later in the list when there was no concurrent task or an easy concurrent task than when there was a more difficult concurrent task. Rehearsal strategies of this type could lead precisely to the result obtained. Indeed, Murdock (1965) interpreted his results in essentially this way without appealing to any dual-trace explanation.

There is actually a study by Bartz and Salehi (1970) that favors Murdock's differential rehearsal interpretation over Glanzer's (1971) dual-trace explanation. According to the Glanzer notion that the subsidiary task affects the long trace, but not the short trace, one should expect to see an effect of the difficulty of the concurrent task on the strength of the long trace at all serial positions of the list. However, according to the differential rehearsal interpretation, one should expect to see it primarily in the initial and medial positions but not the terminal positions of the list. By using an interpolated interference task (backward counting) to eliminate any possible short-term component, Bartz and Salehi were able to show that the effect of the difficulty of the concurrent sorting task was present only at the initial and medical serial positions and not at the terminal serial positions. Thus, the differential rehearsal explanation appears to provide a more satisfactory explanation of these results than the dual-trace explanation.

10. Associative Structure

Glanzer and Schwartz (1971) have demonstrated that the free recall of highly associated word pairs is greater than that of unassociated word pairs at all positions of the list, with a subtraction method being used to determine that the effect was entirely on the hypothesized long trace and not at all on the short trace. A postlist interference task was used to estimate the long trace component without contamination by short trace components. The validity of this evidence depends completely on the validity of the particular subtraction method chosen. In the absence of any knowledge regarding exactly how short traces and long traces combine to produce a decision and interact in other ways, it is difficult to derive great confidence from the result of any particular subtraction analysis. In addition, of course, even if there are two traces operative in the situation, they may well differ only in coding properties and not dynamic properties as discussed previously. Namely, the two traces may be phonetic and semantic traces that differ in decay rates because of different degrees of similarity of the encoding in each modality to the retroactively interfering material. Given that the traces differ in coding properties in this manner, one expects that associative structure would affect primarily or exclusively the degree of acquisition of the semantic trace, not the phonetic trace.

E. Spacing of Repetitions

Bjork (1970) has surveyed the findings with regard to the efficacy of multiple learning traits as a function of the spacing between repetitions and come to the following conclusions: (a) Massed repetitions are superior to spaced repetitions when performance is measured after very short retention intervals (seconds) and (b) spaced repetitions are superior to massed repetitions at longer retention intervals, with the improvement increasing up to an optimum degree of spacing and then declining thereafter. Wickelgren (1970a) gave a dual-trace explanation of these findings: Short retention intervals rely primarily on the short trace and massed repetitions give less time for forgetting in short-term memory. Spaced repetitions improve long-term memory because a period of 10 to 30 seconds is required for consolidation of the long trace for the previous presentation. This explanation is probably wrong even if the dual-trace theory is correct.

In any event, the qualitative results can equally well be given a single-trace explanation. The explanation is as follows: Massed repetitions give higher initial degrees of learning after the last repetition, since little time elapses for decay of the traces from earlier presentations. However, since the decay rate for memory traces decreases with increasing delay (Wickelgren, 1972b), the decay rate of the trace for items after spaced repetitions will be lower than after massed repetitions. Thus, one should obtain a crossover, with lower initial degree of learning for spaced repetitions leading to poorer performance at short retention intervals, but lower decay rate after spaced repetitions leading to better performance at longer retention intervals. Thus, these phenomena are utterly inconclusive with regard to distinguishing between single- and dual-trace theories.

F. Selective Impairment of Auditory Verbal Short-Term Memory

Shallice and Warrington (1970) and Warrington and Shallice (1969, 1972) have recently discovered a patient who has extremely poor performance on all verbal short-term memory tasks using auditory presentation, but whose capacity to learn and remember at both short and long retention intervals is relatively normal with visual presentation. At first, there was some suspicion that the patient had a deficit in short-term memory but no deficit in long-term memory, but now it seems that the early results were merely a consequence of a confounding between the supposedly "long-term" tasks and visual presentation of the material. The deficit appears to be a memory modality deficit without necessarily indicating any reason to distinguish short or long traces within a modality or to conclude that the dynamic character of long traces are different in different modalities.

III. RELEVANT DYNAMIC EVIDENCE

A. Form of the Retention Function

For the reasons mentioned repeatedly earlier in the article, differences in decay rate are not presently sufficient to establish a dynamic distinction between short and long traces. However, if it could be shown that the basic laws of retention for one class of traces that had rapid decay were different from the laws for another class of traces that had slower decay, then there would be sufficient justification for making a dynamic distinction. One of the most basic laws of retention is the mathematical form of the retention function which describes how some measure of the strength of the memory trace changes as a function of retention interval.

In determining the form of the retention function for the long trace, without contamination by the short trace, it is reasonable simply to use long enough retention intervals filled with interfering activity such that the short traces are presumed to be entirely dissipated. Using this method, Wickelgren (1972b) studied long-term retention for a variety of verbal materials using both the continuous and study–test designs, under a variety of different conditions, spanning retention intervals from a minute to over two years. These experiments demonstrated that the long trace cannot be characterized by an exponential decay of strength, but rather required the assumption that susceptibility to decay is continually decreasing. This continual decrease in the susceptibility to decay is handled by assuming that long traces must be characterized by two properties, strength and resistance, with strength decreasing and resistance increasing with delay since learning. The same basic form of retention fits the results of all these studies and may be called an exponential-power decay function: $\ell = \lambda e^{-\psi t^{1-\gamma}}$, where ℓ is the strength of the long trace, λ is the degree of initial acquisition of the long trace, ψ is the rate of decay of the long trace, γ is the exponent of growth of trace resistance, and t is the length of the retention interval.

To study the short trace independently of the long trace is somewhat more difficult, since it presently appears possible, even likely, that the long trace is present at the shortest measurable retention intervals following learning. In any event, it cannot be assumed that the long trace is absent at short delays when it appears to be present at longer delays.

However, there are conditions under which there appears to be no retention at intervals longer than 10 or 20 seconds following learning. Within a dual-trace theory, it is plausible to assume that the retention function in such cases represents only the short trace.

Furthermore, the situations in which no long-term retention appears to be present are precisely those in which a long trace should not be present according to a dual-trace theory. All of the studies that appear to contain no long trace are those for which list items on each trial are selected from a small population with rather little time elapsing between the occurrences of the same item from one trial to the next. Under these circumstances, the long traces for correct and incorrect items on a given trial should be approximately equal. Thus, a measurement of the *difference* in strength between correct and incorrect items on a given trial should reflect only the short component. Probe recognition designs using either digits (Wickelgren & Norman, 1966, 1971) or long lists of letters (Wickelgren, 1970b) fit these requirements for studying only the short trace in isolation from the long trace, and it is precisely these studies that appear to produce no long trace component.

When the form of the retention function for the short trace is analyzed in these studies, the results contrast sharply with those observed for the long trace. Wickelgren and Norman (1966, 1971) and Wickelgren (1970b) found that the short trace followed an exponential decay: $s = \alpha e^{-\beta t}$, where s is the strength of the short trace, α is the initial level of acquisition of the short trace, β is the decay rate, and t is the retention interval. Empirical retention functions in these studies cannot be well fit by the exponential-power function that fits long-term retention.

B. Similarity and Storage Interference

Wickelgren (1972b) has summarized the results of more than a dozen studies that all agree in demonstrating that storage interference (unlearning) for the long trace (as measured by recognition tests at long-retention intervals), is greater, the greater the similarity of interpolated material to original material. Only one study (Bower & Bostrom, 1968) failed to find a difference on a long-term recognition test between the AB–AC paradigm and the AB–CD paradigm. Also, in the most highly publicized such study, namely, Postman and Stark (1969), the difference between AB–AC and AB–CD was not significant, though the difference between AB–ABr and AB–CD was statistically significant. However, in the Postman and Stark study, the difference between AB–AC and AB–CD paradigms was quite large, though too near the 100% correct ceiling to be statistically significant. In all of the other dozen or more studies, the difference between AB–AC and AB–CD paradigms was statistically significant. Thus, there can be no doubt that increasing the similarity of interfering material increases storage interference (unlearning) measured at long-retention intervals.

By contrast, Wickelgren (1967a) demonstrated that in retention measured under the previously mentioned conditions that produce a simple exponentially decaying trace (interpreted to be the short trace), an AB–AC design produces no greater interference than an AB–CD design. This probably does not mean that short-term memory is a passive decay process. Deutsch (1970) showed that learning interpolated material within the same modality produces a greater storage interference effect on the short-term trace than does learning interpolated material in a different modality. Also, the relation between decay rate and presentation rate appears to require the assumption of a type of storage interference effect for the short trace (Wickelgren, 1970b, 1974). However, storage interference for the short trace appears to be independent of a "fine-grain" similarity of the interpolated material to the original material within the same modality.

Wickelgren (1967a) used a serial list design with auditory presentation, and the finding has also been replicated using a paired-associate design with visual presentation. However, this finding for short-term memory really needs to be demonstrated more extensively and by other investigators before the finding can be taken as evidence for the distinctively different character of storage interference for short and long traces. If replicable, this finding stands as good evidence for distinguishing two traces in the absence of any single-trace explanation of such a fundamental difference in storage interference.

C. Long-Acquisition Amnesia

The only frequently cited evidence for the distinction between short and long traces which can be regarded as relevant evidence for this distinction comes from the patients who exhibit relatively normal verbal short-term memory coupled with an almost complete inability to form new verbal long-term memory traces (Drachman & Arbit, 1966; Milner, 1966; Scoville & Milner, 1957). I call this phenomenon "long-acquisition amnesia." These subjects do show a considerable capacity for perceptual motor learning (Corkin, 1968) and a kind of perceptual learning (Milner, Corkin, & Teuber, 1968; Warrington & Weiskrantz, 1968, 1970). But this does not alter the significance of the finding that short-term retention for verbal material is relatively unimpaired, while the ability to form new long traces for the same type of material is grossly impaired.

At a minimum, the phenomenon of long-acquisition amnesia would appear to provide evidence either for two memory traces or for two independent mechanisms (initial learning versus subsequent learning) in the establishment of a single memory trace. The dual-trace explanation appears to be the simpler of the two, and this evidence should, at present, be considered to support the distinction between short and long memory traces.

IV. CONCLUSION

Although a staggering number of different phenomena have been cited in support of the distinction between short and long traces (primary and secondary memory), the vast majority of these phenomena provide no evidence whatsoever for distinguishing two dynamically different memory traces. Nevertheless, there are three phenomena that do appear to support a dynamic distinction between short and long traces. First, the form of the retention function appears to be quite different for the two traces. Second, fine-grain similarity affects storage interference for the long trace, but not for the short trace (which is only affected by a grosser modality similarity). Third, the long-acquisition amnesia phenomena demonstrated by bilateral mesial temporal patients and Korsakoff syndrome patients is somewhat simpler to interpret within a two-trace theory than a single-trace theory.

Although it is reasonable to adopt the two-trace theory as a working hypothesis at present, it is quite important for these phenomena to be investigated further both experimentally and theoretically. In some instances, the results are insufficiently replicated for such an important conclusion, but equally important, it is necessary for many people to think about the significance of these phenomena in order to be sure that alternative single-trace explanations cannot be given for them. One point of this article is to urge that further work concerned with the distinction between short and long traces be devoted to areas that have the potential for being truly relevant to this question, instead of concentrating on irrelevant phenomena. Finally, there appears to be no reason at present to assume more than one dynamic type of long trace. However, much more research is necessary to determine whether the laws of forgetting assessed at retention intervals of minutes are the same as the laws of forgetting assessed at hours, days, and weeks. Although the dual-trace theory has a limited degree of support at present, considerably more experimental and theoretical work concerned with the exact dynamics of each memory trace will be required before this theory can be considered to have extensive support.

REFERENCES

Atkinson, R. C., & Crothers, E. J. A comparison of paired-associate learning models having different acquisition and retention axioms. *Journal of Mathematical Psychology,* 1964, **2,** 285–315.
Bartz, W. H., & Salehi, M. Interference in short- and long-term memory. *Journal of Experimental Psychology,* 1970, **84,** 380–382.
Bjork, R. A. Repetition and rehearsal mechanisms in models for short-term memory. In D. A. Norman (Ed.), *Models of human memory.* New York: Academic Press, 1970.
Bower, G. H., & Bostrom, A. Absence of within-list PI and RI in short-term recognition memory. *Psychonomic Science,* 1968, **10,** 211–212.
Corkin, S. Acquisition of motor skill after bilateral medial temporal-lobe excision. *Neuropsychologia,* 1968, **6,** 255–265.
Craik, F. I. The fate of primary memory items in free recall. *Journal of Verbal Learning and Learning Behavior,* 1970, **9,** 143–148.
Deese, J. Serial organization in the recall of disconnected items. *Psychological Reports,* 1957, **3,** 577–582.
Deutsch, D. Tones and numbers: Specificity of interference in immediate memory. *Science,* 1970, **168,** 1604–1605.
Deutsch, J. A. The physiological basis of memory. *Annual Review of Psychology,* 1969, **20,** 85–104.
Drachman, D. A., & Arbit, J. Memory and the hippocampal complex. *Archives of Neurology,* 1966, **15,** 52–61.
Glanzer, M. Short-term storage and long-term storage in recall. *Journal of Psychiatric Research,* 1971, **8,** 423–438.
Glanzer, M., & Cunitz, A. R. Accuracy of perceptual recall: An analysis of organization. *Journal of Verbal Learning and Verbal Behavior,* 1966, **5,** 351–360.
Glanzer, M., Gianutsos, R., & Dubin, S. The removal of items from short-term storage. *Journal of Verbal Learning and Verbal Behavior,* 1969, **8,** 435–447.
Glanzer, M., & Schwartz, A. Mnemonic structure in free recall: Differential effects on STS and LTS. *Journal of Verbal Learning and Verbal Behavior,* 1971, **10,** 194–198.
Gruneberg, M. M. A dichotomous theory of memory—Unproved and unprovable? *Acta Psychologica,* 1970, **43,** 489–496.

Gruneberg, M. M., Colwill, S. J., Winfrow, P., & Woods, R. W. Acoustic confusion in long-term memory. *Acta Psychologica*, 1970, **32**, 394–398.

Gruneberg, M. M., & Sykes, R. N. Acoustic confusion in long-term memory. *Acta Psychologica*, 1969, **29**, 293–296.

Hellyer, S. Supplementary report: Frequency of stimulus presentation and short-term decrement in recall. *Journal of Experimental Psychology*, 1962, **64**, 650.

Hovland, C. I. Human learning and retention. In S. S. Stevens (Ed.), *Handbook of experimental psychology*. New York: Wiley, 1951.

Milner, B. Amnesia following operation on the temporal lobes. In C. W. M. Whitty & O. L. Zangwill (Eds.), *Amnesia*. London: Butterworths, 1966.

Milner, B., Corkin, S., & Teuber, H.-L. Further analysis of the hippocampal amnesic syndrome: 14-year follow-up study of H. M. *Neuropsychologia*, 1968, **6**, 215–234.

Murdock, B. B., Jr. The serial position effect of free recall. *Journal of Experimental Psychology*, 1962, **64**, 482–48.

Murdock, B. B., Jr. Interpolated recall in short-term memory. *Journal of Experimental Psychology*, 1963, **66**, 525–532.

Murdock, B. B., Jr. Effects of a subsidiary task on short-term memory. *British Journal of Psychology*, 1965, **56**, 413–419.

Murdock, B. B., Jr. Visual and auditory stores in short-term memory. *Quarterly Journal of Experimental Psychology*, 1966, **18**, 206–211.

Murdock, B. B., Jr. Auditory and visual stores in short-term memory. *Acta Psychologica*, 1967, **27**, 316–324.

Murdock, B. B., Jr. Modality effects in short-term memory: Storage or retrieval? *Journal of Experimental Psychology*, 1968, **77**, 79–86.

Murdock, B. B., Jr. Where or when: Modality effects as a function of temporal and spatial distribution of information. *Journal of Verbal Learning and Verbal Behavior*, 1969, **8**, 378–383.

Peterson, L. R., & Peterson, M. J. Short-term retention of individual verbal items. *Journal of Experimental Psychology*, 1959, **58**, 193–198.

Postman, L., & Phillips, L. Short-term temporal changes in free recall. *Quarterly Journal of Experimental Psychology*, 1965, **17**, 132–138.

Postman, L., & Stark, K. The role of response availability in transfer and interference. *Journal of Experimental Psychology*, 1969, **79**, 168–177.

Raffel, G. Two determinants of the effects of primacy. *American Journal of Psychology*, 1936, **48**, 654–657.

Raymond, B. Short-term storage and long-term storage in free recall. *Journal of Verbal Learning and Verbal Behavior*, 1969, **8**, 567–574.

Rundus, D. Paired-associate recall following a distractor task: Initial and second choice performance. *Journal of Mathematical Psychology*, 1970, **7**, 362–370.

Rundus, D., & Atkinson, R. C. Rehearsal processes in free recall: A procedure for direct observation. *Journal of Verbal Learning and Verbal Behavior*, 1970, **9**, 99–105.

Rundus, D., Loftus, G. R., & Atkinson, R. C. Immediate free recall and three-week delayed recognition. *Journal of Verbal Learning and Verbal Behavior*, 1970, **9**, 684–688.

Scoville, W. B., & Milner, B. Loss of recent memory after bilateral hippocampal lesions. *Journal of Neurology, Neurosurgery and Psychiatry*, 1957, **20**, 11–21.

Shallice, T., & Warrington, E. K. Independent functioning of verbal memory stores: A neuro-psychological study. *Quarterly Journal of Experimental Psychology*, 1970, **22**, 261–273.

62   Wayne A. Wickelgren

Shulman, H. G. Encoding and retention of semantic and phonetic information in short-term memory. *Journal of Verbal Learning and Verbal Behavior*, 1970, **9**, 499–508.

Shulman, H. G. Similarity effects in short-term memory. *Psychological Bulletin*, 1971, **75**, 399–415.

Shulman, H. G. Semantic confusion errors in short-term memory. *Journal of Verbal Learning and Verbal Behavior*, 1972, **11**, 221–227.

Silverstein, C., & Glanzer, M. Difficulty of a concurrent task in free recall: Differential effects on STS and LTS. *Psychonomic Science*, 1971, **22**, 367–368.

Smith, E. E., Barresi, J., & Gross, A. E. Imaginal versus verbal coding and the primary-secondary memory distinction. *Journal of Verbal Learning and Verbal Behavior*, 1971, **10**, 597–603.

Sumby, W. H. Word frequency and the serial position effect. *Journal of Verbal Learning and Verbal Behavior*, 1963, **1**, 443–450.

Tulving, E., & Arbuckle, T. Y. Sources of intertrial interference in immediate recall of paired-associates. *Journal of Verbal Learning and Verbal Behavior*, 1963, **1**, 321–324.

Tulving, E., & Arbuckle, T. Y. Input and output interference in short-term associative memory. *Journal of Experimental Psychology*, 1966, **72**, 145–150.

Warrington, E. K., & Shallice, T. The selective impairment of auditory verbal short-term memory. *Brain*, 1969, **92**, 885–896.

Warrington, E. K., & Shallice, T. Neuropsychological evidence of visual storage in short-term memory tasks. *Quarterly Journal of Experimental Psychology*, 1972, **24**, 30–40.

Warrington, E. K., & Weiskrantz, L. New method of testing long-term retention with special reference to amnesic patients. *Nature*, 1968, **217**, 972–974.

Warrington, E. K., & Weiskrantz, L. Amnesic syndrome: Consolidation or retrieval? *Nature*, 1970, **228**, 628–630.

Waugh, N., & Norman, D. Primary memory. *Psychological Review*, 1965, **72**, 89–104.

Wickelgren, W. A. Acoustic similarity and retroactive interference in short-term memory. *Journal of Verbal Learning and Learning Behavior*, 1965, **4**, 53–61. (a)

Wickelgren, W. A. Short-term memory for phonemically similar lists. *American Journal of Psychology*, 1965, **78**, 567–574. (b)

Wickelgren, W. A. Short-term memory for repeated and non-repeated items. *Quarterly Journal of Experimental Psychology*, 1965, **17**, 14–25. (c)

Wickelgren, W. A. Phonetic similarity and interference in short-term memory for single letters. *Journal of Experimental Psychology*, 1966, **71**, 396–404.

Wickelgren, W. A. Exponential decay and independence from irrelevant associations in short-term recognition memory for serial order. *Journal of Experimental Psychology*, 1967, **73**, 165–171. (a)

Wickelgren, W. A. Rehearsal grouping and hierarchical organization of serial position cues in short-term memory. *Quarterly Journal of Experimental Psychology*, 1967, **19**, 97–102. (b)

Wickelgren, W. A. Associative strength theory of recognition memory for pitch. *Journal of Mathematical Psychology*, 1969, **6**, 13–61.

Wickelgren, W. A. Multitrace strength theory. In D. A. Norman (Ed.), *Models of human memory*. New York: Academic Press, 1970. (a)

Wickelgren, W. A. Time, interference, and rate of presentation in short-term recognition memory for items. *Journal of Mathematical Psychology*, 1970, **7**, 219–235. (b)

Wickelgren, W. A. Coding, retrieval, and dynamics of multitrace associative memory. In L. Gregg (Ed.), *Cognition in learning and memory*. New York: Wiley, 1972. (a)

Wickelgren, W. A. Trace resistance and the decay of long-term memory *Journal of Mathematical Psychology*, 1972, **9,** 418–455. (b)

Wickelgren, W. A. Strength-resistance theory of the dynamics of memory storage. In D. H. Krantz, R. C. Atkinson, R. D. Luce, & P. Suppes (Eds.), *Contemporary developments in mathematical psychology*. San Francisco: Freeman, 1974.

Wickelgren, W. A., & Norman, D. A. Strength models and serial position in short-term recognition memory. *Journal of Mathematical Psychology,* 1966, **3,** 316–347.

Wickelgren, W. A., & Norman, D. A. Invariance of forgetting rate with number of repetitions in verbal short-term recognition memory. *Psychonomic Science,* 1971, **22,** 363–364.

CHAPTER

3

MORE ON THE LONG AND SHORT OF MEMORY[1]

WAYNE A. WICKELGREN

A few months after writing the previous article, I generated an alternative single-trace theory that explains even the three phenomena I had thought supported the distinction between short- and long-term memory. The theory was not generated specifically for the purpose of providing a

[1] This work was supported by Grant 3-0097 from the National Institute of Education and by Contract F 44620-73-C-0056 from the Advanced Research Projects Agency, Department of Defense.

single-trace explanation for these phenomena. Instead, I generated a new theory of the long trace to account for a phenomenon contradictory to an earlier version of the theory. Then I realized that this new theory of the long trace would probably eliminate the need to assume any dynamically distinct short trace at all. This appears to be true, and I now believe that the conclusion of the previous paper can be strengthened to say that there is *no* evidence favoring a distinction between short-term and long-term memory.

The purpose of this addendum is to present the single-trace theory briefly and explain how one can account for the form of the retention function, the effects of similarity on storage interference, and long-acquisition amnesia within a single trace formulation. The explanation of the first two of these phenomena follows from the particular single-trace theory described, but the single-trace explanation of long-acquisition amnesia could have been provided in the absence of this particular theory. I simply had a blind spot previously for the inadequacies of the amnesic-patient evidence.

I. SINGLE-TRACE, DUAL-DECAY THEORY

The theory of long-trace storage dynamics described in Wickelgren (1972) was a pure interference theory, that is, the decay of the long trace occurred solely due to storage interference (unlearning) caused by acquiring subsequent similar traces. The results of many studies summarized in Wickelgren (1972) support the existence of a storage interference process acting to reduce the strength of the long trace in proportion to the degree of similarity. However, according to the interference theory described in Wickelgren (1972), the long trace has a second important dynamic property, resistance (to interference). The resistance of the long trace to interference was assumed to increase with increasing trace age. For reasons irrelevant to this discussion, I now assume that the second property is trace fragility, which decreases with increasing trace age. The assumption of gradually decreasing trace fragility appears to be necessary to account for the continual decrease in the rate of forgetting and the temporally defined character of retrograde amnesia and recovery from it. The trace fragility property also accounts for the ability to make recency judgments under conditions that prevent the use of associations to time concepts. Thus, the assumption that the long trace has a second dynamic property that depends only on trace age is well motivated.

However, the combination of the decreasing trace resistance on the one hand with a pure interference theory of forgetting on the other hand leads to the prediction that the storage interference effect of similar learning (AB–AC versus AB–CD) learning will be greater the earlier the similar interfering learning is interpolated during a retention interval. Previous studies using a recall measure (Archer & Underwood, 1951; Houston, 1967; Newton & Wickens, 1956) provide no support for this prediction, but one could argue that the recall studies are confounded by competition effects and other retrieval interference problems that mask the expected storage interference effects. A previous study by Howe (1969) that used a recognition measure also yielded results contradictory to this prediction. However, I was not convinced without doing the experiment myself, so I did two experiments manipulating the delay between original and similar interpolated learning. I found a negative storage interference effect of similar interpolated learning, but one that appeared to be independent of the delay between original and interpolated learning. Thus, a central prediction of the previous theory appeared to be convincingly contradicted.

The most obvious solution to this problem is probably to assume that two factors produce decay of the long trace: (a) storage interference from subsequent similar learning and (b) an interference-free time-decay process. Now one can assume that the decrease in the fragility of the trace affects the time-decay process but has no effect on the interference process (the latter being affected only by the similarity of subsequent learning to original learning).

I resisted formal consideration of this dual-process theory for some time since it seemed more complex than a single-process theory. However, after many fruitless attempts to formulate a theory consistent with all of the previously mentioned phenomena, I was forced to formulate explicitly a differential equation model of the dual-process theory. When I did this, I immediately noticed that the resulting form of the retention function for the long trace was a product of a power function decay term and an exponential decay term. Immediately, I saw that such a more complex form of retention function could provide both the power function decay characteristic of long-term retention and the exponential decay characteristic of certain types of short-term retention. This meant that a single trace with two decay processes (time and interference) might permit one to eliminate the assumption of a separate short-term memory trace altogether. If so, there was nothing *ad hoc* and inelegant about the two-process theory.[2]

---

[2] From a philosophy of science point of view, I think it might be well to note in passing how foolish it would have been not to have considered the two-process

According to the single-trace, two-process theory, the form of the retention function is as follows:

$$d_m = \lambda(1 + \beta t)^{-\psi}(e^{-\pi t})$$

where

$$\alpha, \beta, \psi, \text{ and } \pi > 0$$

In this equation, d_m represents the interval scale d' measure of memory strength, λ represents the degree of learning, β and ψ represent rate parameters characterizing the time decay process, and π represents the rate parameter (degree of similarity) for the interference process.

II. FORM OF THE RETENTION FUNCTION

In the above equation for the long-term retention function, if π is close to zero, the form of the retention function will approximate a power function, as has been obtained for long-term retention (Wickelgren, 1972). On the other hand, if π is large, as will occur when the interpolated material is highly similar in its encoding to the originally learned material, then the form of the retention function will approximate exponential decay, as is characteristic of certain types of short-term retention (Wickelgren & Norman, 1966; Wickelgren, 1970). In fact, the conditions under which power function decay is obtained are precisely those in which encoding is known to be largely semantic in nature and therefore characterized by low similarity between original and interpolated material. The conditions under which exponential decay is obtained are precisely those in which encoding is known to be largely phonetic, characterized by high similarity

---

theory because it seemed like a purely *ad hoc* explanation for a particular phenomena. All new ideas are probably initially *ad hoc* in that they are generated to account for one or at most two phenomena. The important question is not whether a theory is initially *ad hoc,* but whether it remains *ad hoc,* never accounting for additional phenomena. To rule out any consideration of a theory because it is initially *ad hoc* is quite wrong in that it will prevent one from investigating "interesting" theoretical reformulations of data. Thus, one must be quite careful in the uncritical use of the attribution *ad hoc* to a component of a theory. I think we have no better way to judge whether a theoretical idea is worth pursuing than our own intuition that it is "interesting," whatever that may mean. There is nothing more absurd than to reject a useful criterion, such as our intuitive judgment that an idea is interesting, simply because we do not understand that intuition, in favor of a criteria, such as *"ad hocness,"* which we may understand somewhat better, but which is a much less relevant criterion.

between original and interpolated material. In studies of short-term retention in which the intervening material is very dissimilar to the originally learned material, one does not obtain rapid exponential decay. Thus, there appears to be an extremely plausible single-trace explanation for obtaining two different forms of retention functions under these different conditions, and this evidence does not support a two-trace theory.

III. SIMILARITY AND STORAGE INTERFERENCE

As discussed in the preceding paper, the similarity of interpolated learning appears to have no effect on short-term retention in most tasks where a pure exponential decay has been obtained, while greater similarity produces greater interference in the longer-term retention studies characterized by power function decay. This important qualitative difference between the nature of interference can be given a single-trace explanation as well.

According to the single-trace theory, greater similarity of interpolated learning should cause greater storage interference no matter what the conditions. However, the magnitude of this effect will depend on the relative magnitude of the disparity between the high similarity and low similarity conditions of interpolated learning being compared.

In the long-term retention studies characterized by a large degree of semantic encoding, the difference in similarity between an AB–AC condition, on the one hand, and an AB–CD condition, on the other hand, is enormous, because the semantic similarity (π) of any two words (AC) is very low. In fact preliminary testing of the single-trace theory indicates that the π parameter is close to zero for any two words drawn from a population of 10,000 common English words. Thus, one is comparing zero similarity with perhaps 50 per cent similarity in comparing the storage interference effects of AB–CD with AB–AC.

By contrast, in the cases where a rapid exponential decay has been obtained, the encoding is thought to be predominately phonetic and each item has a rather high degree of phonetic similarity on the average to any other item. Thus, the discrepancy between the high similarity characteristic of AB–AC and the unknown but still fairly high similarity characteristic of AB–CD will be much lower in this case. So, one expects to find a much smaller effect of similarity in this case than in the former case. Therefore, the negative results I obtained in these situations cannot be taken to provide any convincing evidence that interference operates differently in this type of memory task than in the other type of memory task. Only the

magnitude of the effect may be different, and that may be grossly different. Thus, a truly enormous number of trials might be necessary to detect
the effect of similarity in these situations whereas only a modest number
of trials is necessary in the former class of situations.

Furthermore, when subjects receive an AC interpolated learning trial
only a few seconds after receiving an AB learning trial, there may be a
greater tendency to go back and rehearse the AB pair (even contrary to
instructions) than when one receives a CD interpolated learning trial.
Such differential uncontrolled rehearsal could mask a small negative storage interference effect. Thus, these phenomena are totally unconvincing as
evidence for the dual-trace theory.

In fact, the single-trace explanation for when a large effect of similarity will be found and when it will not actually accounts for the one
discrepant finding (Bower & Bostrom, 1968) mentioned in regard to the
effects of similar interpolated material in long-term retention. Although
Bower and Bostrum described their findings as applying to short-term
memory, this was because the design was similar to that used in short-
term memory studies and the materials were letter-digit pairs (likely to
have a substantial degree of phonetic encoding). The retention intervals
are actually long enough so most experimental psychologists would consider the study to be tapping long-term memory. Thus, the Bower and
Bostrom finding was actually contradictory to the dual-trace hypothesis
that similarity affected storage interference in long-term memory but not
short-term memory. Since the type of materials and design used by Bower
and Bostrom are of the type likely to produce phonetic encoding, with
high similarity of interpolated and original learning even in the control
condition, the single-trace explanation is actually consistent with the Bower
and Bostrom result, while the dual-trace explanation is inconsistent. Thus,
what little evidence exists actually favors the single-trace explanation over
the dual-trace explanation regarding the effects of similarity on amount of
retroactive interference in recognition memory.

IV. LONG-ACQUISITION AMNESIA

It is now quite clear that amnesic subjects have relatively normal
motor skill and perceptual long-term learning and memory despite their
severe deficits in the establishment of new cognitive long-term memory
(Baddeley & Warrington, 1970; Corkin, 1968; Warrington & Weiskrantz,
1970). Such findings suggest that amnesic subjects have a modality deficit
in the formation of cognitive (semantic) memory traces and do not provide evidence for the reality of dynamically different traces (short-term

and long-term memory) either within or across modalities. The fact that amnesic patients often have relatively small impairments on such short-term memory tasks as the memory span test, while having much larger deficits on tests tapping long-term verbal retention, may be simply due to the patients having a relatively unimpaired capacity for phonetic encoding, while having a severely impaired capacity for establishing new semantic memory traces. Under the conditions characteristic of most of the longer-term verbal learning studies, a phonetic trace will be rapidly interfered with and thus rapidly lost, for reasons discussed in the previous paper. Hence, amnesic patients will show severe deficiencies at long-retention intervals. However, it should be clear that the explanation need not be that they lack the capability of forming long-term memory traces, in general, while retaining the capacity to acquire short-term traces. Rather, the most parsimonious explanation appears to be that amnesic patients lack the capability of forming "higher-level" cognitive (including semantic) memory traces, while often retaining substantial capacity for acquiring "lower-level" sensory and motor memories. The modality explanation clearly seems more attractive at the present time than the dual dynamic trace explanation.

V. CONCLUSION

The arguments presented in this and the preceding paper indicate that there is no psychological support whatsoever for distinguishing two dynamically different memory traces, and that appears to be the long and the short of it.

REFERENCES

Archer, E. J., & Underwood, B. J. Retroactive inhibition of verbal associations as a multiple function of temporal point of interpolation and degree of interpolated learning. *Journal of Experimental Psychology,* 1951, **42**, 283–290.

Baddeley, A. D., & Warrington, E. K. Amnesia and the distinction between long- and short-term memory. *Journal of Verbal Learning and Verbal Behavior,* 1970, **9**, 176–189.

Bower, G. H., & Bostrom, A. Absence of within-list PI and RI in short-term recognition memory. *Psychonomic Science,* 1968, **10**, 211–212.

Corkin, S. Acquisition of motor skill after bilateral medial temporal-lobe excision. *Neuropsychologia,* 1968, **6**, 255–265.

Houston, J. P. Retroactive inhibition and point of interpolation. *Journal of Verbal Learning and Verbal Behavior,* 1967, **6**, 84–88.

Howe, T. S. Effects of delayed interference on list 1 recall. *Journal of Experimental Psychology,* 1969, **80**, 120–124.

Newton, J. M., & Wickens, D. D. Retroactive inhibition as a function of the temporal position of the interpolated learning. *Journal of Experimental Psychology,*
1956, **70,** 237–245.

Warrington, E. K., & Weiskrantz, L. Amnesic syndrome: Consolidation or retrieval?
Nature, 1970, **228,** 628–630.

Wickelgren, W. A. Time, interference, and rate of presentation in short-term recognition memory for items. *Journal of Mathematical Psychology,* 1970, **7,** 219–235.

Wickelgren, W. A. Trace resistance and the decay of long-term memory. *Journal of
Mathematical Psychology,* 1972, **9,** 418–455.

Wickelgren, W. A., & Norman, D. Strength models and serial position in short-term
recognition memory. *Journal of Mathematical Psychology,* 1966, **3,** 316–347.

CHAPTER
4

SHORT-TERM RETENTION, LEARNING, AND RETRIEVAL FROM LONG-TERM MEMORY[1]

HERMAN BUSCHKE

[1] This research was supported by USPHS Grants MH-17733 from NIMH, NB-03356 from NIMS, and HD-01799 from NICHD. I thank Christine Hiney and Susan Berenzweig for their assistance in data analysis.

In this chapter I will consider some aspects of the relationship between short-term retention processes, learning, and retrieval from long-term permanent storage for a better understanding of their function in free recall and learning of lists. While I am persuaded that it is useful, and probably correct, to distinguish between short-term and long-term or permanent retention processes, I do not know whether such retention *processes* involve distinct *storages* or whether both operate in a common permanent storage (Craik & Lockhart, 1972). It is clear, however, that the role of permanent storage in human memory can no longer be ignored in attempting to understand short-term memory. I agree with Bower's remarks in this connection:

> . . . the question is how to characterize what happens when a subject encounters a familiar item, for instance the word *cat,* while studying a list of to-be-remembered words. A variety of hypothesis, metaphors, and analogies have been offered as answers to this theoretical question. Many analogies or metaphorical theories suppose that some specific unit corresponding to a token of the word *cat* is what is stored on this occasion. It is as though a book entitled *cat* were being placed on a circulation shelf of a mental library, or an object labeled *cat* were being tossed into a mental junk box, possibly even a small junk box labeled "List-1," from which recall is to occur by sampling objects and reading off their labels.
>
> Just the converse attitude is my overall orientation. The mind does not take in or soak up new items as single, isolated symbols, like water into a sponge, or new imprints on a waxed tablet, or new books deposited in a mental warehouse. I believe that such analogies are systematically misleading. The subject does not enter the item *cat* into his long-term memory when he sees it on the list; he is not learning the item *cat* at all. He already fully knows that item and all its associates. This and many, many other concepts exist already in the person's "semantic memory," which may possibly be represented by a complex graph structure of relational associations among concepts and properties [Bower, 1972, p. 110].

This chapter represents an attempt to indicate why we should take seriously the view that *recall of an item or of a list of items involves the retrieval of that item or set of items from the appropriate search-space in permanent storage.* (Following Glanzer's [1972] convention, I also will use "the item" when I mean "the information related to the item.") It seems obvious that at some point the item must be found in permanent storage for information retained in either short-term or long-term storage to be recovered by actually recalling the item.

I will begin by reviewing some experiments that illustrate aspects of the relationship between short-term memory and learning and implicate retrieval from permanent storage in free recall. Because these experiments also indicate to me that verbal learning requires search in permanent storage (and that short-term retention processes probably operate in long-term, permanent storage), I will then review some salient features of spontaneous, free retrieval from permanent storage. To indicate the relationship between such spontaneous, free retrieval (of any and all items belonging to a category in permanent storage) and the more conventional free recall of a restricted subset of target items, I will show what happens in restricted retrieval from permanent storage when retrieval is restricted to recall of previously retrieved items.

Next, I will consider free recall of a restricted list of presented items from the same category in permanent storage to show how the method of *selective reminding* may be used to estimate concurrent recall from short-term storage, retrieval from long-term storage, and retention in long-term storage during verbal learning. The use of extended recall and repeated retrieval after only a single presentation of such a list lets us examine recall and retrieval alone, without confounding by further presentation. Since extended, repeated retrieval after a single list presentation allows us to distinguish between those recall failures *before* the first recall of an item that are due to encoding failure and those due to retrieval failure, and to distinguish between those recall failures *after* initial recall that are due to loss from long-term storage and those due to retrieval failure, this approach shows how retrieval from long-term storage is involved in free recall and provides a method to investigate such retrieval. Finally, I will summarize some factors that may influence the retrieval of individual items from long-term storage at different stages of learning, and consider the relationship between recalling or retrieving individual items in a list and recalling or retrieving the list as a whole from long-term storage.

The following terminology and abbreviations will be used. ST means short-term, LT means long-term, STS means short-term storage, and LTS means long-term storage. STR means recall from short-term storage and LTR means retrieval from long-term storage. PS means permanent storage. STS and LTS are meant to refer to short-term and long-term storage mechanisms or retention processes, without necessarily implying that these processes operate in different storage systems, because both may operate in the common permanent storage system. While Glanzer (1972) has thoroughly and persuasively reviewed our current knowledge about STS and the experimental basis for a distinction between STS and LTS, Murdock has reminded us that:

> . . . a second argument for two-store models is based on the experimental separation of the recency effect and the asymptote in studies in short-term memory. Thus in one study, Glanzer and Cunitz (1966) were able to show that interpolated activity eliminated the recency effect, but the presentation rate affected only the asymptote. . . . [W]hile it is certainly true that, *if* there are separate short-term and long-term stores, then experimental separation should be

possible, it does *not* follow that if the recency effect and the asymptote are experimentally separable then there must be a dichotomous memory system [Murdock, 1972, pp. 92–93].

Although I will not refer to either short-term memory or long-term memory as such, I do distinguish short-term *retention* from short-term *memory*. Short-term retention is used here to mean the intra-trial retention (and recall) of items presented on a particular trial; it refers to the task of an *S* in remembering the items presented for immediate recall. In short-term retention of more than a very few items, items are retained by long-term as well as short-term storage processes. If short-term memory is taken to mean short-term storage, then it is important, as Glanzer (1972) has urged, that the STS and LTS components of short-term retention be distinguished.

I. CONCURRENT SHORT-TERM RETENTION AND LEARNING

To indicate some aspects of the interaction of short-term retention, learning, and retrieval from LT or PS, I will begin with some experiments that required learning of repeated items and ST retention of new items at the same time, done with Dr. Walter Ritter. We were interested in how the concurrent ST retention of some items might affect the learning of other items that were repeated from trial to trial, and in whether ST retention of new items from the same category as the repeated items might interfere more with learning the repeated items than ST retention of items from a different category in PS (Ritter, Buschke & Gindes, 1974).

In these experiments the names of 8 birds were repeatedly presented on each of 8 successive trials, together with either 8 *new birds* on each trial, 8 *new trees* on each trial, or 8 trees that also were repeated from trial to trial so that they too could be learned. Lists of 16 items each were presented at a 2 sec rate for free recall immediately after presentation of the list. All lists contained the same 8 repeated birds in random order from trial to trial. In Condition I the 8 repeated birds alternated with 8 new items, which also were birds, on each trial. In Condition II the 8 target birds alternated on each trial with 8 new items, which were from a different category in PS, namely trees. In Condition III the 8 repeated target birds alternated on each trial with 8 repeated trees, which were also randomized from trial to trial.

We expected that the repeated birds would be learned best in Condition III, when the other items (trees) recalled on each trial could also be learned, because more of the limited STS capacity would become available for retention of repeated birds, increasing the number of repeated birds recalled on successive trials. Recall of the repeated birds should be less in Condition II than III, if the new items recalled on each trial required additional STS capacity, decreasing the STS capacity available for retention of the repeated birds. Finally, we expected that recall of the repeated birds in Condition I would be decreased further by requiring concurrent recall of new items from the *same* category on each trial, if the new birds on each trial were retained by STS processes operating in the same LTS involved in the learning of the repeated items, or if information about the new birds on each trial either could enter LTS directly without transfer through STS or was transferred rapidly (and rather completely) from STS to LTS.

Recall of the repeated birds and of the other items presented on each trial of the three conditions is shown in Fig. 4-1. Recall of repeated birds increased most in Condition III, when the repeated trees also were learned. Recall of the repeated birds was not as great in Condition II as in III, but did increase over trials. As the repeated birds were learned in Condition II, the concurrent recall of new trees also increased over trials, suggesting that more STS capacity became available for retention of the new trees as the repeated birds were learned. Finally, recall of the repeated birds in Condition I did not increase over trials when the concurrent retention and recall of new birds (from the same category in PS) also was required on

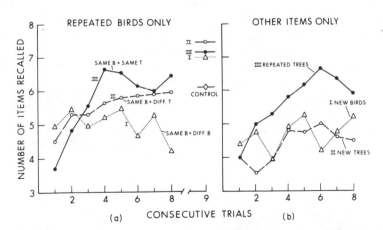

Fig. 4-1. (a) The number of repeated birds recalled only when presented for recall together with new birds (Condition I), new trees (II), or repeated trees (III). Results shown for Trial 9 represent recall of repeated birds alone when presented by themselves. (b) The concurrent recall of new birds (I), new trees (II), or repeated trees (III).(From Ritter, Buschke, & Gindes, 1974. Copyright 1974 by the American Psychological Association. Reprinted by permission.)

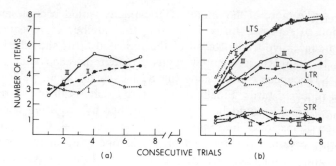

Fig. 4-2. (a) The number of repeated birds that were also recalled on the next trial. (b) Retention in long-term storage (LTS), retrieval from long-term storage (LTR), and recall from short-term storage (STR) for the repeated birds only in Conditions I, II, and III. (From Ritter, Buschke, & Gindes, 1974. Copyright 1974 by the American Psychological Association. Reprinted by permission.)

each trial. Similar results also are seen in Fig. 4-2a, which shows the repeated recall of the same repeated birds from each trial to the next, *i.e.,* the number of repeated birds on each trial that were also recalled on the following trial. This measure of inter-trial retention and recall (Tulving, 1964) evaluates learning of the repeated items somewhat more specifically, although it still includes recall from STS as well as retrieval from LTS.

To show that LTS of the repeated items was similar in all three conditions, we analyzed the recall of the repeated birds over the first 8 trials, separating recall on each trial into STR and LTR by the method of Tulving and Colotla (1970). An item is considered to have been retrieved from LTS if more than 7 other presented or recalled items intervened between the presentation and recall of that item. If 7 or fewer such items intervened between the presentation or recall of an item, an item is considered to have been recalled from STS. While this method may seem slightly arbitrary, it does yield estimates of recall from STS that appear to be reasonable and consistent with those obtained by other methods (Tulving & Colotla, 1970). Fig. 4-2b shows STR and LTR separately for the repeated birds in each of the three conditions. An estimate of retention in LTS was obtained by accumulating the number of repeated items that had been retrieved from LTS at least once by the end of each trial, under the defensible assumption that once an item has been retrieved from (encoded in) LTS it remains in LTS (Buschke, 1974a). While such an estimate of LTS has the desirable property of deriving from actual retrieval, reflecting storage adequate for retrieval, it probably underestimates actual LTS because, as Fig. 4-2b shows, LTR is variable and far from complete. However, as Fig. 4-2b also shows, this estimate of LTS appears to be at least partially independent of retrieval on particular trials, so that different rates of LTR may still yield quite similar estimates of LTS.

Fig. 4-2b shows that retention in LTS was the same in all three conditions, as was recall from STS. The differences in recall of the repeated birds shown in Fig. 4-1a apparently were due to differences in LTR, not to differences in retention by either LTS or STS.

The finding that STR did not differ in the three conditions was surprising to us. The concurrent ST retention and recall of new trees on each trial of Condition II apparently retarded the recall of the repeated birds by requiring more attention and processing time, rather than more STS capacity. Similarly, the concurrent ST retention and recall of new items from the same category in Condition I also apparently interfered with the retrieval of repeated items from LTS rather than with their recall from STS. Thus, these results seem to show that concurrent ST retention and recall of new items on each trial interfered with the concurrent retrieval of repeated items from the same category in PS, rather than with either the LT storage of the repeated birds or their retention in a limited capacity STS.

It is clear that information about items presented only once may be retained in LTS. This might be due to rapid transfer from STS to LTS or independent entry into LTS without transfer through STS (Warrington & Shallice, 1969; Shallice & Warrington, 1970). Comparison of Conditions I and II indicates that the retrieval of the repeated birds from LTS was greater in II when the repeated birds could be distinguished by their category membership from the new trees on each trial. If better retrieval of repeated items from LTS on the basis of category membership involves recognition of category membership, then it would be necessary for some contact to be made with (the representation of information about) each presented item in PS to determine category membership. It is possible that selective retention in STS may be governed at least in part by information coming *to* STS *from* PS to permit selective learning. That is, presented information may go to LTS as well as STS for (semantic) evaluation in LTS, so that items might be retained in STS or transferred from STS to LTS, or lost from STS on the basis of an evaluation made in PS (see Fig. 1 of Posner & Warren, 1972).

These results also suggest the use of directed searching in PS for retrieval of information about presented items from LTS (Ritter & Buschke, in press). A list may be regarded as a directed search in PS, resulting in retrieval of *all* items in that list but *no* items that are not list members. Learning to recall a target subset of items from a larger search-set in PS may involve development of a directed search, resulting in the reliable retrieval of all items in the target set, without the intrusion of other items from the larger search-set that are not members of the set to be recalled. Thus, the recall of repeated birds may not have improved in Condition I because the Ss never had an opportunity to develop such a directed search for (only) the target set of repeated birds, because retrieval of the repeated birds was always part of a different search on each trial to retrieve the repeated birds together with the other newly presented items from the same category. In Condition II a directed search for the repeated target birds could be developed, because they could be retrieved by themselves, without any other items from the same search set, or category. The development of directed search for the repeated target birds in Condition II is reflected in Fig. 4-3, which shows the proportion of items retrieved in the second half of each individual recall across trials. As the repeated birds were learned in Condition II, they were progressively retrieved later in recall, while new items in Condition II were progressively recalled earlier. Such retrieval of the repeated items later in recall developed more slowly and was less marked in Condition I, where the search for retrieval of the repeated birds was always part of a search for retrieval also of new items from the same category in PS. Roberts (1969) has shown that the early recall of new items, first described by Battig, Allen, & Jensen (1965), reduces the loss of new items from output interference (Tulving & Arbuckle, 1963; Roediger, 1974).

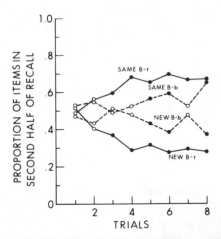

Fig. 4-3. Vincentized recall of repeated and new items in Conditions I and II of Experiment 1, as proportion of each retrieved in the last half of recall. Closed circles show proportions significantly different from 0.50.

II. FREE RETRIEVAL FROM
PERMANENT STORAGE

Understanding retrieval from PS as well as the organization of PS is clearly essential for a satisfactory understanding of human verbal learning and memory. Since much verbal learning involves items about which information is already contained in PS, this verbal learning may be considered to consist of learning how to retrieve information from PS about that subset of items to be recalled. Considerable analysis has suggested that recall involves directed search in PS to find items to be recalled (Yntema & Trask, 1963; Peterson, 1967; Shiffrin & Atkinson, 1969; Kintsch, 1970, 1972; Shiffrin, 1970a, 1970b; Anderson & Bower, 1972). To understand more about the search for and recovery of selected subsets of items from PS, it may be useful to know something about unrestricted search and retrieval from PS when Ss are asked to recall *all* available information in some part of PS. This can be done experimentally by requiring Ss to recall all the items they can from a category in PS (Bousfield & Sedgewick, 1944). To learn more about how retrieval from PS may increase, Dr. Gerald Lazar and I have been studying repeated, spontaneous retrieval from PS by requiring at least two separate, complete retrievals of as many items from one or more categories as an S can recall (Brown, 1923). Such repeated, free retrieval from PS is also of interest because it provides a model for the investigation of learning without specific experimenter input; because the information to be retrieved already is clearly in PS, retrieval alone may be studied.

Table 4-1 shows a typical protocol from one S that illustrates many of the salient features of such spontaneous retrieval. This S attempted to recall all animals he could think of in 5 min (I), then repeated the attempt again in a second, separate and complete retrieval of all the animals he could think of (II). The horizontal lines in Table 4-1 separate the 5-min retrieval periods into 1 min segments to show the number of items recalled in each consecutive minute. This S recalled 19 items in I, only one of which was not again retrieved in II. In II, 18 of the items retrieved in I were recalled again (more rapidly and principally at the beginning of the second retrieval), and 11 new items were added (principally at the end of the second retrieval), for a total of 29 items recalled in II. The rate of retrieval declines sharply in both I and II, even though many items remain in the category to be recalled. (The word in capitals [FROG] in the first column is one not again retrieved. The words in capitals in the second column indicate the 11 new items added.)

TABLE 4-1
Typical Repeated Retrieval of All Items
from a Category in Permanent Storage

I		II
dog	5	horse
cat	6	cow
lion	7	pig
tiger	17	camel
horse	18	mouse
cow	11	zebra
pig	8	alligator
	9	crocodile
alligator	15	turtle
crocodile	3	lion
elephant	4	tiger
zebra	13	jaguar
leopard	12	leopard
jaguar		RAT
FROG	16	bear
lizard	1	dog
turtle	2	cat
	10	elephant
bear	14	lizard
camel		SHEEP
mouse		OX
		DONKEY
		RABBIT
		HAMSTER
		GERBIL
		PANTHER
		DEER
		GUINEA PIG
		MULE

The numbers given in II indicate the sequential position in which those items were first retrieved in I. The obvious juxtaposition of clearly related items in both I and II suggests strongly that such retrieval is not random (Bousfield, 1953). Items that "belong together" tend to appear together, even though their joint position in the second sequence of recall may be quite different from their position in the first recall. For example, horse and cow, cow and pig, dog and cat, alligator and crocodile remain together, and lion and tiger are brought together with leopard and jaguar.

TABLE 4-2

Typical Individual Retrieval of a Category from Permanent Storage
in Terms of Overall Frequency of Retrieval
of Different Items in that Category

	(I)	I	II		(I)	I	II
DOG	35	+	+	CAMEL	14	+	+
HORSE	35	+	+	LLAMA	14		
TIGER	35	+	+	BULL	13		
CAT	33	+	+	MOOSE	13		
LION	33	+	+	ANTELOPE	13		
COW	32	+	+	RACCOON	13		
ELEPHANT	29	+	+	HAMSTER	12		+
BEAR	29	+	+	BUFFALO	12		
ZEBRA	29	+	+	MONKEY	12		
GIRAFFE	28			ALLIGATOR	11	+	+
MOUSE	27	+	+	PANTHER	11		+
DEER	26		+	ELK	11		
RABBIT	25		+	TURTLE	10	+	+
GOAT	24			GERBIL	9		+
SQUIRREL	24			SKUNK	8		
PIG	23	+	+	LAMB	8		
LEOPARD	22	+	+	CROCODILE	7	+	+
RAT	21		+	BEAVER	7		
RHINO	21			GUINEA PIG	6		+
HIPPO	21			FROG	6	+	
WOLF	16			GAZELLE	6		
DONKEY	16		+	LIZARD	6	+	+
SHEEP	15		+	CHEETAH	5		
MULE	15		+	OX	4		+
FOX	15			JAGUAR	3	+	+

Furthermore, related new items tend to appear together in II: rabbit, hamster and gerbil.

Table 4-2 relates the retrieval by this *S* to the overall retrieval by the entire group of 36 *S*s. The 50 items shown in Table 4-2 are listed in order of their relative frequency of first retrieval (I) to show how little concordance there appears to be among *S*s spontaneously recalling well-known items from a familiar category. While this *S* did recall the most frequent items, he failed to recall many available and relatively more frequent items in his first retrieval. It is also apparent that subsequent recall in II of items retrieved in I is practically independent of their initial probability of retrieval. The probability of subsequent recall remains high once an item has been retrieved.

The use of at least two repeated, spontaneous retrievals from permanent storage allows a detailed analysis of retrieval in terms of items retrieved in both first and second retrievals, lost items retrieved only in

I, and new items gained in II (Brown, 1923). The temporal and sequential characteristics of a retrieval also can be analyzed in terms of items lost, gained, or carried over, and this analysis can be extended for investigation of changes in retrieval from PS when more than two retrievals are used (I-II, II-III, *etc.*).

In a study of repeated retrieval from PS (Lazar & Buschke, 1972) each *S* gave two separate, complete, spontaneous retrievals of items in each of two different categories. Three different sequences of the two separate retrievals from two different categories by each *S* (aabb; abab; abba) were used to show that the facilitation of second retrieval by a previous retrieval is category specific, and that exponential decrease in continuous retrieval is not due to fatigue or exhaustion of the pool of available items. The *S*s were simply told to write down as many items from the designated category as they could each time, and they were asked to draw a line under their last response when given a signal every minute of each 5-min retrieval in order to indicate the temporal course of retrieval.

There were no significant differences among the three types of sequence. About 85% of the 24 items retrieved in I were retrieved again in II. Retrieval in II was greater than retrieval in I because about twice as many new items were gained in II as were lost from I. The average number of different items retrieved altogether in I, II, or both was about 31, while the total number of different items retrieved by all *S*s together, averaged across the four categories, was almost 150, indicating that individual *S*s managed to retrieve about 21% of the available items.

Although the number of available items estimated from the overall retrieval by all *S*s may be inflated by idiosyncratic retrieval of some items by only a very few *S*s, examination of the items retrieved indicates that there certainly are many more reasonably common items in PS than were retrieved by any individual *S*. It is clear that *S*s certainly do not retrieve more than half of the items that surely are available in their PS, so that the rapid decrease in temporal retrieval is not due only to exhaustion of the pool of available items.

Analysis of the number of items retrieved each minute during the first and second retrieval from each of two categories in the three different sequences showed that the rate of retrieval was facilitated only by prior retrieval of items in the same category, and that this facilitation was not affected by the sequential and temporal relationships of the first and second retrievals of a category. The facilitation of second retrieval by a previous retrieval of items from the same category was due to an increase in the rate of retrieval of those items previously retrieved in I. The gain of new items was relatively constant throughout II and was about twice as great as the number of items lost from I. Analysis of the relative *sequential*

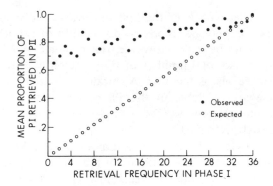

Fig. 4-4. Proportion of items from first retrieval recalled again in second retrieval, as a function of frequency of first retrieval.

retrieval for the different types of items showed that there was a slight tendency for items to be lost from the end of I, and a sharp gain in the number of new items retrieved at the end of II. Those items retrieved in both I and II were retrived relatively equally throughout I, but they were recalled again mostly at the beginning of II.

Given the rapidly declining and surprisingly limited retrieval of the items available in PS, the finding that 85% of those items retrieved in a first retrieval are recalled again in the second retrieval is striking. Fig. 4-4, which shows the probability of recall of animals in II as a function of their initial retrieval frequency during I, indicates that the probability of a second recall was relatively independent of an item's initial probability of retrieval. Once an item has been retrieved from PS, whatever its initial probability of retrieval, the probability of subsequent recall is very high. The facilitation of second retrieval by previous retrieval of items in that category clearly is item-specific, because the recall of previously retrieved items is clearly increased.

III. REPEATED AND RESTRICTED RETRIEVAL FROM PERMANENT STORAGE

One possible explanation for the finding that 85% of the first retrieval is recalled again in the second retrieval might be that this simply represents the overlap of two relatively complete retrievals from the total pool of available items. For example, if a typical S retrieved 18 birds in the first retrieval and 23 birds in the second retrieval, of which 15 had been previously recalled (85% of the first retrieval), and if the total pool of available items was only 27, then the probability of recalling 15 birds in both retrievals would be 0.37. However, this estimate of 27 birds available in PS, given by the total number of different birds retrieved in first, second, or both retrievals, is too low. Accurate evaluation of the number of items in a category available in the PS of any particular S requires either the use of multiple retrievals or a single very extended retrieval for *all* available items to be retrieved.

Bousfield & Barclay (1950) found that individual Ss retrieved approximately 36 birds as a minimal estimate of the number of birds available in PS, so that the probability of recalling 15 birds again in II, if 18 were retrieved in I and 23 in II, is only 0.015. This probability is only 0.008 when an estimate of 50 birds is used, obtained by counting only those birds retrieved by at least two Ss, which an average S would be expected to retrieve eventually. The high probability of again recalling a previously retrieved item does not appear to be due simply to overlap between relatively large samples from the pool of available items.

Another possible explanation for the high probability of recalling previously retrieved items again is that such items simply are more accessible in each S's PS; they are more likely to be recalled again because they are likely to be recalled on any retrieval attempt. However, it seems more reasonable to attribute the individual differences in retrieval of presumably well known items from PS to differences in retrieval search rather than to differences in the structure, content, or accessibility of PS.

To investigate whether individual Ss might tend to retrieve the same items from PS at any time, and to investigate the effect of increasing delay between first and second retrievals, three groups of Ss were studied with delays of 1 hr, 2 days, or 1 week between the first and second retrieval of items from the same category in PS. The Ss were asked to write down as many birds as they could in 5 min on each retrieval, but they were not informed that they would be required to attempt a second retrieval at a later time.

The data from the three groups with different delays between first and second retrieval, shown in Table 4-3, are practically identical except for a significant decrease in the proportion of items from the first retrieval recalled again in the second retrieval and a slight but significant increase in the number of items lost from the first retrieval.

Fig. 4-5 shows that the facilitation of the overall rate of output in the second retrieval persisted for a week. Fig. 4-6 shows that this facilitation was due to an increased rate of recall of previously retrieved items, which persisted for 2 days but was attenuated by 1 week after the first retrieval. This facilitation indicates that a second retrieval is affected by

TABLE 4-3
*Repeated Retrieval from Long-Term Storage
with Delay between First and Second Retrieval*

Interval	I	II	Both	Both I	I Only	II Only	Total[a]	Total Pool[b]
1 hr (N = 24)	17.7	22.3	16.0	90.3	1.7	6.4	24.1	29.7
2 days (N = 19)	18.5	25.1	15.9	86.2	2.5	9.2	27.7	33.0
1 week (N = 24)	17.4	21.7	13.9	79.0	3.5	8.0	25.4	30.6

[a] Mean number of different items retrieved by individual subjects.
[b] Total number of different items retrieved by all subjects.

previous retrieval of same items from the same category, and that the high probability of repeated recall of most of the first retrieval is not due only to idiosyncratic accessibility of particular items retrieved from PS. Previous retrieval does facilitate the subsequent retrieval of items from PS so that they are recalled more rapidly and earlier in a second retrieval.

Finally, to determine whether Ss could selectively recall items they had retrieved before, and whether they could distinguish between previously retrieved and new items, Lazar and I did another experiment in which four groups of 18 Ss either were required to restrict their second retrieval to just those items recalled during I, or were free to recall any and all items from the category again during II. In addition, Ss either were told about this restriction before their first retrieval, or were not told until just before their second retrieval. The first group of Ss was told before their initial retrieval that they would be required to restrict their second retrieval to only those items they had already recalled during the first re-

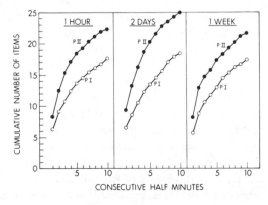

Fig. 4-5. Cumulative overall first (PI) and second (PII) free retrieval from permanent storage with different delays between PI and PII.

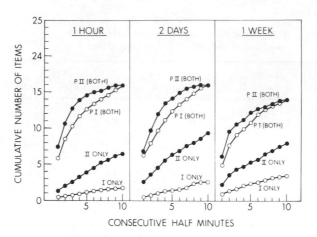

Fig. 4-6. Cumulative components of first (PI) and second (PII) free retrieval from permanent storage with different delays between PI and PII.

trieval. The second group was also given these instructions, but was told just before their second retrieval to retrieve any items in the category rather than just those items already retrieved. The third group was told only before their second retrieval to restrict that retrieval to those items already retrieved, and the fourth group was told just before the second retrieval to retrieve any items in the category. All groups retrieved items from the category, which was four-legged animals, with 5 min for each of the two retrievals. The second and fourth groups, which retrieved all items from the category during their second retrieval, were then asked to discriminate items that had been recalled during the first retrieval from new items, to evaluate their recognition of previously retrieved items.

Table 4-4 shows that Ss were quite successful in selectively recalling only those items previously retrieved. The results of the first and third groups which had been told before their first retrieval that their second retrieval would be restricted to recall of previously retrieved items, show that these Ss recalled a greater percentage of their first retrieval again in II than did those Ss who attempted unrestricted retrieval of all items in their second retrieval, with fewer items lost from I (I Only) and scarcely any intrusion of new items in II (II Only). More impressively, Ss in the third group, who were not told until just before their second retrieval to restrict it to recall of previously retrieved items, were able to recall about as many previously retrieved items as Ss in the fourth group, whose second retrieval was not restricted, without the intrusion of more new items. It is clearly possible for Ss to restrict their retrieval from PS to items previously retrieved without a significant incidence of either misses or false alarms.

TABLE 4-4

Second Retrieval of All Items in the Category and
Second Retrieval Restricted to Recall of Items in First Retrieval

Conditions[a]	I	II	Both	I Only	II Only	Total	Both/I	I Only/I	Both/II	II Only/II
Told Before All (3)	32.3	37.8	27.0	5.3	10.7	43.0	83.4	16.6	71.4	28.6
I Only (1)	24.9	23.0	22.4	2.5	0.6	25.5	89.7	10.3	97.4	2.6
Not Told All (4)	30.4	36.5	23.9	6.5	12.5	42.9	78.5	21.5	65.5	34.5
I Only (2)	27.4	23.1	22.3	5.1	0.8	28.2	82.5	17.5	96.5	3.5

[a] Mean number of different items retrieved by individual subjects.

TABLE 4-5
*Discrimination of Previously Recalled and New Items
in Second Retrieval from Long-Term Storage*

Condition[a]	Correct Responses	Hits	False Alarms	d'	β	Hits / (Hits + False Alarms)
Told Before (3)	$\dfrac{35.9}{37.8} = .94$	$\dfrac{26.2}{27.0} = .96$	$\dfrac{1.1}{10.7} = .10$	4.34	2.89	$\dfrac{26.2}{27.3} = .95$
Not Told Before (4)	$\dfrac{34.2}{36.5} = .93$	$\dfrac{22.6}{23.9} = .94$	$\dfrac{1.1}{12.5} = .08$	4.02	3.13	$\dfrac{22.6}{23.7} = .95$

[a] Either told or not told before first retrieval that the second retrieval would be restricted to recall of items in first retrieval; second retrieval was actually unrestricted.

Table 4-5 shows that Ss in the second and fourth groups, who were free to retrieve any items during their second retrieval, were able to distinguish previously recalled items from new items with great accuracy. Overall, about 93% of their responses were correct, with an average hit rate of 0.95 and false alarm rate of 0.09. It is clear that Ss can discriminate between previously retrieved and new items in retrieval from PS, and can restrict their recall to previously retrieved items.

Do Ss restrict their retrieval to recall of previously retrieved items by recognizing but supressing new items, or by restricting their retrieval search so that only previously retrieved items will be found for recall again? Does such restricted retrieval require discrimination of previously retrieved and new items as well as directed search, or does it result from restricted search alone, without further discrimination between new and previously recalled items? This question also applies to the facilitation of second retrieval by a previous retrieval, which might reflect only facilitation of search for retrieval, or increased item accessibility and discriminability that permits more effective readout and recovery.

If restriction of second retrieval to recall of only previously retrieved items resulted from restricted search alone, without also requiring discrimination of previously retrieved items from new items, then restricted second retrieval should proceed at the same rate as unrestricted second retrieval of all items from the appropriate category in PS. Comparison of the recall of only the previously retrieved items (Both) in restricted second retrieval (I Only) with unrestricted second retrieval of all items (All) shown in Fig. 4-7 clearly indicates that restricted second retrieval of previously retrieved items (I Only) requires discrimination of new and previously recalled items. Previously retrieved items (Both) were not recalled more rapidly in restricted second retrieval (I Only–Both) than in unrestricted second retrieval (All–Both). Restricted second retrieval (I Only) did not

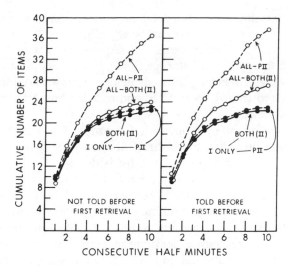

Fig. 4-7. Cumulative free retrieval (All) and restricted retrieval (I Only) from permanent storage (PS).

occur as rapidly as unrestricted retrieval of new and previously retrieved items together (All–PII). If preferentially directed search for previously retrieved items had been used for restricted second retrieval, then the previously retrieved items (I Only–Both) should have been retrieved by the end of the second minute, rather than continuing through the 5-min retrieval period. Restricting second retrieval to recall of previously recalled items seems to require the discrimination of previously retrieved from new items, which we know Ss can do quite successfully.

The finding that restricted retrieval is not due to restricted search for previously retrieved items also indicates that the more rapid, earlier recall of previously retrieved items in a second unrestricted retrieval is not due to facilitation of search for those items, but instead appears to be an item-specific facilitation due to increased item accessibility or discriminability. If the initial facilitation of recall from PS by previous retrieval is due to increased item accessibility rather than differential search, it suggests that a temporary LT storage (similar to temporary computer storages that retain recently used information to decrease the need for retrieval of such information from core memory) might be used for learning and retrieval from PS. Thus, Ss might retain some recently acquired information in a temporary LT storage, from which they can retrieve directly without requiring active search in PS. The information in such a highly accessible, temporary LT storage could be recalled rapidly at any time. Learning a list of items might be viewed as the gradual addition of relevant items to such a highly accessible, temporary LT storage so that, as learning proceeds, more and more of the items can be expeditiously retrieved from this storage, while fewer and fewer items will require active search in PS for retrieval. If such temporary LT storage is simply regarded as a function of STS, then this view of learning a list of items illustrates how information might be transferred from LTS to STS, and indicate how STS might function as an output buffer.

Alternatively, information in such temporary LT storage might be search information providing more direct access to the items in PS. As a suitable search to recover the items in a list is developed, portions of that search might be retained in such a temporary LT storage so that, as learning proceeds, some of the search is relatively rapid because it is highly directed while the remainder is random. This might be thought of as similar to learning to drive from one city to another, with less and less of the trip requiring active searching as learning increases on repeated attempts. It is interesting that the temporal course of recall as list learning proceeds is consistent with this suggestion. Typically, Ss will rapidly recall a few items, then pause and have to search before retrieving more items. The number of items retrieved in the rapid phase of recall, before Ss clearly pause and have to search actively for more items, increases over trials, so that eventually Ss can retrieve all of the items rapidly without active search in PS. This suggests that the development of directed search for items might require the transfer of items from LTS to STS, so that at least two items can be attended to and processed together in order to perceive or establish relationships necessary for their organized retrieval from PS. Almost any cognitive processing that involves more than one item would seem to require that at least two items must be attended to and processed together at the same time. While this might occur in LTS itself, it seems reasonable to expect that concurrent processing of two or more items might be carried out in STS (Glanzer, 1969, 1972).

IV. REMINDED RECALL AND EXTENDED RETRIEVAL

Having reviewed some experiments that support the view that learning to recall a list of items may require directed search in PS for retrieval from LTS, and, having described some salient characteristics of spontaneous free retrieval from PS, I will return to the more usual kind of list learning, using the method of *selective reminding* (rather than presentation of the entire list for each trial) to show how free recall learning may also require directed search in PS for retrieval from LTS. The kind of restricted list of items I will deal with are all from the same category in PS, instead of the more usual list of unrelated items or only partially categorized list. Although the recall of lists of items from the same category has not been studied extensively, it will provide a bridge from the previous discussion of the free retrieval of all items from a category in PS to the restricted recall of a selected subset of items from PS. Laurence (1967) found that such restricted lists were learned better than mixed lists of unrelated items and that aged adult Ss, who did not learn mixed lists as well as young adult Ss, did learn such restricted lists as well as young adult Ss. Craik and Birtwistle (1971) showed that the proactive inhibition of free recall by previous recall of lists of items from the same category was due to interference with retrieval from LTS, and that shifting to recall of items from another category provided release from such proactive inhibition. I have been using lists of items from the same category also because they provide a well-defined search space in PS for extended recall: When an S is asked to increase his recall by persisting in active search for items not yet recalled, he may be more likely to continue active searching if he knows where to search in PS.

When Ss are asked to learn a list of items, it is conventional to present *all* items in the list before *each* recall trial. It is not obvious that this is the best way to teach someone a list of items. A reasonable way to teach someone a list of items might be to "remind" him of those items he has not yet learned rather than to present all items, both learned and unlearned, on each trial. This would have the advantage of directing attention to items that still need to be learned but that might be overlooked when presented together with items already learned. For multi-trial free recall of only the items in a given list regardless of their order, *selective reminding* of only certain items is reasonable and has significant advantages for studies of free-recall verbal learning. One advantage is that selective reminding separates total recall into retrieval from LTS and recall from STS, and provides an estimate of cumulative LT storage during learning; LTS is the cumulative number of items retrieved at least once from LTS.

Selective reminding can be done in several ways (Buschke, 1973). The most obvious form of selective reminding is to present on each trial *only* those items in the list that were *not* recalled on the immediately preceding trial. In this case, the S will be reminded of some items already in LTS, but not retrieved from LTS on the preceding trial, as well as items not yet encoded in LTS but recalled from STS. Alternatively, Ss may be reminded selectively of only those items still to be learned because they are not yet in LTS. The use of selective reminding to show that an item was retrieved from LTS because it was recalled without being presented on a particular trial is an extension of similar techniques for estimating retrieval from LTS used by Glanzer and Cunitz (1966), Craik (1968, 1970), Tulving (1964), Tulving and Colotla (1970), and Waugh and Norman (1965). These techniques involve separating recall from STS and retrieval from LTS on the basis of interference by presented or recalled items intervening between the presentation and recall of each item. When selective reminding is used with lists of any reasonable length, there is substantial interference by items intervening between the last recall of an item and its subsequent recall without further presentation. When an item is recalled without presentation on that trial, the items intervening between the last recall of that item on the preceding trial and its recall on the trial in question include all other items recalled after that item on the preceding trial, all other items presented by selective reminding on that trial, and all other items recalled before that item itself was recalled from LTS on that trial.

Another kind of selective reminding involves presenting items only until they have been recalled once. This is useful for determining whether recall failures following an initial recall represent encoding failures or retrieval failures, and can be used for investigation of retrieval alone after all items have been encoded (Buschke, 1974a). The most extreme version of selective reminding, discussed in detail later, consists of providing only one presentation of all items in the list to be learned, followed by multiple, independent, complete recall trials. Selective reminding with only a single presentation of each item (on the first trial) provides the best evaluation of encoding in LTS because any item retrieved during the subsequent recall trials must have been encoded during that single presentation. Since our estimates of encoding must necessarily depend on retrieval, we may underestimate encoding when items are presented again on subsequent trials if retrieval from LTS is less than perfect. Multiple retrieval attempts following a single initial presentation of the list can show that more items were encoded than is apparent from the initial recall alone.

In order to maximize retrieval from LTS on each trial, it is important also to require extended recall by requesting the S to continue his retrieval attempt even after retrieval becomes difficult. From simple observation of the course of free recall, it is clear that recall occurs in at least two stages. Subjects typically recall a number of items rather rapidly, then pause to search for more items. At first many of the items recalled during the first rapid recall stage are from STS, while most of those recalled later during the slow, second stage are retrieved from LTS. Many Ss apparently prefer to discontinue their recall attempts shortly after concluding the first stage of rapid recall, even though more time may still be available. When the entire list is presented for each recall trial, the S may be less motivated to persist in the second stage of slow retrieval because he can add any missing items on the next trial when all items are again presented. Because additional items may be retrieved from LTS by extending the second slow stage of retrieval, Ss should be requested to persist in their recall attempts in order to maximize estimates of LTS and of retrieval from LTS.

These stages of recall are interesting in themselves and deserve further study. They do not merely represent recall from STS and retrieval from LTS, respectively, because the number of items recalled during the first rapid stage of recall increases over trials as items are learned and retrieved from LTS, until finally, *all* items on the list may be retrieved very rapidly without requiring a second slow stage of retrieval by active searching. This increasingly rapid retrieval of an increasing number of list items from LTS indicates an increased accessibility of the list items in LTS, not just in STS. It is unclear whether this shift from both rapid recall and slow retrieval initially to rapid retrieval alone is due to increased accessibility of individual items, increasingly effective search in PS for retrieval from LTS, or possibly the increasing retention of list items in a temporary LT storage.

The use of selective reminding also helps us to ask more specific questions about the relationship between presentation and recall in terms of encoding, retaining, and retrieving items from STS and LTS. Does the failure to recall an item before the first recall of that item represent encoding failure or retrieval failure? Does the failure to recall an item after it has been recalled once represent loss from STS, failure to encode that item in LTS, loss of that item from LTS, or failure to retrieve that item from LTS? What functions are served by presentation of an item? Possible functions of presenting an item include: (1) ST storage; (2) initial encoding ("tagging") in LTS; (3) increasing item accessibility in LTS by (a) further encoding of more features of an item with multiple attributes, or (b) increasing the discriminability of that item from related items sharing many of the same attributes; (4) preventing the loss of information about that item in LTS by counteracting trace decay, which is due to interference by presentation and recall of other items; (5) restoring to LTS an item that was lost after previous encoding in LTS; (6) restructuring the organization of retrieval search in PS to include the retrieval of items not previously retrieved (*i.e.,* reminding the S to include the retrieval of previously omitted items in the retrieval of the list); and (7) providing a basis for deleting any intrusions from retrieval. One difference between selective reminding and presentation of the entire list on each trial is that in selective reminding there is no basis for deleting any intrusions that arise during recall, because items are not presented again if they are recalled. Although intrusions of items not in the list do occur in selective reminding, it is interesting that Ss can often discriminate their own intrusions (when, for example, they discover that they have recalled too many items). Intrusions during learning by selective re-

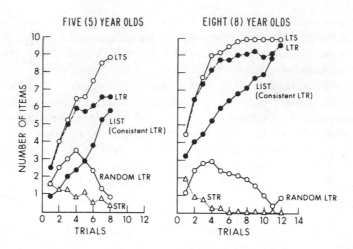

Fig. 4-8. Development in 5-year-old and 8-year-old children of components of memory and learning shown by selective reminding of only those items not recalled on the preceding trial. (From Buschke, H., 1974b.)

minding also do not persist and often disappear spontaneously after a few trials (Buschke, in press,).

The power of selective reminding as a method for studying memory and learning is shown by its application to the investigation of the development of verbal memory and learning in children. Fig. 4-8 shows the detailed differences in the memory and learning of a 10-item list of common animals by 5-year-old and 8-year-old children. LTS is long-term storage (of individual *items*). LTR is total retrieval from long-term storage, and STR is recall from short-term storage. Consistent LTR and random LTR distinguish retrieval from long-term storage due to directed search and random search, respectively. LIST shows list learning, *i.e.,* the degree to which the list has been learned as a list, or the number of items that have been learned as part of a list. It is apparent that selective reminding shows significant changes in all of these components of memory and learning as memory and learning develop. The most striking findings shown in Fig. 4-8 are those that show the development of retrieval from LTS. Total retrieval from LTS is clearly more effective in the 8-year-olds than in the 5-year-olds, due principally to the development of more consistent retrieval from LTS (Buschke, 1974 b).

To determine whether failure to recall items after their first presentation, *i.e.,* before their initial recall, is mainly due to encoding failure or to retrieval failure, and to investigate retrieval from LTS alone unconfounded by encoding, Dr. Paula Altman Fuld and I investigated free recall after the most extreme kind of selective reminding, which required multiple, extended retrievals after only a single presentation of a list of 20 animals. The *S*s were asked to write down each item as it was read aloud during the single presentation to make sure that they paid attention to each item. Then they were given 12 sequential recall trials for complete, extended recall of all items in the list. About 1 week later, they were asked for an additional long-term recall trial without further presentation of the list, followed by a yes-no recognition test for the items in the list.

Fig. 4-9 shows the successive retrieval by a typical *S* after only one presentation of the list, with delayed recall and recognition a week later. Although only 14 items were recalled on the first trial, 19 of the 20 items

SINGLE PRESENTATION ONLY

Extended Free Recall

Four – Footed Animals

		1	2	3	4	5	6	7	8	9	10	11	12	ONE WEEK LATER RECALL	RECOG
1	Dog	(1)	1	1	1	1	1	1	1	1	1	1	1	12	+
2	Fox	(12)	3	12	17	4	4	4	13	4	4	4		4	+
3	Horse	(2)	2	2	2	3	5	2	2	2	2	2	2	2	+
4	Buffalo						(2)	7	5	4	14	5	14		+
5	Lion		(15)	4	11	1	3	3	3	3	3	3	3	3	+
6	Rhinoceros	(10)	7	14	10	16	11	9	13	7	13	11	17	13	+
7	Elephant	(4)	3	5	13	14	8	8	11	5	11	9	12	11	+
8	Antelope	(11)	8	13	9	15	12	10	12	6	12	10	16	12	+
9	Bear	(5)	13	6	4	(16)	5	19		(19)	7	18		14	+
10	Lamb	(9)	(10)	7	6	15	13	10	11	7	15	9		10	+
11	Rat	(3)	9	16	3	4	9	11	6	16	16	16	10	18	+
12	Raccoon	(16)	11	14	5	10	12	7	17	17	17	11		7	+
13	Sheep	(8)	5	9	6	7	14	14	8	10	5	13	8	9	+
14	Llama													(16)	+
15	Goat	(14)				(8)	13	15	9	9	6	14	7	8	+
16	Cheetah	(13)	6	15	16	9	18	18	14	(15)	18	13		17	+
17	Squirrel	(7)	4	8	8	12	6	19	15	8	18	6	6	6	+
18	Beaver	(6)	14	7	5	13	17	6	18	15	8	8	19	15	+
19	Donkey	(11)		(17)	11		(17)	17	14	9			(15)		+
20	Turtle	(12)	10	12	15	10	7	16	16	12	10	12	5	5	+
	Σ Recall	14	16	16	17	17	18	19	19	17	19	18	19	18	20
	# of items retrieved at least once	14	18	18	18	18	19	19	19	19	19	19	19	20	
	LONG-TERM STORAGE (item learning)	20	20	20	20	20	20	20	20	20	20	20	20	20	
	CONSISTENT RETRIEVAL (list learning)	10	13	14	14	15	16	16	16	16	18	18	18		
	RANDOM RETRIEVAL	4	3	2	3	2	2	3	3	1	1	0	1		

Fig. 4-9. Protocol of one *S*s repeated and extended written free recall without any further presentation of items after a single presentation of the entire list on the first trial. Numbers show order of recall on each trial and one week later; + indicates recognition one week later. Circles indicate the first recall of each item. Boxed circles indicate recovery of a previously recalled item after retrieval failure. Underlining marks the onset of consistent retrieval of an item from long-term storage on all subsequent trials; this also shows list learning (*i.e.*, the number of items learned as part of a list so that they are consistently retrieved together).

were recalled by the twelfth trial, and the one remaining item was recovered spontaneously during the delayed recall a week later. Apparently this *S* encoded all 20 items during the single presentation. Four additional items were first recalled on the second retrieval trial, another on the sixth retrieval trial, and the remaining item was retrieved a week later. In this case, all items recalled were retrieved from LTS without any recall from STS. It is apparent that, once an item is retrieved, the probability of subsequent retrieval is extremely high, so that although list learning progressed fairly slowly even though all items were encoded on the first trial, retrieval from LTS by random search was minimal. The boxed circles show that the recovery of a previously recalled item after retrieval failure is the result of extensive searching in PS because these items are retrieved quite late in the recall of the list. The circles indicate that recall failure before initial recall of an item represented retrieval failure, not encoding failure, and the boxed circles indicate that recall failure after initial recall (*i.e.,* after previous retrieval from LTS in this case) represented retrieval failure, not loss from LTS.

Fig. 4-10 shows the overall results of multiple trials of extended free recall following one presentation of this list of 20 animals. The number of items retrieved on successive recalls continues to increase (recall), as does repeated recall of an item from one trial to the next (RR), while the number of items in any recall that were not retrieved on the immediately preceding trial remains constant (NR). The cumulative estimate of initial encoding (LTS) increases over trials to almost 18 items by the twelfth

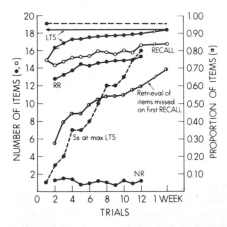

Fig. 4-10. Repeated retrieval after only a single presentation of the entire list on the first trial. RR is recall of items also recalled on the preceding trial, and NR is recall of items not recalled on the preceding trial.

trial. A maximum estimate of initial encoding of 19.06 items in LTS was obtained when the results of delayed recall and recognition a week later were included. Of the total number of items that were not retrieved during the first trial, 27% were retrieved on the second recall trial, with recovery of new items continuing until about 60% of those not retrieved on the first recall had been recovered without further presentation. The slow increase in the number of Ss who had reached their maximum retrieval also shows that these Ss continued to retrieve new items that had been encoded in LTS during the single presentation but had not yet been recalled. These results show quite clearly that retrieval may increase on successive recall attempts following a single presentation of a list. In this case it appears that the number of items recalled was more a function of the effectiveness of retrieval than of encoding, because, although nearly all items were encoded, many recall attempts were required before most of the items in LTS were retrieved. However, once an item was retrieved, it was very likely to be retrieved again subsequently. I cannot account for the difference between these results and those of Estes (1960), who did not find that more new items were retrieved on a second recall attempt without further presentation. These results may be due partly to the use of extended recall and partly to the use of a list of items from the same category in PS, which allowed these Ss to retrieve items from a well-defined search space.

To show that extended free recall, when Ss are asked to persist in searching for additional items, may result in greater retrieval than obtained by standard free recall (when Ss are permitted to discontinue their retrieval and wait for the next trial), we studied two other groups of Ss. The entire list of 20 animals was presented in random order on every trial for standard free recall by one group of 16 Ss and for extended free recall by another group of 16 Ss. For extended free recall, the Ss were urged to persist in their recall attempts and were provided longer intertrial intervals initially; for standard free recall, the Ss were simply asked to recall as many items as they could on each trial during the 2-min intertrial interval following each presentation of the list. In extended free recall, items are typically recalled for the first time earlier than in standard recall; once recalled, they are retrieved more consistently.

Fig. 4-11 compares extended and standard free recall (when the entire list is presented again on each trial) with extended recall after only a single presentation of the list. The more rapid increase of both standard and extended free recall when the entire list is presented before each trial seems to be due mainly to more effective retrieval, because almost all items were encoded during the single presentation alone. When the entire list is presented before each trial, retrieval search can be revised for more complete retrieval of all items in the list.

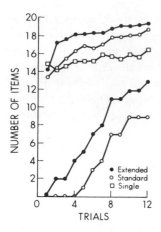

Fig. 4-11. Comparison of extended and standard free recall with repeated retrieval after only a single presentation of the list (top three curves). Lower curves show the number of Ss who recalled all 20 items by extended or standard free recall.

Extended recall also was greater than standard recall. While the rate of increase in standard recall was relatively constant, extended recall increased markedly on the second trial and more slowly thereafter. Fig. 4-11 also shows that the number of Ss who recalled all 20 items for the first time on consecutive trials was greater when extended recall was used. Unlike "forced" recall of associated items from different categories (Cofer, 1967), extended recall of items from the same category is greater than standard free recall. This indicates that continued searching, at least in the well-defined search space given by a category, can increase retrieval from PS.

These results indicate that most of the recall failures, before as well as after the first recall of an item, probably represent retrieval failure rather than either encoding failure or loss from LTS. Continuing presentation of items does not appear necessary for either initial encoding or the maintenance of retrieval once achieved. The major problem in free-recall learning seems to be retrieval of all items together from PS. Further presentation of all items in a list on each trial appears to enhance recall of the list by reminding the S to search for items not previously retrieved, so that their retrieval can be integrated with the retrieval of all other items for more complete retrieval of the list as a whole.

V. CONCLUDING COMMENTS: THE RETRIEVAL OF ITEMS AND LISTS

Free recall of items and lists of selected items, as well as free retrieval of all items from a category, may involve the use of search in PS for retrieval from LTS. The main idea underlying this discussion is that recall and retrieval in verbal learning of items and lists of items is carried out by retrieval of items from LTS. My discussion of STS itself has been limited because it is not yet clear how STS processes function in learning and memory. STS does not contribute much to total recall, and it no longer seems likely that learning or encoding in LTS is necessarily limited by the limited capacity of STS. The experiment with Ritter on concurrent learning and STS indicates either that there is direct access of all presented items to LTS or that transfer from STS to LTS is rapid and complete. That experiment also suggests that STS processes may operate in PS. Craik and Lockhart (1972) have recently urged that "levels of processing" may provide a more productive conceptual basis for further investigation of human memory than is provided by current models of STS and LTS. It seems likely that the major role of STS in learning involves the processing of information necessary for the kind of encoding appropriate for subsequent retrieval of that information from LTS, because, as the experiment with Fuld also indicates, retrieval from LTS may be more of a problem then encoding. Since cognitive analysis of items and lists of items requires concurrent consideration of at least two items together, STS might also be used to retain a limited number of items for concurrent processing in order to appreciate "clustering" and to effect "chunking." Thus STS may also be necessary for the "deeper" level of processing attributed to LTS, and may be more important for processing lists or sets of items than for processing individual items alone.

The experiments discussed here involve memory for items. While the representation of these items in PS may be randomly organized, to permit the addition of new items without requiring reorganization of the entire storage, access to such items is organized, at least in the sense that we can define search spaces in PS for the retrieval of different kinds of items. For example, categories define search spaces in PS, so that, although we may have difficulty finding particular items or retrieving all items in a category, we can search appropriately for items in only that category.

In this discussion I have used items as memoranda, without considering the nature of different kinds of items. These experiments actually involved the recall and retrieval of names, or labels. However, while some items in PS may be only relatively isolated labels, others are labels for items with cognitive or perceptual content. When I retrieve *aardvark* I retrieve only the name of an animal of which I have no image, and about which I have no information beyond the fact that it is an animal. However, when I retrieve *cow* I can retrieve an item with cognitive content (an animal that gives milk, *etc.*) and an image. It may be important to know when *S*s are retrieving items and when they are retrieving just the *names* of items, because while items are related to each other, their labels may not be related to each other due to the arbitrary relationship between an item and its label.

There appears to be a difference between learning to recall individual items and learning to recall a list of items. Although a list may be defined in terms of its component items, items may also be defined in terms of their list membership. While a search in PS for retrieval of the items in a list usually is regarded as a search for the individual items in that list, it should also be regarded as an overall search for that list, in the course of which individual items are retrieved. Although current models of memory are often elaborated in terms of the retrieval of individual items, the data we usually analyze appears to be data about the proportion of the list retrieved. Apparently we assume that we can consider the retrieval of each item independently. However, it is not obvious that the retrieval of individual items in a list is independent of the retrieval of other items in that list. If the retrieval of individual items is the result of a search for the entire list (in the sense that such a search should result in the retrieval—by the shortest, most reliable route—of all items in the list without the intrusion of items not in the list), then the retrieval of any individual item would not necessarily be independent of the retrieval of other items in the list.

The retrieval of individual items could be increased in at least three ways. Since some items in PS are available only for reception by direct access (as in recognition), their retrieval would require that they be made available for retrieval. The independent accessibility of individual items that are already available for retrieval from PS can be increased (Tulving & Pearlstone, 1966). Finally, the retrieval of items as part of a set of items can be increased. That is, the retrieval of an item in conjunction with the retrieval of other items can be increased by integrating its retrieval with the retrieval of all other items in the list. This may also be viewed as decreasing the omission of that item from the retrieval of the list as a whole.

Learning to recall a list of items can be viewed in terms of the relative completeness of retrieval of the list as a whole, rather than just the sum of individual items recalled. The retrieval of lists may be increased in at least three ways. Since learning to recall a restricted list of selected items requires the recall of items in the list without the intrusion of items not in the list, items in the list must somehow be "tagged" so they may be discriminated from other items in the search space that are not in the list. Tagging more items will increase the retrieval of a list. The retrieval of a list may also be increased by increasing the discriminability of items in the list, *i.e.,* differentiating the list items from other items not in the list. Finally, the retrieval of a list may be increased by organizing a directed search so that the probability of finding items in the list is increased. Several kinds of search may be used for retrieval of a list from PS. Retrieval search may be

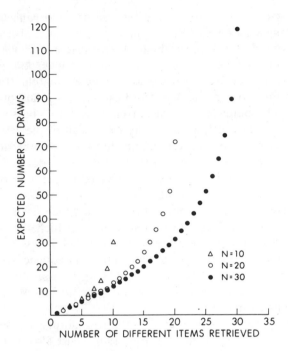

Fig. 4-12. Number of draws expected in order to retrieve increasing numbers of different items by sampling with replacement from sets containing 10, 20, or 30 items.

a random search, or it may be an associative search in which each item points to other items. Retrieval of a list may also result from an organized, directed search into which the retrieval of each item is integrated so that the completeness of retrieval of the list can be increased by reminding a S to include the retrieval of any item omitted.

Incomplete retrieval of a list may indicate the use of at least partially random search in PS for retrieval from LTS. Such random search could be considered as sampling with replacement (from an urn containing only the items in the list). Fig. 4-12 shows the expected number of draws necessary to retrieve increasing numbers of different items by sampling with replacement from lists containing 10, 20, and 30 items. The number of draws for retrieval of the last few items needed to complete retrieval of the list increases very rapidly. For example, retrieval of the last three items necessary for complete retrieval of *all* items in a list of 20 items requires twice as many draws as for the retrieval of the first 17 items. This indicates why extended recall should be used to obtain more complete retrieval during early recall trials when search is still random. Complete retrieval of *all* items in a list would appear to require the use of an organized, directed search (which might be considered as sampling without replacement from an urn containing only the items in the list). Consistent retrieval from trial to trial of all items in a list should be possible only when the retrieval of the items in that list can be organized as a directed search. If a directed search in which the retrieval of each item has its appropriate place cannot be developed, then complete retrieval on each trial will be sporadic and unreliable. This may also help explain why free recall of the selected items in a restricted list may be relatively complete, while free retrieval of all items in a category is so incomplete. It is much easier to develop an organized search for recall of a limited subset of selected items, not only because fewer items must be retrieved, but also because a limited set of items may more easily be encoded in a semantic structure, in which each item has its place, and/or in an organized retrieval scheme, in which the retrieval of each item is integrated with the retrieval of the other items, so that a directed search for all items by appropriate retrieval sequences is possible. The enhancement of retrieval by the use of imagery also may be due in part to the greater ease of organized retrieval from a semantic structure in which each item has its place.

While processing is certainly as important as storage (Craik & Lockhart, 1972), the results of information processing must also be considered. The semantic structures just mentioned would result from processing at a "deeper" level. Consideration of levels of processing and types of storage need not be mutually exclusive. An adequate understanding of human memory will require consideration of the results of processing and how such results are retained and modified, as well as consideration of processing itself. Finally, since processing of new information depends on our previous experience, it will be necessary to understand more about the organization of, and retrieval from, permanent storage.

REFERENCES

Anderson, J. R., & Bower, G. H. Recognition and retrieval processes in free recall. *Psychological Review*, 1972, **79**, 97–123.

Battig, W. F., Allen, M., & Jensen, A. R. Priority of free recall of newly learned items. *Journal of Verbal Learning and Verbal Behavior*, 1965, **4**, 175–179.

Bousfield, W. A. The occurrence of clustering in the recall of randomly arranged associates. *Journal of General Psychology*, 1953, **49**, 229–240.

Bousfield, W. A., & Barclay, W. D. The relationship between order and frequency of occurrence of restricted associative responses. *Journal of Experimental Psychology*, 1950, **40**, 643–647.

Bousfield, W. A., & Sedgewick, C. H. W. An analysis of sequences of restricted associative responses. *Journal of General Psychology,* 1944, **30,** 149–165.

Bower, G. H., A selective review of organizational factors in memory. In E. Tulving & W. Donaldson (Eds.), *Organization of Memory.* New York: Academic Press, 1972.

Brown, W. To what extent is memory measured by a single recall? *Journal of Experimental Psychology,* 1923, **6,** 377–382.

Buschke, H. Selective reminding for analysis of memory and learning. *Journal of Verbal Learning and Verbal Behavior,* 1973, **12,** 543–550.

Buschke, H. Spontaneous remembering after recall failure. *Science,* 1974, **184,** 579–581.(a)

Buschke, H. Components of verbal learning in children: analysis by selective reminding. *Journal of Experimental Child Psychology,* 1974, 18, 488–496. (b)

Buschke, H. Retrieval of categorized items increases without guessing. *Bulletin of the Psychonomic Society,* in press.

Cofer, C. N. Does conceptual organization influence the amount retained in immediate free recall? In B. Kleinmuntz (Ed.), *Concepts and the Structure of Memory.* New York, Wiley, 1967.

Craik, F. I. M. Two components in free recall. *Journal of Verbal Learning and Verbal Behavior,* 1968, **7,** 996–1004.

Craik, F. I. M. The fate of primary memory items in free recall. *Journal of Verbal Learning and Verbal Behavior,* 1970, **9,** 143–148.

Craik, F. I. M., & Birtwistle, J. Proactive inhibition in free recall. *Journal of Experimental Psychology,* 1971, **91,** 120–123.

Craik, F. I. M., & Lockhart, R. S. Levels of processing: A framework for memory research. *Journal of Verbal Learning and Verbal Behavior,* 1972, **11,** 671–684.

Estes, W. K. Learning theory and the new "mental chemistry." *Psychological Review,* 1960, **67,** 207–223.

Glanzer, M. Distance between related words in free recall: Trace of the STS. *Journal of Verbal Learning and Verbal Behavior,* 1969, **8,** 105–111.

Glanzer, M. Storage mechanisms in recall. In G. H. Bower (Ed.), *Psychology of learning and motivation.* Vol. 5. New York: Academic Press, 1972.

Glanzer, M., & Cunitz, A. R., Two storage mechanisms in free recall. *Journal of Verbal Learning and Verbal Behavior,* 1966, **5,** 35–360.

Kintsch, W. Models for free recall and recognition. In D. A. Norman (Ed.), *Models of human memory.* New York: Academic Press, 1970.

Kintsch, W., Notes on the structure of semantic memory. In E. Tulving & W. Donaldson (Eds.), *Organization of memory.* New York: Academic Press, 1972.

Laurence, M. W. A developmental look at the usefulness of list categorization as an aid to free recall. *Canadian Journal of Psychology,* 1967, **21,** 153–165.

Lazar, G., & Buschke, H. Successive retrieval from permanent storage. *Psychonomic Science,* 1972, **29,** 388–390.

Murdock, B. B., Jr. Short-term memory. In G. H. Bower (Ed.), *The psychology of learning and motivation.* New York: Academic Press, 1972.

Peterson, L. R. Search and judgment in memory. In V. Kleinmuntz (Ed.), *Concepts and the structure of memory.* New York: Wiley, 1967.

Posner, M. I., & Warren, R. E. Traces, concepts, and conscious constructions. In A. W. Melton & E. Martin (Eds.), *Coding processes in human memory.* New York: Wiley, 1972.

Roberts, W. A. The priority of recall of new items in transfer from part-list learning to whole-list learning. *Journal of Verbal Learning and Verbal Behavior*, 1969, **8**, 645–652.

Roediger, H. L. Inhibiting effects of recall. *Memory and Cognition*, 1974, **2**, 261–269.

Ritter, W., & Buschke, H. Free, forced, and restricted recall in verbal learning. *Journal of Experimental Psychology*, in press.

Ritter, W., Buschke, H., & Gindes, M. Retrieval of items embedded in changing lists. *Journal of Experimental Psychology*, 1974, **102**, 726–728.

Shallice, T., & Warrington, E. K. Independent functioning of verbal memory stores: A neuropsychological study. *Quarterly Journal of Experimental Psychology*, 1970, **22**, 261–273.

Shiffrin, R. M. Forgetting: Trace erosion or retrieval failure? *Science*, 1970, **168**, 1601–1603. (a)

Shiffrin, R. M. Memory search. In D. A. Norman (Ed.), *Models of human memory*. New York: Academic Press, 1970, 375–447. (b)

Shiffrin, R. M., & Atkinson, R. C. Storage and retrieval processes in long-term memory. *Psychological Review*, 1969, **76**, 179–193.

Tulving, E., Intratrial and intertrial retention: Notes toward a theory of free recall verbal learning. *Psychological Review*, 1964, **71**, 219–237.

Tulving, E., & Arbuckle, T. Y. Sources of intratrial interference in immediate recall of paired associates. *Journal of Verbal Learning and Verbal Behavior*, 1963, **1**, 321–334.

Tulving, E., & Colotla, V. A. Free recall of tri-lingual lists. *Cognitive Psychology*, 1970, **1**, 86–98.

Tulving, E., & Pearlstone, Z. Availability versus accessibility of information in memory for words. *Journal of Verbal Learning and Verbal Behavior*, 1966, **5**, 381–391.

Warrington, E. K., & Shallice, T. The selective impairment of auditory verbal short-term memory. *Brain*, 1969, **92**, 885–896.

Waugh, N., & Norman, D. A. Primary memory. *Psychological Review*, 1965, **72**, 89–104.

Yntema, D. B., & Trask, F. P. Recall as a search process. *Journal of Verbal Learning and Verbal Behavior*, 1963, **2**, 65–74.

CHAPTER

5

THE ORGANIZATION OF SHORT-TERM MEMORY FOR A SINGLE ACOUSTIC ATTRIBUTE[1]

DIANA DEUTSCH

[1] This work was supported by U.S. Public Health Service Grant MH 21001-03.

107

I. INTRODUCTION

In the formation of human memory models, the characteristics of non-verbal information storage have received very little attention. This may be attributed largely to the popularity of the three-stage view of memory as a framework for such models. This view holds that nonverbal information is retained in highly transitory and nonspecific fashion, and that it can be saved from obliteration only by a process of verbal labeling that enables it to enter a linguistic short-term memory store. If the nonverbal store were indeed simply an unstructured buffer that retains information before verbal encoding, the study of its characteristics would clearly be of little general interest. There is growing evidence, however, that this view is incorrect. This chapter reviews such evidence with regard to the duration of the non-verbal memory trace, and then describes a series of experiments exploring the behavior of one specific nonverbal memory system over time periods characteristic of short-term memory. These experiments demonstrate that with the use of simple stimulus materials, which may be precisely and systematically varied, the short-term storage of nonverbal information can be shown to possess a systematization and specificity rivaling any found in verbal memory studies.

II. DURATION OF NONVERBAL MEMORY TRACES

The majority of experiments on the duration of sensory memory have been concerned with visual storage. Here, attention has focused particularly on Sperling's (1963, 1967) model. Sperling hypothesized that visual information first enters a large-capacity visual information store (VIS) where it decays very rapidly, within a second. The information is saved from obliteration by its serial transfer into an auditory short-term store (AIS) of strictly limited capacity, where it is retained through a process of linguistic rehearsal. If visual information survives in memory only by being recoded and retained in a limited-capacity acoustic store, then the amount of information retained in this store should be constant independent of its sensory mode. Various studies involving combined presentation of visual and acoustic materials show that this is not the case (Sanders & Schroots, 1969; Scarborough, 1972a; Henderson, 1972). We can recall substantially more information if some of it is visual and some of it acoustic than if only one stimulus modality is involved.

Other inconsistencies with Sperling's theory are revealed by studies demonstrating the persistence of a visual trace after several seconds filled with auditory-linguistic activity. Parks, Kroll, Salzberg, and Parkinson (1972) required subjects to compare two visually presented letters when these were separated by an 8-sec retention interval filled with auditory shadowing. They found that subjects responded faster to a physically identical match rather than to a name match, even given this delay. Further, Kroll, Parks, Parkinson, Bieber, and Johnson (1972) presented test letters either visually or acoustically and required subjects to recall them after periods of auditory shadowing. The letters were recalled better when they had been presented visually rather than acoustically even after a delay as long as 25 sec (see Chapter VI of this volume for a detailed discussion of these experiments). Scarborough (1972b), using the Peterson technique, found similarly that trigrams were better retained after 18 sec of backward counting when they had been presented visually rather than acoustically.

Experiments on recognition of pictures have demonstrated the persistence of visual traces for even longer periods of time. Such recognition has been shown to be remarkably accurate, even when hundreds of pictures are compared (Nickerson, 1965; Shepard, 1967). In these experiments a delay of many minutes intervened between the initial presentation of a picture and its second presentation in a recognition test. The involvement here of a visual rather than a verbal store is shown by Shepard's finding that recognition of pictures was substantially better than recognition of words or sentences. Shepard found further that even after a delay of a week, memory for pictures was nearly equivalent to memory for verbal materials when the test immediately followed stimulus presentation. Further evidence for the remarkably strong persistence of visual memory comes from a study by Bahrick and Boucher (1968), who concluded that verbal recall of pictures presented after two weeks depended largely on retrieval from visual storage.

Other investigations into the duration of nonverbal memory have been concerned with the acoustic properties of speech. On the basis of a series of experiments on the suffix effect, Crowder and Morton have proposed that auditory information is retained in a "precategorical acoustic store," where it decays within a second or two, and is also subject to displacement by subsequent acoustic events (Crowder & Morton, 1969; Morton, 1970). However, other studies have demonstrated that we can retain the sensory attributes of speech sounds for longer periods. Cole (1973) required subjects to decide whether two spoken letters were the same or different when they were presented either in the same voice or in different voices. He found that even with a retention interval of 8 sec, the subjects took a shorter time to respond "same" when the letters were spoken in the same voice rather than in a different voice. The subjects must therefore have been storing the acoustic attributes of the spoken letters during this period.

Murdock and Walker (1969), on the basis of experiments comparing free recall of words presented either acoustically or visually, also concluded that prelinguistic auditory information was retained in memory for at least 5 to 10 sec.

Further convincing evidence that we can retain the acoustic properties of speech sounds for relatively long periods has been provided by Pollack (1959). He presented subjects first with a test word embedded in noise, and later with a list of words that included the test word. Subjects were required to choose which of the words in the list was the test word. When the number of words in the list was reduced, the subjects showed improved recognition of the test word, and this improvement was manifest even after a 15-sec delay between presentation of the test word and the list of alternatives. The subjects must therefore have been storing some acoustic representation of the test word during the delay. Crossman (1958) obtained a similar finding. He played a test word at half-speed on a tape recorder, and after a delay presented subjects with a list of words containing the original word. Subjects were able to improve their recognition of the test word when the number of words in the list was reduced, even after a 40-sec delay between presentation of the test word and the list of alternatives. Indeed, considering the ease and speed with which we recognize a familiar voice by its intonation, we must be capable of storing the acoustical properties of speech sounds on a very long-term basis.

These studies demonstrate that we can store nonverbal stimulus attributes over substantially longer time periods than those predicted by the three-stage model. It must be concluded that the sensory attributes of a stimulus survive in memory after verbal encoding, and that they continue to be retained in parallel with the verbal attributes. This view has been argued persuasively by Posner in a series of articles (Posner, 1967; Posner, 1972; Posner & Warren, 1972). Posner assumes further that nonverbal attributes compete with verbal attributes for processing capacity in a limited capacity system. This theory is discussed later for the specific case of pitch memory.

Finally, it must also be stressed that there is a basic implausibility about the view that nonverbal memory is only transient. Shepard (1967) and Paivio (1969) have argued persuasively for the role of mental images as precursors of verbal recall. Unfortunately, in the case of memories for which verbal descriptions are possible, one can always argue—even though implausibly—that the basic mode of such information storage is really verbal. There is one incontrovertible example, however, of an enduring nonverbal memory system; this is the system responsible for storing musical information. Although we commonly recognize melodies and long works of music by name and can, with musical training, label abstracted tonal relationships, the basic process of music recognition cannot conceivably be verbally mediated. We constantly recognize melodies as familiar without having learned their names. Further, we can accurately identify very short sequences taken from the middle of long works of music. It is also striking how acutely aware we may be of a single error or distortion in the performance of a musical composition. It is clear from such considerations that musical information must be stored in highly specific form for substantial periods of time.

III. PROPOSED MODELS OF NONVERBAL MEMORY ORGANIZATION CONSIDERED FOR THE CASE OF TONAL PITCH

There are various theories concerning the nature of nonverbal memory. Broadbent (1958, 1963) has proposed that nonverbal information simply decays with time: "The stored information decays very rapidly as a function of time, and not as a function of intervening activity" (Broadbent, 1963). An alternative suggestion was made by Posner (1967), who theorized that the maintenance of precategorical information in memory requires the use of a portion of a limited capacity system: ". . . in verbal terms it may involve covert speech, while in other situations . . . something more akin to concentration may be appropriate" (Posner, 1967). Concerning acoustic information, Crowder and Morton (1969) have hypothesized the existence of a precategorical acoustic store where information is subject both to decay and also to displacement by subsequent acoustic events.

Concerning Broadbent's decay theory, it has indeed been found that memory for tonal pitch deteriorates with time in the absence of intervening stimulation (Koester, 1945; Harris, 1952; Bachem, 1954). However, the rate of decay is much slower than Broadbent supposed. Harris (1952) found that with a retention interval of 15 seconds, the difference threshold for pitch was elevated only by .8 cps or by 3.7 cps, depending on whether the standard stimulus was fixed during the experimental session or whether it varied. Further, Broadbent was incorrect in assuming that the presence of other stimuli during the retention interval would not affect the degree of memory loss. Several studies have shown that the interpolation of a tone during the retention interval between a standard and a comparison tone produces further memory deterioration (Wickelgren, 1966, 1969; Elliott, 1970). Increasing the number of interpolated tones, when the retention interval is held constant, results in increased memory loss (Rimm, 1967; Deutsch, 1970a; Massaro, 1970).

What is the basis for the memory interference produced by interpolated tones? The hypotheses of Posner (1967) and of Crowder and Morton (1969) give rise to testable predictions. If information concerning tonal pitch is held in a short-term memory store of limited channel capacity, then the larger the number of bits of information processed during the retention interval, the greater should be the resultant memory decrement. Alternatively, if this information is held in a precategorical acoustic store that is limited to a certain number of items, then the amount of memory decrement should depend on the number of acoustic items interpolated during the retention interval. Such acoustic items include spoken digits, since these were the stimuli employed by Crowder and Morton (1969) in their experiment on the retention of precategorical acoustic information.

I tested these predictions in two experiments. Basically, I compared the effects on memory of interpolating two different types of information during the interval between a standard and a comparison tone. The first type of interpolated information consisted of other tones, and the second type consisted of spoken numbers of equal loudness to the tones. The number of items in each interpolated sequence remained constant throughout the experiment. Further, the numbers and tones were both chosen from the same size ensemble and so carried the same number of bits of information. Theories of memory loss based on the concept of a limited capacity storage system, either general or precategorical acoustic in nature, would predict the intervening number sequences to cause at least as much disruption in pitch recognition as the intervening tonal sequences. However, if information concerning tonal pitch were stored in a specialized system, the intervening number sequences would not necessarily cause memory disruption equivalent to the disruption caused by intervening tones.

The first experiment consisted of two conditions. In the first condition, pitch recognition was required after a 6-sec interval during which 8 extra tones were played. The second condition was identical to the first, except that instead of tones, 8 spoken numbers were interpolated. The numbers were of equal loudness to the tones and were spaced identically and selected randomly from the same size ensemble. In both conditions, subjects were required to listen to the standard tone, ignore the 8 interpolated items, listen to the comparison tone, and then judge whether the standard and comparison tones were the same or different in pitch. When the interpolated items were further tones, the error rate was very high (40.3%). However, when the interpolated items were spoken numbers, the error rate was close to zero (2.4%).

It would appear from this experiment that memory for tonal pitch is subject to a large interference effect caused specifically by other tones and not due to some general storage limitation. It could, however, be argued that although the subjects were instructed in both conditions to ignore the intervening items, they achieved this much more effectively when these were numbers than when they were tones. The results might therefore be explained in terms of an involuntary selective attention mechanism, which allowed the intervening numbers to be ignored but which compelled attention to the intervening tones. I therefore performed a further experiment, in which recall of the intervening numbers was also required. This insured that the numbers were in fact attended to and stored in memory.

There were four conditions in this second experiment (Deutsch, 1970b). In all conditions, subjects listened to a standard tone that was followed 5 sec later by a comparison tone, and they judged whether the two were the same or different in pitch. In Condition 1, six extra tones were played during the retention interval. In Conditions 2, 3, and 4, six spoken numbers were incorporated instead. These were of equal loudness to the tones and were spaced identically. In Condition 1, subjects were instructed to ignore the intervening tones and indicate whether the standard and comparison tones were the same or different in pitch by writing "S" or "D." In Condition 2, they were similarly instructed to ignore the numbers and compare the pitch of the standard and comparison tones. In Condition 3, in addition to comparing the tones, subjects were required to recall the 6 numbers in their correct order. Having heard the entire sequence they wrote "S" or "D," followed by the numbers. In Condition 4, the pitch of the standard and comparison tones was always the same, and the subjects were informed of this. They were instructed to listen to the total sequence and then to write "S" followed by the numbers in their correct order. Condition D therefore provided a baseline estimate for number recall in the absence of a tonal memory load.

The results of this experiment are shown on Table 5-1. It can be seen that here again, the intervening tones caused considerable memory disruption. However, when numbers were instead interpolated, the error rate was minimal even when recall of these numbers was required. Further, the requirement to remember the standard tone produced no decrement in number recall. The memory disruption produced by interpolated tones could not therefore have been due to general factors, such as prevention of rehearsal, limitation in information-storage capacity, or displacement in a general, precategorical acoustic store of limited capacity. One must conclude that a specialized system exists for the storage of tonal pitch.

The memory dissociation described here is subjectively very compelling; many of the subjects expressed surprise at the lack of strain im-

TABLE 5-1[a]

	Task	
Condition	Pitch Recognition (%)	No. Recall (%)
1. Pitch recognition with intervening tones ignored.	32.3	
2. Pitch recognition with intervening numbers ignored.	2.4	
3. Pitch recognition with intervening numbers recalled.	5.6	25.3
4. Number recall with no pitch recognition required.		27.4

[a] Percent errors in pitch comparison as a function of type of information interpolated during the retention interval. Number recall was judged correct on any trial only if all the numbers were correctly recalled in order. The error rate in Condition 1 was significantly greater than in either Conditions 2 or 3 ($p < .001$ for both comparisons on sign tests). From Deutsch, D., 1970, by permission of *Science*, **168**, 1604–5. Copyright 1970 by the American Association for the Advancement of Science.

posed by the two simultaneous memory tasks. It might be tempting to explain such a striking dissociation in terms of gross anatomical differences in the processing of verbal and musical information. Dichotic listening experiments have shown that right-handed subjects identify verbal stimuli more accurately when these are presented to the right ear rather than to the left (Kimura, 1961; Bryden, 1963; Dirks, 1964). The reverse happens when certain nonverbal materials are dichotically presented. This has been found, for instance, with hummed melodies (King and Kimura, 1972), melodies played on woodwinds and strings (Kimura, 1964), and environmental sounds (Curry, 1967; Knox and Kimura, 1970). One might, therefore, suggest that speech sounds are stored in the dominant hemisphere, tones in the nondominant, and that the present dissociation is due to a lack of interference between the hemispheres. However, recent dichotic listening experiments show the situation to be more complicated. Studdert-Kennedy and Shankweiler (1970) present evidence that the auditory parameters of speech are processed in both hemispheres, with the dominant hemisphere providing further extraction of linguistic features. Further, although consonants are better identified when presented to the right ear, vowels appear either to be better identified when presented to the left ear, or to be equally well processed through either ear (Shankweiler & Studdert-Kennedy, 1967; Kimura, 1967; Shankweiler & Studdert-Kennedy, 1970). Given this evidence, and if we accept the argument that asymmetries in dichotic listening are due to differential processing by the two hemispheres, it appears that both hemispheres in the present experiment would be involved in processing the numbers. Indeed, Crowder (1971) has shown that the properties, which had originally been found to characterize the precategorical acoustic storage of verbal materials, are exhibited by vowels but not by consonants. On this basis, together with the evidence from laterality studies, he proposes that the precategorical acoustic store for verbal materials is a property of the nondominant rather than the dominant hemisphere.

Further, the studies quoted above, which demonstrate a left ear advantage for perception of dichotically presented musical materials, both involved the simultaneous variation of several acoustic attributes, and so cannot be used to draw inferences about the processing of pitch information *per se*. Studies addressed to the processing of more specific musical attributes have produced a rather complicated picture. For instance, Gordon (1970) obtained a significant left ear advantage for dichotically presented chords, but not for melodies. Spellacy (1970) found a significant left ear superiority for perception of dichotically presented violin melodies, but not for timbre, temporal patterns, or patterns of tones varying in frequency alone. Doehring (1972) obtained a significant left ear advantage for monaural intensity discrimination, but not for frequency discrimination.

It would appear from such findings that musical information is indeed processed asymmetrically by the auditory pathways, but that this asymmetry cannot be defined in terms of a simple "if nonverbal, then nondominant" rule. I have investigated this question further as applied to the processing of pitch information, and have come across some very surprising illusions, which add further complexity to the situation.

In my first experiment I presented subjects with stimulus pattern shown in Figs. 5-1a and 2a (Deutsch, 1974b&c). It can be seen that this consisted of a sequence of 250 msec tones. Each tone was either 400 Hz or 800 Hz, and these frequencies were presented in strict alternation. The identical sequence was presented to both ears simultaneously at equal amplitude, except that when one ear received 400 Hz the other ear received 800 Hz, and vice versa. This sequence of alternating tones was presented without pause for 20 sec. The tones were sinusoids, and their phase relationship varied randomly.

Amazingly, this simple dichotic sequence was almost never perceived correctly. Out of well over a hundred listeners, only one reported the correct percept, and this listener had strabismus and the signs of neurological abnormality (which may be coincidental, but may also provide a clue to the neurological basis for the illusory percepts). The illusion most commonly obtained is diagramed in Fig. 5-1b. It can be seen that a single tone was perceived, which oscillated from one ear to the other, and whose pitch also oscillated from one octave to the other in synchrony with the localisa-

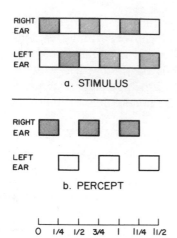

Fig. 5-1. Diagrammatic representation of the first dichotic sequence, and the illusory percept most commonly obtained. Filled boxes represent tones of 800 Hz, and unfilled boxes tones of 400 Hz. From Deutsch, D., 1974, by permission of *Nature, 251,* 307–309. Copyright 1974 by Macmillan Journals, Ltd.

tion shift. This percept is also illustrated in Fig. 5-2b, which reproduces the written report in musical notation of a subject with absolute pitch.

There is clearly no simple way to explain this illusory percept. We can account for the perception of a single tone oscillating from ear to ear by assuming that the listener alternately processes the information from one ear and suppresses the other. But then the pitch of this alternating tone should not shift with a shift in its apparent localisation. We can also account for the perception of a single tone oscillating from one octave to the other by assuming that the listener consistently follows one ear alone; but then the tone should not appear to oscillate from ear to ear. The illusion of a single tone which oscillates simultaneously both in pitch and in localisation appears quite paradoxical.

This illusion has a further surprising aspect: right-handers and left-handers exhibit different patterns of localisation for the two pitches at the two ears. These are shown in Table 5-2. Each subject was presented with the sequence twice for 20 sec each time, with earphones placed first one way and then the other. The order of earphone placement was strictly counterbalanced for both right and left-handed subjects. It can be seen that right-handers tended significantly to maintain a given localisation pattern when the placement of the earphones was reversed, and also to hear the high tone in the right ear and the low tone in the left ($p < .001$, two-tailed, on binomial tests in both instances). (The percept reproduced in Fig. 5-2b is that of a typical right-hander.) On the other hand, the left-handers as a group did not preferentially localise the tones either way, and showed only a marginally significant tendency to maintain a given locali-

Fig. 5-2. Representation in musical notation of the first dichotic sequence, and the percept depicted by a right-handed subject with absolute pitch. $G_4 = 392$ Hz and $G_5 = 784$ Hz; these are closest in the musical scale to the 400 Hz and 800 Hz presented. The subject's own written statement: "Same with earphones reversed" shows that the same asymmetrical percept was obtained regardless of the positioning of the earphones. Fig. 5-2(b) from Deutsch, D., 1974, by permission of *Nature*, *251*, 307–309. Copyright 1974 by Macmillan Journals, Ltd.

a. STIMULUS

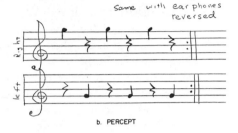

b. PERCEPT

sation pattern when the earphones were placed in reverse position (p = .05, two-tailed, on a binomial test). When these results are related to other findings on patterns of hemispheric dominance and handedness (Hécaen and de Ajuriaguerra, 1964; Brain, 1965), they suggest strongly that we tend to localise high tones to our dominant side and low tones to our non-dominant side.

TABLE 5-2[a]

	RR	LL	Both
Right-handers	25	5	1
Left-handers	6	7	4

[a] Patterns of apparent localization for the two pitches at the two ears in subjects who perceived a single tone oscillating from one octave to the other. Figures show the number of right- or left-handed subjects obtaining a given localization pattern.

RR: High tone localized in the right ear and low tone in the left on both stimulus presentations.

LL: High tone localized in the left ear and low tone in the right on both stimulus presentations.

Both: High tone localized in the right ear and low tone in the left on one presentation; high tone localized in the left ear and low tone in the right on the other. From Deutsch, D., 1974, by permission of *Nature*, 251, 307-309. Copyright 1974 by Macmillan Journals, Ltd.

A further experiment demonstrated that these localisation patterns are based on the pitch relationships between the competing tones, and not on a pattern of ear preference at different pitch levels. Twelve subjects who had consistently localised the 800 Hz tone in the right ear and the 400 Hz tone in the left were presented with sequences alternating between 200 Hz and 400 Hz, 400 Hz and 800 Hz, and 800 Hz and 1600 Hz in the counterbalanced order. With the exception of one report on one sequence, the higher of each pair of tones was always localised in the right ear and the lower in the left. (Thus, for instance, the 800 Hz tone was localised in the right ear when it alternated with the 400 Hz tone, but in the left ear when it alternated with the 1600 Hz tone).

The percept of a single tone oscillating synchronously both in pitch and in localisation was reported by 58% of the right-handers and 52% of the left-handers formally tested. Another 25% of the right-handers and 9% of the left-handers reported, instead, a single tone oscillating from ear to ear, whose pitch either remained constant or changed only slightly as its localisation shifted. In matching experiments the pitch of this oscillating tone was found by some subjects to be closest to that of the 800 Hz tone, and by others to be closest to the 400 Hz tone. The remaining 17% of the right-handers and 39% of the left-handers reported a variety of complex percepts, such as two alternating pitches localised in one ear, and a third pitch appearing intermittently in the other (either synchronized with one of the alternating tones, or out of synchrony with either). A significant difference was found between right- and left-handers in terms of the proportions obtaining these different categories of percept. ($\chi^2 = 6.8$, df $= 2$, $p < .05$.)

We may now ask which ear is followed when the subject perceives a single tone oscillating from one octave to the other. This percept is consistent with following the sequence of pitches presented either to the right ear or to the left, since this same tonal pattern is presented to both ears. A new dichotic sequence was, therefore, constructed in which each ear received a different pattern of pitches. As shown in Figs. 5-3a and 3a', this sequence consisted of three high (800 Hz) tones followed by two low (400 Hz) tones on one channel, and simultaneously three low (400 Hz) tones followed by two high (800 Hz) tones on the other. This pattern was repeated ten times without pause, and each subject listened to the sequence with earphones placed first one way and then the other. (The order of earphone placement was strictly counterbalanced across subjects.)

The results were again surprising. Contrary to expectations from the previous literature, right-handed subjects tended significantly to report the pattern of pitches fed to the *right* ear rather than to the left. (Thus, with channel A to the right ear and channel B to the left, they tended to report three high tones followed by two low tones; with channel B to the right

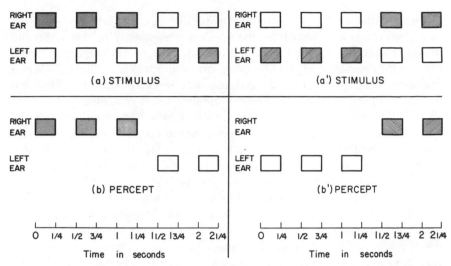

Fig. 5-3. Diagrammatic representation of the second dichotic sequence, and the illusory percept most commonly obtained. Filled boxes represent tones of 800 *Hz* and unfilled boxes tones of 400 *Hz*. (a) Stimulus pattern with channel A to the right ear and channel B to the left ear. (b) Illusory percept with earphones positioned as in a. (a') Stimulus pattern with channel B to the right ear and channel A to the left ear. (b') Illusory percept with earphones positioned as in a'.

ear and channel A to the left, they tended to report three low tones followed by two high tones.) No significant ear preference was demonstrated among left-handers. However, lateralisation of the tones followed a different rule. All subjects lateralised each tone to the ear that received the higher of the two frequencies, regardless of which ear they followed for pitch and regardless of whether the tone was heard as high or low. This combination of two independent rules produced a most paradoxical percept, which is illustrated in Figs. 3b and 3b' for the case of listeners who followed the right ear for pitch. With channel A to the right ear and channel B to the left, these listeners perceived a repetitive presentation of three high tones to the right followed by two low tones to the left. With earphone positions reversed, the same segment of tape was now heard as a repetitive presentation of two high tones to the right followed by three low tones to the left! Clearly this is an impossible auditory object!

So far, the following of pitch information fed to one ear rather than the other suggests a simple inhibitory interaction between pathways from the two ears in determining pitch (but not lateralisation). However, in a further experiment, I presented the sequence shown in Fig. 5-1a channeled through two spatially separated loudspeakers rather than through earphones. To my surprise the illusion was still obtained, even though both sequences were now presented to both ears with only localisation cues to distinguish them. When the listener was positioned equidistant between the two speakers, oriented so that one speaker was exactly on his right and the other exactly on his left, the high tones were heard as coming from the speaker on the right and the low tones from the speaker on the left. When the listener rotated slowly, the tones appeared to move with him (although the speakers were stationary) so that the high tones remained on his right and the low tones on his left. When he stood facing one speaker, with the other speaker behind him, the illusion abruptly disappeared, and a single tone was heard as coming from both speakers simultaneously (as though they had been passed through a mixer). But as the listener continued turning the illusion abruptly reappeared, with the high tones still on the right and the low tones still on the left. Thus when the listener had turned 180% from his original position, the speaker which had originally appeared to be emitting the high tones now appeared to be emitting the low tones, and the speaker which had originally appeared to be emitting the low tones now appeared to be emitting the high tones! This makes a very dramatic demonstration of the illusion, and shows that it must have a complex basis.

The two-channel listening paradigm was further elaborated using a more complicated tonal sequence. As shown on Fig. 5-4a, this new sequence consisted of the *C* major scale with successive tones alternating from ear to ear. This scale was presented simultaneously in both ascending and descending form, such that when a component of the ascending

Fig. 5-4. Representation in musical notation of the third dichotic sequence, and the percept depicted by a right-handed subject with absolute pitch. (a) The C major scale, with successive tones alternating from ear to ear, and played simultaneously in both ascending and descending form. (b) The ascending component alone. (c) The descending component alone. (d) Subject's own report of the dichotic sequence. His written statement: "High tones in right ear with headphones either way" shows that the higher tones were localized in the right ear and the lower tones in the left, regardless of earphone placement.

scale was in one ear, a component of the descending scale was in the other, and vice versa. Figs. 5-4b and 4c show these ascending and descending scales separately; thus the sequence shown in Fig. 5-4a was simply the superposition of the two sequences shown in Figs. 5-4b and 4c. The tones were again sinusoidal, of equal amplitude, and 250 msec in duration; and here there were no gaps between adjacent tones. Each sequence was presented ten times without pause, with earphones positioned first one way and then the other. Subjects reported what they heard verbally and afterwards shadowed the sequences by singing while I monitored the tape on separate earphones (Deutsch, 1974d).

Surprising difficulties were again encountered in perceiving the dichotic sequence, with only one subject out of seventy reporting it correctly. Yet very few subjects misreported the separate ascending or descending sequences, so these difficulties were not due to a simple inability to follow the 250 msec switching rate. Basically, the dichotic sequence was misperceived along two different lines. The majority of subjects reported the correct pattern of pitches, but localised them incorrectly; most commonly, the higher tones were all heard in one ear and the lower tones in the other. Right-handers (but not left-handers) tended significantly to mislocalise the higher tones to the right ear and the lower tones to the left, irrespective of earphone position. This illusory percept is shown in Fig. 5-4d, which reproduces the written report of a right-handed subject with absolute pitch. The remainder of the subjects reported the higher tones, but little or nothing of the lower tones. No subject adopted a different channeling principle, such as reporting the pattern of pitches presented to one ear rather than to the other.

This set of experiments presents a complicated picture of ear advantage in the processing of pitch information. For one type of sequence, tones localised to the dominant side appear to inhibit those localised to the nondominant side in determining pitch (but not lateralisation); for another, the perceived sequence of pitches appears to depend on a principle of channeling that cuts across ear of input. An illusion whereby the higher of two simultaneous tones is mislocalised to the dominant ear, and the lower to the nondominant, adds further complexity to the situation.

Given this ambiguity at the perceptual level, very little can be inferred from dichotic listening studies about the locus of the pitch–memory system. The finding that differences in localisation can produce the same effect as differences in ear of input also raises doubts about the validity of drawing simple inferences about hemispheric specialisation of function from the use of dichotic listening technique. Direct neurological studies are much more convincing, and it is clear from such studies that the nondominant hemisphere is capable of musical information storage (Bogen, 1969). However, it is not clear that memory for pitch *per se* is specifically disrupted by lesions of the nondominant hemisphere; the controlled studies which would answer this question have yet to be performed. At all events, we cannot conclude from the studies reviewed here that the properties of tones and the acoustical properties of words are stored in separate hemispheres. Rather, the evidence points to a specialised system for the retention of pitch information.

IV. ORGANIZATION OF THE PITCH MEMORY SYSTEM

Given the conclusion that tonal information is retained in a specialized system, we can attempt to characterize this system in further detail. An everyday knowledge of music leads to the conclusion that it must contain several subdivisions. For instance, we recognize a transposed melody much more readily than we recognize the key it was played in. Memory for the abstracted relationships between the component tones of the melody must therefore be more enduring than memory for the tones themselves. A similar argument holds for transposition of harmonic sequences. Further, there is considerable evidence that we perceive and remember a tone in terms of its position not only along a "tone-height" continuum, but also within an abstracted octave, or "tone-chroma" continuum. As a related phenomenon, our memory for invertable chords is more enduring than memory for the component tones in the chords. A further complexity exists in the storage of timbre. The experiments of Plomp and his collaborators have shown that the timbral qualities of tones are a function of a highly differentiated multidimensional system (Plomp, 1970).

I do not argue that the different subdivisions of the tonal memory system exist in isolation from each other. The evidence shows that complex and often paradoxical relationships exist, at least at the perceptual level, between our processing of pitch, timbre, chords, and melodies (Erickson, 1975). Rather, I take the view that the properties of various subdivisions of this memory system can be experimentally abstracted, and that relationships between these subdivisions can then be studied in further experiments.

In considering the possible organization of the system that stores the pitch of a single pure tone, a very simple hypothesis presents itself: that *the system that retains this information is organized in many ways along the same principles as the system that receives it.* This hypothesis obviously does not assume an identical organization between sensory and memory systems: their very functions require that they differ in important respects. For instance, a sensory system cannot continue to respond to a stimulus long after its termination, or we would soon cease to have discriminable images. In contrast, a memory system exists precisely to retain information in the absence of the original stimulus. Further, a memory system must have some way of retaining information concerning the time or order in which any given stimulus occurred. This is not required of a purely sensory system. The above hypothesis simply assumes that for those aspects of organization where there is no reason to expect differences between the two systems, important similarities exist.

The system underlying pitch perception has been shown to be highly structured and precisely organized. Facilitatory and inhibitory interactions taking place within it vary systematically as a function of relationships between the elements involved. An internal "tone-height" continuum has therefore been hypothesized along which various interactions occur, which in turn give rise to demonstrable psychoacoustical phenomena. Physiological studies on single units in the auditory pathway reinforce this concept by demonstrating an orderly topographical distribution of neural elements with respect to characteristic frequency, together with specific facilitatory and inhibitory interactions that mirror corresponding psychoacoustical phenomena (Harris, 1972). Our present theory therefore leads us to propose the existence of an analogous continuum underlying the retention of "tone-height" information. Interactions that are a function of distance between the interacting elements are assumed to take place along this continuum. Evidence on the transposition of tunes and chords leads to the further expectation that such a continuum would be organized logarithmically with respect to waveform frequency (Attneave & Olson, 1971).

If this hypothesis is correct, it should be possible to demonstrate interactive relationships in memory for tonal pitch, which vary precisely as a function of the pitch relationships between the elements involved. I performed a further experiment to search for such interactions (Deutsch, 1972a). The effect of a tone that formed part of a sequence interpolated between a standard and comparison tone was studied as a function of its pitch relationship to the standard tone. Subjects were required to compare two tones for pitch when these were separated by a 5-sec retention interval during which 6 other tones were played. The standard and comparison tones were taken from an equal-tempered scale and ranged over an octave, from middle C to the B above. When the standard and comparison tones differed in pitch, this was by a semitone (either higher or lower). The intervening tonal pitches, except as specified by the experimental conditions, were taken from the same scale, and varied randomly from the F♯ below middle C to the F an octave and a half above.

There were eight conditions in this experiment. In every condition but the last, a tone whose pitch bore a critical relationship to the pitch of the standard tone was placed in the second serial position of the intervening sequence. Whenever the standard and comparison tones differed in pitch, the critical intervening tone was placed on the same side of the standard tone along the pitch continuum as the comparison tone was. The relationship between the critical intervening tone and the standard tone varied from identity to a whole-tone separation in the equal-tempered scale. A unique value of pitch separation was incorporated in each of the seven conditions, these values being placed at equal intervals of 1/6 tone within this whole-tone range. Since the musical scale is logarithmic, these intervals were also logarithmic. No such critical tone was incorporated in the eighth experimental condition, but here the pitch of the tone in the second serial position was chosen in the same way as were the other tonal pitches in the intervening sequence. The eighth condition was therefore a null condition.

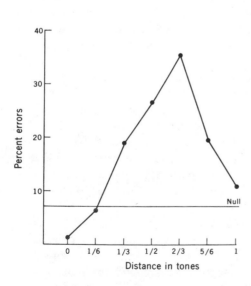

Fig. 5-5. Percent errors in pitch comparisons plotted as a function of the separation in pitch between the critical interpolated tone and the standard tone. The line labeled *Null* shows percent of errors in the control condition, where no tone closer in pitch to the standard tone than 1½ tones was included in the intervening sequence. A separation of 1/6 tone, in the range of pitches used here, is equal to 5 Hz at the lowest standard tone pitch used, and 9 Hz at the highest. Errors were significantly fewer in the condition where the critical interpolated tone was identical in pitch to the standard tone than in the null condition ($p = .02$, two-tailed, on a Wilcoxon test). The increase in errors produced by the interpolated tone was statistically significant for each condition using a value of pitch separation within and including 1/3 tone to 5/6 tone (in each case $p < .01$, two-tailed, on a Wilcoxon test). (From Deutsch, D., 1972, by permission of *Science, 175*, 1020–1022. Copyright 1972 by the American Association for the Advancement of Science.)

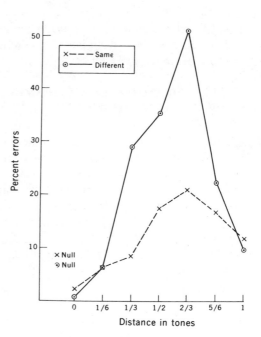

Fig. 5-6. Percent errors in pitch comparisons plotted as in Fig. 5-5, but separately by whether the standard and comparison tones were the same or different in pitch. When the standard and comparison tones differed, the critical interpolated tone was always placed on the same side of the standard tone along the pitch continuum as was the comparison tone. The two null points refer to the same control condition as described in Fig. 5-5. (From Deutsch, D., 1972, by permission of *Science,* **175,** 1020–1022. Copyright 1972 by the American Association for the Advancement of Science.)

The error rates in the different conditions of this experiment are plotted in Figs. 5-5 and 5-6. It can be seen that systematic interference effects do indeed occur. When the critical intervening tone is identical in pitch to the standard tone, memory facilitation is produced. Errors rise progressively with increasing pitch separation between the standard tone and the critical intervening tone, peak at a separation of ⅔ tone, and decline roughly to baseline at a whole tone separation.

The maps shown in Figs. 5-5 and 5-6 were obtained by superimposing plots derived from the sequences in which the standard tones were in different positions along the pitch continuum. Since the musical scale is logarithmic, an identical musical interval is based on an increased difference in waveform frequency as the scale is ascended. This difference doubles at each octave, which is the range used in this experiment. It follows that if the pitch memory store were organized in any fashion other than logarithmic, there should be a systematic shift in the peak of errors as the standard tones shift their position along the pitch continuum. For example, if the pitch memory store were linearly arranged, then as the standard tone shifted upward in pitch, the peak of errors should move progressively closer to the pitch of the standard tone on a logarithmic plot. Yet no such peak shift was present in the experimental records. This leads to the conclusion that the pitch memory store is laid out logarithmically, at least within the range of tonal frequencies used in this experiment.

The above study demonstrates that highly specific systematic interactions occur within the system retaining pitch information. I explored possible bases for these effects in further experiments.

V. SPECIFIC SOURCES OF DISRUPTION IN PITCH MEMORY

It can be seen from Fig. 5-6 that the plot of errors obtained from sequences in which the standard and comparison tones differ in pitch rises much more steeply and is more sharply peaked than the plot obtained from sequences in which the standard and comparison tones are identical. One might speculate, therefore, that these two functions have different underlying bases. In order to explore this hypothesis in detail, I made a systematic study of the effects on pitch memory of including in an interpolated tonal sequence a tone that was a semitone removed from the standard tone (Deutsch, 1973a). It was found that, when the standard and comparison tones were the same in pitch, including in the intervening sequence a tone either a semitone higher or a semitone lower produced an increase in errors. Including in the same intervening sequence both a tone a semitone higher and a tone a semitone lower produced a significantly greater increase in errors (Table 5-3). Further, when the standard

TABLE 5-3[a]

Condition	Percentage Errors
S and C Tones Same	
1. Tone a semitone higher included in intervening sequence.	7.9
2. Tone a semitone lower included in intervening sequence.	6.9
3. Two tones, one a semitone higher and the other a semitone lower, included in intervening sequence.	18.5
4. No tone a semitone higher or lower included in intervening sequence.	2.8
5. S and C tones different.	7.5

[a] Percent errors in pitch comparisons as a function of the presence in the intervening sequence of either one or two tones bearing a semitone relationship to the standard tone. This experiment studied the effects in sequences where the standard and comparison tones were identical in pitch. These were interspersed between sequences where the standard and comparison tones differed, and where there was no systematic inclusion or exclusion of tones on the basis of a semitone separation from the standard tone. Errors were significantly increased in both Conditions 1 and 2 compared with Condition 4; and in Condition 3 compared with Conditions 1 and 2 ($p < .01$, two-tailed on Wilcoxon tests in all cases). (From Deutsch, D., *Journal of Experimental Psychology*, 1973, **100**, 228–231. Copyright 1973 by the American Psychological Association. Reprinted by permission.

and comparison tones differed in pitch by a semitone, including in the intervening sequence a tone identical in pitch to the comparison tone produced a substantial increase in errors. A significantly smaller increase in errors was produced when the critical intervening tone was a semitone removed from the standard tone, but on the opposite side of the pitch continuum to the comparison tone. Including both of these critical tones in the same intervening sequence produced a significantly greater increase in errors than including either one (Table 5-4).

This experiment demonstrates the presence of at least two separable disruptive effects on pitch memory. First, the inclusion of a tone a semitone removed from the standard tone produces a small but significant disruptive effect that cumulates in size when two such tones, one on either side of the standard tone, are included. Second, a significantly larger disruptive effect occurs when the standard and comparison tones differ in pitch, and the critical interpolated tone is identical in pitch to the comparison tone.

Returning to the earlier study (Deutsch, 1972a), it will be recalled that here, whenever the standard and comparison tones differed in pitch,

TABLE 5-4[a]

Condition	Percentage Errors
S and C tones different	
1. Tone of the same pitch as the C tone included in intervening sequence.	20.1
2. Tone a semitone from S tone, but on the opposite side of pitch continuum than C tone, included in intervening sequence.	7.4
3. Two tones, one as in Condition 1 and the other as in Condition 2, including in intervening sequence.	25.2
4. No tone a semitone removed from S tone included in intervening sequence.	3.2
5. S and C tones same.	6.6

[a] Percent errors in pitch comparisons as a function of the presence in the intervening sequence of either one or two tones bearing a semitone relationship to the standard tone. This experiment studied the effects in sequences where the standard and comparison tones differed in pitch by a semitone. These were interspersed between sequences where the standard and comparison tones were identical, and where there was no systematic inclusion or exclusion of tones on the basis of a semitone separation from the standard tone. Errors were significantly increased in both Conditions 1 and 2 compared with Condition 4; Condition 1 differed significantly from Condition 2; and Condition 3 differed significantly from both Conditions 1 and 2 ($p < .01$, two-tailed, on Wilcoxon tests in all cases). From Deutsch, D., *Journal of Experimental Psychology*, 1973, **100**, 228–231. Copyright 1973 by The American Psychological Association. Reprinted by permission.

the critical intervening tone was placed on the same side of the pitch continuum relative to the standard tone as was the comparison tone. (That
is, when the comparison tone was higher in pitch than the standard tone,
the critical intervening tone was also higher. When the comparison tone
was lower, the critical intervening tone was also lower.) The critical intervening tone was therefore identical in pitch to the comparison tone
whenever these two tones bore the same relationship to the standard tone.
The large error function plotted for these sequences on Fig. 5-6 could
therefore also have been based on a relationship of identity or close similarity between the critical intervening tone and the comparison tone.

What could be the basis for this large disruptive effect? One might
suggest that errors here are due to a deterioration of information along a
temporal continuum. As a result of such deterioration, when the comparison tone is played, the subject recognizes correctly that a tone of this pitch
has occurred, but assumes incorrectly that this was the standard tone.
This hypothesis is described in detail elsewhere (Deutsch, 1972b). It gives
rise to two predictions. First, the amount of disruption produced by the
critical intervening tone should vary systematically as a function of its
position in the intervening sequence. The closer the position of this critical tone relative to the standard tone, the more difficult it should be to
discriminate their two positions along a temporal continuum, and so the
greater should be the number of resultant confusions. Second, when this
effect is plotted as a function of the pitch of the critical intervening tone
relative to the pitch of the comparison tone, the peak of errors should occur when the critical intervening tone is identical in pitch to the comparison tone. Thus, a shift in the pitch of the comparison tone, when the pitch
of the standard tone is held constant, should produce a parallel shift in the
peak of errors produced by the critical intervening tone.

These two predictions were put to experimental test. One study measured the effect of including a tone of the same pitch as the comparison
tone early as compared with late in the intervening sequence. In all the
experimental trials, 6 tones were interpolated in the interval between the
standard and comparison tones. In half of these sequences, the standard
and comparison tones differed in pitch. A tone of the same pitch as the
comparison tone was included either in the second serial position of the
intervening sequence, or in the fifth, or not at all. It can be seen from Fig.
5-7 that the critical included tone produced substantially more disruption
when it was included early rather than late in the intervening sequence.
This is as predicted on the hypothesis of a gradual deterioration of information along a temporal continuum.

In another study the pitch of the comparison tone was varied systematically relative to the pitch of the standard tone. The standard and com-

Fig. 5-7. Percent errors in pitch comparisons for sequences where the standard and comparison tones differed in pitch by a semitone, and a tone of the same pitch as the comparison tone was included in the interpolated sequence. Errors are shown separately for sequences where the critical interpolated ton was placed in the second and the fifth serial position of an interpolated sequence of 6 tones. Errors at each serial position differed significantly from baseline, and they also differed significantly from each other ($p < .01$, two-tailed, on Wilcoxon tests for all comparisons).

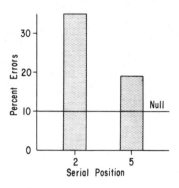

parison tones differed in pitch in half of the sequences; when they differed, this was either by ⅓ tone, or by ½ tone, or by ⅔ tone. Errors were then plotted as a function of the pitch of a further tone that formed part of an interpolated sequence, using the same method as in Deutsch (1972a). The critical interpolated tone was always placed on the same side of the standard tone along the pitch continuum as was the comparison tone. That is, when the comparison tone was higher in pitch than the standard tone, the critical intervening tone was also higher; when the comparison tone was lower, the critical intervening tone was also lower. The critical intervening tone and the comparison tone were therefore identical in pitch whenever they bore the same relationship to the standard tone.

Fig. 5-8 shows the plot of errors as a function of the pitch of the critical interpolated tone relative to the standard tone, with the standard and comparison tones differing in pitch either by ⅓ tone, or by ½ tone, or by ⅔ tone. It can be seen that when the standard and comparison tones were ⅓ tone apart, errors peaked when the critical interpolated tone was also separated from the standard tone by ⅓ tone, and was therefore identical in pitch to the comparison tone. Similarly, when the standard and comparison tones were ⅔ tone apart, errors peaked when the critical interpolated tone was also separated from the standard tone by ⅔ tone. Thus a shift in the pitch of the comparison tone produced a parallel shift in the peak of errors produced by the interpolated tone. This peak shift is as predicted on the above hypothesis. However, when the standard and comparison tones were ½ tone apart, the peak of errors occurred when the critical interpolated tone was separated from the standard tone not by ½ tone but by ⅔ tone. Though the difference in errors at ⅔ tone compared with ½ tone is not statistically significant, it is noteworthy because, extrapolating from the other two curves, one would expect the difference to be in the opposite direction. A similar peak at ⅔ tone also occurs in Fig.

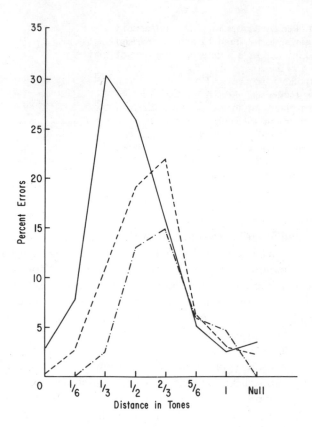

Fig. 5-8. Percent errors in pitch comparisons in sequences where the standard and comparison tones differed in pitch, and the critical interpolated tone was placed on the same side of the standard tone along the pitch continuum as was the comparison tone. Errors were plotted as a function of the amount of pitch separation between the standard tone and the critical interpolated tone, as in Figs. 5-5 and 5-6. The three separate plots show functions obtained when the standard and comparison tones were separated in pitch by ⅓ tone (———), ½ tone (– – – –), and ⅔ tone (– · – ·). For both the ½ tone and the ⅔ tone plots, errors were significantly greater when the standard tone and the critical interpolated tones were separated by ⅔ tone than when they were separated by ⅓ tone. However, for the ⅓ tone plot, errors were significantly greater when the standard tone and the critical interpolated tone were separated by ⅓ tone than when they were separated by ⅔ tone ($p < .01$, two-tailed, on Wilcoxon tests for all comparisons).

5-6, where the standard and comparison tones were also ½ tone apart. This suggests that some fixed disruptive effect that peaks at ⅔ tone is superimposed on the shiftable effect demonstrated by comparing the ⅓-tone curve with the ⅔-tone curve.

The functions plotted in Fig. 5-8 were derived from sessions in which the standard and comparison tones were either identical in pitch or were separated by a constant amount (*i.e.*, by either ⅓ tone, ½ tone, or ⅔ tone). In contrast to the findings in sequences where the standard and comparison tones differed, the peak of errors in sequences where they were identical remained constant at or around a separation of ⅔ tone between the standard tone and critical intervening tone, irrespective of the amount of pitch separation between the standard and comparison tones in the interspersed sequences.

The source of disruption in sequences where the standard and comparison tones are identical also behaves differently in terms of serial position. As shown in Fig. 5-9, when the standard and comparison tones are identical in pitch, the increase in errors due to interpolating a tone that is a semitone removed from the standard tone is of the same magnitude regardless of whether the critical tone is included early or late in the intervening sequence. The sequences from which this plot was derived were interspersed randomly between sequences producing the plot in Fig. 5-7. The two sets of sequences were identical in their parameters, except for whether or not the standard and comparison tones differed in pitch. This large difference in dependence on serial position therefore provides further evidence that we are studying disruptive effects of different origin.

What type of process might we invoke to account for this second source of memory disruption? In searching for analogous findings, intriguing points of similarity emerge between this and lateral inhibitory interactions that have been demonstrated both psychophysically and physiologically in various sensory systems (Ratliff, 1965; Hartline, Ratliff, & Miller, 1961; Alpern & David, 1959; Von Békésy, 1960a, 1960b; Carterette, Freidman, & Lovell, 1969, 1970; Zwislocki, 1970; Houtgast, 1972; Sachs & Kiang, 1968; Kiang, 1968; Klinke, Boerger, & Gruber, 1969, 1970). First, the present effect cumulates when instead of one disruptive tone, two

Fig. 5-9. Percent errors in pitch comparisons for sequences where the standard and comparison tones were identical in pitch, and a tone a semitone removed from the standard tone was included in the interpolated sequence. Errors are shown separately for sequences where the critical interpolated tone was placed in the second and in the fifth serial position of an interpolated sequence of six tones. Errors at each serial position differed significantly from baseline ($p < .01$, two-tailed, on Wilcoxon tests for both comparisons) but there was clearly no difference in errors upon comparing the two serial positions.

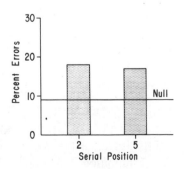

are presented, each placed on either side of the standard tone along the pitch continuum (Table 5-3; Deutsch, 1973a). Such cumulation of disruption from stimuli placed on either side of the test stimulus is typical of lateral inhibition (Ratliff, 1965). Second, the relative frequency range over which this disruptive effect occurs corresponds well with the relative frequency range over which centrally acting lateral inhibition has been found in physiological studies (Klinke *et al.*, 1969, 1970).

At this point we might wonder whether there are reasonable grounds for expecting a memory system to be subject to lateral inhibitory interactions. Two main functions have been proposed for lateral inhibition in sensory and perceptual systems. The first is sharpening the projected image (Ratliff, 1965; Cornsweet, 1970; Von Békésy, 1928, 1960a; Huggins & Licklider, 1951; Carterette *et al.*, 1969, 1970). Upon consideration it can be seen that this function of sharpening should play an equally important role in a sensory memory store. We have everything to gain by mechanisms that help preserve the fineness of a memory image. The second proposed function involves the processing of higher-order information. Several such processes have been suggested to result from inhibitory as well as excitatory interactions. In vision, for instance, the responses of directionally sensitive ganglion cells in the rabbit retina are very probably influenced by lateral inhibition (Barlow & Levick, 1965). In audition, neurons in the central nervous system have been found that respond to a tone only if its frequency is changing. Often the change of frequency must be in a certain direction for a response to occur (Whitfield & Evans, 1965; Suga, 1964). It has been suggested that such behavior also results from an interplay of excitatory and inhibitory effects. If such functions are indeed performed in the case of stimuli that are presented simultaneously or near-simultaneously, they should assume at least as much importance in the case of stimuli presented successively. The system that processes higher-order tonal relationships is clearly very complex and, given what is known of neural function, extremely likely to involve inhibitory as well as excitatory interactions.

As an explanation of the present disruptive effect on pitch memory, the lateral inhibition hypothesis so far rests on three pieces of evidence: the general shape of the function, the cumulation of inhibition produced by stimuli on either side of the test stimulus along the pitch continuum, and the range within which the effect operates. A further experiment provides persuasive evidence for this hypothesis. It has been found in peripheral receptors that when a unit that is inhibiting a neighboring unit is itself inhibited by a third unit, this releases the originally inhibited unit from inhibition (Hartline & Ratliff, 1954, 1957). This phenomenon is known as disinhibition and is a property of recurrent but not noncurrent inhibitory networks. Thus, although it is not a necessary consequence of lateral inhibitory interactions, its demonstration should provide persuasive evidence that such a network indeed underlies the present phenomena. In our present situation, one would expect that if there were placed in the intervening sequence two critical tones, one always two-third tone removed from the standard tone, and the other further removed along the pitch continuum, then errors should be a function of the pitch relationship be-

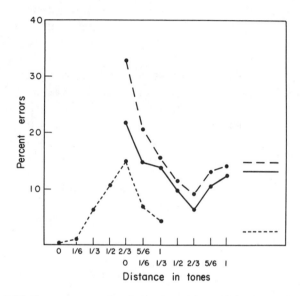

Fig. 5-10. Percent errors in pitch recognition obtained experimentally and predicted theoretically. The dotted line ($\cdot \cdot \cdot \cdot \cdot$) plots percent errors in the baseline experiment, which varies the pitch relationship between the standard tone and a critical interpolated tone. (The horizontal dotted line at right shows percent errors where no tones were interpolated within the critical range under study.) The solid line (————) displays percent errors in the experiment where a tone that is ⅔ tone removed from the standard tone is always interpolated. Errors are plotted as a function of the pitch relationship between this tone and a second critical interpolated tone that is further removed along the pitch continuum. The dashed line (— — — — —) displays percent errors for the same experimental conditions predicted theoretically from the lateral inhibition model. (The horizontal solid and dashed lines at right show percent errors obtained experimentally and assumed theoretically where no further critical tone is interpolated.) When the second critical interpolated tone was identical in pitch to the first, errors were significantly enhanced compared with the baseline condition where no further critical tone was interpolated ($p < .005$, one-tailed, on a Wilcoxon test). When the second critical tone was ⅔ tone removed from the first, errors were significantly reduced compared with the baseline ($p < .01$, one-tailed, on a Wilcoxon test). Data from Deutsch, D., and Feroe, J. *Perception and Psychophysics,* in press.

tween the two critical intervening tones. Errors should be greatest when these two tones are the same in pitch, decline as the second critical tone moves away from the first, dip maximally at a two-third tone separation, and then return to baseline. In other words, the curve produced should be roughly inverse of the curve plotting the original disruptive effect. In an experiment to test this hypothesis, there was always placed in the second serial position of a sequence of 6 intervening tones a tone that was two-third tone removed from the standard tone. Errors were then plotted as a function of the pitch of a further tone, placed in the fourth serial position, whose relationship to the tone in the second serial position varied systematically from identity to a whole tone separation (Deutsch & Feroe, in press).

It can be seen from Fig. 5-10 that the predicted disinhibition function was indeed obtained. The parameters of the baseline inhibitory effect were then plotted for subjects selected on the same criterion as for the disinhibition study. This function was then used to obtain a precise quantitative prediction of the disinhibition effect. These baseline and theoretically predicted disinhibition functions are also plotted on Fig. 5-10. It can be seen that there is a close correspondence between the disinhibition plots obtained experimentally and derived theoretically. This argues persuasively that the elements of the system underlying the short-term retention of tonal pitch are arranged as a lateral inhibitory network, analogous to those in systems handling incoming sensory information.

VI. MEMORY CONSOLIDATION

When a tone that is identical in pitch to the standard tone is included in an intervening sequence, its effect on memory is facilitatory rather than disruptive. A small facilitatory effect is apparent in Figs. 5-5 and 5-6, taken from a study in which the subjects had been selected for displaying a very low baseline error rate, so as to permit accurate plotting of the disruptive effects. With higher baseline errors, a substantial and highly significant reduction in errors is produced by the repeated tone, both in sequences where the standard and comparison tones are identical in pitch, and also where they differ (Deutsch, 1970c, 1972b).

This facilitatory effect is highly sensitive to serial position. In one experiment, a sequence of 6 tones was interpolated between the standard and comparison tones. A tone of the same pitch as the standard tone was included either in the second serial position of the intervening sequence, or in the fifth, or not at all. Fig. 5-11 shows the serial position effect for sequences in which the standard and comparison tones are identical in

Fig. 5-11. Percent errors in pitch comparisons where the standard and comparison tones were identical in pitch, and a further tone of identical pitch was included in the intervening sequence. Errors are shown separately for sequences where the critical interpolated tone was placed in the second and in the fifth serial position of an interpolated sequence of 6 tones. Errors at the second serial position differed significantly from baseline ($p < .01$, two-tailed, on a Wilcoxon test) but errors at the fifth serial position did not. A significant difference was manifest between errors at the second and the fifth serial positions ($p < .01$, two-tailed, on a Wilcoxon test). Data from Deutsch, D., *Memory and cognition,* in press.

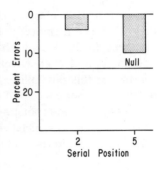

pitch, and Fig. 5-12 shows the effect when they differ. It can be seen from both plots that errors are reduced substantially more when the standard tone is repeated early rather than late in the intervening sequence. Indeed, for each plot the reduction in errors is statistically significant only for sequences in which the repeated tone occurs in the early serial position (Deutsch, in press).

This serial position effect is similar to the effect shown in Fig. 5-9, which plots the errors produced by including a tone that is identical in pitch to the comparison tone, when the standard and comparison tones differ in pitch. One may hypothesize that these two effects are based on the same process—the spread along a temporal continuum of the distributions representing the component tones, with their resultant overlap and summation. This line of argument is developed in detail elsewhere (Deutsch, 1972b). If this hypothesis is correct, the repeated tone produces consolidation of memory for the standard tone by trace enhancement. Such an effect would also be expected to occur proactively. Alternatively, the decrease in errors here produced by the repeated tone might be due to the subject's adopting a particular strategy. When the standard tone is repeated,

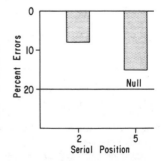

Fig. 5-12. Percent errors in pitch comparisons where the standard and comparison tones differed in pitch, and a tone of identical pitch to the standard tone was included in the interpolated sequence. The same pattern of significances occurred here as in Fig. 5-11. Data from Deutsch, D., *Memory and cognition,* in press.

136   **Diana Deutsch**

the subject recognizes it, and as a result holds the new trace rather than the old one in memory; that is, the repeated tone becomes the new standard tone. In this way, both the number of intervening items and the retention interval are effectively reduced, and so errors are decreased. To control for this possibility, a further experiment was performed. The interpolation of a sequence of 4 randomly chosen tones (Condition 1) was compared with the interpolation of 6, in which a tone of the same pitch as the standard tone was included in the second serial position (Condition 2) and with the interpolation of 6 randomly chosen tones (Condition 3). Thus in the first two conditions, an identical retention interval and an identical number of interpolated tones separated the standard from the comparison tone (Fig. 5-13). If the facilitatory effect of repeating the standard tone were due to the subject adopting the repeated tone as the new standard, no difference in performance between Conditions 1 and 2 should be expected. However, if the repeated tone produced true consolidation, errors should be fewer in Condition 2 although here the number of interpolated tones in the total sequence was in fact larger. It can be seen from Fig. 5-13 that the hypothesis of true consolidation is borne out. Errors in Condition 2 are fewer than in either Condition 1 or Condition 3.

According to the three-stage model of memory, consolidation processes occur only when the information is coded or labeled. Indeed, consolidation is assumed to take place only when the information is in a form suitable for long-term storage. Turvey (1967) describes an experiment that he interprets as evidence for this view. Using the partial report procedure, he presented digit slides tachistoscopically for 50 msec. When one slide was repeated 54 times with other slides interpolated between repetitions, no cumulative effect of repetition was found. This result contrasts with the present finding of consolidation in sensory memory. However, the interpo-

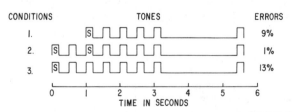

Fig. 5-13. Percent errors in pitch comparisons as a function of number of interpolated tones and repetition of the standard tone pitch. The symbol "S" stands for the pitch of the standard tone. Errors in Condition 3 were significantly greater than in Condition 1, yet errors in Condition 2 were significantly fewer than in either Conditions 1 or 3 ($p < .01$, two-tailed, on Wilcoxon tests for all comparisons). Data from Deutsch, D., *Memory and cognition*, in press.

lated nonrepeated slides could well have interfered with the sensory trace, as might be expected from the findings of Steffy and Ericksen (1965). Such interference could have prevented memory cumulation due to repetition in this situation. But whatever the interpretation of Turvey's negative results, the present findings represent an example of consolidation in sensory memory.

VII. TONE HEIGHT AND TONE CHROMA

There is abundant evidence that we code information concerning tonal pitch not only along a monotonic dimension of "tone height" but also in terms of its position within an abstracted octave. Tones that are separated by octaves, *i.e.,* whose waveform frequencies stand in the ratio of a power of 2:1, have long been known to have an essential similarity. Indeed, the musical scale is based on this similarity, since tones separated exactly by octaves are given the same name (C, C♯, D, *etc.*). People with absolute pitch may often name a note correctly but place it in the wrong octave (Baird, 1917; Bachem, 1954). Octave generalization in response to tonal stimuli has been demonstrated not only in man (Humphreys, 1939) but even in the rat (Blackwell & Schlosberg, 1943). A complex tone made up of components separated by octaves sounds like a single organ-like tone rather than like a chord (Shepard, 1964). Inverted chords (*i.e.,* chords in which the component tones have the same name but are placed in different octaves) are treated in traditional music as harmonically equivalent to their root forms (Rimsky-Korsakov, 1930); they do indeed sound strikingly similar. (To be strictly accurate, the subjective octave is slightly larger than the physical octave, and also varies slightly as a function of frequency (Ward, 1954). This does not, however, affect the general argument).

Given such considerations, various investigators have maintained that tonal pitch should not be treated as a unidimensional stimulus, but should rather be analyzed along two dimensions: *i.e.,* tone height, which represents overall pitch level, and tone chroma, which defines the pitch of a tone within the octave (Meyer, 1904, 1914; Révész, 1913; Ruckmick, 1929; Bachem, 1948; Shepard, 1964). Various bases have been suggested for this bidimensional representation. For instance, it has been proposed that tonal pitch be represented as a helix, with tones separated by an octave lying in closest proximity within each turn of the helix (Drobisch, 1846). A similar suggestion involving a bell-shaped spiral instead of a helix has been made (Ruckmick, 1929).

The problem, however, with hypothesizing a single three-dimensional array to accommodate both "tone height" and "tone chroma" is that this would predict octave generalization in all musical situations. Yet the evidence from music indicates that although simultaneously presented tonal combinations are invertible, successive tonal combinations are not. This question can also be tested experimentally. If successive intervals involving notes of the same name but placed in different octaves were treated by us as equivalent, then we should be able to use octave generalization to recognize tunes. But if inverted successive intervals were treated as independent entities, we should be unable to do this. Reasoning along these lines, I performed the following experiment. I played the first half of the tune *Yankee Doodle* to groups of people in any one of three octaves, and it was universally recognized. Yet when I played the same sequence in identical fashion, except that each note was chosen randomly from one of the same three octaves, the percentage correct recognition was not significantly different from that obtained when the sequence was played as a series of clicks with the pitch information omitted but the rhythmic information retained (Deutsch, 1974 a).It must be concluded that tune recognition takes place along a channel that is independent of that which gives rise to octave generalization.

Elsewhere I have proposed a scheme for the abstraction of tonal relationships that accommodates both "tone-chroma" phenomena and also the finding that octave generalization does not occur in tune recognition (Deutsch, 1969). According to this scheme, abstraction of tonal information takes place along two independent channels, each of which consists of two stages of information transformation (Fig. 5-14). The first channel is concerned with tonal transposition, and is described in detail later. The second channel underlies "tone-chroma" phenomena. In the first stage of transformation along the "tone-chroma" channel, there is convergence of frequency-specific units onto second-order units in such a way that units responding to tones separated exactly by octaves are joined together (Fig. 5-15). This second-order array thus provides a basis for the "tone-chroma" dimension. In the second stage of transformation along this channel, second-order units are joined to third-order units, which respond only to simultaneous input. This third-order array thus provides for chord inversion. It is further assumed that each of these memory arrays has its own retention characteristics, in terms of susceptibility to specific interference effects, rate of decay, consolidation patterns, *etc.* From an everyday knowledge of music it would appear that the higher-order the array, the more enduring its memory characteristics.

One may ask whether disruptive effects on immediate memory for tonal pitch take place along the dimension of "tone height," "tone chroma," or both. This question can be investigated by studying the possible generalization patterns across octaves for these interference effects. Such octave

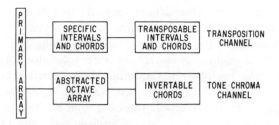

Fig. 5-14. Flow diagram for abstraction of pitch relationships. On this scheme, the information is simultaneously transformed along two parallel channels, one forming the basis for transposition phenomena, and the other for "tone-chroma" phenomena. It is assumed that the information at each stage of both channels is stored in a unique fashion. (Adapted from Deutsch, D., *Psychological Review,* 1969, **76,** 300–307. Copyright 1969 by the American Psychological Association. Reprinted by permission.)

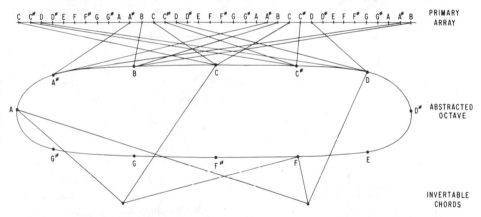

Fig. 5-15. Confluence of information along the two stages of the "tone-chroma" channel. Units corresponding to the traditional musical scale are here used for purposes of clarity, but these simply represent arbitrary points on a continuum of log frequency. (Adapted from Deutsch, D., *Psychological Review,* 1969, **76,** 300–307. Copyright 1969 by the American Psychological Association. Reprinted by permission.)

generalization would be evidence for the involvement of a "tone-chroma" dimension.

In one experiment, I found that large disruptive effects in pitch recognition were produced by interpolating tones taken from the octave above or below the octave from which the standard and comparison tones were taken (Deutsch, 1973c). In a further experiment, I studied the effect of interpolating tones in the intervening sequence that bore the same relationship to the standard and comparison tones as had been found earlier to produce disruption, but that were further removed by an octave (Deutsch, 1973b). Two sources of interference were used. The first was that produced by the interpolation of two tones, one a semitone higher than the standard tone, and the other a semitone lower, when the standard and comparison tones were identical in pitch (Deutsch, 1973a). The second was that produced by the interpolation of a tone of the same pitch as the comparison tone, when the standard and comparison tones differed in pitch (Deutsch, 1970b, 1972b, 1973a).

It was found that both sources of interference exhibit octave generalization. It can be seen from Table 5-5 that the generalization from the higher octave is extremely strong, and that from the lower octave, though statistically significant, is weaker. The finding of substantial and significant

TABLE 5-5[a]

Conditions	Percentage Errors
S and C Tones Different	
1. No tone at pitch of C tone, or displaced by an octave from C tone, included in intervening sequence.	4.6
2. Tone at pitch of C tone included in intervening sequence.	26.7
3. Critical included tone as in Condition 2, but displaced an octave higher.	20.2
4. Critical included tone as in Condition 2, but displaced an octave lower.	12.1
S and C Tones Same	
5. No tone a semitone removed from S (and C) tone, or displaced from such a tone by an octave, included in intervening sequence.	5.6
6. Two tones, one a semitone higher and the other a semitone lower, included in intervening sequence.	24.4
7. Critical included tones as in Condition 6, but displaced an octave higher.	21.0
8. Critical included tones as in Condition 6, but displaced an octave lower.	11.3

[a] Percent errors in pitch comparisons as a function of the presence in the intervening sequence of tones displaced by an octave from those known to produce disruption. Errors in sequences where the disruptive tones were displaced by an octave were significantly greater than baseline errors for all conditions ($p < .01$, two-tailed, on Wilcoxon tests in all cases). A weaker pattern of generalization from the lower compared with the higher octave was also manifest: significant differences occurred between Conditions 3 and 4 ($p < .02$, two-tailed, on a Wilcoxon test) and Conditions 7 and 8 ($p < .01$, two-tailed, on a Wilcoxon test). From Deutsch, D., 1973, by permission of *Perception & Psychophysics*, **13**, 271–275. Copyright 1973 by The Psychonomic Society, Inc.

octave generalization demonstrates the involvement of a "tone-chroma" dimension in these effects. However, the finding that such generalization is not absolute demonstrates that these effects also take place along a "tone-height" dimension. In terms of the scheme described above (Deutsch, 1969), it would appear that these interactions take place along both the primary array and the abstracted octave array (Fig. 5-15). At all events, one must conclude that the memory store within which such interactions take place is bidimensional in nature.

VIII. INTERACTIONS WITH THE SYSTEM RETAINING PITCH RELATIONSHIPS

It is clear from an analysis of music recognition that memory for tonal relationships must exist independently of memory for the component tonal pitches. Pairs of tones appear to stand in the same relationship to each other when their waveform frequencies are related by roughly the same ratio. The question of whether this equivalence is based on pure ratios or some approximation of these ratios is a matter of current debate, but does not affect the general principle of transposition. Plomp, Wagenaar, & Mimpen (1973) have shown, however, that we do not rate intervals for similarity on the basis of their relative ranks on a scale of ratio simplicity. At all events, when tonal combinations are transposed from one key to another, the component tonal pitches are altered, but the relationships between them remain the same. It is these relationships that are stored in memory and provide the basis for transposition. Under such circumstances, provided sufficient time or interfering activity occurs between the initial presentation of the combination and its later presentation in transposed form, the combination will be recognized as the same and the fact of its transposition may go unnoticed. This finding leads to the conclusion that memory for abstracted tonal relationships is more enduring than memory for the pitches of the component tones. Attneave and Olson (1971) have demonstrated that even musically untrained subjects will transpose successive tonal relationships in a log frequency medium, especially when they can use enduring long-term traces for the abstracted tonal information.

According to the above scheme for abstraction of pitch information, transposition takes place in two stages along one of two parallel channels (Fig. 5-16). In the first stage, frequency-specific units converge onto second-order units in groups of two or three. These second-order units therefore respond to intervals and chords only when they are formed by tones of specific pitch. Second-order units responding to two-tone combinations fall into three categories: those responding to simultaneous tonal combi-

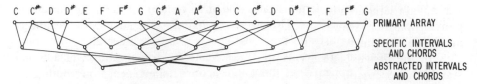

Fig. 5-16. Confluence of information along the two stages of the transposition channel. As in Fig. 5-15, units corresponding to the traditional musical scale are here chosen solely for the purposes of clarity. (Adapted from Deutsch, D., *Psychological Review,* 1969, **76,** 300–307. Copyright 1969 by the American Psychological Association. Reprinted by permission.)

nations, those responding to ascending intervals, and those responding to descending intervals. In the second stage of transformation along the transposition channel, second-order units are joined to third-order units in such a way that there is convergence of units responding to a given tonal relationship. The third-order units therefore respond to the abstracted relationships independently of the component pitches involved. This third-order array thus provides the basis for transposition.

As with the parallel "tone-chroma" channel, it is assumed that each of the proposed memory arrays along the transposition channel exhibits a unique set of retention characteristics. Again, it is expected that the higher-order the array, the more enduring its retention characteristics. For example, we remember and learn melodies much better than we remember or learn what key they are played in. It follows that the abstracted information concerning the successive tonal relationships is learned and retained much better than the information concerning the absolute pitches of the component tones. In terms of the present scheme, the third-order array along the transposition channel retains information much longer, and has the power to consolidate information much more efficiently than does the primary array. Similar considerations apply to transposed chords.

In further studies the retention of abstracted tonal relationships in immediate memory was explored (Deutsch & Roll, in press). The paradigm used was very similar to that used in previous experiments, except that the standard and comparison tones always occurred simultaneously with other tones of lower pitch. The two tones of each combination were fed separately to each ear, so as to avoid the introduction of artifacts into the physical stimulus. On each trial the standard and comparison tonal combinations were separated by a sequence of 6 intervening tones. The subject was instructed to listen to the upper tone of the first combination and ignore the lower tone, to ignore the 6 intervening tones, and then to judge whether the upper tone of the second combination was the same or different in pitch from the upper tone of the first combination. The standard tone was always separated by 7 semitones (*i.e.,* a musical fifth) from its accompanying partner. However, the relationship between the comparison tone and its partner varied.

In the first experiment, two conditions were compared in which the standard and comparison tones were the same in pitch. In the first condition, the tone accompanying the comparison tone was the same in pitch as the tone accompanying the standard tone. In the second condition the lower tone shifted either upward or downward in pitch by a semitone. As shown in Table 5-6, errors were substantially more numerous in the second condition than in the first. This is consistent with an interpretation in terms of misjudgment of the comparison tone based on its altered relationship to its accompanying tone. However, the subjects might have been mistakenly judging the wrong tone. So in a further study the subjects were required to judge not only whether the standard and comparison tones differed in pitch, but also the direction in which they differed. No correlation was found between the direction of incorrect "different" judgments and the actual direction in which the lower tones of the combinations varied.

Two conditions were compared in which the standard and comparison tones differed in pitch. In the first condition, the tone accompanying the comparison tone was the same in pitch as the tone accompanying the standard tone. In the second condition it shifted in parallel with the pitch difference between the standard and comparison tones. That is, when the

TABLE 5-6[a]

Conditions	Errors
Standard and Comparison Tones Same	
1. Simultaneous tone same.	8%
2. Simultaneous tone different.	29%
Standard and Comparison Tones Different	
1. Simultaneous tone same.	18%
2. Simultaneous tone moves in parallel with an upward shift of the comparison tone.	31%
3. Simultaneous tone moves in parallel with a downward shift of the comparison tone.	31%

[a] Percent errors in pitch comparisons as a function of the relationships between the standard and comparison tones and their accompanying partners. When the standard and comparison tones were the same in pitch, errors increased when the accompanying tone shifted in pitch. When the comparison tone differed in pitch from the standard tone, errors increased when the accompanying tone moved in the same direction, thus preserving the relationship within the combination ($p < .01$ in both cases).

All standard tone combinations form a musical fifth. All shifts are of one semitone. Data from Deutsch, D., and Roll, P. L., *Journal of Experimental Psychology*, in press.

comparison tone was a semitone higher than the standard, the accompanying tone was also a semitone higher. When the comparison tone was a
semitone lower, the accompanying tone was also a semitone lower. In this
way the interval formed by the simultaneous combination was preserved.
As shown in Table 5-6, errors were substantially greater in the second condition than in the first. In this case, the increased errors could not have
been due to the subjects' mistakenly judging the wrong tone, since both
tones of the combination moved in the same direction. This provides strong
evidence that misrecognition was based on the storage of abstracted relational information.

It might alternatively be argued that when the lower tones of the test
tone combinations were the same in pitch, these lower tones served as some
kind of anchor to facilitate discrimination of the standard from the comparison tone. I therefore performed another experiment that was essentially a replication of the first, except that the two tones of the test-tone
combinations moved in opposite directions rather than in parallel. That is,
when the comparison tone was a semitone higher than the standard tone,
its accompanying tone shifted downward by a semitone. When the comparison tone was a semitone lower, its accompanying tone shifted a semitone upwards. Here a very interesting finding emerged. It will be recalled
that a "fourth" is a musical inversion of a "fifth." When the two components of the combination shifted toward each other, the relationship between them changed from a "fifth" to a "fourth." When they shifted away
from each other, the new relationship became a "sixth." It was found that
errors were significantly greater when the two components of the combination shifted inward than when they shifted outward. That is, errors increased when the comparison tone combination stood in the same abstracted and inverted relationship as the standard tone combination (Table
5-7). It would appear that errors here were based on the storage of a tonal
relationship that was both transposed and inverted.

To ensure that these results were not due to verbal labeling of the
intervals, the subjects were asked at the end of the experiment to name the
intervals used. Because none of them was able to do this, it must be concluded that the pattern of errors was due to the retention of information
that was abstracted and yet not verbally labeled.

The above experiment may be related to an interesting study by Plomp
et al. (1973), who examined patterns of confusion in judgments of intervals that varied in semitone steps between a minor second and an octave.
They found that subjects generally confused intervals on the basis of their
size; however, the subjects tended in addition to confuse intervals that were
inverted. That is, a "fifth" and a "fourth" were confused with each other
more than either with a "diminished fifth." Confusions between "seconds"

TABLE 5-7[a]

Conditions	Errors
Standard and Comparison Tones Same	
1. Simultaneous tone same.	10%
2. Simultaneous tone different.	29%
Standard and Comparison Tones Different	
1. Simultaneous tone same.	21%
2. Simultaneous tone moves in opposite direction to an upward shift of the comparison tone.	16%
3. Simultaneous tone moves in opposite direction to a downward shift of the comparison tone.	26%

[a] Percent errors in pitch comparisons as a function of the relationships between the standard and comparison tones and their accompanying partners. As on Table 5-6, when the standard and comparison tones were the same in pitch, errors increased when the accompanying tone shifted in pitch ($p < .01$). When the standard and comparison tones differed, shifting the pitch of the accompanying tone in the opposite direction produced no overall effect. However, in sequences where the accompanying tones shifted, the error rate was significantly enhanced when the comparison combination formed a relationship that was an inversion of the relationship formed by the standard combination ($p < .05$).

All standard tone combinations form a musical fifth. All shifts are of one semitone. Data from Deutsch, D., and Roll, P. L., *Journal of Experimental Psychology*, in press.

and "sevenths," and between "thirds" and "sixths," also emerged. This experiment provides further evidence for storage of inverted intervals.

IX. CONCLUSION

In conclusion, various general questions concerning nonverbal memory are considered in light of these experiments. The first concerns the amount of differentiation within the precategorical information storage system. It was initially assumed that all precategorical information was retained in a single nonspecific large-capacity store (Broadbent, 1958). Then, as evidence accumulated that nonverbal memory exhibited modality-dependent characteristics, the nonverbal storage system was divided into several stores, separated on the basis of input modality alone (Atkinson & Shiffrin, 1968). However, the characteristics of memory for tonal pitch show separation by input modality to be insufficient. The acoustical properties of words interfere only minimally with memory for tonal pitch, whereas other tones interfere considerably. Further, it is clear on general grounds that memory for abstracted tonal relations is considerably more enduring than memory for absolute pitch values. A more realistic principle for subdividing precategorical memory would appear to be by the type of perceptual operation performed on the information, rather than by the nature of the end-organ involved.

A related question concerns the nature of the influence producing forgetting in nonverbal memory. Various diffuse factors, such as decay or displacement, have been proposed (Broadbent, 1958; Crowder & Morton, 1969). However, the experiments described here show interference in memory for tonal pitch to be a systematic function of similarity between the tone to be remembered and the interfering tone. Indeed, the evidence strongly indicates that interactive effects in pitch memory are analogous to known effects operating in systems handling incoming sensory information. On this basis it is here proposed that the memory system that retains sensory information is organized in many ways along the same principles as the system that receives it.

A final question concerns the form of information storage required for consolidation. It is generally held that consolidation processes occur only when information has been coded verbally in a form suitable for long-term storage. However, experiments described here demonstrate consolidation through repetition in memory for the pitch of a single tone. This argues strongly against the view that a specific type of coding is necessary for memory consolidation.

In conclusion, the findings described in this chapter show that the short-term retention of tonal pitch is the function of a system possessing a high degree of organization and specificity. It is likely that similar characteristics will be uncovered in other sensory memory systems.

REFERENCES

Alpern, M., & David, H. The additivity of contrast in the human eye. *Journal of General Physiology,* 1959, **43,** 109–126.

Atkinson, R. C., & Shiffrin, R. M. Human memory: A proposed system and its control processes. In K. W. Spence & J. T. Spence (Eds.), *The psychology of learning and motivation: Advances in research and theory,* Vol. II. New York: Academic Press, 1968.

Attneave, F., & Olson, R. K. Pitch as a medium: A new approach to psychophysical scaling. *American Journal of Psychology,* 1971, **84,** 147–165.

Bachem, A. Note on Neu's review of the literature on absolute pitch. *Psychological Bulletin,* 1948, **45,** 161–162.

Bachem, A. Time factors in relative and absolute pitch determination. *Journal of the Acoustical Society of America,* 1954, **26,** 751–753.

Bahrick, H. P., & Boucher, B. Retention of visual and verbal codes of the same stimuli. *Journal of Experimental Psychology*, 1968, **78**, 417–422.

Baird, J. W. Memory for absolute pitch: Studies in psychology. In *Titchener commemorative volume*. Worcester, Mass.: L. N. Wilson, 1917.

Barlow, H. B., & Levick, W. R. The mechanism of directionally selective units in the rabbit's retina. *Journal of Physiology*, 1965, **178**, 477–504.

Blackwell, H. R., & Schlosberg, H. Octave generalization, pitch discrimination, and loudness thresholds in the white rat. *Journal of Experimental Psychology*, 1943, **33**, 407–419.

Bogen, J. E. The other side of the brain. II: An appositional mind. *Bulletin of the Los Angeles Neurological Society*, 1969, **34**, 135–162.

Brain, R. *Speech disorders*, 2nd ed. London: Buttersworth, 1965.

Broadbent, D. E. *Perception and communication*. New York: Pergammon Press, 1958.

Broadbent, D. E. Flow of information within the organism. *Journal of Verbal Learning and Verbal Behavior*, 1963, **2**, 34–39.

Bryden, M. P. Ear preference in auditory perception. *Journal of Experimental Psychology*, 1963, **65**, 103–105.

Carterette, E. C., Friedman, M. P., & Lovell, J. D. Mach bands in hearing. *Journal of the Acoustical Society of America*, 1969, **45**, 986–998.

Carterette, E. C., Friedman, M. P., & Lovell, J. D. Mach bands in auditory perception. In R. Plomp & G. F. Smoorenburg (Eds.), *Frequency analysis and periodicity detection in hearing*. Sijthoff: Leiden, 1970.

Cole, R. A. Different memory functions for consonants and vowels. *Cognitive Psychology*, 1973, **4**, 39–54.

Cornsweet, T. N. *Visual perception*. New York: Academic Press, 1970.

Crossman, E. R. F. W. Discussion on the paper by J. Brown in "The Mechanization of Thought Processes," National Physical Laboratory Symposium. London: HMSO, 1958.

Crowder, R. G. The sound of vowels and consonants in immediate memory. *Journal of Verbal Learning and Verbal Behavior*, 1971, **10**, 587–596.

Crowder, R. G., & Morton, J. Precategorical acoustic storage (PAS). *Perception & Psychophysics*, 1969, **5**, 365–373.

Curry, F. K. W. A comparison of left-handed and right-handed subjects in verbal and nonverbal dichotic listening tasks. *Cortex*, 1967, **3**, 343–352.

Deutsch, D. Music recognition. *Psychological Review*, 1969, **76**, 300–307.

Deutsch, D. The deterioration of pitch information in memory. Unpublished doctoral dissertation, University of California at San Diego, 1970. (a)

Deutsch, D. Tones and numbers: Specificity of interference in short-term memory. *Science*, 1970, **168**, 1604–1605. (b)

Deutsch, D. Dislocation of tones in a musical sequence: A memory illusion. *Nature*, 1970, **226**, 286. (c)

Deutsch, D. Mapping of interactions in the pitch memory store. *Science*, 1972, **175**, 1020–1022. (a)

Deutsch, D. Effect of repetition of standard and comparison tones on recognition memory for pitch. *Journal of Experimental Psychology*, 1972, **93**, 156–162. (b)

Deutsch, D. Octave generalization and tune recognition. *Perception and Psychophysics*, 1972, **11**, 411–412. (c)

Deutsch, D. Interference in memory between tones adjacent in the musical scale. *Journal of Experimental Psychology*, 1973, **100**, 228–231. (a)

Deutsch, D. Octave generalization of specific interference effects in memory for tonal pitch. *Perception & Psychophysics*, 1973, **13**, 271–275. (b)

Deutsch, D. Generality of interference by tonal stimuli in recognition memory for pitch. *Quarterly Journal of Experimental Psychology*, 1974, **26**, 229–234. (a)

Deutsch, D. An auditory illusion. *Journal of the Acoustical Society of America*, 1974, **55**, 518–19. (b)

Deutsch, D. An auditory illusion. *Nature*, 1974, **251**, 307–309. (c)

Deutsch, D. An illusion with musical scales. *Journal of the Acoustical Society of America*, 1974, **56**, 525. (d)

Deutsch, D. Facilitation by repetition in recognition memory for tonal pitch. *Memory and cognition*, in press.

Deutsch, D. & Feroe, J. Evidence for lateral inhibition in the pitch memory system, *Perception and Psychophysics*, in press.

Deutsch, D. and Roll, P. Error patterns in delayed pitch comparison as a function of relational context. *Journal of Experimental Psychology*, in press.

Dirks, D. Perception of dichotic and monaural verbal material and cerebral dominance for speech. *Acta Oto-Laryngologica*, 1964, **58**, 73–80.

Doehring, D. G. Ear asymmetry in the discrimination of monaural tonal sequences. *Canadian Journal of Psychology*, 1972, **26**, 106–110.

Drobisch, M. W. *Über die mathematische Bestimmung der Musikalischen Intervalle.* In Fürstlich, *Jablonowskischen Gesellschaft der Wissenschaften.* Leipzig: Weidmann'sche Buchlandlung, 1846; Abhandenagen bei Begründung der Vërnighich Sächsz'schen Gesellschaft der Wissenschaften am Tageder Zweihudertjähzingen Gebwizfeier Leibnizens Lerausgeben von der Fürslich Jablonowskischen Gesellschaft.

Elliott, L. L. Pitch memory for short tones. *Perception & Psychophysics*, 1970, **8**, 379–384.

Erickson, R. Sound Structure in Music. University of California Press, Berkeley, 1975, in press.

Gordon, H. W. Hemispheric asymmetries in the perception of musical chords. *Cortex*, 1970, **6**, 387–398.

Harris, J. D. The decline of pitch discrimination with time. *Journal of Experimental Psychology*, 1952, **43**, 96–99.

Harris, J. D. Audition. *Annual Review of Psychology*, 1972, **23**, 313–346.

Hartline, H. K., & Ratliff, F. Spatial summation of inhibitory influences in the eye of Limulus. *Science*, 1954, **120**, 781.

Hartline, H. K., & Ratliff, F. Inhibitory interactions of receptor units in the eye of Limulus. *Journal of General Physiology*, 1957, **40**, 357–376.

Hartline, H. K., Ratliff, F., & Miller, W. H. Inhibitory interaction in the retina and its significance in vision. In E. Florey (Ed.), *Nervous inhibition.* New York: Pergammon Press, 1961.

Hecaen, H., & de Ajuriaguerra, J. *Left-Handedness.* New York: Grune and Stratten, 1964.

Helmholtz, H. L. F. *On the sensations of tone, as a physiological basis of music* (1862). New York: Dover, 1954.

Henderson, L. Spatial and verbal codes and the capacity of STM. *Quarterly Journal of Experimental Psychology*, 1972, **24**, 485–495.

Houtgast, T. Psychophysical evidence for lateral inhibition in hearing. *Journal of the Acoustical Society of America*, 1972, **51**, 1885–1894.

Humphreys, L. F. Generalization as a function of method of reinforcement. *Journal of Experimental Psychology*, 1939, **25**, 361–372.

Huggins, W. H., & Licklider, J. C. R. Place mechanisms of auditory frequency analysis. *Journal of the Acoustical Society of America*, 1951, **23**, 290–299.

Kiang, N. Y-S. A survey of recent developments in the study of auditory physiology. *Annuals of Otology, Rhinology, and Laryngology*, 1968, **77**, 656–676.

Kimura, D. Cerebral dominance and the perception of verbal stimuli. *Canadian Journal of Psychology*, 1961, **15**, 166–171.

Kimura, D. Left-right differences in the perception of melodies. *Quarterly Journal of Experimental Psychology*, 1964, **16**, 355–358.

Kimura, D. Functional assymetry of the brain in dichotic listening. *Cortex*, 1967, **3**, 163–178.

King, F. L., & Kimura, D. Left-ear superiority in dichotic perception of vocal non-verbal sounds. *Canadian Journal of Psychology*, 1972, **26**, 111–116.

Klinke, R., Boerger, G., & Gruber, J. Alteration of afferent, tone-evoked activity of neurons of the cochlear nucleus following acoustic stimulation of the contralateral ear. *Journal of the Acoustical Society of America*, 1969, **45**, 788–789.

Klinke, R., Boerger, G., & Gruber, J. The influence of the frequency relation in dichotic stimulation upon the cochlear nucleus activity. In R. Plomp & G. F. Smoorenburg (Eds.), *Frequency analysis and periodicity detection in hearing*. Sijthoff: Leiden, 1970.

Knox, C. and Kimura, D. Cerebral processing of nonverbal sounds in boys and girls. *Neuropsychologia*, 1970, **8**, 227–237.

Koester, T. The time error in pitch and loudness discrimination as a function of time interval and stimulus level. *Archives of Psychology*, 1945, **297**, whole issue.

Kroll, N. E. A., Parks, T., Parkinson, S. R., Bieber, S. L., & Johnson, A. L. Short-term memory while shadowing: Recall of visually and of aurally presented letters. *Journal of Experimental Psychology*, 1970, **85**, 220–224.

Massaro, D. W. Retroactive interference in short-term recognition memory of pitch. *Journal of Experimental Psychology*, 1970, **83**, 32–39.

Mcyer, M. On the attributes of the sensations. *Psychological Review*, 1904, **11**, 83–103.

Meyer, M. Review of G. Révés, "Zur Grundleguncy der Tonpsychologie." *Psychological Bulletin*, 1914, **11**, 349–352.

Morton, J. A functional model for memory. In D. A. Norman (Ed.), *Models for human memory*. New York: Academic Press, 1970.

Murdock, B. B., Jr., & Walker, K. D. Modality effects in free recall. *Journal of Verbal Learning and Verbal Behavior*, 1969, **8**, 665–676.

Nickerson, R. S. Short-term memory for complex meaningful visual configurations: A demonstration of capacity. *Canadian Journal of Psychology*, 1965, **19**, 155–160.

Paivio, A. Mental imagery in associative learning and memory. *Psychological Review*, 1969, **76**, 241–263.

Parks, T. E., Kroll, N. E. A., Salzberg, P. M., & Parkinson, S. R. Persistence of visual memory as indicated by decision time in a matching task. *Journal of Experimental Psychology*, 1972, **92**, 437–438.

Plomp, R. Timbre as a multidimensional attribute of complex tones. In R. Plomp & G. F. Smoorenburg (Eds.), *Frequency analysis and periodicity detection in hearing*. Sijthoff: Leiden, 1970.

Plomp, R., Wagenaar, W. A., & Mimpen, A. M. Musical interval recognition with simultaneous tones. *Acustica*, 1973, **29**, 101–109.

Pollack, I. Message uncertainty and message reception. *Journal of the Acoustical Society of America*, 1959, **31**, 1500–1508.

Posner, M. I. Short-term memory systems in human information processing. In A. F. Sanders (Ed.), *Attention and performance*. Amsterdam: North Holland, 1967.

Posner, M. I. Coordination of internal codes. Paper presented to the 8th Carnegie Symposium of Cognitive Psychology, Pittsburgh, May 1972.

Posner, M. I., & Warren, R. Traces, concepts, and conscious constructions. In A. W. Melton & E. Martin (Eds.), *Coding in learning and memory*. New York: Scripture, 1972.

Ratliff, F. *Mach bands: Quantitative studies of neural networks in the retina*. San Francisco: Holden-Day, 1965.

Révész, G. *Zur Grundleguncy der Tonpsychologie*. Leipzig: Feit, 1913.

Rimm, D. C. The effect of interpolated stimulation on short-term memory for tones. *Psychological Record*, 1967, **17**, 429–435.

Rimsky-Korsakov, N. *Practical manual of harmony*, 12th ed. New York: Fischer, 1930.

Ruckmick, C. A. A new classification of tonal qualities. *Psychological Review*, 1929, **36**, 172–180.

Sachs, M. B., & Kiang, N. Y-S. Two-tone inhibition in auditory nerve fibers. *Journal of the Acoustical Society of America*, 1968, **43**, 1120–1128.

Sanders, A. F., & Schroots, J. J. F. Cognitive categories and the memory span: III. Effects of similarity on recall. *Quarterly Journal of Experimental Psychology*, 1969, **21**, 21–28.

Scarborough, D. L. Memory for brief visual displays of symbols. *Cognitive Psychology*, 1972, **3**, 408–429. (a)

Scarborough, D. L. Stimulus modality effects on forgetting in short-term memory. *Journal of Experimental Psychology*, 1972, **95**, 285–289. (b)

Scharf, B. Critical bands. In J. V. Tobias (Ed.), *Foundations of modern auditory theory*, Vol. 1. New York: Academic Press, 1970.

Shankweiler, D., & Studdert-Kennedy, M. Identification of consonants and vowels presented to left and right ears. *Quarterly Journal of Experimental Psychology*, 1967, **19**, 59–63.

Shankweiler, D., & Studdert-Kennedy. Hemispheric specialization for speech perception. *Journal of the Acoustical Society of America*, 1970, **48**, 579–594.

Shepard, R. N. Circularity in judgments of relative pitch. *Journal of the Acoustical Society of America*, 1964, **36**, 2345–2353.

Shepard, R. N. Recognition memory for words, sentences, and pictures. *Journal of Verbal Learning and Verbal Behavior*, 1967, **6**, 156–163.

Spellacy, F. Lateral preferences in the identification of patterned stimuli. *Journal of the Acoustical Society in America*, 1970, **47**, 574–578.

Sperling, G. A model for visual memory tasks. *Human Factors*, 1963, **5**, 19–31.

Sperling, G. Successive approximations to a model for short-term memory. In A. F. Sanders (Ed.), *Attention and performance*. Amsterdam: North Holland, 1967.

Steffy, R. A., and Ericksen, C. W. Short-term perceptual recognition memory for tachistoscopically presented nonsense forms. *Journal of Experimental Psychology*, 1965, **70**, 277–283.

Studdert-Kennedy, M., & Shankweiler, D. Hemispheric specialization for speech perception. *Journal of the Acoustical Society of America*, 1970, **48**, 579–594.

Suga, N. Recovery cycles and responses to frequency-modulated tone pulses in auditory neurons of echo-locating bats. *Journal of Physiology*, 1964, **175**, 50–80.

Turvey, M. T. Repetition and the preperceptual information store. *Journal of Experimental Psychology*, 1967, **74**, 289–93.

Von Békésy, G. *Zur Theorie des Hörens, Die Schwingungsform der Basilarmembran.* Physikalische Zeitschrift, 1928, **29**, 793–810.

Von Békésy, G. *Experiments in hearing.* New York: McGraw-Hill, 1960. (a)

Von Békésy, G. Neural inhibitory units of the eye and skin: Quantitative description of contrast phenomena. *Journal of the Optical Society of America*, 1960, **50**, 1060–1070. (b)

Ward, W. D. Subjective musical pitch. *Journal of the Acoustical Society of America*, 1954, **26**, 369–380.

Whitfield, I. C., & Evans, E. F. Responses of auditory cortical neurons to stimuli of changing frequency. *Journal of Neurophysiology*, 1965, **28**, 655–672.

Wickelgren, W. A. Consolidation and retroactive interference in short-term recognition memory for pitch. *Journal of Experimental Psychology*, 1966, **72**, 250–259.

Wickelgren, W. A. Associative strength theory of recognition memory for pitch. *Journal of Mathematical Psychology*, 1969, **6**, 13–61.

Zwislocki, J. J. Central masking and auditory frequency selectivity. In R. Plomp & G. F. Snoorenburg (Eds.), *Frequency analysis and periodicity detection in hearing.* Sijthoff: Leiden, 1970.

CHAPTER

6

VISUAL SHORT-TERM MEMORY[1]

NEAL E. A. KROLL

[1] The research and much of the theory reported here has been the joint effort of a number of people. Those most central to this project have been Stanley R. Parkinson, Theodore E. Parks, Michael H. Kellicutt, and Philip M. Salzberg. I also wish to acknowledge the editorial assistance of my wife, Bonnie.

I. INTRODUCTION

A. Visually Presented Memory Stimuli Are Often Remembered Subvocally

Research conducted in the late 1950s and throughout the 1960s emphasized the adult human subject's tendency to recode visually presented stimuli into subvocal memory codes. As indicated by Sperling and Speelman (1970), three general lines of experimental evidence were developed, all demonstrating that the subject's ability to recall visual stimuli was a function of the names of the stimuli.[2]

One line of evidence was based on the finding of a high correlation between the memory intrusion errors made while recalling visually presented stimuli (e.g., letters of the alphabet) and the perceptual errors made while listening to the same information presented aurally (e.g., Conrad, 1964). That is, the name of the subjects' recall errors tended to sound like the names of memory stimuli, even if these stimuli had been presented visually.

A second line of evidence comes from the effects of the acoustic composition of the memory stimulus itself. For example, Kintsch and Buschke (1969, Experiment II) presented lists of 16 words containing either homophone pairs or unrelated words. After each list, one of the words in the sequence was presented as a probe for the subject to recall the word that had followed the probe word in the list. They found that the recall of the most recently presented words of a list was poorer when the list contained homophones.

A third line of evidence for subvocal recoding came from experiments studying the amount of interference caused by various distractor tasks as a function of the acoustic similarity between the memory item and the distractor task. (A distractor task is a task performed by the subject during the retention interval.) For example, if a distractor task requires the subject to make particular verbal responses during the retention interval, memory is often worse when the words in the distractor task sound like the name of the visually presented memory stimulus than when they do not (e.g., Dale & Gregory, 1966).

B. The Visual Memory Trace Seems to Drop Out Rapidly

While the evidence of subvocal recoding was accumulating, other experimental results were supporting the position that the visual trace itself

---

[2] See Sperling and Speelman (1970, p. 152) for a more extensive bibliography.

was extremely short lived. For example, Posner and Keele (1967) used a reaction-time technique wherein the subject was first shown a memory letter and then, following a brief retention interval, a test letter. After seeing the test letter, the subject indicated as rapidly as possible if the memory and test letters had the same name. With extremely brief retention intervals, subjects responded most rapidly when the memory and test letters were physically identical, but when the retention interval reached 1.5 sec, the subject responded as quickly to name-same, case-different pairs (*e.g.,* "a" and "A") as to name-same, case-same pairs (*e.g.,* "A" and "A"). This suggested that, with the briefer retention interval, subjects were comparing the first letter's visual memory trace with the form of the test letter on the screen. With slightly longer retention intervals, however, they were apparently using some nonvisual memory code (such as a subvocal name code) that was independent of letter case.

The apparent brevity of visual memory was also demonstrated when subjects were asked to remember lists. Auditory presentation of list items seemed to result in better memory than visual presentation, regardless of whether memory was tested by the probe technique (Murdock, 1968), by free recall (Murdock & Walker, 1969), by serial recall (Conrad & Hull, 1968), or even by several different recognition procedures (Murdock, 1968). The superiority of auditory presentation is most consistent across testing procedures within the recency portion of the serial position curve (*i.e.,* those items presented toward the end of the list). It is this portion of the curve that many see as reflecting the short-term, or primary, memory component (see Craik, 1971, p. 233). Laughery and Pinkus (1966) interpreted this modality difference as being consistent with the hypothesis that the visual input must be transformed into a subvocal code in order to be retained in short-term memory (*e.g.,* Sperling, 1963).

As a result of the apparent prevalence of subvocal recoding and the apparent short life of visual memories, the theories of memory developed during this period considered covert rehearsal to be primarily, if not entirely, via the repetition of subvocal memory codes (Broadbent, 1958; Sperling, 1967; Atkinson & Shiffrin, 1968; Laughery, 1969). However, not all experimental psychologists in the 1950s and 1960s had completely abandoned the possibilities of visual imagery. Posner and Keele (1967), for example, ended their interpretation of their reaction time experiment, which demonstrated the loss of the visual trace over a 1.5-sec retention interval, with the statement: "This should not be taken to mean that subjects would be unable to preserve the visual information of the first letter if, in fact, they desired to do so." Murdock, whose experiments were often interpreted by others as demonstrating the lack of visual short-term memory, interpreted his own results as "clearly inconsistent with a . . . one-

store model. . . . Instead [they reaffirm] that there are separate prelinguistic auditory and visual short-term stores . . ." (Murdock & Walker,
1969, p. 665).

Most of the earlier experiments purporting to demonstrate visual
short-term memory, however, were always open to the criticism that the
subject might actually have been using subvocal coding (*e.g.,* Atkinson &
Shiffrin, 1968, p. 100). To avoid this and other criticisms, it was necessary
to develop a task that would: (1) place enough pressure on the subject
so as to make mnemonic coding (that is, the use of natural language
mediators, Prytulak, 1971) unlikely; (2) make subvocal recoding a very
poor strategy; and (3) allow a direct comparison between conditions that
should result in visual coding with those conditions that should result in
subvocal coding. This was deemed necessary not only to support the existence of visual imagery (which is intuitively obvious to most humans,
though not to all—see Neisser, 1970), but also to develop tools to measure
the characteristics of visual imagery and its relationships to other memory
processes.

II. THE SEARCH FOR VISUAL
MEMORY

A. The Use of Shadowing as a Distractor Task

1. General Experimental Procedure

The voice of a practiced female reader was recorded reading letters
of the alphabet at a rate of 2/sec. The subjects were then taught to shadow
this recording. ("To shadow" means to say the letter being heard over
earphones; there is typically a 2-letter lag between hearing and saying a
letter.) The subjects were given practice shadowing until they reached
about 80% accuracy. This level of accuracy means that the subject is good
enough so there will be no large gaps in the shadowing, but not so good
that shadowing has become completely automatic and requiring little or
no attention.

After the subject reached the required proficiency in the shadow task,
the memory task was introduced. In the auditory memory letter (AML)
condition, a male-voiced letter was inserted into the shadow list; *i.e.,* a
female-voiced shadow letter was removed and replaced by the male-voiced
AML. The subject was instructed to shadow all letters, but to remember
only the male-voiced letter (the AML). In the visual memory letter (VML)
condition, a letter was flashed onto a screen while the subject was shadow-

ing. In this case, the subject was instructed to continue shadowing the female voice, which did not stop during VML presentation.

Mowbray (1964) had used this technique earlier, but with one notable difference. He had kept the auditory and visual conditions more analogous by presenting the shadow letters to one ear and the auditory memory stimulus to the other ear while the subject continued to shadow. Although this seems to make the conditions more equivalent logically, in fact it makes them less equivalent. As Mowbray admitted, the presentation of two simultaneous auditory signals—one to shadow and one to remember—results in a very poor perception of the AML. Consequently, in Mowbray's procedure the subject often did not hear the AML properly. The current procedure (replacing a shadow letter with a differentiated memory letter) results in nearly equal perception. If anything, initial perception should slightly favor the AML because the subject both hears and says it, while the VML is seen only while hearing and saying other letters.

2. Rationale of the Shadow Experiments

The following assumptions were made: (1) On most trials, the memory letter must be rehearsed during the retention interval to protect this memory letter from the proactive interference built up over previous trials. (The proactive interference observed in these experiments will be discussed in detail in Section III-B-2.) (2) The shadow task requires considerable attention and, therefore, ordinarily (exceptions will be discussed below) precludes recoding the memory stimulus into a different mode. Thus the memory stimulus is most often rehearsed in the same form in which it was received; *i.e.,* visual imagery is used to rehearse VMLs and auditory imagery is used to rehearse AMLs. (3) Both types of rehearsals require the subject's attention, and thus compete with the ongoing shadow task. The auditory code of the AML has the additional disadvantage of being similar to the shadow task. This similarity should cause confusions that result in more mutual interference between shadow and memory tasks with an AML than with a VML. One would therefore predict that trials with VMLs would result in both better memory and better shadow performance.

3. Basic Findings

The first experiment in the series (Kroll, Parks, Parkinson, Bieber, & Johnson, 1970) used only a single memory letter per trial. The letter was presented either visually or auditorily and tested at retention intervals of 1, 10, and 25 sec. At the 1-sec retention interval, subjects recalled VMLs and AMLs equally well (96.5% for VMLs, 96.0% for AMLs), suggesting that they were perceived equally well. However, the AMLs were forgotten at a much faster rate and after the 25-sec retention interval, recall of the AMLs had dropped to 40% while the recall of VMLs had dropped to only 68.6%. As predicted, subjects also made more errors in their shadow task during the retention intervals following AMLs than those following VMLs.

Nearly every subject shows this effect and reports seeing the VML during the retention interval. There are, however, a few exceptions. A very small percentage of subjects in this type of task report subvocal rehearsal of the VML, and their performance with VMLs is typically as poor as with AMLs. Another small percentage report the ability to visualize even the AML and they usually do very well in both VML and AML conditions. Most subjects report associating occasionally, usually when the memory letter is an initial of their name or the name of a very close friend. In the early experiments of this series, very few subjects reported using associations to any great degree, but those who did performed very well in both conditions.

To summarize, this first experiment demonstrated that, if the subject is shadowing, visual memory letter presentations are recalled more accurately than are auditory presentations and that VMLs interfere less with the shadowing than do AMLs. Since this was precisely what was predicted on the basis of assuming the existence of both visual and auditory short-term memory processes, we were convinced that we had the tool that we wanted. However the prevailing degree of faith in the ubiquitous nature of subvocal recording, and the corresponding skepticism in the existence of visual imagery, seemed to necessitate the demonstration of: (1) the lack of contamination from any appreciable amount of subvocal recoding of the VMLs, and (2) the actual visual nature of the memory involved with the VMLs.

B. Testing for Subvocal Recoding of the Visual Memory Stimulus

As mentioned above, there have been three techniques developed to test for subvocal recoding: (1) acoustic intrusion errors, (2) acoustic intra-item interference, and (3) acoustic interference from distractor tasks. We have not designed experiments specifically to use the first two tests, but we have looked at the existing data from a number of our experiments for applicable patterns. With respect to acoustic intrusions, for example, we combined the data from many of our shadow experiments that required the recall of single memory letters. We found some tendency for subjects, when incorrectly recalling an AML, to respond with a letter that sounded like the memory letter (e.g., responding "B" when the AML was "V"); there was absolutely no such tendency when attempting to recall VMLs. This comparison did not seem too exciting, however, since even for the AMLs the tendency was quite weak.

We have very little data pertaining to intra-item interference since we always try to minimize acoustic similarity within a multiple-letter memory stimulus. Our memory stimuli thus have very little variability along this dimension. What little evidence we do have suggests that intra-item acoustic similarity has no effect on the memory of either AML combinations or VML combinations. This is not surprising since even experiments designed specifically to measure this effect have difficulty in finding it within the distractor task paradigm (*e.g.,* Adams, Thorsheim, & McIntyre, 1969a, 1969b).

The third method of testing for subvocal memory codes—acoustic interference from the distractor task—seemed the most relevant to the shadow experiments. Our first experiment in this series (Kroll *et al.*, 1970) had half the shadow lists with no letters acoustically similar to the memory letters with which they were paired, while the other half of the shadow lists did. A shadow list in the acoustically similar condition had approximately every third letter acoustically similar to the memory letter used on that same trial. In this experiment, there was no tendency for acoustic similarity to affect the recall of the VML while there was a tendency for the AML to be recalled less often when followed by the acoustically similar shadow list.

Since this interaction was not significant, we set out to replicate the effect. Our next series of attempts (Parkinson, Parks, & Kroll, 1971, Experiment III), was eventually successful but the interpretation was much more complicated than one would like. This was because we had, knowingly, confounded the acoustic similarity between shadow letters and memory letters with the acoustic similarity within the shadow list itself, under the assumption that this latter variable would not affect memory. It happens to have a very large effect, which will be discussed below (Section III-B-1). With respect to the immediate question, however, a demonstration of a large, significant, and clear-cut interaction between the effects of presentation modality (VML *vs.* AML) and acoustic similarity between shadow list and memory letter was still needed. Our third attempt (Salzberg, Parks, Kroll, & Parkinson, 1971) proved to be the charm. In this experiment, to prevent any possible confounding like those encountered in the Parkinson *et al.* (1971) series, the same memory letters and the exact same recordings of shadow lists were used in both high and low acoustically similar conditions. Only the paring of memory letter to shadow list differentiated the conditions. Thus a shadow list containing "A" and "J" would be a high similarity list if paired with the memory letter "K," but that same list would be a low similarity list if paired with the memory letter "S."

The design contained an additional variable. In the previous experiments, it appeared that acoustic similarity had its greatest interference effect when the shadow letters similar to the AML occurred within the first 5 or 6 sec of the retention interval. To determine if this were true, and to increase the sensitivity of the experiment in case it were, this experiment divided the high-similarity lists into two conditions: half the lists had the letters that were acoustically similar to the memory letter appear very early in the retention interval, and the other half had them appear very late.

This experiment found that the only interference effect due to acoustic similarity between memory letters and shadow letters is with AMLs, and then only if the acoustically similar shadow letters appear soon after the memory letter. The most important finding here is the complete lack of acoustic interference on the VML. The pattern of acoustic interference with the AML is also interesting, however, and will be reconsidered during the discussion of auditory memory (Section III-A-2).

C. Testing the "Visual" Nature of Memory

While the experiments reported above seem to rule out subvocal coding as the method of remembering the VMLs, they do not, except for the subjects' introspective reports, demonstrate that the VMLs are, in fact, remembered visually—only that they are remembered differently than are the AMLs. There are a number of alternative explanations that could easily explain the results thus far. For example, perhaps VMLs are more easily associated with words and thereby remembered better. As a matter of fact, this has been shown to be a serious consideration in some experiments (e.g., Adams et al., 1969a).

Another possibility, suggested by several colleagues, is that these shadow experiments were simply extensions of the von Restorff effect. The traditional method of obtaining the von Restorff effect is to ask the subject to remember a list of items, most of which are very similar to one another, but at least one of which is markedly different from the rest. The unique (or isolated) item is found to be remembered better than it would have been in a list in which it was not unique (see Wallace, 1965, for a recent review). It has been suggested that the shadow experiment may accomplish a similar result by isolating the memory letter from the shadow letters. The difficulty with this explanation is that the von Restorff effect is not well understood and may itself involve visual imagery. Nevertheless, this possibility does throw doubt upon our interpretation of the shadow experiments.

What is needed, then, is a method of directly demonstrating that the memory of the VML is based on a visual image. The Posner and Keele (1967) reaction-time technique seems to be ideally suited for this demonstration. While this experiment found that the visual memory trace disappeared within 2 sec, they suggested it would last longer if there were a way to entice the subject into retaining it. In fact, later evidence obtained by Posner and his students (Posner, Boies, Eichelman, & Taylor, 1969, Experiment III; Boies, 1970, Experiment II) suggested that the visual trace was still strong after a retention interval of 2 sec when subjects were given sufficient incentive to maintain their visual trace.

Unfortunately, they did not use retention intervals longer than 2 sec. However, both they (Posner *et al.*, 1969, Experiment IV) and Tversky (1969) provided convincing demonstrations that subjects can construct visual images (or, alternatively, recall these visual images from a long-term store) and then base decisions on these images. From these experiments, it seems very likely that, with the proper incentive, subjects could maintain visual images over the 5–60-sec intervals typically used in short-term memory experiments. We believed, obviously, that the shadow task provided such an incentive because it made subvocal recoding so inefficient. Therefore the reaction time superiority of case-same pairs (*e.g.*, "A" and "A") over case-different pairs (*e.g.*, "a" and "A") should remain over much longer retention intervals than 2 sec if the time between memory letter and test letter presentations were filled with shadowing. Our first attempt (Parks, Kroll, Salzberg, & Parkinson, 1972) found this to be the case.[3]

Not only should there be a difference in reaction time, there should also be a difference in errors between trial types. If the subject is responding on the basis of physical shape on the case-same trials, then he might mistakenly respond "false" (*i.e.*, "different name") on those name-same trials where the case changes (*e.g.*, "a" to "A"). There is no analogous situation with the trials where the names are actually different. Thus there should be more errors with the name-same, case-different trials than with any of the other types of trials—all of which should be nearly equal. This is exactly what was found.

There is a danger involved when using the reaction time procedure to test the visual nature of the memory involved in the general shadow task experiment: recognition may not be testing the same memory processes as recall. One indication that it is, at least within the shadow experiments, is

---

[3] Reaction time experiments require many trials because: (1) reaction times for the error responses are obviously not considered in the analysis, and, more important, (2) half of the trials must be name-different trials, which also do not contribute to the most important comparison. Consequently, to save time and to prevent the subject from obtaining too much shadow practice, the longest retention interval used in these experiments was 8 sec. Since the effects were still strong at this retention interval, which is four times as long as the longest used previously, this seemed sufficient for our purposes.

the finding that the error rates, when corrected for guessing, are the same for recall and recognition tests (Parkinson *et al.*, 1971, Experiments I and II; Parks *et al.*, 1972).[4]

1. A Further Test of "Visual" Memory

M. H. Kellicutt devised an even more stringent test of visual memory. If the memory traces used by the subjects do indeed maintain the form of the memory letters, then any procedure that makes naming the letters more difficult, while not affecting the visual complexity, should increase both reaction time and error rate differences between case-same and case-different conditions. The procedure here is essentially the same as in the Posner and Keele paradigm except that in half of the trials both memory and test letters are presented backward (*i.e.*, in mirror image), while in the other half of the trials, both memory and test letters are presented forward. (The subject is never asked to compare backward memory letters with forward test letters or vice versa. Either both memory and test letters are backward or both are forward. See Fig. 6-1.)

Being backward should make the letters more difficult to read and, therefore, name-same, case-different trials—where the subject is forced to read—should increase in difficulty. This increased difficulty should result in slower reaction times and more errors than in the analogous forward condition. However, since it is assumed that in the name-same, case-same condition the subjects are relying primarily on a comparison between memory and perceptual forms and are not reading the letters, there should be little or no difference between forward and backward.

The pattern of results in the initial experiment (Kellicutt, Parks, Kroll, & Salzberg, 1973) was close to the above predictions. The error data fit the prediction precisely: same number of errors for forward and backward letters under the name-same, case-same condition; more errors with backward than with forward letters under the name-same, case-different condition. The reaction time data did show the expected interaction; *i.e.*, the difference between backward and forward was greater under the name-same, case-different condition than under the name-same, case-same condition. However, contrary to predictions, the difference between forward and backward letters was significant even under the name-same, case-same condi-

---

[4] The corrected error rate has been equivalent for recognition and recall experiments, except for the name-same, case-different recognition trials where the error rate is actually higher than predicted from the recall data. This discrepancy is probably due to the reason discussed above; *i.e.*, the subject, attempting to respond as quickly as possible, responds on the basis of the physical difference rather than on the basis of the same name.

| FORWARD CONDITION | | NAME | CASE | BACKWARD CONDITION | |
MEMORY PAIR	TEST PAIR			MEMORY PAIR	TEST PAIR
Gr	Gr	SAME	SAME	ıפ	ıפ
gR	Gr	SAME	DIFFERENT	Яפ	ıפ
Xr	Gr	DIFFERENT	SAME	ıX	ıפ
xR	Gr	DIFFERENT	DIFFERENT	Яx	ıפ

Fig. 6-1. Examples of trial types used in the Kellicutt *et al.* (1973) experiment. In this experiment a pair of letters was used for the memory stimulus and a second pair for the test stimulus. The subject was instructed to press the "same" key if the names of the test pair were the same as the names of the memory pair, and to press the "different" key if one of the letters in the test pair had a different name from those in the memory pair. The forward and backward trials were blocked and run on separate days.

tion. We suspected that this unexpected difference was caused either by the subjects occasionally double-checking their visual match with a name match, or, alternatively, that even fundamental perceptual processes may be slower for unfamiliar stimuli (Egeth & Blecker, 1971). We therefore gave subjects a great deal more experience with the reaction time task and found that the reaction time difference between forward and backward letters disappeared under the name-same, case-same condition, while the rest of the pattern remained as in the main experiment. (See Figs. 6-2 and 6-3.)

2. How "Visual" Is Visual Memory?

The above experiments demonstrate that the visual form of the memory letters is retained over the 8-sec retention interval when shadowing is used as a distractor task. Our present ongoing series of experiments is designed to discover: (1) which visual properties are maintained automatically as an essential component of the visual image, (2) which can be maintained or discarded, depending on the demands of the task, and (3) which, if any, are exceedingly difficult or impossible to maintain.

For example, size and orientation (*i.e.*, upright, slanted left, slanted right) are both compounded with form and should, therefore, be essential components of the visual memory image. However, with the use of long-term memory, the subject should be able to transform the trace of the memory stimulus into an image with that form, size, and orientation that is most easily compared with the expected test stimulus. Indeed, this has been shown to be the case with form (Posner *et al.*, 1969; Tversky, 1969; Cruse & Clifton, 1973) and is believed to occur when subjects compare

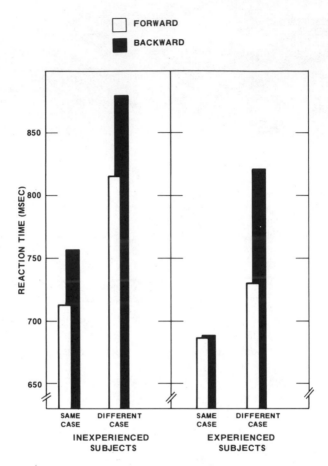

Fig. 6-2. Average reaction times for inexperienced and experienced subjects in the Kellicutt *et al.* (1973) experiment.

stimuli at two different orientations (*e.g.*, Shepard & Metzler, 1971). One interesting and testable possibility is that, in the absence of any information about the orientation of the test stimulus, the subject will rotate the visual image of a slanted memory stimulus so that it can be maintained (perhaps stored or rehearsed) in the more familiar upright orientation.

The color of a stimulus seems to be sufficiently independent of its form that the subject would not necessarily preserve the color if only the form were relevant. Well and Green (1972), using simultaneous comparisons, found that "same" judgments (for either form or name identity) were slowed when the letters compared were of different colors. Using this tech-

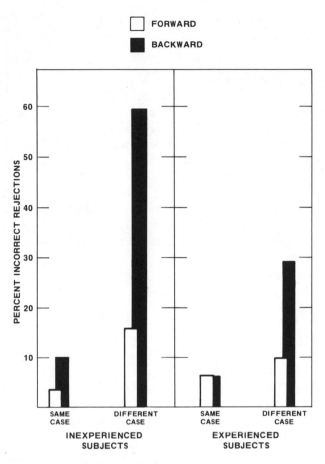

Fig. 6-3. Percent incorrect rejection for inexperienced and experienced subjects in the Kellicutt *et al.* (1973) experiment.

nique with a retention interval, we have found that a change in the irrelevant color dimension slows "same" judgments with short retention intervals (0.8-sec), but does not affect the reaction time of "same" judgments with longer (8-sec) intervals between memory and test stimuli. It is as if the subject does not maintain the irrelevant (and distracting) color information. However, when subjects are forced to retain the color of the memory letters (*i.e.,* they are instructed to recall the color after making their "same" or "different" name response), the color variable has the same effect at 8 sec that it did at 0.8 sec. Under this latter condition, it is as if the color is maintained as part of the visual memory image (Kroll, Kelli-cutt, Berrian, & Kreisler, 1974).

III. LEVELS OF MEMORY

Having concluded that there are memory processes that do have visual properties, the next step is to see how they operate. In terms of multistore models (*e.g.*, Broadbent, 1958; Waugh & Norman, 1965; Sperling, 1967; Atkinson & Shiffrin, 1968; Crowder & Morton, 1969), one would like to know which stages of memory are involved with visual imagery. In terms of information processing models (*e.g.*, Norman, 1968; Cermak, 1972, Chapter 12; Craik & Lockhart, 1972), one would like to know how processing the visual information of the memory stimulus compares and interacts with other forms of processing. Consequently, this discussion will now turn to a theoretical development of the levels of processing involved in the distractor-task memory experiment.

A. Preattentive Memory Processes

The first stage of most multistore memory models is concerned with initial registration of the stimulus information. Atkinson and Shiffrin (1968) have referred to these processes as the "sensory registers." This has also been referred to as the "precategorical" level of processing, which Crowder and Morton defined as follows:

> At the precategorical level, we suppose that there is no effective connection between the visual and auditory stores and that performance . . . of these stores will be describable in terms of purely "sensory" psychology. Of course, it is inevitable that within these preperceptual stores there will be some information reduction with respect to the original stimulus, *at least* information reduction deriving from the limited resolving power of the receptor (Neisser, 1967, p. 200). *At most,* information [at the precategorical level] could be processed and coded to the level of feature analysis. . . . [I]nformation stored precategorically is raw in the sense of not yet having made contact with [the subject's] overlearned linguistic repertoire; however it may well not be completely unprocessed information [1969, p. 366].

For reasons discussed in Section III-A-2, the term "precategorical" is unfortunate since some sort of categorization, or identification, does seem to be a necessary component in some instances. The term "sensory register" also seems too restrictive for the requirements of the immediate discussion. Hence the term "preattentive stores" will be used here, its features being:

(1) As the name suggests, the preattentive stores do not *require* attention, although it will be assumed that one may attend to a particular preattentive store and, in fact, must do so if the information is to be processed and stored more permanently.

(2) Information in the preattentive stores decays fairly rapidly. The rate of decay may be different for the various sensory modalities.

(3) The information in the preattentive stores may also be distorted, or masked, by new stimulation to the same sensory receptor, even if that new information does not require processing.

(4) The preattentive stores themselves are little affected by ongoing information processing; i.e., information stays in the preattentive store for approximately the same time regardless of whether the individual is doing nothing, thinking through a mathematics problem, or whatever, as long as the external stimulation is held constant across conditions of mental activity.

1. Preattentive Visual Storage (PVS)

Coltheart (1972) has an excellent review of this storage system with a thorough documentation of features (1) through (3) above. For an investigation of feature (4), see Doost and Turvey (1971).

The purpose of this discussion of the PVS is to note that its role in the shadowing experiments is probably quite small. While the PVS decays very rapidly and is usually gone by 2 sec—and certainly by 5 sec (Averbach & Sperling, 1961, Part I)—the shadow experiments find evidence of strong visual memory even after 25 sec (Kroll *et al.*, 1970). While the PVS is subject to masking by later visual stimulation, the visual memory in the shadow experiments does not seem to show any tendency of being so affected (Parkinson, Kroll, & Parks, 1973).

2. Preattentive Acoustic Storage (PAS)

Processes Involved in PAS. Unlike the PVS, which can receive and briefly store a great deal of independent information in a simultaneous fashion (*i.e.*, an array of letters), the PAS is pretty much limited to dealing with sequentially presented stimuli. This limitation seems reasonable since several acoustic stimuli received in the same ear at the same time are likely to distort one another. Another major difference between the modalities is that the PAS seems to be "capable of holding information sufficiently long enough to affect [*i.e.*, improve] the immediate memory . . . at least on the order of a few seconds" (Crowder & Morton, 1969, p. 366). Their evidence for this statement comes from a series of experiments on the recency portion of the serial position curve obtained from the immediate recall of a serial list. Massaro (1972, pp. 140–142) has argued that these experiments are not dealing with precategorical storage since "each item in the serial list presentation should have been identified before the following item is presented" (p. 140). Because of this, Massaro believes that Crowder and Morton are studying short-term memory rather than what he calls preperceptual memory. In fact, the recency effect of immediate recall is considered by many to be a relatively pure measure of short-term memory (see Craik, 1971, p. 233). The term "short-term memory" has an unfortunately large number of inconsistent usages. If, however, short-term memory processes are concerned with attention, rehearsals, and other cognitive processes, as many models assume (*e.g.*, Atkinson & Shiffrin, 1971), then this disagreement is more than just a problem of semantics. It is, rather, a fundamental disagreement over the memory processes at work.

Since the subject is clearly attending to the information presented in the Crowder and Morton experiments, at least at time of input, it is somewhat difficult to argue from those experiments that the memory being studied does not depend on attention. It is more difficult to claim that attention is playing a role in the following experiment. Glucksberg and Cowen (1970) had their subjects shadowing the message being played to one ear while a digit was sometimes embedded in the unattended message being played to the other ear. This technique was devised to prevent the subject from attending to the digit at the time of input and, on the basis of subjective reports, it appeared to be quite successful in doing so. With this technique—which not only prevented attention but also provided a great deal of potentially distorting stimulation to the PAS—they found evidence suggesting that the PAS lasted as long as 5.3 sec. This is certainly longer than the PVS has been found to last even in the absence of distorting or masking stimulation.

Assuming that Crowder and Morton (1969) and Glucksberg and Cowen (1970) are both studying the same memory process, this process does seem to qualify as PAS. It is preattentive (*i.e.*, does not *require* attention), it is subject to masking by new stimulation to the same sensory receptor (Crowder & Morton, 1969; Morton, 1970), and it is relatively unaffected by ongoing information processing (Bryden, 1971).

Does this mean that this long lasting PAS system is truly precategorical as Crowder and Morton suggest? [5] Probably not. There are a number of reasons to believe that a great deal of processing, including some categorization, *i.e.*, interaction with linguistic memory, has taken place in order for the PAS to last this long. For one thing, only familiar speech sounds (vowels) seem to be so retained (*e.g.*, Crowder, 1971) and only new

---

[5] In fact, the "p" in *their* PAS was for "precategorical" rather than "preattentive." The latter term comes from Neisser, 1967.

speech sounds can mask the information being so stored (Crowder & Morton, 1969). In other words, Massaro may be correct when he states that stimuli must be "identified" in order to be held longer than 250 msec; however, he is probably incorrect when he assumes that this identification *of speech sounds* requires attention. One possibility is that this longer-lasting PAS includes an abstraction process that may require attention in the very young, but—perhaps through the demands of speech—becomes an overlearned "subroutine" that no longer requires attention in the adult. One indication of the degree of processing of speech sounds that is possible without attention (or, at most, with very minimal attention) is seen in the experiment by Corteen and Wood (1972). They demonstrated that subjects in a dichotic listening situation give autonomic responses to words that had been previously associated with electric shock, even though the subjects were not aware of the words (as measured by subjective reports and by errors in shadowing the attended message).[6]

What this might suggest is that there are a number of different processes involved in preattentive memory. Perhaps when sequential linguistic stimuli are presented to normal, mature humans, a great deal of processing can occur automatically (*i.e.,* with little or no demand on attention) if these stimuli are presented auditorily. As a result of this automatic processing, auditorily presented linguistic information remains available for a number of seconds even in the absence of initial awareness. If these stimuli are presented visually and sequentially, attention may be required to process them to the level of obtaining any of the linguistic information. This would help to account for the typical finding of an advantage of auditory presentation when memory over short time periods is measured—particularly when there are fairly heavy attentional demands. One might argue that most of us also have a tremendous amount of experience with visually presented linguistic information through reading and, therefore, there should be similar, nearly-automatic processes involved with reading. Reading, however, is probably a poor analogy to listening since the linguistic information is typically being registered in much larger "chunks"; *i.e.,* entire words and even phrases are observed simultaneously. Thus any automatic linguistic processing of visual material may be much more likely to take place with simultaneous than with sequential presentation. One far-fetched but interesting possibility is that the deaf, forced to deal with sequential hand signals rather than speech signals, may "overlearn" a visual abstraction process with properties similar to those of the PAS.

---

[6] Corteen has since replicated this finding several times (personal communication). Unfortunately, Mr. Kirk Wardlaw and I have been attempting to reproduce the effect in our laboratory for the past year and a half without success.

PAS in Shadow Experiments. Parkinson (1972) extended our basic experiment on memory while shadowing (Kroll *et al.*, 1970) by using more than a single memory letter. Trials with one, two, three, and four memory letters were used with auditory and with visual memory letter presentation. The AMLs were presented at a rate of 2/sec in place of the female-voiced shadow letters. As with earlier experiments, VMLs were presented while the subject shadowed different, female-voiced letters. There were two methods of visual presentations. The sequential VMLs were presented at a rate of 2/sec with an on-time of approximately 0.2 sec each. The simultaneous VMLs were presented together for 0.5 sec. Two retention intervals were used: 1 sec and 20 sec. With the 20-sec interval, the VMLs were recalled better under simultaneous than under sequential presentation. (This is usually the case; see Mackworth, 1962.) Even the sequential VMLs were recalled better than the AMLs and the degree of superiority appeared to be the same for 1, 2, 3, and 4 memory letters. What was surprising, however, was that with only a 1-sec retention interval, AMLs were recalled better than VMLs, especially on the trials with four memory letters.

It was assumed that the superior recall of AMLs at the short retention interval was due to the PAS. The next experiment (Kroll, Parkinson, & Parks, 1972) was an attempt to chart the effects of PAS while shadowing. In this experiment, there were 5 memory letters and four different retention intervals of 0, 2, 6, or 20 sec. In addition to the usual blocks of VML trials and AML trials, there was also a block of trials where the memory letters were presented both visually and auditorily (V + AMLs). On these trials, the visual representation of each memory letter flashed on the screen at approximately the same time that the male voice was saying that letter.

The following assumptions and predictions were made concerning the memory processes involved with each method of memory letter presentation: (1) AMLs: The PAS should last for approximately 5 sec (Glucksberg & Cowen, 1970), but the subject should find it very difficult to rehearse the AMLs while shadowing (Kroll, *et al.,* 1970). Therefore, recall of AMLs should be good at the short retention intervals, but very poor at the longer retention intervals. (2) VMLs: The PVS should be so short as to play virtually no role (Averbach & Sperling, 1961; Parkinson *et al.*, 1973), but it should be relatively easy to rehearse the visual stimulus even while shadowing (*e.g.,* Parks, *et al.,* 1972). Therefore, recall at the shorter retention intervals should be poorer than for AMLs, but it should not drop much lower with longer retention intervals, resulting in better recall than for AMLs at the longer retention intervals. (3) V + AMLs: It is assumed that the PAS is relatively independent of attention, while the visual rehearsals are an attentional process. Therefore, at extremely short retention intervals, it should be possible to predict the probability of recalling the V + AMLs from the simple additive formula: P(V + A) = P(V) + P(A) − P(V)P(A), where P(V) and P(A) are the probabilities associated with the subject recalling the VMLs and the AMLs, respectively. With longer retention intervals, the subjects should continue to renew the visual memory trace via visual rehearsals, but not attempt to renew the auditory memory trace. The lack of AML rehearsal here is expected because the AMLs are completely redundant to the VMLs, which are easier to renew while shadowing. Therefore, as the retention intervals get longer, the advantage that V + AMLs have over VMLs should decrease until eventually (*i.e.,* beyond the duration of PAS) memory for V + AMLs should equal that for VMLs.

TABLE 6-1

Percentage of Correct Responses Observed under Visual, Auditory, and Visual + Auditory Conditions[a]

Condition	0 sec	2 sec	6 sec	20 sec
Observed				
P(V)	69	56	47	47
P(A)	91	72	46	35
P(V + A)	96	81	57	49
Predicted[b]				
P(V + A)′	97	88	71	66
P(V + A)′ − P(V + A)	1	7	14	17
P(V) − P(V + A)	−22	−25	−10	−2
Estimated[c]				
PAS	87	57	19	4

[a] (Kroll, Parkinson, & Parks, 1972)
[b] $P(V + A)' = P(V) + P(A) - P(V)P(A)$.
[c] $PAS = \dfrac{P(V + A) - P(V)}{1.00 - P(V)}$.

Table 6-1 presents the results of this experiment. As predicted, the recall of V + AMLs is very close to that predicted by the additive model at immediate recall, but is much closer to the recall of VMLs by the 20-sec retention interval. The last line of Table 6-1 estimates the role played by the PAS in the recall of V + AMLs, and these points are plotted in Fig. 6-4. Using the intersection of the line through the 0-, 2-, and 6-sec points with a horizontal line through the 20-sec point, the PAS was estimated to last approximately 7 sec. (See Fig. 6-4.) This is somewhat longer than the estimate obtained by Glucksberg and Cowen, but then this experiment: (1) did not provide as much masking stimulation (*e.g.,* the shadow message was in a different voice and both ears were hearing the same message),

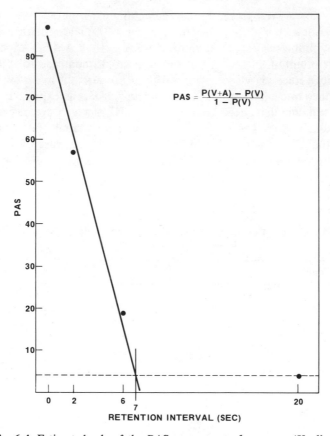

$$PAS = \frac{P(V+A) - P(V)}{1 - P(V)}$$

Fig. 6-4. Estimated role of the PAS component of memory (Kroll *et al.*, 1972).

and (2) allowed for subject to attend to the memory stimulus during presentation. All things considered, the agreement seems reasonable.

B. Active and Long-Term Memory Processes

Those memory processes requiring a great deal of attention will be called "active memory." It will be assumed that, when working with familiar memory stimuli in a typical short-term memory task (*e.g.*, one using a distractor technique), active memory is primarily concerned with "activating" various long-term memory codes relevant to the memory stimuli being used on that particular trial. In this situation, the major function of rehearsal (*i.e.*, thinking about the memory stimuli in any way) is not to place the memory stimuli into long-term storage—in most cases it is already there—but is rather to differentiate the memory stimuli being used on this particular trial. There are, of course, even within these situations, additional functions of rehearsal depending upon the exact task: *e.g.*, maintaining the serial order information in a list of items. The functions of active memory when dealing with unfamiliar stimuli are certainly more complex, and probably more interesting, but beyond the scope of the present discussion.

Often it is easiest to differentiate the items being remembered by simply repeating them covertly during the retention interval; *i.e.*, rote rehearsal. The exact form of these rehearsals will depend on the prior experience of the subject, the way in which the memory stimuli are presented, and any other attentional demands placed on the subject concurrent with memory item presentation and/or retention. In some situations the subject will rehearse via a subvocal memory code, even if the memory stimulus is presented visually (*e.g.*, Conrad, 1964), while in others the subject will rehearse via visual imagery even though the memory stimulus is presented verbally (*e.g.*, Posner *et al.*, 1969). Since these modality transformations with familiar stimuli seem to be quite easy for most adults, experimenters wishing to study one particular form of rote rehearsal will have to do more than simply present the memory stimulus to the relevant modality.

While rote rehearsal is an easy way to differentiate the most recent memory stimulus (*i.e.*, an individual rote rehearsal requires minimal attentional time and effort), many such rehearsals are needed throughout the retention interval. In the terminology of Yntema and Trask (1963), the "time tag" or "recency tag" must be continually renewed if it is to serve any retrieval function. Regardless of the number of such rehearsals allowed, a short period without them results in rapid forgetting (*e.g.*, Meunier, Ritz, & Meunier, 1972). Associating memory letters with particular words (i.e., by using natural language mediators, NLMs, Prytulak, 1971) probably takes greater initial attentional investment, but it may pay off by requiring less frequent renewals. The more semantic processes brought into play, the less time-dependent is the differentiation (Baddeley, 1972).

The more primitive forms of preattentive storage, the sensory registers, are seen to be qualitatively different from active memory. The sensory registers, unlike active memory, do not require attention or long-term storage. However, preattentive storage is seen here as a continuum with the sensory registers at one end and with active memory just across the border from the opposite end. In between are a number of processes that require minimal attention—less as they are practiced more—but definitely interacting with long-term storage. Since preattentive storage is viewed as a continuum, the placement of the border between it and active memory is arbitrary. Thus it may often be more profitable to ask questions like "How much processing occurred?" and "What kind of processing was used?" than it would be to ask "Which 'box' is it in?"

In summary, the memory processes involved in the typical distractor technique are as follows: (1) preattentive processes last for a short time after presentation, typically much longer for auditory than for visual presentation. (These preattentive processes aid recall directly at the shorter retention intervals, but also aid recall at the longer retention intervals by extending the effective duration of the stimulus and, thereby, improving the quality of initial rehearsals.) (2) Long-term storage actually holds the information over the longer retention intervals. (3) Active (attentional) memory processes differentiate the relevant long-term traces from the many other traces held in long-term memory.

1. Sources of Retroactive Interference

At least two dimensions of a distractor task must be considered when studying its interfering influence on memory (Loess & McBurney, 1965). One is the similarity between the memory stimuli and the distractor task and the other is the degree of attentional involvement required by the distractor task.

Similarity between Memory and Distractor Tasks. Bower (1970, p. 506) found that a distractor task requiring visually guided tracking interfered more with learning by visual imagery than did a similar task requiring tactile-guided tracking. However the two tasks interfered equally when the learning was by rote repetition. Similarly, as mentioned earlier, acoustic similarity between the shadow letters and the names of the memory letters interferes with memory only if the memory letters are presented aurally (*e.g.,* Salzberg *et al.,* 1971). The primary cause of interference from a similar distractor task seems to be that the similar elements of the distractor task are confused with the rehearsals of the memory items. For example, Kroll (1972) presented subjects with three VMLs or three AMLs while they shadowed either numbers or letters. The memory of the VMLs was the same under both shadow conditions, presumably because the visual rehearsals were easily distinguishable from the auditory shadow task. The AMLs were remembered much better while shadowing numbers than while shadowing letters. The confusion between rehearsals of the AMLs and the shadow letters was also evident in the large number of intrusions of shadow letters when the subject attempted to recall the AMLs. Parenthetically, it should be noted that one advantage of using natural language mediators (NLMs) here is that they are more distinguishable from the shadow letters than are the memory letters themselves.

Attentional Demands of the Distractor Task. Since it is assumed that active memory requires attention, additional demands placed on attention by the distractor task should decrease the ability of active memory to rehearse. Thus we have found that, while the acoustic similarity between shadow letters and the names of the VMLs does not affect recall, the recall of VMLs *is* reduced by making the shadow letters more acoustically similar to one another since it makes them more difficult to shadow (Parkinson *et al.,* 1971). We have also found that subjects counting backwards by sevens not only remember less than subjects counting backwards by threes, they also report fewer rehearsals (Kroll & Kellicutt, 1972). When shadowing letters, however, subjects report the same number of rehearsals for VMLs and AMLs. The rehearsals just seem less effective for AMLs—probably because subvocal rehearsals are more easily confused with the shadow letters than are visual rehearsals (Kroll & Kellicutt, 1972, Experiment II).

One would also expect that the more difficult the distractor task, the more difficult it would be to use NLMs since, presumably, the act of associating also requires attention. Paradoxically, we have found in a number of pilot studies that if we make the distractor task too difficult, the subjects begin to report more, rather than fewer, NLMs. Subjective reports suggest that as the distractor task increases in difficulty, subjects find it more difficult to rehearse and they realize they are performing poorly. Once they do associate the memory letters with words (usually the initials of a familiar name), they are immediately struck by the much greater ease of semantic memory. After that they actively try for associations on most trials.

2. Sources of Proactive Interference

The memory model proposed above assumes that between rehearsals the memory trace is in long-term storage and that the major function of the rehearsals is to differentiate the relevant trace. If this is the case, a major cause of forgetting should be proactive interference from preceding memory items. In fact, one does find a build-up of proactive interference over trials using similar memory stimuli and a "release of interference" when a memory stimulus easily differentiated from earlier stimuli is presented (*e.g.,* Wickens, 1970; Gardiner, Craik, & Birtwistle, 1972). However attempts to demonstrate a release of interference resulting from a shift in sensory modality have been inconsistent in their results (*e.g.,* see Hopkins, Edwards, & Gavelek, 1971). As a result of these inconsistencies, it had been suggested that it might be necessary either to (1) drop the assumption that auditory and visual memory stimuli are encoded differently, or (2) drop the assumption that the release phenomenon measures important features of the memory code. Another possibility is that earlier attempts were not successful in getting their subjects to use memory codes isomorphic with the presentation modality. Since the use of shadowing as a distractor task seems generally to result in such isomorphic codes, Kroll, Bee, and Gurski (1973) used shadowing as the distractor task while measuring the effect of modality shift on proactive interference. A large release effect was found both for shifts from AMLs to VMLs and for shifts from VMLs to AMLs. A dramatic shift in the source of intrusions was also found, with large numbers of intrusions from the previous trial being made only when the previous trial had used the same presentation modality.

IV. CONCLUSIONS

The model of memory presented here is not new. It has all been said before by others. However it is hoped that this particular recombination of earlier thoughts, with its own angle of orientation, and with its own collection of supporting evidence, will be of some assistence in obtaining a fuller understanding of human memory. So far the model seems to handle extremely well those experiments using familiar memory stimuli in conjunction with the distractor technique. Our next task is to extend it to other techniques of studying short-term memory processes and to the recall of unfamiliar stimuli.

REFERENCES

Adams, J. A., Thorsheim, H. I., & McIntyre, J. S. Item length, acoustic similarity, and natural language mediation as variables in short-term memory. *Journal of Experimental Psychology,* 1969, **80,** 39–46. (a)

Adams, J. A., Thorsheim, H. I., & McIntyre, J. S. Short-term memory and acoustic similarity. *Psychonomic Science,* 1969, **15,** 77–78. (b)

Atkinson, R. C., & Shiffrin, R. M. Human memory: A proposed system and its control processes. In K. W. Spence & J. T. Spence (Eds.), *The psychology of learning and motivation: Advances in research and theory,* Vol. 2. New York: Academic Press, 1968.

Atkinson, R. C., & Shiffrin, R. M. The control processes of short-term memory. *Scientific American,* 1971, **225,** 82–90.

Averbach, E., & Sperling, G. Short-term storage of information in vision. In E. C. Cherry (Ed.), *Fourth London symposium on information theory.* London: Butterworths, 1961.

Baddeley, A. D. Retrieval rules and semantic coding in short-term memory. *Psychological Bulletin,* 1972, **78,** 379–385.

Boies, S. J. Retention of visual information from a single letter. Unpublished doctoral dissertation, University of Oregon, 1970.

Bower, G. H. Analysis of a mnemonic device. *American Scientist,* 1970, **58,** 496–510.

Broadbent, D. E. *Perception and communication.* Oxford: Pergammon Press, 1958.

Bryden, M. P. Attentional strategies and short-term memory in dichotic listening. *Cognitive Psychology,* 1971, **2,** 99–116.

Conrad, R. Acoustic confusions in immediate memory. *British Journal of Psychology,* 1964, **55,** 75–84.

Conrad, R., & Hull, A. J. Input modality and the serial position curve in short-term memory. *Psychonomic Science,* 1968, **10,** 135–136.

Cermak, L. S. *Human memory: Research and theory.* New York: Ronald, 1972.

Coltheart, M. Visual information-processing. In P. C. Dodwell (Ed.), *New Horizons in Psychology,* Vol. 2. Middlesex: Penguin, 1972.

Corteen, R. S., & Wood, B. Autonomic responses to shock-associated words in an un-attended channel. *Journal of Experimental Psychology,* 1972, **94,** 308–313.

Craik, F. I. M. Modality effects in short-term storage. *Journal of Verbal Learning and Verbal Behavior,* 1969, **8,** 658–664.

Craik, F. I. M. Primary memory. *British Medical Bulletin,* 1971, **27** (3), 232–236.

Craik, F. I. M., & Lockhart, R. S. Levels of processing: A framework for memory research. *Journal of Verbal Learning and Verbal Behavior,* 1972, **11,** 671–684.

Crowder, R. G. The sound of vowels and consonants in immediate memory. *Journal of Verbal Learning and Verbal Behavior,* 1971, **10,** 587–596.

Crowder, R. G., & Morton, J. Precategorical acoustic storage (PAS). *Perception and Psychophysics,* 1969, **5,** 365–373.

Cruse, D., & Clifton, C., Jr. Recoding strategies and the retrieval of information from memory. *Cognitive Psychology,* 1973, **4,** 157–193.

Dale, H. C. A., & Gregory, M. Evidence of semantic coding in short-term memory. *Psychonomic Science,* 1966, **5,** 75–76.

Doost, R., & Turvey, M. T. Iconic memory and central processing capacity. *Perception and Psychophysics,* 1971, **9,** 269–274.

Egeth, H., & Blecker, D. Differential effects of familiarity on judgments of sameness and difference. *Perception and Psychophysics,* 1971, **9,** 321–326.

Gardiner, J. M. Craik, F. I. M., & Birtwistle, J. Retrieval cues and release from pro-active inhibition. *Journal of Verbal Learning and Verbal Behavior,* 1972, **11,** 778–783.

Glucksberg, S., & Cowen, G. N., Jr. Memory for nonattended auditory material. *Cognitive Psychology,* 1970, **1,** 149–156.

Hopkins, R. H., Edwards, R. E., & Gavelek, J. R. Presentation modality as an encoding variable in short-term memory. *Journal of Experimental Psychology,* 1971, **90,** 319–325.

Kellicutt, M. H., Parks, T. E., Kroll, N. E. A., & Salzberg, P. M. Visual memory as indicated by the latency of recognition for normal and reversed letters, *Journal of Experimental Psychology,* 1973, **97,** 387–390.

Kintsch, W., & Buschke, H. Homophones and synonyms in short-term memory. *Journal of Experimental Psychology,* 1969, **80,** 403–407.

Kroll, N. E. A. Short-term memory and the nature of interference from concurrent shadowing. *Quarterly Journal of Experimental Psychology,* 1972, **24,** 414–419.

Kroll, N. E. A., Bee, J., & Gurski, G. Release of proactive interference as a result of changing presentation modality. *Journal of Experimental Psychology,* 1973.

Kroll, N. E. A., & Kellicutt, M. H. Short-term recall as a function of covert rehearsal and of intervening task. *Journal of Verbal Learning and Verbal Behavior,* 1972, **11,** 196–204.

Kroll, N. E. A., Kellicutt, M. H., Berrian, R. W., & Kreisler, A. F. The effects of irrelevant color changes on speed of visual recognition following short retention intervals. *Journal of Experimental Psychology,* 1974, **103,** 97–106.

Kroll, N. E. A., Parkinson, S. R., & Parks, T. E. Sensory and active storage of compound visual and auditory stimuli. *Journal of Experimental Psychology,* 1972, **95,** 32–38.

Kroll, N. E. A., Parks, T., Parkinson, S. R., Bieber, S. L., & Johnson, A. L. Short-term memory while shadowing: Recall of visually and of aurally presented letters. *Journal of Experimental Psychology,* 1970, **85,** 220–224.

Laughery, K. R. Computer simulation of short-term memory: A component decay model. In J. T. Spence & G. H. Bower (Eds.), *Advances in the psychology of learning and motivation research and theory,* Vol. 3. New York: Academic Press, 1969.

Laughery, K. R., & Pinkus, A. L. Short-term memory: Effects of acoustic similarity, presentation rate, and presentation mode. *Psychonomic Science,* 1966, **6,** 285–286.

Loess, H., & McBurney, J. Short-term memory and retention-interval activity. *Proceedings of the 73rd annual convention of the American Psychological Association,* 1965, 85–86.

Mackworth, J. F. The effect of display time on the recall of digits. *Canadian Journal of Psychology,* 1962, **16,** 48–54.

Massaro, D. W. Preperceptual images, processing time, and perceptual units in auditory perception. *Psychological Review,* 1972, **79,** 124–145.

Meunier, G. F., Ritz, D., & Meunier, J. A. Rehearsal of individual items in short-term memory. *Journal of Experimental Psychology,* 1972, **95,** 465–467.

Morton, J. A functional model of memory. In D. A. Norman (Ed.), *Models of human memory.* New York: Academic Press, 1970.

Mowbray, G. H. Perception and retention of verbal information presented during auditory shadowing. *Journal of the Acoustical Society of America,* 1964, **36,** 1459–1469.

Murdock, B. B., Jr. Modality effects in short-term memory: Storage or retrieval? *Journal of Experimental Psychology,* 1968, **77,** 79–86.

Murdock, B. B., Jr., & Walker, K. D. Modality effects in free recall. *Journal of Verbal Learning and Verbal Behavior,* 1969, **8,** 655–676.

Neisser, U. *Cognitive psychology.* New York: Appleton-Century-Crofts, 1967.

Neisser, U. Visual imagery as process and as experience. In J. S. Antrobus (Ed.), *Cognition and affect.* Boston: Little, Brown & Company, 1970.

Norman, D. A. Toward a theory of memory and attention. *Psychological Review,* 1968, **75,** 522–536.

Parkinson, S. R. Short-term memory while shadowing: Multiple-item recall of visually and of aurally presented letters. *Journal of Experimental Psychology,* 1972, **92,** 256–265.

Parkinson, S. R., Kroll, N. E. A., & Parks, T. E. Short-term retention of superimposed and of spatially distinct multi-letter visual arrays. *Memory and Cognition,* 1973, **1,** 301–303.

Parkinson, S. R., Parks, T. E., & Kroll, N. E. A. Visual and auditory short-term memory: Effects of phonemically similar auditory shadow material during the retention interval. *Journal of Experimental Psychology,* 1971, **87,** 274–280.

Parks, T. E., Kroll, N. E. A., Salzberg, P. M., & Parkinson, S. R. Persistence of visual memory as indicated by decision time in a matching task. *Journal of Experimental Psychology*, 1972, **92**, 437–438.

Posner, M. I., Boies, S. J., Eichelman, W. H., & Taylor, R. L. Retention of visual and name codes of single letters. *Journal of Experimental Psychology*, 1969, **79**, 1–16.

Posner, M. I., & Keele, S. W. Decay of visual information from a single letter. *Science*, 1967, **158**, 137–139.

Prytulak, L. S. Natural language mediation. *Cognitive Psychology*, 1971, **2**, 1–56.

Salzberg, P. M., Parks, T. E., Kroll, N. E. A., & Parkinson, S. R. Retroactive effects of phonemic similarity on short-term recall of visual and auditory stimuli. *Journal of Experimental Psychology*, 1971, **91**, 43–46.

Shepard, R., & Metzler, J. Mental rotation of three-dimensional objects. *Science*, 1971, **171**, 701–703.

Sperling, G. A. A model for visual memory tasks. *Human Factors*, 1963, **5**, 19–31.

Sperling, G. A. Successive approximations to a model for short-term memory. *Acta Psychologica*, 1967, **27**, 285–292.

Sperling, G., & Speelman, R. G. Acoustic similarity and auditory short-term memory: Experiments and a model. In D. A. Norman (Ed.), *Models of human memory*. New York: Academic Press, 1970.

Tversky, B. Pictorial and verbal encoding in a short-term memory task. *Perception and Psychophysics*, 1969, **6**, 225–233.

Wallace, W. P. Review of the historical, empirical, and theoretical status of the von Restorff phenomenon. *Psychological Review*, 1965, **63**, 410–424.

Waugh, N. C., & Norman, D. A. Primary memory. *Psychological Review*, 1965, **72**, 89–104.

Well, A. D., & Green, J. Effects of color differences in a letter matching task. *Psychonomic Science*, 1972, **29**, 109–110.

Wickens, D. D. Encoding categories of words: An empirical approach to meaning. *Psychological Review*, 1970, **77**, 1–15.

Yntema, D. B., & Trask, F. P. Recall as a search process. *Journal of Verbal Learn- and Verbal Behavior*, 1963, **2**, 65–74.

CHAPTER

7

VISUAL MEMORY PROCESSES IN DYSLEXIA[1]

GORDON STANLEY

[1] This project was supported in part by a grant from the Buckland Fund. The author is grateful to the Director of Special Services and the Psychology and Counseling Service of the Education Department of the State of Victoria for access to schools, and to Rodney Hall and Ida Kaplan, who collected the data. This chapter was prepared while the author was on study leave from the University of Melbourne and a visitor at the Center for Human Information Processing, University of California at San Diego.

181

I. INTRODUCTION

A. The Visual Information Processing Paradigm

The skill of reading normally involves the rapid sequential scanning of letters and groups of letters as the eye moves across and down the page. Such scanning provides the input to a visual recognition memory process. Although a vast literature exists on the psychological study of reading and its disorders (see Hartstein, 1971; Levin & Williams, 1970; Money, 1966; Vernon, 1960), the recent methodology and techniques associated with the study of human visual information processing (Haber, 1969a) provide a new focus for such study. The possible relevance of this approach has been noted (Young & Lindsley, 1970), but to date little direct research within this framework has been reported in the literature dealing with reading disorders.

Current conceptions of visual information processing (Haber, 1969b; Neisser, 1967; Sperling, 1963) imply that the information contained in a brief visual stimulus is represented in different forms at different times after stimulus offset. At first the image is retained in a high-capacity, short-lived storage referred to as the icon (Neisser, 1967) or visual information store (VIS). This VIS decays rapidly, usually disappearing in less than a second. An encoding process transfers a smaller, more manageable amount of this information into the next stage of the memory system, which is called primary memory (Waugh & Norman, 1965) or short-term memory (STM). The STM is more resistant to decay but of considerably more limited capacity. It is strengthened by rehearsal processes and lasts long enough to provide information for subsequent responding. From STM, information is transferred into long-term memory (LTM), a more or less permanent store from which information can be retrieved.

Clearly, learning to read will involve all three stages of the process. In terms of the distinctions just made, much of the previous literature on dyslexia has been concerned with aspects of the transfer from STM to LTM. The main emphasis of the research to be discussed here is on the earlier stages of processing, and in particular with the properties of VIS

and the transfer of information into STM. It is important to know whether
or not dyslexics manifest abnormalities at this level. Perhaps many of the
idiosyncratic features of dyslexic children are due to a basic deficit in the
early stages of information processing. Before pursuing this theme, two
preliminary discussions are necessary to introduce the experimental data.
First, the term *dyslexia* will be defined; second, some properties of VIS will
be considered.

B. The Concept of Dyslexia

Rudolph Berlin, a German ophthalmologist, initially introduced the
term to describe difficulty in the interpretation of written symbols by people
of otherwise average or above-average intelligence (Keeney, 1971). Since
that time the term has often been used to refer to any reading disability
without regard to other cognitive functions. For present purposes the following definition will be accepted (from World Federation of Neurology
Research Group on Developmental Dyslexia, 1968): "*Dyslexia:* A disorder in children, who, despite conventional classroom experience, fail to
attain the language skills of reading, writing, and spelling commensurate
with their intellectual abilities."

Much of the literature on dyslexia derives from case studies and
clinical experience with small samples. Disagreement over specific symp-
tomatology is undoubtedly related to the absence of appropriate control
groups to assess the extent to which presumed symptoms are unique. For
this reason the research by this author and associates at the University of
Melbourne has involved the use of a control group drawn from the same
schools as the dyslexic sample. For the data to be reported here, a sample
of 66 children, 33 dyslexics and 33 normals, was selected from four inner
suburban primary schools in the Melbourne area. Each of these schools
had a remedial teacher who selected the dyslexic children according to the
following criteria: (1) the children were to be characterized as having a
specific reading disability of 2.5 yr or greater while functioning at average
or better levels in other subjects, and (2) they were not to have any gross
behavioral problems or record of organic disorders. The controls were
selected by their class teachers as being average-to-bright students. Ages
ranged from 8 to 12 yr, the dyslexics having a mean age of 10.88 ± 1.27
yr and the controls 10.52 ± 1.28 yr. As a check on the level of cognitive
functioning in the two groups of children, a standard Piagetian test of con-
servation of quantity was administered. Forty-seven of the children con-
served quantity and there was no significant difference between the number
of conservers in the two groups. This, together with the finding that the two

groups performed at the same level on two spatial tests, provides evidence that the sample does meet the basic criteria of the classic concept of dyslexia.

C. Properties of VIS

Before considering the results obtained in comparing normal and dyslexic children on measures of VIS, some clarification of the concept is desirable. In particular it is important to discuss how VIS is measured and to know the extent to which its duration is affected by different stimulus conditions.

Averbach and Coriell (1961) and Sperling (1960) obtained evidence for the existence of VIS by presenting an overload of information in a brief visual display. Following termination of the display some milliseconds later, the subject was presented with a cue indicating which element or subset of elements he should report. The temporal limit of VIS was estimated from accuracy of performance, which was found to be a decreasing function of delay of the post-stimulus cue up to delays of 200–300 msec. Even greater delays were obtained with dark pre- and post-fields, suggesting that VIS is basically sensory in nature and dependent on stimulus factors (Averbach & Sperling, 1961).

Haber and his colleagues (Haber & Nathanson, 1968; Haber & Standing, 1969, 1970) developed alternative measures of VIS duration in which direct estimates of visual persistence were obtained. Three measures used to assess persistence were: (1) recycling flashes of low physical persistence and obtaining judgments of inter-flash persistence, (2) presentation of an oscillating outline figure through a narrow slit less than the width of the figure and measuring oscillation speeds at which the entire figure was visible, (3) adjusting the asynchrony of a flash and click so that the click in turn was made in phase with the onset and offset of the flash. Under normal room illumination the direct estimates of persistence yielded values around 250 msec. This value is close to that obtained in the research by Averbach and Sperling (1961).

Eriksen and Collins (1968) introduced another means of measuring VIS duration. They used two-part visual stimuli constructed so that each part by itself appeared as a random collection of dots. When superimposed, these two parts were seen as a three-letter nonsense syllable. Varying the temporal interval (ISI) between the presentation of the two stimulus halves resulted in decreasing perception of the nonsense syllable for ISIs in excess of 100 msec. They accounted for their results in terms of a psychological moment acting in conjunction with a decaying sensory trace. Depending on stimulus conditions, estimates of the duration of the psychological moment typically vary from 50 to 200 msec. (Kristofferson, 1965; Stroud, 1956; White, 1963). If VIS is considered in terms of this literature, then its duration would be somewhat less than suggested by the other techniques of measurement. Whatever the exact relationship between the two concepts, the temporal separation threshold appears to be a useful measure. As it implies a simple response criterion, it was used as a measure in the Melbourne project.

II. COMPARISONS BETWEEN DYSLEXICS AND NORMALS

A. VIS in Normals and Dyslexics

Using the sample of 33 normals and 33 dyslexics, we presented 2-part displays (Fig. 7-1) comprising the letters N and O, 2 halves of a cross, and a cross surrounded by a square (SQCR). The stimuli were displayed on a Hewlett-Packard oscilloscope with a P15 phosphor. The P15 phosphor fades to 1% relative brightness 10 μsec after intensification ceases, effectively eliminating phosphor persistence artifacts. Time parameters of the display were under the control of a PDP 11/20 computer. The children sat at a distance of approximately 37 cm from the screen, and the stimuli were 30 mm in height. Each part of the stimulus was presented for 20 msec with a variable-length ISI. Increments of ISI were made in 20 msec steps until criterion was reached. Two judgments were required: judgment of separation of the elements and identification of the separated elements. The children were given the option of either describing verbally or drawing exactly what they saw after each presentation. The criterion for the separation measure was the ISI at which two parts were first reported, and the identification criterion was the ISI for which the child could correctly identify the two separate parts of the display on three successive presentations.

In terms of VIS duration, the separation measure was considered to be the appropriate index because it requires less cognitive processing for a response than the identification measure. For this reason, identification thresholds will be considered under the topic of transfer from VIS to STM. The separation thresholds obtained with the two groups are shown in Table 7-1. An analysis of variance of this data yielded a significant difference between the groups ($F(1,192) = 9.41$, $p < .01$), nonsignificant differences between the tasks, and a nonsignificant task times group-interaction effect. The values for the normal children are close to those obtained by Eriksen and Collins (1968) for college students. John Ross, working with undergraduates and using similar computergraphic displays at the University of

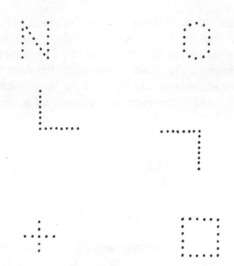

Fig. 7-1. The two-part stimuli used in the separation and identification tasks. The part on the right was spatially superimposed on the left part to produce the appearance of a spatially and temporally composite figure at short ISIs.

Western Australia, found that a 100-msec rule applied for the perception of configurality (personal communication, 1971). His 100 msec referred to onset-onset time rather than ISI, which means that the present sample of normal children required about 20 msec longer than his subjects for separation to occur.

As can be seen in Table 7-1, dyslexics as a group have about 30 to 50 msec longer separation times than have normals. In view of the non-independence of measures of VIS from stimulus conditions, it is probably most useful to express the longer values obtained with the dyslexics as a percentage of the normal value. On this basis it would seem that dyslexics have approximately 30–50% longer VIS duration than normals. Indirect support for the conclusion that dyslexics have longer VIS duration comes from a study by Zelhart and Johnson (1971), who found that a group of

TABLE 7-1
Mean Separation ISI (msec)

Task	Normals ($n = 33$)	Dyslexics ($n = 33$)
No	100.62	136.38
Cross	106.06	130.91
SQCR	101.82	154.55
Mean	102.82	140.61

poor readers performed significantly better than controls in a test for eidetic imagery. The measure of eidetic imagery used was a task dependent on visual persistence.

Having a greater duration may seem to be an advantage, but if the transfer from VIS to STM is also longer, then no advantage would occur. If VIS duration is related to eye fixation duration as suggested by Haber (1971), then long VIS should mean longer fixations. Evidence on eye-movements is somewhat equivocal, but dyslexics appear to take more fixations than normals as well as manifesting other abnormalities of eye-movement (Goldberg, 1968). Conceivably, some of the basic symptoms in dyslexia could be due to an asynchrony of fixation duration and VIS duration. We will return to this point later.

B. Transfer from VIS to STM

The identification durations on the no, cross, and SQCR tasks also differed between the two groups, as can be seen in Table 7-2. Analysis of variance yielded a significant difference ($F(1,192) = 12.54$, $p < .01$) between the groups, nonsignificant differences between the tasks and a non-significant task times group-interaction effect. Identification presumably involves some memory scan process and the transfer of information from VIS to STM. The implication of the present result is that the scan and retrieval process takes longer for dyslexics than for normals. Subtracting the separation ISI values from the identification ISI values shows that this stage of processing takes over twice as long for the dyslexics as for the normals. While these results are suggestive, the identification task is not a particularly satisfactory measure of transfer and processing rate. The sequential displays involve a certain amount of interference between the parts of the display, as indicated by the apparent movement effects spontaneously reported by the subjects. Probably, such effects would produce greater delay in processing. Another measure of transfer rate was developed by Sperling (1963).

Sperling (1963) argued that information is transferred from VIS in a serial manner. He assumed that for most alphabetical material, items would

TABLE 7-2
Mean Identification ISI (msec)

Task	Normals ($n = 33$)	Dyslexics ($n = 33$)
No	191.52	363.64
Cross	170.91	283.03
SQCR	184.85	334.55
Mean	182.42	327.07

be encoded in a left-to-right manner, so that features making up the farthest left letter of a string of letters would be processed first. This would be followed by naming of the letter, after which the next letter's features would be processed, and so on. The design adopted by Sperling to study the processing rate involved presentation of a linear array of letters for varying durations. This presentation was followed immediately by visual noise designed to erase or interfere with VIS, so that information transfer from it would cease. Sperling found that for each 10 msec during which the stimulus is available before it is masked, the subject is capable of processing one additional letter. Although there has been some argument as to the level of processing at which the mask operates (Liss, 1968; Spencer, 1969; Spencer & Shuntich, 1970), the evidence shows that masking limits the recovery of information.

   Two backward masking tasks were run with the dyslexic and control subjects (Fig. 7-2). In the first task one of the consonants C, F, H, J, K, M, R, or S was presented on the oscilloscope screen for 20 msec, followed by a dot mask pattern for 20 msec, with varying ISIs. For task 2, the letters U or O were presented, followed by the mask at varying ISIs. The order of presentation of the consonants was random, as was the order of the U or O. The ISI was incremented and the dependent variable was the ISI at which the subject could correctly identify a particular letter on three successive presentations. The children were told that they would be shown a letter that would be covered up with dots and their task was to tell which letter had been shown. For neither masking task were the children told which stimuli to expect. The mean ISI for the normals on the consonant masking task was 56 msec, and that of the dyslexics was 64 msec. On the U and O masking task, the main ISIs were 92 and 122 msec, respectively. Analysis of variance indicated a significant difference between groups ($F(1,128) = 29.22$, $p < .01$), a significant task difference ($F(1,128) = 5.00$, $p < .05$), and nonsignificant interaction.

   Hence the results from the masking tasks also indicate that dyslexics have a slower processing time than normals. The significant task difference may be due to higher confusability in recognizing U and O compared to the consonants. Note that the values obtained are much longer than the 10 msec obtained by Sperling (1963). However, Sperling reported that pre-adaptation of the subject influenced the time at which processing began. For example, with a pre-field of visual noise it takes the subject 20 to 30 msec before processing begins. Hence without systematic manipulation of this variable, the present results should not be taken as an index of absolute rate of processing, but rather as an indication of the relative differences in rate of processing between normals and dyslexics.

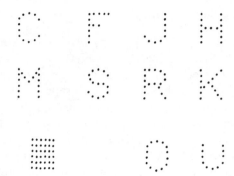

Fig. 7-2. The letter set and masker used in the masking experiment.

C. STM Differences between Normals and Dyslexics

Although there are many possible measures of STM functioning, the visual sequential memory (VSM) and auditory sequential memory (ASM) tasks from the revised Illinois Test of Psycholinguistic Abilities were used with both the normal and dyslexic samples. In the VSM task the child is shown a sequence card displaying symmetrical but unfamiliar geometric forms. The sequence is shown for 5 sec and then removed. Next the child is given a set of plastic chips in a disarrayed order and asked to reproduce the original sequence. The ASM test is essentially a digit span task in which a sequence of digits is read to the child who is required to repeat the sequence in the correct order.

The mean VSM score for the dyslexics was 17.85 and that for the normals 21.85, the difference being significant ($t = 4.40$, $p < .05$). Similarly, the mean ASM score for the dyslexics was 31.00 and that for the normals was 41.42, the difference again being significant ($t = 4.81$, $p < .05$). Thus on both tests the dyslexics performed at a lower level than the normals. Analogous results for sequential memory have been found by a number of other workers (Hartstein, 1971; Silver & Hagin, 1970) and were implicit in the early finding by Hinshelwood (1917, reported in Ingram, 1970) that dyslexics were unable to write to dictation, even though they could copy the unwritten material.

Silver and Hagin (1970) interpret problems in visual sequential memory in children with reading disorders as primarily defects in spatial orientation. The common symptom of reversals and inversions of letters (Wagner, 1971) would suggest difficulties relating to memory for location of orientation in space (see also Critchley, 1968).

D. Spatial Transformation Ability

Shepard and Metzler (1971), using two shapes similar to those in Fig. 7-3, claimed that adult subjects matched the pairs as same or different by using a process of mental rotation. Evidence for this notion came from the linear relation observed between angular separation in degrees of the two identical shapes and the mean reaction time for same responding. The ability to transform objects in space mentally is particularly important in a number of academic disciplines (Poole & Stanley, 1972).

Dyslexic and normal children were presented with 26 photographs of the forms shown in Fig. 7-3, one photograph being presented at a time. Each photograph displayed three wooden blocks whose locations and angular rotations were randomly ordered. Two of the three blocks were the same and the subjects' task was to identify the different form. The mean correct identification score for the dyslexics was 15.27 and that for the normals 14.73. These differences were not statistically significant ($t < 1$, $p > .05$), but greater than the chance rate of 8.66. Hence as far as this

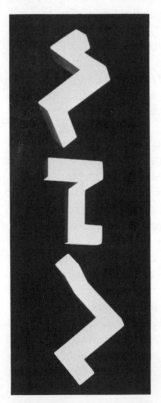

Fig. 7-3. An example of the figures used in the spatial transformation ability test.

measure of spatial transformation ability is concerned, the dyslexics function at the same level as normals. This result suggests that perhaps it is memory for transformation rather than the ability to transform that is deficient in dyslexics.

Wooden replicas of the two different shapes shown in Fig. 7-3 were made. These were presented sequentially in sets of three (two same, one different) with the instructions to say whether the different one was presented first, second, or third. Six combinations of three were presented in random order. The child felt the blocks with his eyes closed. The mean score for the dyslexic group was 3.00 and that for the normal group 3.33, the difference not being significant ($t < 1$, $p > .05$). The mean level of performance for both groups was above the chance level of two. On the basis of this result it would seem that there is little difference between the abilities of normals and dyslexics on tasks involving tactual memory for sequences of shapes. As both visual and auditory sequential memory appear to be impaired in dyslexics, it could be considered that the tactual mode would be useful in providing an aid to sequential memory. However, the relatively poor performance level in absolute terms on this task, for both normals and dyslexics, suggests that tactual sequential memory is fairly limited in scope.

III. METHODOLOGICAL ISSUES

A. Other Interpretations of the Data

Two issues relating to the interpretation of the experimental data need to be considered. First, it could be argued that the sample referred to as dyslexic is not representative of the syndrome of reading difficulty. Although there is a current trend in educational circles to treat all reading difficulties without regard to diagnostics, it is our belief that there is some value in a careful differentiation of subgroups of children with reading failure. The criteria on which we selected our sample are explicit, and although data were not collected systematically from all the dyslexic sample, other symptoms of dyslexia, such as letter reversals, were observed.

A second issue relates to the possibility that the differences in performance could be accounted for in motivational rather than cognitive terms. It may be argued that the dyslexics' past experiences of failure means that they come to the experimental situation with lower motivation than normals. While this is always a possible influence, its effects were probably minimal. Participation in the experiment involved time out from the usual routine of school and a visit to a university computer laboratory, an experience that all subjects seemed to enjoy. Moreover, a primarily motivational interpretation would not account for those tasks on which no differences were found between the groups.

B. Evaluation of the Framework

This research program has been interpreted within a simplistic version of the visual information processing framework. It has been assumed that the experimental manipulations and response measures provide relatively direct access to the different stages of memory in the processing of visual information. However, in discussing the research, it has been noted that there are differences of opinion as to the appropriate interpretation of the processes underlying different experimental measures. For example, it was pointed out that the separation measure of VIS is not equivalent to the more direct persistence measure used by Haber and Standing (1969), and that there is some question as to the role of the masker in a masking measure of transfer rate. Recently, Ross (1972) questioned the current notion of visual persistence and argued that preattentive processes and configurational rules determine the nature of the percept obtained after brief visual stimulation. Drawing on different data, Hochberg (1970) has argued a similar case. Given the current state of the framework, it is clear that process interpretations of the present data with dyslexics and normals must be viewed tentatively, pending further research.

IV. CONCLUSION

This research supports the view that in dyslexics there are specific limitations at the early stages of visual information processing. The results were interpreted as providing evidence that visual persistence or VIS duration as well as transfer rate is greater in dyslexics than in normals. The slowness of processing at this stage probably accounts for the universal difficulty that dyslexics experience with sequential memory tasks. If VIS duration is not intrinsically related to eye-movements in dyslexics, then many of their confusions may result from eye-movements feeding new information into the visual system before the old information has been processed or masked. Thus there may be some overlay of visual information in storage. The abnormal eye-movement patterns manifested by dyslexics (Goldberg, 1968) could be due to the system trying to correct by searching for information that produces less interference.

Although the results obtained in the present experiments are encouraging, much more research is needed to clarify and substantiate the defects in visual information processing in dyslexics suggested by the data.

REFERENCES

Averbach, E., & Coriell, A. S. Short-term memory in vision. *Bell System Technical Journal,* 1961, **40,** 309–328.

Averbach, E., & Sperling, G. Short-term storage of information in vision. In C. Cherry (Ed.), *Information Theory.* London: Butterworths, 1961.

Critchley, M. Minor neurologic defects in developmental dyslexia. In A. H. Keeney & V. T. Keeney (Eds.), *Dyslexia: Diagnosis and treatment of reading disorders.* St. Louis: Mosby, 1968.

Eriksen, C. W., & Collins, J. F. Sensory traces versus the psychological moment in the temporal organization of form. *Journal of Experimental Psychology,* 1968, **77,** 376–382.

Goldberg, H. K. Vision, perception, and related defects in dyslexia. In A. H. Keeney & V. T. Keeney (Eds.), *Dyslexia: Diagnosis and treatment of reading disorders.* St. Louis: Mosby, 1968.

Haber, R. N. *Information-processing approaches to visual perception.* New York: Holt, Rinehart & Winston, 1969. (a)

Haber, R. N. Perceptual processes and general cognitive activity. In J. F. Voss (Ed.), *Approaches to thought.* Columbus: Merrill, 1969. (b)

Haber, R. N. Where are the visions in visual perception? In S. S. Segal (Ed.), *Imagery: Current cognitive approaches.* New York: Academic Press, 1971.

Haber, R. N., & Nathanson, L. S. Post-retinal storage? Parks' camel as seen through the eye of a needle. *Perception and Psychophysics,* 1968, **3,** 349–355.

Haber, R. N., & Standing, L. Direct measures of short-term visual storage. *Quarterly Journal of Experimental Psychology,* 1969, **21,** 43–54.

Haber, R. N., & Standing, L. Direct estimates of apparent duration of a flash followed by visual noise. *Canadian Journal of Psychology,* 1970, **24,** 216–229.

Hartstein, J. (Ed.) *Current concepts in dyslexia.* St. Louis: Mosby, 1971.

Hochberg, J. Attention, organization, and consciousness. In D. I. Mostofsky (Ed.) *Attention: Contemporary theory and analysis.* New York: Appleton-Century-Crofts, 1970.

Ingram, T. T. S. The nature of dyslexia. In F. A. Young & D. B. Lindsley (Eds.), *Early experience and visual information processing in perceptual and reading disorders.* Washington, D.C.: National Academy of Sciences, 1970.

Keeney, A. H. Introduction. In J. Hartstein (Ed.), *Current concepts in dyslexia.* St. Louis: Mosby, 1971.

Kristofferson, A. B. Attention in time discrimination and reaction time. *Technical Report,* 1965, Contract No. CR-194, National Aeronautics and Space Administration.

Levin, H., & Williams, J. P. (Eds.) *Basic studies on reading.* New York: Basic Books, 1970.

Liss, P. Does backward masking by visual noise stop stimulus processing? *Perception and Psychophysics,* 1968, **4,** 328–330.

Money, J. (Ed.) *The disabled reader: Education of the dyslexic child.* Baltimore: Johns Hopkins Press, 1966.

Neisser, U. *Cognitive psychology*. New York: Appelton-Century-Crofts, 1967.

Poole, C., & Stanley, G. A factorial and predictive study of spatial abilities. *Australian Journal of Psychology*, 1972, **24**, 317–320.

Ross, J. Analysis before perception. *University of Western Australia Psychology Research Report 4*, June 1972.

Shepard, R. N., & Metzler, J. Mental rotation of three-dimensional objects. *Science*, 1971, **171**, 701–703.

Silver, A. A., & Hagin, R. A. Visual perception in children with reading disabilities. In F. A. Young & D. B. Lindsley (Eds.), *Early experience and visual information processing in perceptual and reading disorders*. Washington, D.C.: National Academy of Sciences, 1970.

Spencer, T. J. Some effects of different masking stimuli on iconic storage. *Journal of Experimental Psychology*, 1969, **81**, 132–140.

Spencer, T. J., & Shuntich, R. Evidence for an interruption theory of backward masking. *Journal of Experimental Psychology*, 1970, **85**, 198–203.

Sperling, G. The information available in brief visual presentations. *Psychological Monographs*, 1960, **74** (11), entire issue.

Sperling, G. A model for visual memory tasks. *Human Factors*, 1963, **5**, 19–31.

Stroud, J. M. The fine structure of psychological time. In H. Quastler (Ed.), *Information theory in psychology*. Glencoe, Ill.: Free Press, 1956.

Vernon, M. D. *Backwardness in reading*. Cambridge: University Press, 1960.

Wagner, R. F. *Dyslexia and your child*. New York: Harper & Row, 1971.

Waugh, N. C., & Norman, D. A. Primary memory. *Psychological Review*, 1965, **72**, 89–104.

White, C. T. Temporal numerosity and the psychological unit of duration. *Psychological Monographs*, 1963, **77** (575), entire issue.

Young, F. A., & Lindsley, D. B. (Eds.) *Early experience and visual information processing in perceptual and reading disorders*. Washington, D.C.: National Academy of Sciences, 1970.

Zelhart, P., & Johnson, R. C. An investigation of eidetic imagery. Western Psychological Association Paper, San Jose, California, 1959. Reported in H. Munsinger. *Fundamentals of Child Development*. New York: Holt, Rinehart & Winston, 1971.

CHAPTER

8

MEMORY SCANNING: NEW FINDINGS AND CURRENT CONTROVERSIES[1]

SAUL STERNBERG

[1] This paper is based on the Fourth Sir Frederic Bartlett Lecture, delivered to the Experimental Psychology Society in London, January 1973. I thank the Society for this opportunity to honor the memory of F. C. Bartlett. I also thank the John Simon Guggenheim Memorial Foundation for its fellowship support during the period when this paper was initially drafted, and the Department of Psychology of University College London for its hospitality. I am grateful to R. L. Knoll, T. K. Landauer, D. E. Meyer, and A. M. Wing for helpful criticism of the manuscript. Reprinted, with permission of the Experimental Psychology Society, from a slightly more detailed version in the *Quarterly Journal of Experimental Psychology* (Sternberg, 1975).

I. INTRODUCTION: THE REACTION-TIME METHOD IN MEMORY RESEARCH

Human memory has traditionally been studied by examining how and when it fails—by considering the frequency and pattern of errors in recall or recognition. These errors may result from failures of learning, retention, or retrieval, and one difficulty in the traditional approach is the disentangling of these alternative sources of error.

During the past decade a complementary approach to the study of memory has become increasingly popular. Here memory is examined under conditions in which it functions successfully and produces virtually errorless performance. By applying time pressure to the subject under these conditions, the experimenter can induce some of the mechanisms at work to reveal themselves, not by how they fail, but by how much time they need in order to succeed. The questions addressed by such reaction-time (RT) studies have focused on mechanisms of memory retrieval for information in both short-term and long-term memory, but the approach is also being widely used to confront issues such as what information is stored and how it is coded and organized (see, *e.g.,* Landauer & Meyer, 1972). All this is part of a general revival in the use of RT methods to infer the organization of perceptual and cognitive processes. Our current desire to analyze the processing of information into its functional components (particularly when combined with the hypothesis that component processes are arranged in stages) leads naturally to RT methods and to an interest in the temporal structure of processing. The power of these methods compared to others lies partly in the fact that the appropriate scale of measurement can be specified on the basis of relatively weak assumptions (Sternberg, 1969b). This means that quantitative aspects of data, such as additivity and linearity of effects, come to have powerful implications.

In this paper I shall focus on studies of the recognition of items in relatively short memorized lists. I start by briefly reviewing some of the experiments, now about 10 years old, that led me to infer the existence of a particularly simple but curious process of internal scanning (Sternberg, 1963, 1966, 1969a). Then I discuss, on the one hand, some of the extensions and generalizations of the early findings, obtained in a number of laboratories, and, on the other hand, several of the findings that appear to create serious difficulties for the scanning model. These findings have led others to propose alternative models; I consider three contrasting examples of alternative models and point out some of their strengths and weaknesses. Finally I review several new findings from various laboratories—findings that particularly intrigue me and that bear on the elaboration or extension of the original scanning model.

II. THE ITEM-RECOGNITION PARADIGM

In the item-recognition paradigm we shall be considering the *stimulus ensemble* consists of all the items that might appear as test stimuli. In the early experiments, for example, the ensemble was made up of 1-digit numerals. From among the ensemble a set of elements is selected arbitrarily and is defined as the *positive set;* these items are presented as a list for the subject to memorize. The remaining items are called the *negative set.* In general, positive and negative sets are not distinguished by any simple physical or semantic feature. When a *test-stimulus* is presented the subject must decide whether it is a member of the positive set. If it is, he makes a *positive response,* for example, by pressing one of two buttons. If it is not, he makes a *negative response* by pressing the other button. The RT is measured from the onset of the test stimulus to the response. The task is easy enough so that without time pressure, performance would be virtually perfect. Even with time pressure, the error rate can be held to 1% or 2% by paying subjects in such a way as to penalize errors heavily while rewarding speed, although in some experiments the error rate is somewhat higher.

Two of the procedures that have been used within the item-recognition paradigm are shown in Fig. 8-1. In the *varied-set procedure,* the subject must memorize a new positive set on each trial. The set might be presented serially, followed by a retention interval of two or three seconds during which the subject is free to rehearse if he wishes, then a warning signal, and then a test stimulus. In the *fixed-set procedure,* the same positive set is used for a long series of trials, and a trial consists only of warning signal, test stimulus, and response.

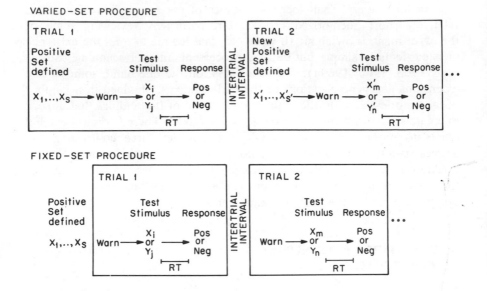

Fig. 8-1. Varied-set and fixed-set procedures in item recognition. Y represents an item in the negative set. Primes are used in representing Trial 2 of the varied-set procedure to show that both the items in the positive set ($X_1, \ldots, X_s$) and its size (s) may change from trial to trial.

III. EARLY FINDINGS AND INTERPRETATIONS: THE EXHAUSTIVE-SEARCH MODEL

I and many other researchers have studied the effects of a large number of experimental factors on performance in the item-recognition paradigm. The focus of most attention is the effect of varying the size of the positive set, while keeping constant the relative frequency with which positive and negative responses are required. The effect of this factor in an experiment using the varied-set procedure is shown in Fig. 8-2a. The ensemble contained the 10 digits, and the positive set could contain from 1 to 6 different digits. Mean RT is plotted as a function of the size of the positive set. Four features of these data should be noted: (1) mean RT increases approximately linearly with set size; (2) the rate of increase is the same for positive and negative responses; (3) the rate of increase is about 38 msec for each item in the positive set; and (4) the zero intercept is about 400 msec.

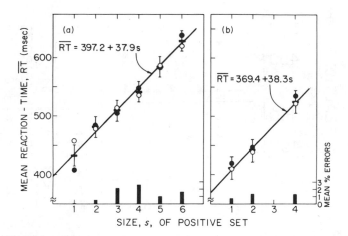

Fig. 8-2. Results from item-recognition experiments with varied-set (a, 8 subjects) and fixed-set (b, 6 subjects) procedures. Mean latencies of positive responses (filled circles) and negative responses (open circles) as functions of size of positive set. Overall means (heavy bars) and estimates of $\pm SE$. Lines were fitted by least squares to overall means.

Fig. 8-2b shows the effect of the same factor in an experiment using the fixed-set procedure, where the positive set could contain 1, 2, or 4 different digits, and a subject worked with each set for 180 trials. The results are similar: a roughly linear increase, at the same rate for positive and negative responses, with the slope of the fitted function about 38 msec, and the zero intercept about 400 msec. (In this experiment, the positive response was required on 27% of the trials. When the two responses are equiprobable in the fixed-set procedure, positive responses are produced about 40 msec faster than negatives, at each set size.) The phenomenon seems to be the same, whether the positive set is fixed over a long series of trials or is varied from trial to trial.

Now, since the ensemble was constant in these experiments, changes in the size of the positive set induced complementary changes in the size of the negative set. Results of two other early experiments (Sternberg, 1963), which permit us to ignore this confounding, are shown in Fig. 8-3. In each of these experiments, the fixed-set procedure was used, the stimulus ensemble consisted of the 10 digits, the size of the positive set was fixed, and the size of the negative set was varied. In all conditions, subjects were told the members of both positive and negative sets in advance, and the positive response was required on half of the trials. Results are shown at the top of the figure for positive sets of size two, and at the bottom for

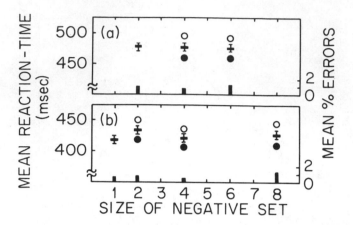

Fig. 8-3. Results of two experiments in which size of the negative set was varied. Mean latencies of correct responses (heavy bars) with estimates of $\pm SE$, as functions of size of negative set, for positive sets of size 1 (b, 8 subjects, about 640 observations per point, F [3, 18] = 1.01) and size 2 (a, 6 subjects, about 720 observations per point, F [2, 8] = 0.02). Also shown, for conditions where the two sets differ in size, are separate means for responses to stimuli in the smaller, positive set (filled circles) and for responses to stimuli in the larger, negative set (open circles).

positive sets of size one. Here, mean RT is plotted as a function of the size of the negative set. (In the fixed-set procedure, the only feature that distinguishes the two sets is that the positive set is the smaller. When the two sets are made equal in size this asymmetry disappears. Results for the smallest values of negative set size in each experiment, for which the characteristic that distinguishes positive and negative sets is missing, should therefore be considered separately from the other data.) In neither experiment was there a significant effect on the overall mean RT of the size of the negative set. Notice that this means that stimulus probability *per se* had no effect, and also that ensemble size *per se* had no effect, since both of them varied with negative set size. In short, there is a striking asymmetry between the effects of positive and negative set size, at least when the items are digits. Positive set size influences the latencies of both positive and negative responses, and in the same way. Negative set size influences neither. As we shall see later, this finding has new importance in relation to some recent theoretical proposals.

How does a person decide whether the test stimulus is contained in the positive set? The early results discussed above, together with others, suggested a search through the positive set in which the test item is compared serially to each of the memorized items, and each comparison results in either a match or a mismatch. The data indicate two remarkable features of such a scanning process. First, the fact that positive and negative latency functions have equal slopes means that the search is *exhaustive:* even when a match has occurred, scanning continues through the entire positive set. Otherwise, if the scanning process terminated on the occurrence of a match, the positive function would have half the slope of the negative. (This follows from the fact that in *self-terminating* search of a set of s elements, the test item is compared to all s elements before negative responses, whereas it is compared to $(s + 1)/2$ elements, on average, before positive responses; the rates at which these two numbers increase with s are in the ratio 2:1.) The second remarkable feature is the speed of the search process: each additional member of the positive set adds 1 to the number of comparisons producing mismatches that must occur in the course of the search. The time taken by each mismatching comparison is therefore estimated by the slope of the function, which is between 35 and 40 msec per item in the examples we have seen. This implies a scanning rate of about 30 items per sec. Thus, the process is exhaustive and is substantially faster than estimates of the rate of covert speech (Landauer, 1962; Clifton & Tash, 1973). Judging from what subjects report, the search is not accessible to introspection.

Furthermore, the process seems largely unaffected by how well the set has been learned. The varied-set procedure is a short-term memory procedure: the test item is presented only 2 or 3 sec after a single presentation of the set. On the other hand, on the average test trial in the fixed-set procedure whose results are shown in Fig. 8-2b, a subject had been working with the same positive set for 10 min; subjects could recall the sets they worked with several days later. In this case the sets must have been stored in long-term memory. Nonetheless, the similarity of the data led to the conjecture that the same memory was being searched in the two procedures: even if a set is well learned, when it is needed in the item-recognition task its members are "activated," or transferred into an "active memory," perhaps equivalent to the short-term store, where they are more rapidly accessible. Other experiments have confirmed this conjecture (*e.g.,* Sternberg, 1969a, Experiment 5).

The height of the zero intercepts indicates that a large fraction of the RT reflects the duration of processes other than scanning. Even if we subtract estimates of input and output times (based, *e.g.,* on simple visual RT data) we are left with more than 200 msec to account for. In other early item-recognition experiments, other experimental factors were studied. The effects of those factors, and certain additive relations among them (Sternberg, 1969b), pointed to the existence of at least three additional processes, arranged in stages, as shown in Fig. 8-4, whose durations contribute to the zero-intercepts. Also shown are four experimental factors

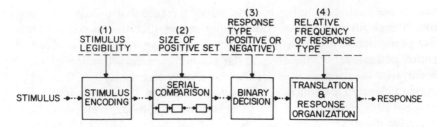

Fig. 8-4. Four processing stages in item recognition. Above the broken line are shown four experimental factors believed to influence the stages. Vertical arrows show each factor influencing only one stage. The additivity of the effects of factor pairs 1 and 2 (after a session of practice), 1 and 3, 2 and 3, 2 and 4, and 3 and 4 was the main reason for inferring the existence of the stages and the selectivity of factor effects (Sternberg, 1969b). Other factors, not shown, may also influence these same stages, and dots between arrows indicate the possibility of additional stages, as yet unknown.

whose influence on the stages appeared to be selective after a session's practice. The legibility of the test stimulus influences the duration of an encoding stage in which an internal representation of the stimulus is formed. This representation is then used in the serial-comparison stage, whose duration increases linearly with positive-set size; in each of a series of substages, the representation is compared to a memory representation of one member of the set. In the third stage a binary decision is made that depends on whether a match has occurred during the serial-comparison stage that precedes it; the mean duration of the third stage is greater for negative than for positive decisions. The selection and output of a response based on the decision is accomplished in a fourth stage, whose duration is influenced by the relative frequency with which a response of that type is required. (Other factors, not shown in the figure, may also influence these same stages, of course.)

IV. GENERALIZATIONS AND
EXTENSIONS OF PARADIGM
AND PHENOMENON

Now let us move on from early data and theory to the question of the generality and robustness of the phenomenon. Reaction-time functions that are approximately linear, and with roughly equal slopes for positive and negative responses, have now been observed in various laboratories with a large variety of stimulus ensembles, both auditory and visual.

(Later we shall come to some important exceptions, however.) The stimuli that have been used include visual and auditory digits and letters, 2- and 3-digit numerals, shapes, pictures of faces, drawings of common objects, words of various lengths, colors, and phonemes (*e.g.,* Burrows & Okada, 1973; Chase & Calfee, 1969; Clifton & Tash, 1973; Foss & Dowell, 1971; Hoving, Morin, & Konick, 1970; Sternberg, 1969a; Swanson, Johnsen, & Briggs, 1972; Wingfield, 1973). The slopes of the functions are not the same for different ensembles, however; they appear to differ systematically from one ensemble to another, and in an orderly way, as described in Section VII-E. The RT functions have been observed to remain linear and parallel in studies with positive sets containing up to 10 letters (Wingfield & Branca, 1970), and up to 12 common words (Naus, 1974).

Changes in the relative frequencies with which positive and negative responses are required alter the zero-intercepts of the RT functions but leave their slopes and linearity relatively invariant (Sternberg, 1963; 1969b). And, so long as errors do not exceed about 10%, the slope and shape of the functions change very little when subjects are instructed to increase their speed at the cost of accuracy (Swanson & Briggs, 1969; Lyons & Briggs, 1971; Pachella, 1972; but see also Coots & Johnston, 1972; Lively, 1972).

The phenomenon has been observed in people of various ages, ranging from children to elderly adults, and in normals, alcoholics, schizophrenics, and brain-damaged mental retardates. For some of these groups the slopes and/or intercepts of the RT functions are elevated relative to those of young adults; for example, aging and mental retardation both appear to produce increased slopes (Anders, Fozard, & Lillyquist, 1972; Eriksen, Hamlin, & Daye, 1973; Harris & Fleer, 1974). More remarkable, perhaps, is the absence of slope differences among certain groups of people, despite the existence of reliable individual differences within groups. Thus, children as young as 8 produce RT functions with higher intercepts but the same slope as young adults (Hoving *et al.,* 1970; Harris & Fleer, 1974). And, as shown in Fig. 8-5, except for their zero-intercepts, schizophrenics and alcoholics look surprisingly similar to each other and to normals.[2] Of all the groups studied, only aphasics produce data that are qualitatively (rather than merely parametrically) unusual, as discussed in Section VII-C (Swinney & Taylor, 1971).

Finally, let us consider the effect of extended practice in the item-

[2] I thank S. F. Checkosky of Bell Laboratories, Holmdel, N.J., for furnishing me with details of this extensive unpublished study.

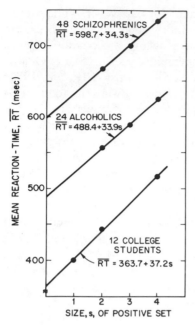

Fig. 8-5. Results from item-recognition experiments with three groups of subjects. Overall mean RTs as functions of size of positive set, and lines fitted by least squares. Data for schizophrenics (average hospitalization, 15 months) and alcoholics (average hospitalization, 8 months) from an unpublished study by S. F. Checkosky. For both groups the standard error of the mean slope was about 2.2 msec, and slopes of separately fitted functions for positive and negative responses differed by less than 2.5 msec. Data show performance after an average of 1728 trials practice (8 test days preceded by 4 practice days, with 216 trials per day). Data for college students from a similar study shown for comparison (Sternberg, 1967a, Session 2); data show performance after an average of 630 trials practice. *SE* of the mean slope for these data was about 3.4 msec.

recognition task. This effect seems to depend very much on details of procedure. Several studies have shown that when subjects practice with the same fixed sets over many days, the RT functions become flatter and negatively accelerated. This is particularly true if members of the ensemble are consistently associated with particular responses, so that a stimulus that is in any positive set for a subject can never be in any negative set, and vice versa (Ross, 1970; Kristofferson, 1972b). On the other hand, when sets are changed either from trial to trial (Nickerson, 1966, Experiment 4), or from session to session (Kristofferson, 1972a), and stimuli are not consistently assigned to particular responses, extended practice seems to have virtually no effect on the phenomenon. The most complete experiment that demonstrates this invariance with practice was recently reported by Kristofferson (1972a). She used 7 subjects who worked for 144 trials per day for 30 days with an ensemble of digits, and with positive sets that changed from day to day. Results are shown in Fig. 8-6, averaged over positive and negative responses. Practice appears to affect only the zero-intercept. The average slope stayed very close to 36 msec per digit, deviation from linearity did not change systematically with practice, and the difference between mean positive and negative slope estimates, which are not shown here, was never more than 4 msec. Finally, for each 5-day period for each subject, the percentage of the variance of set-size means accounted for by linear regression was never less than 97.

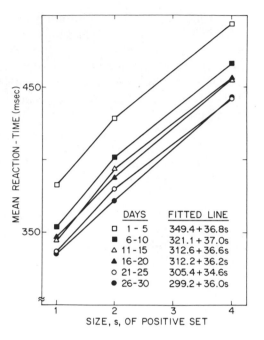

Fig. 8-6. Effects of extended practice on item-recognition performance: data from a study by M. W. Kristofferson (1972a). Mean RTs for 7 subjects averaged over positive and negative responses for 6 consecutive groups of 5 days. Data points from each 5-day period are joined by line segments; also shown for each period is equation of best-fitting linear function.

DAYS		FITTED LINE
□	1 - 5	349.4 + 36.8s
■	6 -10	321.1 + 37.0s
△	11 -15	312.6 + 36.6s
▲	16 -20	312.2 + 36.2s
○	21 -25	305.4 + 34.6s
●	26 -30	299.2 + 36.0s

V. FINDINGS THAT CHALLENGE THE MODEL OR LIMIT ITS SCOPE, AND WHAT TO DO ABOUT THEM

The robustness of the set-size effect indicates that it is a phenomenon worth explaining. But there are a number of reasons for questioning its explanation in terms of a high-speed exhaustive scanning process. Some of these reasons can be disputed, since they depend on judgments of plausibility. For example, the exhaustiveness of the inferred comparison process is difficult for many psychologists to accept because it seems inefficient.

Plausibility judgments, however, are highly subjective. I recently described some of this work to a group of Bell Laboratories engineers concerned with the design of special-purpose computers for telephone switching. They were obviously surprised when I commented on the implausibility of exhaustiveness; and when I asked about this later, they said that there were several instances of similar scanning processes being wired into the computer hardware, for the very reason that in those instances they were *faster,* on the average. It is easy to imagine systems in which the average search time is *less* for an exhaustive process than a self-terminating one (Sternberg, 1969a, Section 11). See Section VII-C for new findings supporting the idea that human memory retrieval depends on such a system.

There seem to be several other reasons why the scanning model puts a strain on psychologists' intuition, and why we feel the need to seek alternative models. These include the high speed of the process (relative to rates of covert speech or to rates of overt sequences of discrete actions), the fact that subjects are not aware of it (even when introspections include a search, it is reported to be slow and self-terminating), the paucity of connections with theories of memory that have been designed primarily to explain forgetting, and the widespread belief (Kintsch, 1970; McCormack, 1972) that recognition depends on a stimulus having direct access to its representation in memory, rather than on any search process.

More serious for the scanning model than considerations of plausibility and intuition are several features of performance occasionally observed in item-recognition tasks. Some of these merely suggest limitations on the scope of the model. But others suggest that it must either be elaborated or discarded altogether. Discussed below are three of the more interesting challenges to the model, three strategies for elaborating the model to accommodate them, and one kind of finding that should, I feel, be used to limit the model's scope rather than to develop it further.

Let us consider first the serial-position function in the varied-set procedure. For each set size, this function relates the mean latency of positive responses to the position in the memorized list of the item that is matched by the test stimulus. Now, scanning processes lead very easily to predictions of serial-position effects if they are self-terminating—that is, if a positive response is initiated as soon as a match occurs. For example, in such a process, if scanning proceeded systematically from the beginning of the list, the serial-position function would increase monotonically. Different scanning orders and different mixtures of such orders could generate a large variety of serial-position curves so long as the search is self-terminating. But in an exhaustive search, this obvious source of serial-position effects is lacking. Since all items are searched, even on positive trials, the number of items searched before the match occurs should have no effect. Without elaboration, the model leads us to expect flat serial-position functions, and in many experiments this is what has been observed. But other item-recognition experiments have produced substantial serial-position effects. They vary in form, some showing recency effects (*e.g.,* Clifton & Birenbaum, 1970), others primacy effects (*e.g.,* Klatzky, Juola, & Atkinson, 1971), and others both (*e.g.,* Burrows & Okada, 1971). It is particularly embarrassing for the model if a procedure that gives rise to serial-position effects also produces set-size functions that are linear and parallel, since the latter suggests strongly that the situation is one to which the model ought to apply. A number of experiments showing position effects failed to demonstrate the basic phenomenon, because only one or two set sizes were used, the RT functions were nonlinear or nonparallel, error rates were unusually high, or RTs were outside of the normal range. But unhappily for the model, data from a few experiments whose gross features *are* consistent with the model have also shown serial-position effects. These effects appear to be most marked when the list to be memorized is presented rapidly and the interval between list and test stimulus is brief.

A second finding from the varied-set procedure that presents difficulties for the model arises when the same item appears more than once in a memorized list instead of all items being distinct. More data need to be collected with lists containing duplications. But on the basis of experiments by Baddeley and Ecob (1973) and unpublished data of my own, we can say—at least tentatively—that if the trials on which the duplicated item is itself the test stimulus are excluded, then the set-size function is not unusual; moreover, the effective set size is the same as if all the items in the list were distinct. The difficulty for the model arises when the duplicated item itself is tested, because on such trials the RT is unusually short. Again, the scanning model, as it stands, cannot account for this.

A third troublesome finding is related to the probabilities with which the different members of the positive set are presented as test stimuli. In most experiments these probabilities are equal. But a few experimenters have unbalanced the probabilities in the positive set, either by varying relative frequency in a fixed-set procedure (*e.g.,* Miller & Pachella, 1973; Theios, Smith, Haviland, Traupmann, & Moy, 1973; Biederman & Stacy, 1974), or by cueing the subject between presentation of the set and the test stimulus in a varied-set procedure (Klatzky & Smith, 1972). Responses to high-probability positives in a set are faster than to low-probability positives in the same set. If search were self-terminating, and probability influenced the order of search, such effects of probability could be readily explained. But in an exhaustive process this natural source of the probability effects is missing.

Let us now turn to some of the alternative theorizing strategies we might apply in dealing with these challenges to the model. Most investigators are strongly biased to place the burden of explanation on the second stage shown in Fig. 8-4—the serial-comparison process. Perhaps because the set-size effect is itself explained in terms of changes in the number of mismatching comparisons, so other effects, they apparently feel, should be explained in the same terms; since the exhaustive-scanning model does not permit this, it must be discarded and replaced. This is one strategy of theorizing. In Section VI, I discuss three of the models that have been proposed as replacements.

A second strategy is to preserve the second stage, but elaborate the model elsewhere, explaining these effects in terms of changes in the duration of other processing stages, such as the encoding stage or the binary-decision stage. For example, it is not inconceivable that the time needed to form an internal representation of the test stimulus in the encoding stage might depend on how frequently or recently that stimulus had been presented, or on the extent to which it was expected, thereby producing effects of trial sequence and stimulus probability. And it is possible when an item that appears twice in the positive set is tested, and two matches occur, that this increases the strength of the internal signal indicating a match, so that the binary decision is facilitated. Of course, unless conjectures like these are made precise and subjected to quantitative experimental tests, the model becomes too flexible. We will see later that the additivity of the effects of stimulus probability and set size can be regarded as one such test.

A third strategy is to invoke the idea of a probabilistic mixture of processes, as shown in Fig. 8-7. On the basis of an early analysis of the stimulus, a branch occurs, so that the serial-comparison process is executed on a proportion, P, of the trials, and an alternative process on the remaining trials. For example, in a fixed-set procedure, the test stimulus could first be compared to a representation of the previous test stimulus. If they matched, the previous response would be repeated, and if not, the positive set would be scanned. Again, the quantitative implications of such mixtures have to be determined and tested. For example, depending on details, mixtures need not affect the linearity of the set-size function.

Some versions of the item-recognition paradigm produce findings that are sufficiently different from the early ones so that in my opinion they should be used to suggest limitations in the scope or generality of the model, rather than ways in which it ought to be elaborated, at least for the present. Some procedures, for example, consistently produce nonlinear set-size functions, particularly after practice. In one class of procedures where this occurs, members of positive sets are distinguished from members of negative sets by semantic or physical features (*e.g.,* Marcel, 1970;

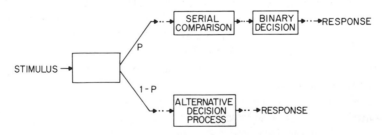

Fig. 8-7. A probabilistic mixture model. An early analysis of the stimulus on each trial determines whether the serial-comparison process or some alternative process will be used as the basis of the binary decision. The two processes are invoked with probabilities P and $1 - P$, respectively; P may vary across conditions within an experiment.

Foss & Dowell, 1971), by large differences in familiarity or in frequency of presentation (*e.g.,* Swanson & Briggs, 1969; Clifton, 1973), or by an assignment of responses to stimuli that is consistent over many trials or even sessions (*e.g.,* Kristofferson, 1972b; Ross, 1970; Simpson, 1972; Swanson, 1974). One possibility is that such procedures provide an alternative basis for the positive-negative decision that subjects may find to be more efficient than the scanning process, at least for large sets.

VI. ALTERNATIVE MODELS OF THE COMPARISON PROCESS

A. Self-Terminating Search

We turn now to three of the mechanisms that have been proposed as alternatives to the exhaustive comparison stage.

Theios (1973; Theios *et al.,* 1973) has proposed a model whose aim is to account for data from a fixed-set procedure in which stimulus probabilities are unbalanced, and probability effects as well as parallel and linear set-size functions are observed. The proposed process is one of serial self-terminating search, but the list that is searched contains the entire ensemble of test stimuli rather than being limited to members of the positive set. Each item in the searched list is assumed to be stored in association with a code that indicates the correct response for that item. Positive and negative items are mixed together in the list. The stored list functions as a "push-down stack," whose members are rearranged from trial to trial in response to stimulus events. As a result, the more recent and more frequent stimuli tend to be located near the beginning of the list. The test stimulus is compared to one member of the ensemble after another until a match occurs, at which point the indicated response is initiated. The model does reasonably well in accounting for both stimulus-probability and set-size effects in experiments in which the positive and negative sets are of equal size. (Under these circumstances, for example, if the two responses are required with equal frequency, a simple version of the model implies that for any set size the average amount of search preceding positive responses is as great as that preceding negatives, hence the parallel set-size functions.)

One limitation of this model is that it cannot account in a natural way for findings from the more typical procedure, where positive and negative set sizes are unequal. To fit the model here, two special assumptions have been added to it: First, positive stimuli are much more likely than negatives to move to the beginning of the stored list after being presented. Second, when the positive set has s members, searching the list beyond position $s + 1$ contributes no additional time to the RT. Even with these assumptions, however, the model appears incapable of producing equal effects of positive-set size on RTs of positive and negative responses at the same time as it produces no effects of negative-set size.

A second limitation is that the model, tailored as it is to the fixed-set procedure, cannot readily account for results from the varied-set procedure, without adding special assumptions about how associations involving items in the negative set on each trial are stored and ordered. (In the varied-set procedure the negative set on a trial is defined only indirectly and by exclusion; hence these negative associations would have only the 2 or 3 sec that elapse between presentation of positive set and test stimulus to be generated and intermingled among the positive associations in the stored list.) The equivalence of results from fixed-set and varied-set procedures seems to me to be a very strong argument for seeking one model that can explain the performance in both procedures.

A third problem for any explanation in terms of self-terminating search is related to the behavior of the minimum of the RT distribution, as set size is increased. For a self-terminating process the minimum must be invariant with set size. The reason is that regardless of set size, there is some probability that the first comparison will produce the match. (Unlike some of the other properties of the RT distributions produced by self-terminating search, this property does not depend on assuming the durations of successive comparisons either to have equal means or to be stochastically independent.) Now, without making unacceptably strong distributional assumptions one cannot guarantee that any particular sample estimate of the population minimum is unbiased, or that its bias is independent of set size. However, the fact that the sample minimum has been found to increase systematically with set size whenever it has been examined strongly suggests that the true minimum RT does not have the required invariance property (Lively, 1972; Lively & Sanford, 1972). (Furthermore, other statistics can be devised that capture this aspect of self-terminating search, but do not suffer from the estimation difficulties of the minimum; the observed behavior of these statistics also provides evidence against self-terminating search, either through the entire stimulus ensemble or through the positive set only [Sternberg, 1973].)

Finally, experimental support is accumulating for the idea that stimulus probability produces its effects by influencing one or more stages *other* than the serial-comparison stage, and the encoding stage has been proposed as one possibility. There are two sources of evidence: First, in the three experiments where the question could be asked, the effects of absolute stimulus probability and set size were found to be additive, within the limits of experimental precision (Klatzky & Smith, 1972; Theios *et al.,*

1973; Biederman & Stacy, 1974). The additivity is evidence that the two factors influence different processing stages. Secondly, it has been shown that the effects of stimulus legibility and stimulus probability are not additive, which indicates that they influence a common stage (Miller & Pachella, 1973). Given the assumption that stimulus legibility has its effect by influencing an encoding stage, this finding locates at least part of the probability effect in that stage.

In some models the self-terminating search is restricted to members of the positive set, at least on trials requiring positive responses. In such cases, and when the stimuli in the positive set are equally probable, one can derive a theoretical relation between the increase in mean RT as a function of set size, and the increase in RT variance. (The derivation does not require one to assume that components of the RT are stochastically independent.) Although the variance is observed to increase markedly with set size, it does not increase fast enough relative to the mean to satisfy this relation. Such failures provide evidence against this variety of self-terminating search. But the variance increase, which is approximately linear with set size and equal in rate for positive and negative responses, is what one would expect from an exhaustive search process with stochastically independent comparison times (Sternberg, 1964).

B. Trace-Strength Discrimination

A second class of candidates for replacing the exhaustive-scanning model has appealed to several investigators as a way to extend more traditional concepts about memory to this domain; they can be described as pure trace-strength models (Baddeley & Ecob, 1973; Corballis, Kirby, & Miller, 1972; Nickerson, 1972). In these models there is no search; instead there is direct access to an internal representation of the test stimulus. Members of the positive set are assumed to have acquired greater strength than nonmembers as a result of their presentation or rehearsal; the binary decision can thus be based on the strength of the accessed test-stimulus representation, as in a "signal detection" analysis. Such models can be made to generate variations in RT by assuming a functional relation between the trace strength (and possibly also an adjustable strength criterion) and the duration of the strength-discrimination process. The models differ in the particular functions assumed and in the rules by which trace strengths are assigned to items.

In the particular models proposed by Corballis et al. (1972) and Nickerson (1972), the most recently presented or rehearsed item in the positive set has the same trace strength, whatever the size of the set. One implication is that the minimum of the RT distribution for positive responses should not increase with the size of the positive set, just as described in Section VI-A for a self-terminating search. Since this implication is violated by existing data, I consider only the particular model proposed by Baddeley and Ecob (1973, Model I), which does not have the above property. Their aim was to account, in the varied-set procedure, for effects of serial position and item duplication within the positive set, as well as linear and parallel RT functions. According to their model, a fixed amount (C) of trace strength is divided among the s members of the positive set. As the set is increased in size, therefore, the difference between the average strengths of the positive and negative items $(C/s$ and zero, respectively) is reduced, making the discrimination more difficult. The duration of the discrimination process is assumed proportional to the reciprocal of the difference between test-stimulus strength and an adjustable strength criterion. To account for the fact that the latencies of negative as well as positive responses increase with set size, the criterion is assumed to be moved closer to zero as set size grows. In particular, the criterion is assumed to be adjusted to $C/2s$, midway between the average strengths of positives and negatives, causing their RT functions to be parallel and linear.[3] The repetition effect can be accounted for by assuming that repeating an item in the set gives it a larger proportion of the available strength. Effects of serial-position on RT can be accounted for by variation in strength from item to item as a function of serial position.

At this point in its development there are at least three objections that can be leveled against the trace-strength model. The first and most serious is based on what happens when subjects have to retain a small number of additional items in short-term memory that are not relevant to the positive–negative decision, but are presented at the same time as the positive set and have to be recalled after the decision is made. If the irrelevant symbols must share in the limited available trace strength, the RT should increase with the number of such symbols that have to be retained. But a recent study (Darley, Klatzky, & Atkinson, 1972) has shown that even in the varied-set procedure the RT is virtually unaffected by the additional load on short-term memory. This finding presents a serious problem for the strength theory. To avoid this difficulty, a trace-strength theory would seem to require a special limited supply of trace strength that can be shared only by members of the positive set.

[3] Insofar as the total trace strength, C, is distributed unequally among the members of the positive set, the linearity of the RT function for positive responses is only approximate: mean discrimination time is proportional to the mean of the reciprocal strengths, which is not identical to the reciprocal of the mean strength.

The second objection is that a natural interpretation of "trace strength" makes it difficult for the model to account for performance when the positive set is well learned, as in the fixed-set procedure, and when negative stimuli have been presented as often as positives over a series of test trials, so that they should be equally familiar. Despite the large differences in stimulus frequency and degree of learning between these conditions and those of the varied-set procedure, the two procedures produce results that are virtually identical. To explain this, it has to be assumed that frequency of presentation *per se,* which is usually regarded as a critical determinant of strength in long-term memory, has no effect on the trace strength that is used in the decision process.

Finally, since the strength criterion used in the decision is adjustable, it should vary as a function of the relative frequency with which positive and negative responses are required, in order to minimize the mean RT. But it can be shown that such adjustment would change the relative slopes of the latency functions for positive and negative responses, as well as their zero intercepts. And such slope changes are not observed when the relative frequency of the responses is varied (Sternberg, 1963, 1969b, Experiment 4).

C. Parallel Comparisons

The final alternative to the exhaustive-scanning stage that is considered here is a model in which the test stimulus is compared in parallel to all the members of the positive set. In most models of this type that have recently been considered, each of the simultaneous comparisons is assumed to require processing capacity; the increase of mean RT with set size is assumed to result from the sharing of a fixed capacity among these increasing demands, thereby reducing the capacity available for each comparison, which determines its duration.[4] By suitably relating the capacity concept to processing time, a linear set-size function can be generated (Atkinson, Holmgren, & Juola, 1969; Corcoran, 1971; Townsend, 1971).

The particular parallel model that has attracted most attention has been considered by Atkinson *et al.* (1969) and by Townsend (1971). All comparisons start simultaneously and have durations that are expo-

[4] Parallel models in which the duration of any particular comparison is *not* influenced by the number of other ongoing comparisons, or by when they are completed, can be rejected because the effect of number of comparisons (set size) on the mean is too great relative to an estimate of the comparison-time variance (Sternberg, 1963, 1966).

nentially distributed. The available capacity is assumed to be equally divided among those comparisons not yet completed, and the mean comparison time is assumed proportional to the reciprocal of the assigned capacity. The mean of the exponential distributions is therefore proportional to the number of ongoing comparisons. As soon as one comparison is completed, the limited capacity is instantaneously reallocated to the others, reducing their means. This continues until the final comparison is completed. If the process is assumed to be exhaustive, the resulting RT functions are linear and parallel. A model like this is proposed, not to account for effects that a serial process cannot explain, but rather as an alternative of possibly equal power.

My first comment about this model also applies to other parallel models that invoke the concept of a limited shared capacity. What is the limited capacity used for, other than the comparison process? Any concurrent task whose introduction has no effect on the RT function cannot be sharing in the same capacity. I mentioned above that introducing a small memory load that is not relevant to the decision has virtually no effect on the RT (Darley *et al.*, 1972). It has also been shown that adding a concurrent size discrimination to the item-recognition task leaves the RT function unchanged (Ellis & Chase, 1971). Therefore neither of these additional processing operations can be sharing the same limited capacity that is used by the scanning process.

One concurrent task that is always present in item recognition, at least in the varied-set procedure, is maintaining the memory of the positive set. In the particular parallel model mentioned above, it is (implicitly) assumed that any capacity required by this process is either fixed, regardless of the size of the memory load, or that its source is different from the capacity used by the scanning process.

Finally, difficulties are presented for this model in accounting for the RT function when it *is* changed by additional processing demands. Pure changes in slope, with no change in zero-intercept, are easy to explain by assuming that added demands consume a fixed amount of the available capacity, independent of the size of the positive set. But pure intercept changes require a different rule for capacity sharing, in which the capacity allocated to the additional demand is reduced as the positive set is increased in size. Thus, Wattenbarger and Pachella (1972) found that embedding an arrows–keys binary choice task in an item-recognition experiment increased only the intercept of the RT function. Since performance in the embedded task was the same, regardless of the size of the positive set, any capacity allocated to it would have to be constant. But a constant reduction in the capacity available for the scanning process should have changed the slope of the RT function rather than its intercept. Here, again, the embedded task cannot have been sharing the same capacity. These constraints that are required on the capacity concept seem to me to reduce its appeal considerably.

My second comment concerns the use of the exponential distribution to represent the duration of a processing operation. Despite its popularity and simplicity, and its success in describing aspects of radioactivity and telephone traffic, I think it can be argued that the Markov (no memory) property of the exponential is fundamentally inconsistent with what we normally mean by the concept of processing over time. Consider the processing of a single item. Given an exponential distribution it follows that, no matter how much time has elapsed, so long as processing is not yet complete the expected remaining time needed to complete it is unchanged. This means that at any point in time the processing that has been accomplished is either all or none and therefore that the processing of an item must be instantaneous. What is arranged in parallel in the particular model proposed by Atkinson *et al.* (1969) and by Townsend (1971), then, is not a set of processing operations, but a set of waiting times prior to processing. The processing itself occurs at a series of points in time.

VII. NEW FINDINGS

A. The Translation Effect

For the remainder of this paper I turn my attention away from alternative explanations of the set-size effect, and act as if there is an exhaustive serial-comparison process. In this context I consider some intriguing new findings that bear on several issues that can be raised about the process, and also present new puzzles.

In the assumed scanning process, some internal representation of the test stimulus is compared to internal representations of items in the positive set. What is the nature of the internal codes that can be compared at such high speed? An equivalent question is: to what level is the test stimulus processed before it enters into the series of comparisons? To what extent do the codes depend on the format or sensory modality in which the stimuli are presented?

Experiments that bear on this issue in a number of laboratories have revealed what can be called a *translation effect*. These experiments are concerned with what happens when the test stimulus is not identical to a possible member of the positive set, but is related to it by association. In some instances the associations were known by the subject before he arrived in the laboratory, such as the relation between printed letters and their spoken names. In other instances the associations were learned in the laboratory.

In one of their experiments, for example, Cruse and Clifton (1973) taught subjects a set of 8 letter–digit associations. In the item-recognition experiment that followed, which used sets that changed from trial to trial, a set could contain either all letters or all digits, and the test stimulus could be either a letter or a digit, with equal probability. Consider a trial on which the set contains digits. If the test stimulus is also a digit, we have the standard task. But if the test stimulus is a letter, the subject must decide whether the digit associated with that letter is contained in the set. If the subject did this by translating the test stimulus into the "language" of the set and then searched for the translation, one might expect an increase in the zero-intercept, reflecting the translation time, but no change in the slope. Exactly the reverse occurred: when the "languages" of set and test-stimulus differed so they were related by association, the slopes of the RT functions for both positive and negative responses increased substantially —from 37 to 94 msec/item, on the average—but there was no increase in the zero-intercepts. The same effect occurs, although less dramatically, when the two languages are printed letters and their spoken names, even when the subject knows the sensory modality of the test stimulus in advance (Chase & Calfee, 1969). Similar effects have been observed in several other cases, with slope increases ranging from 20% to over 100% (*e.g.,* Swanson, Johnsen, & Briggs, 1972; see also Burrows & Okada, 1973; Juola & Atkinson, 1971; and Klatzky *et al.,* 1971).

Several explanations are available, and it is too early to decide among them. The most obvious is that for some reason yet to be determined, if their "languages" differ, each member of the set is translated into the code of the test stimulus, or into some common code, after the test stimulus is presented. If each translation operation added the same mean increment to the RT, the result would be a change in slope, but no change in intercept, as observed. (If the test stimulus instead of the set were translated, the effect should be seen in the intercept, but not the slope.)

Two recent findings by Clifton and his associates, however, have led them to question this explanation: first, increases in the rate at which the positive set is presented that do not change the RT function under normal conditions increase its intercept when translation is required (Clifton, Cruse, & Gutschera, 1973). Second, variations in the learned associations that change the associative latencies for overt translation do not always change the slope of the RT function when covert translation is required in the recognition task (Clifton, Gutschera, Brewer, & Cruse, 1973). An alternative explanation for the effect they consider is that both direct and translated representations of the positive set are generated before the test stimulus is presented, but that the translated representation is stored in a less "active" form that is scanned more slowly than the direct representation.

Whatever the explanation of the translation effect, it seems evident from its existence that even after several seconds the memory code of the positive set may strongly reflect the form in which the stimuli were presented. This idea appears to conflict sharply with the ideas about recoding (of, *e.g.,* visual stimuli into their spoken names) that psychologists have been led to by the study of errors in short-term memory.

B. Partial Selectivity of Search

The second set of findings I would like to consider bear on the selectivity of the scanning process. In most item-recognition experiments the memorized list that defines the positive set is relatively homogeneous, and there is no basis on which search could be selective. Suppose instead that the list is partitioned into distinct sublists, each containing a different category of items. It would presumably benefit the subject if he could confine his search to the "relevant" sublist—that is, the sublist containing the category to which the test stimulus belongs. For scanning to be selective in this way, two conditions must be met. First, the category of the test stimulus must be ascertained. Second, the list must be organized in memory in such a way that selective access to the relevant sublist is possible. In considering findings related to this question it is worth noting that if the scanning process is sufficiently fast and categorizing sufficiently slow, then selective search might be slower, on the average, than unselective search, so that selective search might not occur, even if selective access was possible.

It has been shown that if the subject is informed of a relevant subset sufficiently in advance of the test stimulus, he can scan selectively, even while maintaining the "irrelevant" items in short-term memory. That is, the subject is not obliged to search the entire set of recently presented items, even though they may be required for later recall (Darley *et al.,* 1972). But perhaps more interesting is whether selective scanning occurs when there is no advance warning: is scanning of a recently memorized list that contains two or more well-defined sublists limited to the sublist whose category matches that of the test stimulus? A series of experiments by Naus *et al.* (1972; Naus, 1974) addressed this question. They used ensembles of common words organized into several different semantic categories. In one experiment (Naus *et al.,* 1972), for example, the words were either girls' names or animal names. The positive set contained either words from just one category or equal-size sublists of words from the two different categories. The category of the test stimulus was always represented by at least one of the words in the positive set. For both kinds of sets the RT functions for positive and negative responses were linear and parallel. However, when the list contained two semantic categories rather than one, the slope was reduced by 25%, and there was no substantial intercept difference. If scanning were completely selective, the slope would have been reduced by 50%, because only half of the words would have been scanned. On the other hand, if scanning were completely unselective, and if we assume that relevant and irrelevant words are scanned at the same rate, then the slopes would have been equal. Neither of these was the case.

The 25% reduction suggests two simple interpretations. One is that on the average, exactly half of the irrelevant words, as well as all of the relevant words, are scanned at the standard rate. This was the interpretation made by Naus *et al.* (1972). It means that search is partially but not wholly selective. The alternative interpretation is that search is not selective at all, but that irrelevant words are scanned at exactly twice the rate of relevant ones. I use the word "exactly" because of results when the experiment was generalized to lists containing three and four equal-length sublists from different categories (Naus, 1974). The more categories, the smaller the fraction of the list containing words from the relevant category, and the greater the slope reduction. In each case, the observed slope of the RT function was within 1% of what would be expected from either of these interpretations.

A model of the process that corresponds to the Naus *et al.* interpretation is as follows. Words in the memorized list are stored in a set of bins, with one category per bin. Either because the bins are unmarked, or because the category of the test word is not ascertained, selective access does not occur. Instead, the bins are entered and searched successively in random order. The words in each bin are searched exhaustively, and at the standard rate, whether or not they are in the same category as the test word. However, when the bin containing the relevant category is entered, this fact is detected, and the search stops as soon as this bin has been scanned. Given this model, an irrelevant bin has a probability of exactly one-half of being searched, but the relevant bin is always searched. Hence, irrelevant words add half as much time, on the average, as relevant words.

How is the detection of category relevance achieved? Naus *et al.* suggest that the category "label" of the test word, $L(t)$, is compared to the category label, $L(b)$, of the bin words, and that this occurs at the same time as the contents of the bin are being scanned. But the data for short lists would then require that retrieving $L(t)$ and comparing it to $L(b)$ be very brief processes. An alternative is that the categorical identity of test word and bin word (t and b) or of test word and bin label [t and $L(b)$]

can be recognized "directly," without having to delay the search by the time required to retrieve the category, $L(t)$, of the test word. In either case it is an open question why the search should be exhaustive within bins but not across bins.

Before we leave this topic, it is perhaps worth mentioning two objections to the alternative interpretation, according to which all the irrelevant words are scanned, but at twice the rate. This interpretation has the advantage of being more consistent with results of studies (using different kinds of items and different procedures from Naus *et al.*) in which the test stimulus could be drawn from a category not represented in the positive set. For such stimuli the RT function typically has a slope that is neither as small as zero—which would indicate no search—nor as large as the slope for same-category stimuli—which would indicate search at the normal rate (Homa, 1973; Lively & Sanford, 1972; Milles & Morin, 1970; but see also Okada & Burrows, 1973). However, one objection is that the exact 2:1 ratio between mismatching times for words from same and different categories that is required for the Naus *et al.* data calls for an explanation in terms of process structure rather than parameter values. The other objection is based on the existence of some data indicating that when the words from various categories are scrambled in the list, rather than being arranged into sublists, and subjects do not rearrange them in memory, then the effect disappears (Naus, 1974).

C. Relation between Search Structure and Search Rate

If we had an acceptable explanation for the exhaustiveness of the scanning process in item recognition, this would seem to reduce the pressure to find alternative models. I turn next to some recent data that bear on this issue and seem to support the explanation I put forward some time ago (Sternberg, 1966; 1969a). The difficulty with exhaustiveness is that it strikes one as inefficient. Why should scanning continue after a match has occurred? But suppose we have a system in which a separate match-testing operation is needed to determine whether a match has occurred. If match-testing takes time and cannot occur concurrently with scanning, then, for a self-terminating search, the scanning process would have to be interrupted after each comparison. The response depends only on whether there is a match, not on which item produces it. Therefore it might be faster, on the average, to store information that a match had occurred in a location that was examined only after all comparisons had been completed. But this would depend delicately on the relative speeds of scanning versus match-testing. Roughly speaking, the slower the scanning process, the less efficiency to be gained from exhaustiveness.

Some support for this explanation seemed to be provided by the discovery that when the task was changed so that the response depended on which item produced the match, the scanning process became substantially slower and appeared self-terminating (Sternberg, 1967b). But this finding could be explained in other ways as well.

Table 8-1 shows results from five recent studies that provide evidence for self-terminating search in the item-recognition task itself, for either some subjects or some treatments. The evidence is based on the relation between the slopes of the RT functions from positive and negative responses: for a self-terminating search the slope ratio expected is 0.5, for an exhaustive search, 1.0. There is a fine dividing line between this kind of *post-hoc* analysis and numerology, but I feel that the results are at least suggestive. What is interesting is the association between small slope ratios and slow scanning rates; this association fits with the idea that it is the exhaustiveness of the process that makes its high speed possible, that the rate of self-terminating search is slower because of the time consumed by checking for the occurrence of a match after each comparison, and that although self-termination can sometimes speed positive responses, it must slow negatives. Except possibly for the first two sets of data, this association cannot have resulted from a selection artifact.

In the Clifton and Birenbaum (1970) study, among 12 subjects, 9 had slope ratios near 1.0 (range .80–1.25) and 3 had ratios near 0.5 (range .41 to .56). The mean scanning rate for the 3 was 50% slower. In the Corballis and Miller (1973, Group R) study, among 10 subjects, 6 had slope ratios near 1.0 (range .83–1.25) and 4 had ratios near 0.5 (range .50–.65). The mean scanning rate for the 4 was 89% slower. In the Klatzky and Atkinson (1970) study, I divided subjects into two groups on the basis of the means of positive and negative slopes.

TABLE 8-1

Experiment	Group or condition	Mean slope negative responses (msec/item)	Mean slope ratio (positive/negative)
Clifton & Birnbaum (1970)	9 subjects	31	0.99
	3 subjects	47	0.47
Corballis & Miller (1973, Group R)	6 subjects	45	1.02
	4 subjects	85	0.58
Klatzky & Atkinson (1970)	5 flattest	37	1.00
	5 steepest	113	0.44
Pachella (1972)	before	50	1.0
	after	105	0.6
Swinney & Taylor (1971)	normals	44	1.18
	aphasics	121	0.55

Again, the slow-scanning group displays a mean slope ratio near 0.5, and the others, who show the normal scanning rate, have a mean ratio of 1.0. In the Pachella (1972) study the treatment placed extreme emphasis on speed. This led to a reduction in intercept, but at the same time seems to have changed subjects from fast and exhaustive to slow and self-terminating. Finally, in the Swinney and Taylor (1971) study, the normals appear to be fast and exhaustive, and the aphasics slow and self-terminating.[5]

In addition to supporting an explanation of exhaustiveness, some of these data seem to indicate a bunching of slope ratios in the vicinity of 0.5 and 1.0. If this could be better documented in other studies, it would represent strong evidence against some of the models (such as those involving trace strength or processing capacity considered in Sections VI-B and VI-C) that explain the set-size effect without a scanning process.

D. Exhaustive Search in Long-Term Memory

A number of experimenters are currently using RT methods to explore the processes underlying relatively accurate retrieval of information from large lists or categories that are well learned and presumably stored in long-term memory (e.g., Atkinson & Juola, 1974; Indow & Togano, 1970; Landauer & Meyer, 1972; Lovelace & Snodgrass, 1971). Several reasons prompt me to discuss the model developed on the basis of a recent set of studies by Juola, Atkinson, and colleagues, in which the item-recognition paradigm has been extended to well-learned ordered lists of up to 30 random words (Juola, Fischler, & Wood, 1971; Atkinson & Juola, 1973, 1974). First, these studies suggest that familiarity (or trace strength) does play a role in such tasks, while also showing how its role is limited, relative to the one assumed for it in the models of pure trace-strength discrimination discussed in Section VI-B. Second, they reveal a search process in long-term memory that is qualitatively similar but quantitatively different from the exhaustive-scanning process we have been considering. And third, they suggest a possibly fruitful elaboration of the exhaustive-scanning model, as applied to the original paradigm.

According to the model developed by Juola and Atkinson, the learning of a list of words has two effects. One is that the familiarity value associated with a representation of each word in a lexical memory is increased; the other is that in a different part of the long-term memory the words are stored as an array. Thus, two alternative bases for a recognition decision are established. When a test stimulus is presented, there is direct

[5] I thank C. Clifton, Jr., and M. C. Corballis for furnishing me with unpublished details of their data.

access to its representation in the lexical memory, where its level of familiarity can be determined. The difficulty with making the decision at this point is that even when positive items are from well-learned lists, and negative items have not been seen before in the experiment, familiarity is not a reliable indicator of list membership. This idea is represented in Fig. 8-8a. Although responses based exclusively on familiarity would be uniformly fast, they would contain many errors. Therefore, when higher accuracy is called for, the process indicated in Fig. 8-8b is used. When the familiarity level is either high enough or low enough to be reliable, fast responses are made, based on familiarity discrimination alone. The speed of these responses does not depend on how extreme a familiarity value the test stimulus has, and they lead to some small number of errors. But when the familiarity level falls in the range of unreliability that lies between the two adjustable criteria, a search of the stored array is performed, which leads to an accurate response.

The result is a special instance of the probabilistic mixture of processes discussed in Section V and illustrated in Fig. 8-7, in which both the mixing probability, P, and the mean RT on nonsearch trials are independent of list length.[6] As shown in Fig. 8-8c, the obtained RT function is a probabilistic mixture (weighted average) of two functions, one constant and the other increasing linearly; relative to the latter, the mixture is still linear, but has a reduced slope and intercept.

Parameter values in the fitted model that represent effects of list length on the search time for positive versus negative responses tell us that the search is exhaustive, and that although it takes about 70 msec longer to initiate than a search of short-term memory, it proceeds at the higher rate of about 10 msec (rather than 35 msec) per word.[7] These parameter

---

[6] Given that the RT function is based on correct responses only, the proportion, P, is a mean of two proportions, one for positive test stimuli, determined by the relation between the criteria (C_N and C_P) and the familiarity distribution for positive stimuli, and the other for negative test stimuli and determined by the relation between the criteria and the familiarity distribution for negative stimuli.

[7] These values unfortunately suggest an inconsistency with experiments using short lists. According to the parameter estimates, if the RT function produced by a search in active memory is $T_A = \alpha + 35s$ msec, then the function produced by a search in long-term memory is $T_L = \alpha + 70 + 10s$ msec. For a list of length $s = 1$ or 2 that is contained in both memories (as in the fixed-set procedure), T_A is the smaller, so the active-memory search should be used. But for a list of length $s = 3$ or more, the search in long-term memory is the faster. These considerations would be hard to reconcile with the similarity of results from varied-set and fixed-set procedures (Fig. 8-2) if this similarity could be demonstrated for words as it has been for digits. They are also hard to reconcile with the effects on the RT function of fully loading the active memory with irrelevant material (Sternberg, 1969a, Experiment 5).

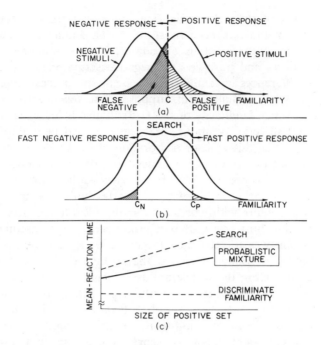

Fig. 8-8. The Atkinson-Juola (1974) model. (a) Overlapping familiarity distributions for positive and negative stimuli. In the middle range of values, the familiarity measure available by direct access to the representation of the test word in the lexical memory is not a reliable indicator of list membership. (b) Hence decisions are based on familiarity discrimination alone only outside the middle range of familiarity values. When the value is inside this range, a search of the stored array is performed that uses more time, but guarantees perfect accuracy. (c) Mean RT function when search time (top function) is linear with list length, and mean RT on nonsearch trials (bottom function) and mixing probability are independent of list length. The overall RT function is a weighted average of the two contributing functions.

estimates are remarkably invariant across experiments and procedures, an outcome that lends considerable support to the model, as does its overall goodness of fit to results from several studies. On the other hand, several of the special assumptions that play a critical role are open to question. First, the familiarity distribution of the memorized words, which presumably depends on degree of learning, is assumed to be independent of list length. Second, the adjustable criteria are assumed to be independent of list length, even though lists of different lengths are learned by different subjects. Third, all errors are assumed to be generated by the familiarity-discrimination process; search trials are totally error free.

Elaborations of the exhaustive-scanning model for short lists contained in active memory, similar in spirit to the Juola–Atkinson model, would seem to be worth pursuing. Of course, if the ensemble is small, as it has usually been, and positive and negative sets are not distinguished by systematic differences in familiarity, the scanning process might be bypassed only very occasionally. But suppose these few occasions tend to be the trials on which familiarity of the test stimulus is high because it was drawn from certain serial positions, or because it had been duplicated in the positive set. Then this kind of elaboration of the model might be able to explain some of the troublesome effects considered in Section V.[8]

Atkinson and Juola (1974) have successfully applied such an elaborated model to an experiment by C. Darley and P. Arabie that used the varied-set procedure with words as stimuli, but differed from the typical procedure with short lists in that it used a very large ensemble of test stimuli. Their aim was to introduce large familiarity differences between positive and negative stimuli. Whereas the positive words on a trial were presented shortly before the test stimulus, a negative test stimulus might never have been seen in the course of the experiment. Some of the negatives were deliberately made more familiar, however, by being drawn from the previous positive set. According to the model, responses to such negatives should include more decisions based on scanning, and fewer based on familiarity discrimination. This implies that their RT function should be steeper than the function for negative words that were novel, and this is what was observed.

It is interesting that even for the novel negative words, the model tells us that search occurred on more than half of the trials and that if, instead, all decisions about these words had been based on familiarity discrimination, about 20% of the responses would have been errors. This result can be taken as further evidence of the inadequacy of a pure trace-strength model for explaining accurate performance.

E. Relation Between Memory Search and the Memory Span

The similarity between retrieval mechanisms in short-term and long-term memory that is suggested by the work discussed above, along with

[8] One difficulty in applying the model as it stands to experiments using short lists and typical procedures is that changes either in overall error rate or in the relative speeds of positive and negative responses would presumably be mediated by adjustment of one or both criteria, and would therefore require concomitant changes in slopes of the RT functions. But, as discussed in Section IV, changes in error rates and zero-intercepts have been produced by experimental variations that leave slopes relatively constant.

its elucidation of the role of familiarity, seems to help integrate results and interpretations from the item-recognition paradigm with more traditional concepts and issues of memory. But nothing that I have yet said explicitly links measures of accuracy when there is no time pressure, with measures of speed when there is. Indeed, an important general question that is not often raised in relation to RT studies is to what extent the processes invoked in speeded tasks are the same as those used in tasks without great time pressure. At the very least, it would be comforting to know that important parameters of performance in studies both of RT and of accuracy depend on the same factors. For this reason, I find particularly encouraging the result shown in Fig. 8-9, from a study by Cavanagh (1972), which is the last new finding I shall mention.

Cavanagh found seven classes of items, ranging from digits to nonsense syllables, for which both memory-span and memory-scanning data

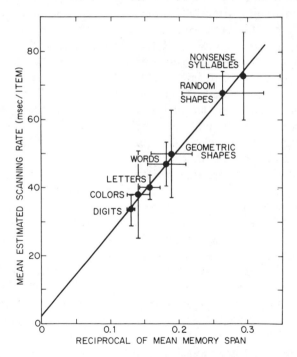

Fig. 8-9. The relation discovered by Cavanagh (1972) between mean slope of the RT function in item recognition (time per item; unit is 1 msec) and reciprocal of the mean memory span (space per item; unit is one memory span). Estimates of ± SE are based on pooled variance between studies, within classes of items. Intercept and slope of fitted line are 2.4 msec/item (not significantly different from zero) and 245.5 msec/span, respectively. Based on data from 45 experiments.

had been obtained for similar groups of subjects under similar conditions. Thirteen studies in the literature provided traditional measures of the immediate memory span for ordered sequences of items from these classes. These values were averaged for each class, and it is their reciprocals that are plotted on the abscissa. If one uses a space metaphor for immediate memory capacity, and thinks of memory span as the number of items that fill a fixed space, then the reciprocal is a measure of the space required per item. (Proportionately less of the fixed available space is presumably used by an item list that is shorter than the memory span.) For these same classes of items, 32 studies in the literature provided measures of the memory-scanning rate, in terms of slopes of the best-fitting linear functions of RT versus set size. These values of time required per item are plotted on the ordinate. What Cavanagh discovered, then, is that the time per item in the RT task is proportional to the space per item in the recall task.

Suppose that this remarkable relation could be confirmed and made more precise in studies specifically designed for the purpose. Its simplicity would then suggest that both measures are in some sense unitary or pure. It would suggest, for example, that the immediate-memory span indeed reflects the capacity of a single, short-term or active memory, rather than depending on contributions from more than one memory system as has recently been argued (Craik, 1971; but see also Shallice, 1975). The relation would support the idea that a straight line provides a meaningful approximation to the RT function; a simple quantitative law would be even more surprising if it involved the slope of a line fitted to what was really a curve. It would also suggest that so long as they are reliable, small slope differences in item recognition may be important.

Several directions of interpretation suggest themselves (see Cavanagh, 1972). One possibility is that the average number of features that make up the internal representation of an item varies from one class of items to another. If the memory space required by an item, as well as the duration of mismatching comparisons involving that item, are both proportional to the number of features in its representation, then Cavanagh's finding would be expected. One possible difficulty for this kind of interpretation (and one that makes the finding itself particularly surprising) arises if we consider the effects of adding features to the items that are redundant, but that nonetheless must be recalled in the memory-span task. (An example would be adding a different color to each member of a digit ensemble.) It seems likely that this would reduce the memory span without necessarily influencing performance in the item-recognition task, where the redundant feature could be ignored. If so, one would expect natural variations in redundancy from one class of items to another to similarly disrupt the relation between tasks.

On a dynamic theory of the memory span, involving a recycling "rehearsal" process that refreshes a decaying trace (*e.g.,* Broadbent, 1958), Cavanagh's finding could mean that the rehearsal rate and memory-scanning rate are proportional. But if the process that refreshes the trace is the same rehearsal often identified with covert speech, this interpretation is violated by a recent experiment (Clifton & Tash, 1973), which showed that syllabic word length influences the rate of covert speech, but not the memory-scanning rate.

VIII. SUMMARY

This paper has been concerned with the recognition of items in relatively short memorized lists, investigated with RT methods. First I described some of the early experiments that led to the idea of a high-speed, exhaustive scanning process, and indicated some of the other processing stages that the data seem to require. Then I considered extensions and generalizations of the early findings that show the phenomenon to be relatively robust, and the estimated scanning rate to be remarkably invariant across subject populations and practice. But effects of duplication, serial position, and probability show the scanning model to be either wrong or insufficiently detailed in its description of how these effects might arise in the encoding and decision stages. Such effects have led others to propose alternative models, involving self-terminating search, trace-strength discrimination, or parallel comparisons. Each of these alternatives has weaknesses that appear to be at least as serious as the inadequacies of the exhaustive-scanning model. My current preference is for a strategy of theorizing that retains the exhaustive-scanning process and elaborates the model by investigating the other processing stages and considering mixtures of processes.

Finally I described five recent developments that I find intriguing and that seem to shed more light on the scanning process as well as on other issues in memory research. The translation effect tells us about the coding of information in memory. Work with lists of words that are organized into categories suggests that search is partially but not wholly selective. The correlation between slopes and their ratios supports the idea that the high speed of the scanning process may depend on its exhaustiveness. Extension of the paradigm to long lists in long-term memory illuminates the role of familiarity in recognition and suggests elaborations of the scanning model for the case of short-term memory. And the relations between the scanning rate and the immediate memory-span links the recognition-RT approach to more traditional studies of recall accuracy.

REFERENCES

Anders, T. R., Fozard, J. L., & Lillyquist, T. D. Effects of age upon retrieval from short-term memory. *Developmental Psychology,* 1972, **6,** 214–217.

Atkinson, R. C., Holmgren, J. E., & Juola, J. F. Processing time as influenced by the number of elements in a visual display. *Perception & Psychophysics,* 1969, **6,** 321–327.

Atkinson, R. C., & Juola, J. F. Factors influencing speed and accuracy of word recognition. In S. Kornblum (Ed.), *Attention and performance,* Vol. 4. New York: Academic Press, 1973.

Atkinson, R. C., & Juola, J. F. Search and decision processes in recognition memory. In D. H. Krantz, R. C. Atkinson, R. D. Luce, & P. Suppes (Eds.), *Contemporary developments in mathematical psychology.* Vol. 1. San Francisco: W. H. Freeman, 1974.

Baddeley, A. D., & Ecob, J. R. Reaction time and short-term memory: Implications of repetition effects for the high-speed exhaustive scan hypothesis. *Quarterly Journal of Experimental Psychology,* 1973, **25,** 229–240.

Biederman, I., & Stacy, E. W., Jr. Stimulus probability and stimulus set size in memory scanning. *Journal of Experimental Psychology,* 1974, **102,** 1100–1107.

Broadbent, D. E. *Perception and communication.* New York: Pergammon Press, 1958.

Burrows, D., & Okada, R. Serial position effects in high-speed memory search. *Perception & Psychophysics,* 1971, **10,** 305–308.

Burrows, D., & Okada, R. Parallel scanning of semantic and formal information. *Journal of Experimental Psychology,* 1973, **97,** 254–257.

Cavanagh, J. P. Relation between the immediate memory span and the memory search rate. *Psychological Review,* 1972, **79,** 525–530.

Chase, W. G., & Calfee, R. C. Modality and similarity effects in short-term recognition memory. *Journal of Experimental Psychology,* 1969, **81,** 510–514.

Clifton, C., Jr. Must overlearned lists be scanned? *Memory & Cognition,* 1973, **1,** 121–123.

Clifton, C., Jr., & Birenbaum, S. Effects of serial position and delay of probe in a memory scan task. *Journal of Experimental Psychology,* 1970, **86,** 69–76.

Clifton, C., Jr., Cruse, D., & Gutschera, K. D. Recoding processes in recognition: Some effects of presentation rate. *Memory & Cognition,* 1973, **1,** 387–394.

Clifton, C., Jr., Gutschera, K. D., Brewer, E., & Cruse, D. Recoding in a character classification task: Some inconsistent effects of recoding difficulty. Unpublished report, Cognitive Processes Laboratory, University of Massachusetts, 1973.

Clifton, C., Jr., & Tash, J. Effect of syllabic word length on memory-search rate. *Journal of Experimental Psychology,* 1973, **99,** 231–235.

Coots, J. H., & Johnston, W. A. The effects of speed and accuracy strategies in an information-reduction task. *Perception & Psychophysics,* 1972, **12,** 1–4.

Corballis, M. C., Kirby, J., & Miller, A. Access to elements of a memorized list. *Journal of Experimental Psychology,* 1972, **94,** 185–190.

Corballis, M. C., & Miller, A. Scanning and decision processes in recognition memory. *Journal of Experimental Psychology,* 1973, **98,** 379–386.

Corcoran, D. W. J. *Pattern recognition.* New York: Penguin, 1971.

Craik, F. I. M. Primary memory. *British Medical Bulletin,* 1971, **27,** 232–236.

Cruse, D., & Clifton, C., Jr. Recoding strategies and the retrieval of information from memory. *Cognitive Psychology*, 1973, **4**, 157–193.

Darley, C. F., Klatzky, R. L., & Atkinson, R. C. Effects of memory load on reaction time. *Journal of Experimental Psychology*, 1972, **96**, 232–234.

Ellis, S. H., & Chase, W. G. Parallel processing in item recognition. *Perception & Psychophysics*, 1971, **10**, 379–384.

Eriksen, C. W., Hamlin, R. M., & Daye, C. Aging adults and rate of memory scan. *Bulletin of the Psychonomic Society*, 1973, **1**, 259–260.

Foss, D. J., & Dowell, B. E. High-speed memory retrieval with auditorily presented stimuli. *Perception & Psychophysics*, 1971, **9**, 465–468.

Harris, G. J., & Fleer, R. E. High speed memory scanning in mental retardates: Evidence for a central processing deficit. *Journal of Experimental Child Psychology*, 1974, **17**, 452–459.

Homa, D. Organization and long-term memory search. *Memory & Cognition*, 1973, **1**, 369–379.

Hoving, K. L., Morin, R. E., & Konick, D. S. Recognition reaction time and size of the memory set: A developmental study. *Psychonomic Science*, 1970, **21**, 247–248.

Indow, T., & Togano, K. On retrieving sequence from long-term memory. *Psychological Review*, 1970, **77**, 317–331.

Juola, J. F., & Atkinson, R. C. Memory scanning for words versus categories. *Journal of Verbal Learning and Verbal Behavior*, 1971, **10**, 522–527.

Juola, J. F., Fischler, I., Wood, C. T., & Atkinson, R. C. Recognition time for information stored in long-term memory. *Perception & Psychophysics*, 1971, **10**, 8–14.

Kintsch, W. Models for recall and recognition. In D. A. Norman (Ed.), *Models of human memory*. New York: Academic Press, 1970.

Klatzky, R. L., & Atkinson, R. C. Memory scans based on alternative test-stimulus representations. *Perception & Psychophysics*, 1970, **8**, 113–117.

Klatzky, R. L., Juola, J. F., & Atkinson, R. C. Test stimulus representation and experimental context effects in memory scanning. *Journal of Experimental Psychology*, 1971, **87**, 281–288.

Klatzky, R. L., & Smith, E. E. Stimulus expectancy and retrieval from short-term memory. *Journal of Experimental Psychology*, 1972, **94**, 101–107.

Kristofferson, M. W. Effects of practice on character-classification performance. *Canadian Journal of Psychology*, 1972, **26**, 540–560. (a)

Kristofferson, M. W. When item recognition and visual search functions are similar. *Perception & Psychophysics*, 1972, **12**, 379–384. (b)

Landauer, T. K. Rate of implicit speech. *Perceptual and Motor Skills*, 1962, **15**, 646.

Landauer, T. K., & Meyer, D. E. Category size and semantic-memory retrieval. *Journal of Verbal Learning and Verbal Behavior*, 1972, **11**, 539–549.

Lively, B. L. Speed/accuracy trade-off and practice as determinants of stage durations in a memory search task. *Journal of Experimental Psychology*, 1972, **96**, 97–103.

Lively, B. L., & Sanford, B. J. The use of category information in a memory search task. *Journal of Experimental Psychology*, 1972, **93**, 379–385.

Lovelace, E. A., & Snodgrass, R. D. Decision times for alphabetic order of letter pairs. *Journal of Experimental Psychology*, 1971, **88**, 258–264.

Lyons, J. J., & Briggs, G. E. Speed-accuracy trade-off with different types of stimuli. *Journal of Experimental Psychology*, 1971, **91**, 115–119.

Marcel, A. J. Some constraints on sequential and parallel processing, and the limits of attention. In A. F. Sanders (Ed.), *Attention and performance III. Acta Psychologica*, 1970, **33**, 77–92.

McCormack, P. D. Recognition memory: How complex a retrieval system? *Canadian Journal of Psychology*, 1972, **26**, 19–41.

Miller, J. O., & Pachella, R. G. Locus of the stimulus probability effect. *Journal of Experimental Psychology*, 1973, **101**, 227–231.

Milles, K. P., & Morin, R. E. The effect of a basis for stimulus classification on recognition reaction time. Paper presented at a meeting of the Midwestern Psychological Association, Cincinnati, May 1970.

Naus, M. J. Memory search of categorized lists: A consideration of alternative self-terminating search strategies. *Journal of Experimental Psychology*, 1974, **102**, 992–1000.

Naus, M. J., Glucksberg, S., and Ornstein, P. A. Taxonomic word categories and memory search. *Cognitive Psychology*, 1972, **3**, 643–654.

Nickerson, R. S. Response times with a memory-dependent decision task. *Journal of Experimental Psychology*, 1966, **72**, 761–769.

Nickerson, R. S. Binary-classification reaction time: A review of some studies of human information-processing capabilities. *Psychonomic Monograph Supplements*, 1972, **4**, 275–318 (whole number 65).

Okada, R., & Burrows, D. Organizational factors in high-speed scanning. *Journal of Experimental Psychology*, 1973, **101**, 77–81.

Pachella, R. G. Memory scanning under speed stress. Paper presented at a meeting of the Midwestern Psychological Association, Cleveland, May 1972.

Ross, J. Extended practice with a single-character classification task. *Perception & Psychophysics*, 1970, **8**, 276–278.

Shallice, T. On the contents of primary memory. In P. M. A. Rabbitt & Dornic, S. (Eds.), *Attention and performance, 5.* New York: Academic Press, 1975.

Simpson, P. J. High-speed memory scanning: Stability and generality. *Journal of Experimental Psychology*, 1972, **96**, 239–246.

Sternberg, S. Retrieval from recent memory: Some reaction-time experiments and a search theory. Paper presented at a meeting of the Psychonomic Society, Bryn Mawr, August 1963.

Sternberg, S. Estimating the distribution of additive reaction-time components. Paper presented at a meeting of the Psychometric Society, Niagara Falls, Ontario, October 1964.

Sternberg, S. High-speed scanning in human memory. *Science,* 1966, **153**, 652–654.

Sternberg, S. Two operations in character recognition: Some evidence from reaction-time measurements. *Perception & Psychophysics*, 1967, **2**, 45–53. (a)

Sternberg, S. Retrieval of contextual information from memory. *Psychonomic Science,* 1967, **8**, 55–56. (b)

Sternberg, S. Memory-scanning: Mental processes revealed by reaction-time experiments. *American Scientist*, 1969, **57**, 421–457. (a)

Sternberg, S. The discovery of processing stages: Extensions of Donders' method. In W. G. Koster (Ed.), *Attention and performance. II. Acta Psychologica,* 1969, **30**, 276–315. (b)

Sternberg, S. Evidence against self-terminating memory search from properties of RT distributions. Paper presented at a meeting of the Psychonomic Society, St. Louis, November 1973.

Sternberg, S. Memory scanning: New findings and current controversies. *Quarterly Journal of Experimental Psychology*, 1975, **27**, 1–32.

Swanson, J. M. The neglected negative set. *Journal of Experimental Psychology,* 1974, **103,** 1019–1026.

Swanson, J. M., & Briggs, G. E. Information processing as a function of speed versus accuracy. *Journal of Experimental Psychology,* 1969, **81,** 223–229.

Swanson, J. M., Johnsen, A. M., & Briggs, G. E. Recoding in a memory search task. *Journal of Experimental Psychology,* 1972, **93,** 1–9.

Swinney, D. A., & Taylor, O. L. Short-term memory recognition search in aphasics. *Journal of Speech and Hearing Research,* 1971, **14,** 578–588.

Theios, J. Reaction time measurements in the study of memory processes: Theory and data. In G. H. Bower (Ed.), *The psychology of learning and motivation,* Vol. 7. New York: Academic Press, 1973.

Theios, J., Smith, P. G., Haviland, S. E., Traupmann, J., & Moy, M. C. Memory scanning as a serial self-terminating process. *Journal of Experimental Psychology,* 1973, **97,** 323–336.

Townsend, J. T. A note on the identifiability of parallel and serial processes. *Perception & Psychophysics,* 1971, **10,** 161–163.

Wattenbarger, B. L., & Pachella, R. G. The effect of memory load on reaction time in character classification. *Perception & Psychophysics,* 1972, **12,** 100–102.

Wingfield, A. Effects of serial position and set size in auditory recognition memory. *Memory & Cognition,* 1973, **1,** 53–55.

Wingfield, A., & Branca, A. A. Strategy in high-speed memory search. *Journal of Experimental Psychology,* 1970, **83,** 63–67.

CHAPTER

9

DYNAMICS OF RETRIEVAL[1]

WAYNE A. WICKELGREN

When a subject attempts to recall or recognize many items or pairs of items over an extended period of time (15 sec or more), the retrieval

[1] This work was supported by Grant MH 17958 from NIMH.

process appears to be extremely complicated and it is difficult to describe the dynamics of such complex retrieval processes with mathematical precision. For this reason, complex retrieval tasks, such as free recall and ordered recall of entire lists, will be largely ignored in this paper.

This paper will try to draw some tentative conclusions concerning the retrieval processes in what might be called "elementary" recall and recognition tasks. Tasks that probe for recall or recognition of a single item or pair of items in a short period of time (less than 5 sec) are assumed to be tapping elementary retrieval processes that can be characterized in a precise and simple theory. According to this hypothesis, complex retrieval tasks, such as those involved in free recall or everyday recall of large amounts of information, are composed of sequences of elementary retrieval processes plus logical or other cognitive operations being applied to draw deduction from these retrieved memories.

Three elementary retrieval processes will be assumed: recognition, recall, and recency judgments. This paper defends the direct-access strength theory of elementary recognition and recall. According to this theory, presentation of a single item in a recognition test elicits a feeling of familiarity for the item as associated to a particular experimental context; the greater the strength of association between the item and the context, the greater the feeling of familiarity that is elicited. If a pair of items is presented, the greater the strength of association between the pair of items, the greater the feeling of familiarity that is elicited.

Following the criterion decision rule of Thurstonian Scaling and signal-detection theory, the subject is assumed to say "yes" to a test item or pair in a recognition task, if and only if the strength of that item or pair exceeds a variable recognition criterion. In multiple-choice recognition memory or recall with a small number of alternatives, an individual is assumed to choose the alternative that has the greatest associative strength in memory. In recall, with an extremely large number of alternative responses, let us assume that the correct response will be selected only if its associative strength exceeds some (high) recall threshold.

Elsewhere, I have speculated that some recency judgments are based on a second property of the long-term memory trace, namely, its resistance, which increases monotonically with delay since learning (Wickelgren, 1972). However, recency judgments can clearly be mediated indirectly by recalling associations to time concepts (serial position, times of the day, dates, periods in one's life, etc.). Because comparatively little research has been done on recency memory, and that research has not generally attempted to rule out indirect mediation of recency judgments via associations to time concepts, little can be concluded regarding the reality of any elementary recency retrieval process, let alone determining its logical character and dynamics. For this reason, this chapter will be concerned only with analyzing the dynamics of elementary recall and recognition.

Recently there has been some interest in comparing recognition with free recall. Such comparisons are of little theoretical interest because free recall is certain to be a very complex task involving a complicated sequence of elementary recall and recognition retrieval operations over a considerable period of time. Also, experimental control of the cues used in free recall is typically very poor, and subjects must generate most of the cues (typically category labels) themselves if they are to recall any reasonable number of items. There are bound to be many differences between the retrieval processes involved in recognition and free recall, and such comparisons tell us very little concerning the precise nature of the retrieval processes involved in elementary recognition or recall. The more illuminating comparisons are of probe recognition and probe recall with retrieval times limited to a few seconds.

I. STRENGTH VERSUS SCANNING THEORIES OF RETRIEVAL

At least three major stages of the memory usage process need to be distinguished: (1) the time to perceive the test stimulus, (2) the time to retrieve memory traces in some way connected to the trace stimulus, and (3) the time to make a response. The memory-retrieval phase of this process is sometimes divided into two subphases: (a) the time to access one or more memory traces and (b) the time to make a decision, or choose a response, based on the memory traces that have been accessed.

There are two basic classes of retrieval theories: strength theory (Baddeley & Ecob, 1970; Corballis, Kirby, & Miller, 1972; Norman & Wickelgren, 1969; Okada, 1971; Wickelgren & Norman, 1966) and scanning theory (Sternberg, 1966, 1967, 1969). The theory of Juola, Fischler, Wood, & Atkinson (1971) incorporates a mixture of strength and scanning theories.

Strength theory assumes that a test item directly accesses its internal representation in memory without the need for memory scanning, or search. Associated with this internal representative is a memory-trace strength that provides the input to the decision-making system, which selects the response. In addition, strength theory postulates that the output of the memory-accessing process is a continuous real-valued variable (strength), rather than a discrete (all-or-none, finite-state) variable. A continuous speed–accuracy tradeoff in memory retrieval can be realized within a strength theory, if the output of the memory-accessing processes increases in some continuous way with the time allowed for retrieval.

Memory-scanning theories assume that memory accessing involves a search of a number of storage locations, looking for a match between a stored item and the test item. In recognition, the output of the memory-accessing process is a one–zero (all-or-none) variable indicating the presence or absence of a match between the test item and an item in some storage location. In probe recall, after a match is found, the subject recalls the item in the next storage location. Since, in general, several memory locations are searched, a vector of ones and zeros will be output from the memory-accessing process as input to the decision process. The memory-search process is almost always assumed to be sequential, and the output of the process is assumed to be a series of discrete (zero *vs.* one) variables. Although one could postulate the output of the matching process to be a vector of continuous variables, representing the degrees of similarity between the test items and the items in storage locations, this sort of hybrid model has never, to my knowledge, been proposed. A scanning theory could account for continuous speed–accuracy tradeoff in retrieval by assuming that the scanning rate was variable and that, at faster scan rates, the probability of an error occurring in matching was higher than at slower scan rates.

Although the memory-scanning theory achieved almost instant popularity following the initial Sternberg (1966) study, and many subsequent studies concerned with the dynamics of memory retrieval have presented interpretations of their results in terms of scanning theory, the accumulated evidence strongly favors some form of strength theory over any form of scanning theory for both recall and recognition. The remainder of this section is concerned with documenting this assertion.

A. Recognition Memory

1. Short-Term Memory

Sternberg (1966) investigated reaction time in probe recognition memory with target sets in short-term memory consisting of from 1 to 6 digits. The task for a subject was to decide whether or not the test digit was a member of a previously memorized list (target set) consisting of from some 1 to 6 digits. Sternberg found that the time to make this decision increased linearly with the length of the target list, with the same slope constant obtaining for both negative and positive responses. Furthermore, Sternberg found no significant differences in reaction time as a function of serial position within a list of a given length. From these results, Sternberg concluded that the access process in recognition memory retrieval was an exhaustive serial scan of the target list. That is to say, subjects were assumed to scan every item in the target list for a match with the test item and make their yes–no decision on the basis of whether any match was achieved after scanning the entire list. It might seem more natural to assume that the scan would terminate when a match was achieved, but the scanning theory appears to require the assumption that all items in the target list are scanned, primarily in order to account for the fact that the slope for negative and positive items was identical in the Sternberg study. Although none of these results is inconsistent with strength theory, any strength theory accounting for these results would be relatively *ad hoc* and would not account for the results in the elegant manner provided by the exhaustive-scanning theory.

Although Sternberg's results have been replicated many times when there has been strict adherence to certain critical aspects of experimental procedure, it is also quite clear that Sternberg's findings are not generally true under other experimental procedures. The results under these other conditions favor strength theory over scanning theory. Furthermore, it is clearly the case that insufficient attention has been paid to the problem of speed–accuracy tradeoff in retrieval in those experiments alleged to support the scanning theory. When attention is paid to this problem, the results in those studies (*e.g.,* Sternberg, 1966) may not support memory-scanning theory either. Finally, there is evidence using the standard Sternberg (1966) conditions that is contrary to memory-scanning theory (Baddeley & Ecob, 1970).

Basically, the Sternberg results are replicated when presentation rate for the elements in the target set is relatively slow (about 1 sec per item or slower), and a relatively long (2 sec) interval elapses between the end of the list and the presentation of the test stimulus. Slow presentation rate and substantial delays between list presentation and test allow ample opportunity for rehearsal. Such rehearsal could easily eliminate the strong recency effect and any differences in degrees of learning (primacy effects) that would be expected by a strength theory. Consistent with this interpretation, when presentation rates are faster and delays between presentation and test are shorter, strong serial-position effects are obtained that are dominated by the recency effect, precisely as expected by strength theory (Baddeley & Ecob, 1970; Burrows & Okada, 1971; Corballis, 1967; Corballis *et al.,* 1972; Kirsner & Craik, 1971; Morin, DeRosa, & Stulz, 1967; Morin, DeRosa, & Ulm, 1967). In addition, Okada (1971) found a monotonic increase in "hit" latency with increasing lag in a continuous-recognition memory task.

Although only a few studies actually reject the original Sternberg (1966) finding of a linear increase in recognition-memory reaction time with increasing list length, many other studies show gross but not significant deviations from linearity. Furthermore, in every study known to me in which error rates have been reported, the error rates increase monotonically (and usually substantially from a relative point of view) with list length. If there is some type of speed–accuracy tradeoff operating in recognition memory, then such results indicate that the recognition-memory latencies at long list lengths are underestimated. In the absence of any knowledge concerning the form of speed–accuracy tradeoff, we cannot know whether this is a major or minor effect. However, at some point, we must assume that only small increases in accuracy occur with increasing decision latency. That is to say, after some time, it may require a relatively large amount of additional decision time in order to achieve a relatively small increase in recognition-memory accuracy. If only some of the decision times found in the memory-scanning studies lie in this range, small differences in recognition-memory accuracy could translate into very large differences in recognition time. This would mean that the obtained reaction times for long list lengths are *grossly* underestimated in relation to the reaction times for short list lengths.

The mistake is frequently made in interpreting error differences as a function of list length that a difference in error rate of 1% *vs.* 3%, or 0.1% *vs.* 1%, is a small difference in recognition memory accuracy. This is surely false from the point of view of strength theory, though it could be true with some memory-scanning theory. However, the general point is we cannot know at present what differences in recognition memory accuracy are "small" and insignificant in their biasing effects on retrieval time.

Also, the dynamic range of the independent variable (target set size) is so small in most studies (generally less than a range from 1 to 6 or 2 to 6 items), that a large variety of different functions will provide a reasonable fit to the increase in recognition memory-reaction time as a function of list length.

For all these reasons, there is little reason to have confidence in the alleged linear functions relating short-term recognition-memory time to list length.

Finally, even in the standard Sternberg conditions for a short-term memory recognition time experiment with slow presentation rate (1.2 sec per digit) and a 2 sec delay interpolated between presentation of the list and presentation of the test item, Baddeley and Ecob (1970) found that increasing the frequency of presentation of digits in the target list reduced the recognition-memory reaction-time for these digits by comparison to nonrepeated digits in the same target list and by comparison to comparable items in lists without repeats. These results are exactly what would be expected by a strength theory and are clearly inconsistent with the scanning theory. The inconsistency with a scanning theory is especially dramatic, since in one of the Baddeley and Ecob experiments, a linear increase in reaction time with increasing list length was obtained accompanied by an absence of serial-position effects. This demonstrates that the principal results claimed as support for the scanning theory can be obtained under conditions where a strength theory clearly appears to be necessary in order to account for the results.

2. Long-Term Memory

As Baddeley and Ecob (1970) and Corballis *et al.* (1972) point out, it was never reasonable to imagine that a serial-scanning process operated as a general model of the recognition-memory process. To apply the memory-scanning theory to long-term recognition memory, one must, at a minimum, assume that subjects can directly access some relevant list of location to scan, as it is obviously false to assume that we scan all our long-term memory-storage locations at even the "high-speed" scanning rates found by Sternberg (1966). Long-term recognition memory would simply take far longer than it does take.

The most favorable context for evaluating the scanning theory in retrieval from long-term memory is that of deciding whether a target word is a member of a verbal category (bird, animal, woman's name, *etc.*). In these studies, it has been shown that recognition-memory time generally increases with the number of instances in the category (Juola & Atkinson, 1971; Landauer & Freedman, 1968; Meyer, 1970; Wilkins, 1971). But there have also been two failures to find any significant effect of category size (Collins & Quillian, 1970, Experiment I; Egeth, Marcus, & Bevan, 1972). The two failures come from radically different experimental contexts and represent gross extremes in the manipulation of category size. Thus, we cannot conclude that category size has any effect on retrieval time from long-term memory. However, even if this conclusion could be substantiated, it is undoubtedly predicted by both scanning and strength theories, since the strength of an association between a category and an instance of a category very likely decreases on the average for categories with larger numbers of examples.

Furthermore, there are discrepancies from any simple scanning model apparent in the data for both recognition-memory retrieval from well-established long-term categories (Juola & Atkinson, 1971) and categories newly established by presentation of a group of instances in the same experimental context (Fischler & Juola, 1971; Juola *et al.,* 1971). The principal discrepancies in the case of the experimentally established "categories" are recency effects (items presented more recently have shorter recognition-memory reaction times) and frequency effects (positive items presented more frequently have shorter recognition times than items presented less frequently and distractors presented more frequently have longer recognition latencies than distractors presented less frequently). These effects are, of course, exactly what a strength theory would expect. Faster recognition times for more recent and more frequent items have also been found in a continuous recognition memory task by Hintzman (1969).

Thus, despite an enormous body of work done from the perspective of memory-scanning theory, the results, at present, unequivocally support a strength theory over a scanning theory for recognition-memory retrieval time for both long-term and short-term memory.

B. Recall

1. Short-Term Memory

The dynamics of retrieval via a recall test have not been as extensively or systematically investigated as for recognition tests. Nevertheless, it can be said that the results on the whole are somewhat more consistent with the strength theory than with the scanning theory of retrieval in recall.

The scanning theory proposed by Sternberg (1967) for recall postulated a self-terminating serial scanning, rather than an exhaustive serial scanning (as in the case of recognition memory). The basic reason Sternberg postulated self-terminating scanning was that recall time increased monotonically (and approximately linearly) with position in the list, the fastest times being for the first position and the slowest times being for the last position in the list. However, it was clear from the data that one could not assume that all subjects were beginning their scan at the beginning of the list, since the time to recall the second item, given the first item as a probe, increased as a function of list length. Furthermore, the slope of the function plotting recall time against serial position was not equal to twice the slope of the function plotting recall time against list length, as it should have been according to a self-terminating serial-scanning strategy.

To resolve these discrepancies, Sternberg proposed that subjects sometimes begin at other positions in the list and scan cyclically. In support of this interpretation, the results for two different subjects were plotted with the different subjects showing vastly different rates of increase in recall time as a function of serial position. Sternberg claims that the average recall data reflect a mixture of starting strategies from different subjects.

However, it is at least equally plausible to assume that under the conditions used by Sternberg (which encouraged extensive rehearsal of the list between presentation and test), strengths of associations decreased systematically as a function of serial position. Assuming that recall time decreases with increasing associative strength, the Sternberg results can be accounted for by a strength theory.

Once again, the reality of the linear increase in recall time as a function of list length is very questionable considering the fact that errors in recall increase markedly as a function of list length. As mentioned previously, consideration of the possibility of speed–accuracy tradeoff in recall would indicate that under these conditions, the recall times for long lists are underestimated relative to the recall times for short lists. Whether consideration of the matter would make the form of the function nonlinear is unknown, but it is a possibility.

The monotonic increase in recall latencies as a function of serial position (pure primacy effect) is very rarely observed in either short-term or long-term recall experiments. A straight recency effect was found in short-term recall times by Norman (1966), and both primacy and recency effects on recall time have been found in a task that presumably involves a combination of short- and long-term memory by Waugh (1970) and in a long-term memory task by Kennedy (1968). DeRosa and Baumgarte (1971) find both primacy and recency effects on recall time and also find effects on recall time induced by inserting, in the middle of the list, brief pauses that induce a grouping structure. These enormous variations of recall time as a function of serial position are essentially equally easy or equally difficult for either memory scanning or strength theory to account for, but they indicate how little can be concluded from the serial-position results obtained by Sternberg (1967).

2. Long-Term Memory

Once again, as was the case for recognition time, greater frequency of presentation of a pair of items decreases the probe-recall latency for the response item given the stimulus item, even for a very large number of trials beyond the last error (Eimas, 1964; Eimas & Zeaman, 1963; Hall, 1969; Millward, 1964; Peterson, 1965; Schlag-Rey, Groen, & Suppes, 1965; Suppes, Groen, & Schlag-Rey, 1966; Theios, 1965; and Wiggins, 1957).

Although frequency and recency effects are the stock-in-trade of direct-access theories (whether finite-state or strength theories), note that very likely some type of scanning theory can be devised to account for such effects, but it would have to be a great deal more complex than the scanning theories proposed so far.

The variable of primary significance according to a scanning theory is the size of the category through which the scan takes place. In the case of long-term recall, it is possible to find conditions, such as in Metlay, Handley, & Kaplan (1971), in which subjects do appear to search sequentially through the instances of a category name, such as the 12 zodiac names, looking for a name containing the letter "n" (*e.g.,* Gemini, Cancer, and Capricorn). However, Freedman and Loftus (1971) have shown that the number of examples in a category has no necessary effect on recall re-action times when the cues are more strongly associated to correct re-sponse items, for instance, producing an animal name that starts with the letter "z," such as "zebra." For tasks such as these, where both the category name and the initial letter are strongly associated to a target word or words, there appears to be no effect of either the number of instances in the noun category or the number of possible correct instances. Such find-ings seem strongly inconsistent with serial scanning as a general model of retrieval in recall from long-term memory.

That the strength of association between the cues and the response items constitutes the principal factor in determining whether a memory-search process needs to be initiated was also indicated by the results of Ceraso, Bader, and Silverstein (1970), who found that the effects of list length on response latency in paired-associate recall declined with in-creasing degree of learning of the lists.

On the whole, it would seem that the evidence favors some type of strength theory of retrieval in recall as well as in recognition memory.

II. SPEED–ACCURACY TRADEOFF IN MEMORY RETRIEVAL

As was mentioned in the preceding sections, our lack of knowledge concerning the possibility of speed–accuracy tradeoff in memory retrieval limits our ability to draw conclusions about retrieval dynamics on the basis of recognition and recall times. Stating the issue in strength-theory terms, the issue is whether the strength of the accessed (retrieved) memory trace increases in a gradual way as a function of retrieval time or suddenly ap-pears in an all-or-none manner at some fixed time following the initiation of the retrieval process. As usual, it does not appear to be possible at present to distinguish a gradual incremental increase in retrieved strength as a function of retrieval time from an all-or-none retrieval process with some appropriate probability density function for finishing times. Each would produce a continuous speed–accuracy tradeoff function, and these two theories will be lumped together and considered in opposition to a theory in which retrieval time is relatively fixed.

If retrieved-memory strength varies in a relatively continuous manner with retrieval time, then presumably one could obtain a family of func-tions such as that shown in Fig. 9-1.

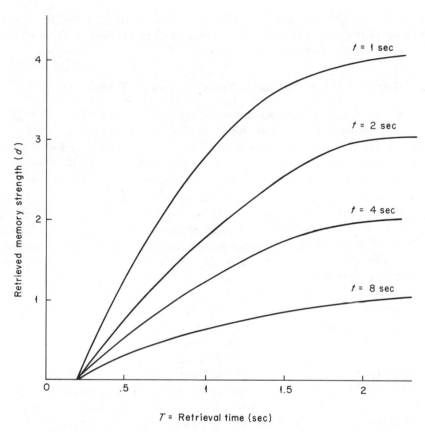

Fig. 9-1. Hypothetical speed–accuracy tradeoff functions for memory retrieval in a short-term memory task with retention interval (t) as the parameter.

The hypothetical speed–accuracy tradeoff function shown in Fig. 9-1 indicates the possibility of an initial latent period of perhaps 200 msec in which the memory-retrieval process would not produce any strength output. After this, the retrieved-memory strength is presumed to increase as a function of retrieval time (T), at a monotonically decreasing rate, to an asymptote set by the strength of the memory trace in store at that time. In Fig. 9-1 this is shown as a function of retention interval (t) in a short-term memory task, where the strength of the trace in storage is presumed to decrease markedly over a retention interval from 1 to 10 sec. Previous studies deriving the strength of the memory trace from recognition or recall-accuracy (choice) data presumably yield the asymptotic values of the function shown in Fig. 9-1. That is to say, if subjects are allowed at least 3 or 4 sec for retrieval, they are presumed to be at or near the asymptote in terms of retrieved strength as a function of retrieval time. Some evidence in support of this assumption will be discussed later.

A. Methods Used to Determine Speed–Accuracy Tradeoff Functions

In determining a speed–accuracy tradeoff function for recognition memory retrieval such as that shown in Fig. 9-1, it is important that the reaction time be an independent (manipulated) variable rather than a dependent (measured) variable. Subjects should be induced to respond at different speeds in different sessions or different blocks of the same experimental session. This procedure for inducing subjects to respond at different speeds might involve the use of different payoff matrices for correct vs. incorrect responses emitted at different response times, although this procedure often appears to encourage subjects to make fast *random* guesses.

Alternatively, one could use simple instructions to the subjects to respond in different time windows or before some deadline time with the window or the deadline time being varied across different sessions or blocks of a session. In using either procedure, it is probably helpful to provide subjects with some feedback concerning their reaction time following each trial.

In my opinion, the best method of manipulating response time is to provide an external cue telling the subject when to respond. This is the method used by Schouten and Bekker (1967), and it appears to produce response-time distributions with very low variance. Low variance response-time distributions minimize the distortions of the speed–accuracy tradeoff function that are produced by pooling results over large sections of nonlinear functions (such as the functions in Fig. 9-1).

Fortunately, perceptual speed–accuracy tradeoff functions have primarily been determined using manipulated response times (see Pachella & Fisher, 1972, Fig. 2; and Schouten & Bekker, 1967, Figs. 2, 3, 4, and 6).

However, recently, several papers have appeared in the perceptual speed–accuracy area (Lappin & Disch, 1972a, and 1972b; Rabbitt & Vyas, 1970) in which speed–accuracy tradeoff functions (called latency operating characteristics by Lappin & Disch) have been derived using measured reaction times instead of manipulated reaction times. The procedure involved determining the accuracy measure for responses emitted with reaction times lying within some interval and doing this for all intervals of reaction time for which a sufficient number of responses were obtained in the experiment. Then accuracy is plotted as a function of the mean or median reaction time for each interval. This procedure is theoretically deficient for the following reason: The responses selected within each reaction-time interval do not necessarily arise from the same underlying sensory (or memory) strength distribution. It is reasonable to suppose and indeed many models of perceptual or memory reaction time assume that events with greater strength will be responded to more rapidly than events with lesser strength. To the extent that strength under a constant experimental condition is a random variable with some substantial variance, a "constant" experimental condition will generate a distribution of strength values. According to the present conception, the trials on which the condition has greater strength will initiate responses at shorter latencies on the average than trials with lesser strengths.

Direct evidence for the validity of this hypothesis has been provided for the recognition memory area by Norman and Wickelgren (1969), who showed that yes-no responses that were subsequently given high confidence were initiated with short latencies. In the presence of this confounding factor, the effect of plotting accuracy against measured reaction time is to overestimate the accuracy at short reaction times and underestimate the accuracy at long reaction times by comparison to a procedure that generates speed–accuracy tradeoff functions by manipulating rather than measuring reaction times.

Schouten and Bekker (1967) obtained speed–accuracy tradeoff functions using both procedures. What they called the "free" procedure used measured reaction times, and the "forced" procedure used manipulated reaction times. Comparing their Figs. 1 and 2 demonstrates a huge overestimation of accuracy at short latencies using measured reaction times, confirming the present argument. There was no possibility of seeing the predicted underestimation at longer latencies in their task because performance became perfect at long latencies (floor effect).

B. Universal Retrieval Function?

It would be particularly simple if it could be shown that the speed–accuracy tradeoff functions for memory retrieval could always be factored into two functions: one expressing the level of the asymptote as a function of various experimental conditions (such as learning time and retention interval) and the other function expressing the approach to this asymptote as a function of retrieval time. For the family of functions shown in Fig. 9-1. such factoring could be given by the following equation: $d(t, T) = m(t) \cdot r(T)$, where $m(t)$ represents the strength of the memory trace in storage as a function of retention interval and $r(T)$ represents the universal memory-retrieval function. Of course, there might be different memory-retrieval functions for recall and recognition, different modalities, and as a function of who knows what other conditions. This discussion is meant to indicate only the possibility that speed–accuracy tradeoff functions could have a very simple lawful character.

One particularly simple and plausible form for the "universal" retrieval function might be: $r(T) = 1 - e^{-\gamma[T-\delta]}$, meaning an exponential approach to a limit following a lag of δ, with $[T - \delta] = T - \delta$ for $T > \delta$ and $[T - \delta] = 0$ for $T \leq \delta$. Different retrieval functions for recall *vs.* recognition, short- *vs.* long-term memory might be simply characterized by different values of the parameters, γ and δ.

C. Incremental Tradeoff versus Fast-Guess Theory

Of course, one could obtain empirical curves similar to those shown in Fig. 9-1 without there being a continuous increase in retrieved memory strength as a function of retrieval time, but rather as a result of a changing mixture of fixed (long latency) accurate responses and fast guesses with chance accuracy. In perceptual reaction time contexts, some results have favored a pure fast-guess theory (Swensson & Edwards, 1971; Yellott, 1971), and some results have favored a continuous speed–accuracy trade-off (Swensson, 1972).

There is little doubt that subjects can make fast chance guesses. The really important question is whether subjects can adjust to retrieval times in some manner that yields incremental growth of accuracy. If it is possible to trade off accuracy for speed in a relatively continuous manner over some range of retrieval times, then this is a critical aspect of memory dynamics for which the laws have yet to be determined. If this is not possible, it would be important to know that it is not possible.

Several previous studies concerned with speed–accuracy tradeoff in memory retrieval suffer from the possibility of interpretation purely in terms of the fast-guess theory and do not unequivocably demonstrate continuous speed–accuracy tradeoff in either recognition memory (*e.g.,* Lively, 1972; Swanson & Briggs, 1969) or recall (Murdock, 1968).

However, a recent study by Reed (1973) obtained continuous speed–accuracy tradeoff in recognition memory, using a method somewhat similar to that used by Schouten and Bekker (1967), in which the results precluded interpretation in terms of fast guesses. The results were consistent with an exponential growth to a limit, though Reed favors a different theoretical function.

Reed's results indicate that the recognition retrieval function for short-term memory is close to its asymptote by about 2 sec after the onset of the test item. This agrees with the results of Murdock (1968) for short-term recall. Thus, we can probably assume that all the choice data obtained with retrieval times of 3 or 4 sec or more are obtained from the asymptotic section of the retrieval function and thus are relatively insensitive to latency differences. Both Reed and Murdock found the bulk of the increase in memory accuracy within the first second, indicating that this is the primary region of interest in investigating speed–accuracy tradeoff in (short-term) memory. Finally, the weak qualitative agreement of the Reed and Murdock studies suggests, very tentatively, the possibility that the retrieval dynamics of short-term recall and recognition memory are identical.

III. RETRIEVAL INTERFERENCE

Response Competition and Blocking

For many decades now it has been recognized that forgetting as measured by the increasing inability to produce the B member of an AB paired associate is not due only to decreasing strength of the association from A to B. Learning a list of AB paired associates followed by learning a list of AC paired associates creates problems in the subsequent recall of either the first or second list associates of the A stimulus due to factors other than the strengths of the associations from A to B and A to C. If subjects are asked to recall only the first (or the second) associates of the A items, they will show poorer performance following the learning of an AC list than a CD list in part because subjects do not discriminate perfectly which (B or C) response was paired with the A stimulus in the first (or second) list. When only one item may be recalled, retroactive and proactive interference designs that pair two responses with the same stimulus would create competition between the two responses, even if there were no storage interference effects on associative strengths due to learning two responses to the same stimulus.

In modified modified free recall (MMFR) designs, subjects are allowed to produce two responses to a stimulus item. While MMFR is designed to eliminate the logically necessary competition involved in having two responses to the same stimulus, it may not eliminate all interfering effects of an AC association on recall of an AB association. A strong AC associate appears to block recall of an AB associate as evidenced by the fact that actually supplying the second list (C) associate of an A stimulus item depresses recall of the first list (B) associate by comparison to an ordinary MMFR procedure (Postman, Stark, & Fraser, 1968). Also, in free recall of the 50 states in the U.S., prior study of a subset of 25 state names depresses recall of the remaining 25 state names (Brown, 1968;

Karchmer & Winograd, 1971). Thus, recall tests may involve an unconscious blocking of weaker associates by stronger associates, in addition to any conscious response competition.

It seems very reasonable to assume that a recognition test in which one presented both the A and B members of the pair sometimes correctly paired (A_iB_i) and sometimes incorrectly paired (A_iB_j) would get around competition and blocking. In addition to this being reasonable, there is also direct evidence that the presence of a strong AC associate does not diminish the discriminability of correct (A_iB_i) from incorrect (A_iB_j) paired associates in a short-term recognition memory task (Wickelgren, 1967). This independence from irrelevant associations in a recognition task could be demonstrated for short-term memory because learning an AC associate in short-term memory does not appear to depress the strength of an AB associate in storage any more than does learning a CD associate depress the strength of the AB associate. Storage interference in short-term memory appears to be independent of this type of fine-grain similarity (although storage interference in short-term memory is not independent of grosser modality similarity of interpolated learning).

Unfortunately, storage interference in long-term memory does appear to be similarity dependent. See Wickelgren (1972) for a long list of studies supporting the similarity dependence of storage interference in long-term memory. Thus, it is somewhat more difficult to demonstrate the independence from this type of retrieval interference in recognition based on long-term traces. It is possible to test for independence from irrelevant associations in recognition based on long-term memory traces with a PI design, where the AC or CD learning is done prior to the AB learning. AB learning should be to the same criterion in both cases. If long-term recognition tests are also free from associative competition and blocking, then subsequent tests of AB recognition should be identical in both cases. That is, recognition tests should show no PI. Evidence for the absence of PI in recognition matching tests has been obtained by Postman *et al.* (1968), confirming this prediction.

B. Response Suppression

Recently, there has been some evidence to support the notion that one of the factors producing declines on recall tests as a function of time is the loss by a subject of his "set" for the responses. This loss of availability of the responses (possibly active reponse suppression) combines with blocking and losses in specific associative strength to produce the forgetting shown in recall tests (Birnbaum, 1972; Cofer, Faile, & Horton, 1971; Postman *et al.*, 1968).

To my knowledge no one has ever suggested that there could be any analogue of response suppression operative in a recognition-memory task, and it is difficult to see any logical possibility for this. Certainly the availability of the yes–no responses could not in any sense be thought to be reduced over the retention interval. Thus, it is difficult if not impossible to imagine any analogue of this loss of response availability operating as an interference factor in a recognition test.

C. Context Effects

It has sometimes been claimed that cues from the background context become strongly associated to the material being learned, and the presence or absence of these contextual cues at the time of retrieval affects the probability of correct recall or recognition. In discussing the effects of changes in context from the time of learning to the time of retrieval, it is important to make the distinction between changes in "irrelevant" cues and changes in "relevant" cues.

Irrelevant cues refer to cues that are held constant throughout the learning of a list. Irrelevant context factors include such properties as the color of the stimulus items, the color of the ground in which the stimulus items are presented, the sex of the experimenter, various characteristics of the testing room, the time of day, the posture of the subject, the physical nature of the apparatus used to present the stimuli and record responses, the presence or absence of background music or other auditory background, *etc.*

However, if the color of each stimulus item is changed systematically from one paired associate to another with the A_1 item always appearing in red, the A_2 item always appearing in blue, and the A_3 item always appearing in green, *etc.,* then the color of the stimulus item can no longer be considered an irrelevant context cue. This latter case must be considered to be an example of paired-associate learning with compound stimuli, where either the color or the verbal character of the stimulus or both could be used as a specific relevant cue to be associated to the response.

McGeoch and Irion (1952, pp. 448–451) listed a number of studies supporting the importance of contextual change as a retrieval interference factor in memory. However, closer examination of this experimental work and other studies on the effects of changing background contexts reveals only a few studies that find significant effects of altering truly irrelevant background contextual cues. Many studies that have been alleged to show the importance of background context were actually experiments in which compound (relevant) stimuli were changed from learning to test. There is every reason to expect that changing or eliminating one of the relevant attributes of the stimulus would depress memory performance. Most of the studies that involve varying truly irrelevant background context have failed to find significant effects of altering such context. Unpublished work of my own has also failed to reveal significant effects of contextual change on either recall or recognition of Russian–English word pairs, though the effect of contextual change on recall was almost significant. Since some of the alterations in experimental context have been deliberately designed to be quite extreme, the negligible or unreliable effect of the contextual changes argues strongly that irrelevant context often plays little role in the coding and retrieval processes of memory.

However, there has recently been a resurgence of interest in the effects of alterations in background context as a possible retrieval interference factor in recognition memory (DaPolito, Barker, & Wiant, 1971; Light & Carter–Sobell, 1970, Thomson, 1972; Tulving & Thomson, 1971; Winograd & Conn, 1971; Winograd, Karchmer, & Russell, 1971). Although the specific designs of these various studies have differed somewhat, the nature of the context effects found for recognition memory can be illustrated by considering the initial study by Light and Carter–Sobell. In this study, recognition memory for nouns that have at least two very different meanings was studied, for example, the noun "jam" as in "raspberry jam" and as in "traffic jam." Although subjects at the time of the recognition test were only asked to identify whether the noun "jam" had occurred earlier, this noun was accompanied at the time of test by an adjective that biased one or another meaning for jam. This adjective could be the same as the adjective presented with the noun during learning of the list (*e.g.*, "raspberry jam" in both cases), or a different adjective, but one that biased the same meaning of the noun ("strawberry jam" in learning followed by "raspberry jam" in the test), or a different adjective that biased a different meaning for the noun ("traffic jam" followed by "raspberry jam"). Changes in the adjective context lowered the discriminability of presented from unpresented nouns by a substantial amount, though recognition in this and all studies of nouns presented in new semantic contexts is far above chance.

However, once again, there has been a failure to recognize the distinction between changes in irrelevant and relevant cues. In the Light and Carter–Sobell study, subjects were not informed at the time of learning that the adjectives were irrelevant and, in any event, the adjectives were different from one noun to another, which would certainly have caused them to have been learned by the subjects and strongly associated to their respective nouns. Thus, this is a study of the effects of varying a relevant part of a compound stimulus, which is logically distinguishable from varying irrelevant context. The same criticism applies to all the other studies and thus these studies provide no support for the role of irrelevant context in recognition memory. All such studies show is what we already knew: that very frequently two cues are better than one. That is, if one learned two relevant cues, then the presence of both cues at the time of the retention test will enhance performance as compared to a condition where only one relevant cue is available.

However, this work does support the hypothesis that, to some extent, what we associate in our minds are the internal representatives of the *meanings* of words (concepts), in addition to, or instead of, associating the internal representatives of *words,* though there does also appear to be a substantial word-strength component to memory in these tasks (Davis, Lockhart, & Thomson, 1972). Also, it is now well established that mnemonics based on the meanings of words in a pair can substantially improve one's learning and retention of paired associates. Thus, this work raises the question concerning what would happen if a subject thought of a different meaning for a word at the time of the test from the meaning thought of at the time of learning. To the extent that some of the memory trace is tied to the specific meaning and not available at the time of retrieval if a different meaning is thought of, there should be a depression of recognition-memory performance. The studies cited earlier demonstrate that this can occur under special circumstances, though I hope it is clear from the preceding discussion that these effects of altering compound stimuli do not prove anything concerning the effects of small changes in irrelevant context in ordinary list-learning tasks. It may well be that the probability that a subject thinks of the same meaning or sets of meanings at the time of retention as he did at the time of original learning is so high in most learning and memory tasks that these potentially significant retrieval interference effects can, in practice, be completely ignored.

At present, we do not know what portion of the forgetting shown by recognition tests is due to a change in the representation of the stimulus item as a function of retention interval and what portion is due to a change in the strength of association from the representation of the stimulus to the representation of the response as a function of retention interval. Also, it seems perfectly reasonable, at present, to imagine that a change in the representation in the stimulus item is as much a storage interference factor as is a change in the association from the representation of the stimulus to the representation of the response.

If the probability of interpreting the stimulus in a different manner at retrieval from the interpretation given at the time of learning is constant as a function of retention interval (as it is in the studies where the change of interpretation was induced experimentally), then such an effect can truly be referred to as a retrieval-interference factor that is operative in recognition memory. As argued previously, this factor may or may not be operative in ordinary recognition memory, though it clearly was operative in the abnormal compound-stimulus recognition-memory tasks employed in the previously mentioned studies.

If such a retrieval interference factor is operative in ordinary recognition memory with a constant probability as a function of delay interval, then the effect would probably be to reduce strength recognition retention functions by a constant factor at all retention intervals. Although such retrieval interference effects are of some slight interest in themselves, they are of no significance for the function of recognition tests in studying losses in storage. What would be of greater consequence for the proposition that recognition memory discriminability is linearly related to the strength of the memory trace in storage would be a demonstration that this or some other type of retrieval interference increased systematically in magnitude as a function of retention interval and accounted for all or a substantial part of the forgetting observed on such recognition memory tasks. If this could be demonstrated, it would revive the old uncertainty concerning whether there are any losses in memory storage or whether, in fact, all "forgetting" is simply due to increasing retrieval interference.

I think there is no reason at present to believe that changes in the interpretation of the stimulus item as a function of delay accounts for any substantial portion of the forgetting observed in memory for an AB paired associate, for example. If the interpretation of an item were substantially changing as a function of retention interval, then any previously strongly learned AC associates should be equally seriously affected, as well as more recently and more weakly learned AB associates. Because it is relatively easy to: (1) learn a strong AC paired associate, (2) learn an AB associate to some low criterion, and (3) observe substantial forgetting of the AB associate along with very little forgetting with the AC associate, this specific form of the retrieval interference hypothesis must be rejected.

Another hypothesis is that the A stimulus item is perturbed to some new form by presentation of the AB pair and then systematically drifts back over the retention interval to the interpretation appropriate for old AC pairs. However, any explicit form of this theory would undoubtedly require that the rate of return to the original interpretation to be a function of the strength of the AC paired associate(s). This would yield a prediction that forgetting of an AB pair on a recognition test should be faster following AC learning than following CD learning. The results of Wickelgren (in press) falsifies this prediction.

In conclusion, I think it is possible to say that changes in the interpretation of the stimulus item from learning to test will depress recognition-memory performance. It is not possible to say whether this occurs to any substantial extent under ordinary recognition learning and test conditions, and even if it does occur, it seems unlikely to be responsible in any significant way for the forgetting observed as a function of retention interval in recognition tests. At most, there may be a constant multiplicative retrieval-interference effect on the strength-retention function across all delays.

REFERENCES

Baddeley, A. D., & Ecob, J. R. Reaction time and short-term memory: A trace strength alternative to the high-speed exhaustive scanning hypothesis. *Center for Human Information Processing,* Report No. 13. University of California, San Diego, 1970.

Birnbaum, I. M. General and specific components of retroactive inhibition in the AB, AC paradigm. *Journal of Experimental Psychology,* 1972, **93,** 188–192.

Brown, J. Reciprocal facilitation and impairment of free recall. *Psychonomic Science,* 1968, **10,** 41–42.

Burrows, D., & Okada, R. Serial position effects in high-speed memory search. *Perception and Psychophysics,* 1971, **10,** 305–308.

Ceraso, J., Bader, L., & Silverstein, M. Response latency as a function of list length in paired-associate learning. *Psychonomic Science,* 1970, **19,** 239–240.

Cofer, C. N., Faile, N. F., & Horton, D. L. Retroactive inhibition following reinstatement or maintenance of first-list responses by means of free recall. *Journal of Experimental Psychology,* 1971, **90,** 197–205.

Collins, A. M., & Quillian, M. R. Does category size affect categorization time? *Journal of Verbal Learning and Verbal Behavior,* 1970, **9,** 432–438.

Corballis, M. C. Serial order in recognition and recall. *Journal of Experimental Psychology,* 1967, **74,** 99–105.

Corballis, M. C., Kirby, J., & Miller, A. Access to elements of a memorized list. *Journal of Experimental Psychology,* 1972, **94,** 185–190.

DaPolito, F., Barker, D., & Wiant, J. Context in semantic information retrieval. *Psychonomic Science,* 1971, **24,** 180–182.

Davis, J. C., Lockhart, R. S., & Thomson, D. M. Repetition and context effects in recognition memory. *Journal of Experimental Psychology,* 1972, **92,** 96–102.

DeRosa, D. V., & Baumgarte, R. Probe digit recall of items from temporally organized memory sets. *Journal of Experimental Psychology,* 1971, **91,** 154–158.

Egeth, H., Marcus, N., & Bevan, W. Target-set and response-set interaction: Implications for models of human information processing. *Science,* 1972, **176,** 1447–1448.

Eimas, P. D. Subjective reinforcement in the paired-associate learning of retarded and normal children. *Canadian Journal of Psychology,* 1964, **18,** 183–196.

Eimas, P. D., & Zeaman, D. Response speed changes in an Estes' paired-associate "miniature" experiment. *Journal of Verbal Learning and Verbal Behavior,* 1963, **1,** 384–388.

Fischler, I., & Juola, J. F. Effects of repeated tests on recognition time for information in long-term memory. *Journal of Experimental Psychology,* 1971, **91,** 54–58.

Freedman, J. L., & Loftus, E. F. Retrieval of words from long-term memory. *Journal of Verbal Learning and Verbal Behavior,* 1971, **10,** 107–115.

Hall, R. F. The effect of number of response alternatives on response frequency and latency in paired-associate learning. *British Journal of Mathematical and Statistical Psychology,* 1969, **22,** 115–130.

Hintzman, D. L. Recognition time: Effects of recency, frequency, and the spacing of repetitions. *Journal of Experimental Psychology*, 1969, **1**, 192–194.

Juola, J. F., & Atkinson, R. C. Memory scanning for words versus categories. *Journal of Verbal Learning and Verbal Behavior*, 1971, **10**, 522–527.

Juola, J. F., Fischler, I., Wood, C. T., & Atkinson, R. C. Recognition time for information stored in long-term memory. *Perception and Psychophysics*, 1971, **10**, 8–14.

Karchmer, M. A., & Winograd, E. Effects of studying a subset of familiar items on recall of the remaining items: The John Brown effect. *Psychonomic Science*, 1971, **25**, 224–225.

Kennedy, A. Response latency in the serial learning of short lists. *British Journal of Psychology*, 1968, **59**, 1–5.

Kirsner, K., & Craik, F. I. M. Naming and decision processes in short-term recognition memory. *Journal of Experimental Psychology*, 1971, **88**, 149–157.

Landauer, T. K., & Freedman, J. L. Information retrieval from long-term memory: Category size and recognition time. *Journal of Verbal Learning and Verbal Behavior*, 1968, **7**, 291–295.

Lappin, J. S., & Disch, K. The latency operating characteristic: I. Effects of stimulus probability on choice reaction time. *Journal of Experimental Psychology*, 1972, **92**, 419–427. (a)

Lappin, J. S., & Disch, K. The latency operating characteristic: II. Effects of visual stimulus intensity on choice reaction time. *Journal of Experimental Psychology*, 1972, **93**, 367–372. (b)

Light, L. L., & Carter-Sobell, L. Effects of changed semantic context on recognition memory. *Journal of Verbal Learning and Verbal Behavior*, 1970, **9**, 1–11.

Lively, B. L. Speed/accuracy tradeoff and practice as determinants of stage durations in a memory-search task. *Journal of Experimental Psychology*, 1972, **96**, 97–103.

McGeoch, J. A., & Irion, A. L. *The Psychology of Human Learning*. New York: Longmans, Green, 1952.

Metlay, W., Handley, A., & Kaplan, I. T. Memory search through categories of varying size. *Journal of Experimental Psychology*, 1971, **91**, 215–219.

Meyer, D. E. On the representation and retrieval of stored semantic information. *Cognitive Psychology*, 1970, **1**, 242–300.

Millward, R. Latency in a modified paired-associative learning experiment. *Journal of Verbal Learning and Verbal Behavior*, 1964, **3**, 309–316.

Morin, R. E., DeRosa, D. V., & Stultz, V. Recognition memory and reaction time. *Acta Psychologica*, 1967, **27**, 298–305.

Morin, R. E., DeRosa, D. V., & Ulm, R. Short-term recognition memory for spatially isolated items. *Psychonomic Science*, 1967, **9**, 617–618.

Murdock, B. B., Jr. Response latencies in short-term memory. *Quarterly Journal of Experimental Psychology*, 1968, **20**, 79–82.

Norman, D. A. Acquisition and retention in short-term memory. *Journal of Experimental Psychology*, 1966, **72**, 369–381.

Norman, D. A., & Wickelgren, W. A. Strength theory of decision rules and latency in retrieval from short-term memory. *Journal of Mathematical Psychology*, 1969, **6**, 192–208.

Okada, R. Decision latencies in short-term recognition memory. *Journal of Experimental Psychology*, 1971, **90**, 27–32.

Pachella, R. G., & Fisher, D. Hick's law and the speed-accuracy tradeoff in absolute judgment. *Journal of Experimental Psychology*, 1972, **92**, 378–384.

Peterson, L. R. Paired-associate latencies after the last error. *Psychonomic Science*, 1965, **2**, 167–168.

Postman, L., Stark, K., & Fraser, J. Temporal changes in interference. *Journal of Verbal Learning and Verbal Behavior*, 1968, **7**, 672–694.

Rabbitt, P. M. A., & Vyas, S. M. An elementary preliminary taxonomy for some errors in laboratory choice RT tasks. *Acta Psychologica*, 1970, **33**, 56–76.

Reed, A. Speed-accuracy tradeoff in recognition memory. *Science*, 1973, **18**, 574–576.

Schlag-Rey, M., Groen, G., & Suppes, P. Latencies on last error in paired associate learning. *Psychonomic Science*, 1965, **2**, 15–16.

Schouten, J. F., & Bekker, J. A. M. Reaction time and accuracy. *Acta Psychologica*, 1967, **27**, 143–153.

Sternberg, S. High-speed scanning in human memory. *Science*, 1966, **153**, 652–654.

Sternberg, S. Retrieval of contextual information from memory. *Psychonomic Science*, 1967, **8**, 55–56.

Sternberg, S. Memory-scanning: Mental processes revealed by reaction-time experiments. *American Scientist*, 1969, **57**, 421–457.

Suppes, P., Groen, G., & Schlag-Rey, M. A model for response latency in paired-associate learning. *Journal of Mathematical Psychology*, 1966, **3**, 99–128.

Swanson, J. M., & Briggs, G. E. Information processing as a function of speed vs. accuracy. *Journal of Experimental Psychology*, 1969, **81**, 223–229.

Swensson, R. G. The elusive tradeoff: Speed vs. accuracy in visual discrimination tasks. *Perception and Psychophysics*, 1972, **12**, 16–32.

Swensson, R. G., & Edwards, W. Response strategies in a two-choice reaction task with a continuous cost for time. *Journal of Experimental Psychology*, 1971, **88**, 67–81.

Theios, J. Prediction of paired-associate latencies after the last error by an all-or-none learning model. *Psychonomic Science*, 1965, **2**, 311–312.

Thomson, D. M. Context effects in recognition memory. *Journal of Verbal Learning and Verbal Behavior*, 1972, **11**, 497–511.

Tulving, E., & Thomson, D. M. Retrieval processes in recognition memory: Effects of associative context. *Journal of Experimental Psychology*, 1971, **87**, 116–124.

Waugh, N. C. Retrieval time in short-term memory. *British Journal of Psychology*, 1970, **61**, 1–12.

Wickelgren, W. A. Exponential decay and independence from irrelevant associations in short-term recognition memory for serial order. *Journal of Experimental Psychology*, 1967, **73**, 165–171.

Wickelgren, W. A. Trace resistance and the decay of long-term memory. *Journal of Mathematical Psychology*, 1972, **9**, 418–455.

Wickelgren, W. A. Single-trace fragility theory of memory dynamics. *Memory and Cognition*, in press.

Wickelgren, W. A., & Norman, D. A. Strength models and serial position in short-term recognition memory. *Journal of Mathematical Psychology*, 1966, **3**, 316–347.

Wiggins, J. S. Two determinants of associative reaction time. *Journal of Experimental Psychology*, 1957, **54**, 144–147.

Wilkins, A. J. Conjoint frequency, category size, and categorization time. *Journal of Verbal Learning and Verbal Behavior*, 1971, **10**, 382–385.

Winograd, E., & Conn, C. P. Evidence from recognition memory for specific encoding of unmodified homographs. *Journal of Verbal Learning and Verbal Behavior*, 1971, **10**, 702–706.

Winograd, E., Karchmer, M. A., & Russell, I. S. Role of encoding unitization in cued recognition memory. *Journal of Verbal Learning and Verbal Behavior*, 1971, **10**, 199–206.

Yellott, J. I., Jr. Correction for fast guessing and the speed-accuracy tradeoff in choice reaction time. *Journal of Mathematical Psychology*, 1971, **8**, 159–199.

CHAPTER

10

SHORT-TERM MEMORY PROCESSES AND THE AMNESIC SYNDROME

MARCEL KINSBOURNE
AND
FRANK WOOD

I. USE OF THE AMNESIC SYNDROME FOR THEORIES OF NORMAL SHORT-TERM MEMORY

Although the amnesic syndrome is an interesting clinical and neurological phenomenon in its own right, it has also in recent years been understood to have important implications for the understanding of normal memory processes. Clinically, the amnesic syndrome manifests itself as follows: Following damage to a system that consists of the hippocampus, the roof and walls of the third ventricle, and connecting projections (Victor, 1969), patients suffer a profound impairment of their ability to recover a wide range of memories and to learn new information. The amnesic syndrome has been surgically induced by bilateral temporal lobe excision (Scoville & Milner, 1957) and simulated by bilateral deep temporal (Bickford, Mulder, Dodge, Svien, & Rome, 1958) and amygdaloid (Chapman, Walter, Markham, Rand, & Crandall, 1967) stimulation. Amnesics can hold as much material within the focus of their immediate awareness as controls. Thus they characteristically have a normal span of immediate memory (Talland, 1965; Wickelgren, 1968) and experience no difficulty in following normal conversation. They also retain the ability to unitize information (Mandler, 1967) and hold its essence in working memory pending the conclusion of the spoken thought. However, once the information has been displaced from immediate awareness on account of overloading, distraction, or change in mental set, amnesics find that information particularly hard to recover. Debate has centered on whether this vulnerability of memories to distraction is due to imperfect initial encoding, loss of information while in store, impaired ability to retrieve, or a combination of these factors.

Amnesics have difficulty remembering information about both events that followed the abrupt onset of their disease and events that occurred well before that time. Occasionally the retrograde amnesia gradually diminishes in severity. The fact that some memories then become available shows that this information must have been held intact in store, but was inaccessible on account of defective retrieval processes. Patients sometimes confabulate, offering spurious episodes in place of those they fail to retrieve. Finally, amnesics are described as inert and lethargic in personality (Talland, 1965).

The theoretical implications that have been drawn from the amnesic syndrome fall into three general classes. First, the syndrome has been used as evidence for the structural distinction between short- and long-term memory (Milner, 1966, 1969, 1970). Milner describes a patient who had a bilateral medial temporal lobectomy removing both hippocampi. Postoperatively, he seemed able to recover information normally from the earlier parts of his life, but in the years following surgery seemed unable to add any new information (for example, the names of visitors) to his working knowledge. He was clearly deficient on a number of experimental tasks that required retention of a memory after intervening distraction. Milner interpreted the patient's difficulties as an inability to consolidate information from short-term memory into long-term memory and suggested that the hippocampal regions were involved in precisely this sort of con- solidation. This observation led Atkinson and Schiffrin (1968) to term the amnesic syndrome as the "single most convincing demonstration of a dichotomy in the memory system." In fact, they used the amnesic syndrome as one of the most basic evidentiary justifications for their theory, which stressed a structural distinction between short-term and long-term memory. This particular use of the amnesic syndrome is widespread, and one finds it frequently in the current literature (Jarho, 1973; Wickelgren, 1974). If it has not become a consensus on the theoretical implications of the amnesic syndrome, it has nevertheless become the single most widely accepted view.

A second use of the syndrome has been to delineate those particular kinds of memory processing that are disproportionately affected, and thus to isolate functionally discrete processing capabilities that are important for normal memory. The principal theorist in this regard was Talland (1965) who, after an extensive review of case material and experimental results concluded that the amnesic syndrome consisted mainly in a defective activation. There was a premature closure of the cycle of arousal necessary for the registration of memory; likewise, there was a premature closure of the searching cycle when retrieval was demanded. Talland (1965) did not specify that the registration or the retrieval processes were affected out of proportion to each other but assumed that the activation deficiency applied in principle, at least, to both processes. (Later, he did suggest that the majority of the amnesic impairment was probably at retrieval [Talland, 1968].) The registration or encoding side of this defect has been experi- mentally investigated most recently by Cermak and Butters and associates. They have concluded that the defect is most specifically a deficiency in the semantic encoding of verbal material (Cermak, Butters & Gerrein, 1973; Cermak, Butters & Moreines, 1974). A variation on the notion of regis- tration difficulty has been proposed by Meissner (1966). His view was that the defect was in the sequential ordering of inputs, so that when their number exceeded about three, they could not be successfully registered. Warrington and Weiskrantz (1970a, 1970b) have, on the other hand, proposed that the amnesic difficulty consists in excessive interference in memory storage. Amnesics therefore suffer unduly from proactive inter- ference. Learning is difficult because the material cannot be sufficiently well segregated from previously learned material in memory storage. Note, however, that Warrington and Weiskrantz do not believe that this difficulty operates in short-term memory. It is confined to retrieval from long-term memory storage. They support the structural distinction between short- and long-term memory, but they stress an interference process that has its deleterious effect on retrieval rather than a registration difficulty or a de-connection of short- and long-term memory stores.

The third theoretical use of the amnesic syndrome is to specify the neuroanatomical structures that are responsible for memory. Milner (1970) has stated that material-specific memory disorders are associated with uni-lateral loss of medial temporal lobe tissue—verbal memory is selectively lost with left medial temporal damage, visual with right. Milner's findings derive from a study of a series of surgical cases. Two other recent studies add generality to hers. Patten (1972) reported a series consisting mostly of vascular and tumor cases where good localization was possible and showed the same verbal–visual laterality dissociation as did Milner's case material. Moreover, Patten found that gustatory memory losses were associated with left hemisphere damage, olfactory with right. Barbizet and Cany (1969) refer to a series of patients with cerebral damage of varying etiology who likewise show the same visual–verbal laterality effect. These material- or modality-specific memory disorders that arise from unilateral lesions are not in general severe or disabling. Should these medial temporal lesions extend bilaterally, however, the memory defect becomes severe, and the classic amnesic syndrome results.

In all these studies (Milner, 1970; Patten, 1972; Barbizet & Cany, 1969), bilateral damage to the hippocampal area was the critical lesion for the full amnesic syndrome. Another recent study, of Finnish war veterans (Jarho, 1973), permitted the conclusion that wound tracks extending bi-laterally through the diencephalon were necessary conditions for the occur-rence of the amnesic syndrome. The work of Victor, Adams, and Collins (1971) has likewise implicated medial diencephalic pathology in alcoholic amnesia, with the probability of precise localization in the medial dorsal nucleus of the thalamus.

These studies suggest that lesions responsible for memory loss can be localized in hippocampal and diencephalic structures. But one cannot use the lesion evidence as a guide to deciding what kinds of memory processes are destroyed. The work of John (1967), Adey (1964), and Vinogradova (1970) contains the theoretical suggestion that these structures are in-volved in the post-perceptual coding, for memory, of stimulus events. The evidence suggests that electrical recordings from these structures show a longer persistence of stimulus-evoked activity than is found in most other brain structures. In other ways, also, the electrical activity of these structures correlates with memory and learning performance. Such evidence does not yet compel the belief that these structures do in fact register memories. The physiological studies still need behavioral elaboration.

II. THEORETICAL SIGNIFICANCE OF THE PETERSON AND PETERSON SHORT-TERM MEMORY PARADIGM

A wide diversity of experimental tasks has been reported in the literature on amnesia. These have, no doubt, contributed to our initial progress in understanding amnesia, because a wide evidentiary net must be cast in order to gain a rough understanding of the boundaries of amnesia's major impact. Nevertheless, if we wish to understand in theoretically adequate detail what amnesia does to memory, and certainly if we wish to select between alternative theories, we need standardized paradigms that can be evaluated consensually and readily replicated. We therefore choose to concentrate our discussion on the Peterson and Peterson (1959) short-term memory paradigm and the impact of the amnesic syndrome on performance in that paradigm. When necessary, we will cite corroborating evidence from other memory paradigms.

The Peterson and Peterson (1959) procedure was: (1) present a consonant trigram to the subject; (2) engage the subject in a distractor task to prevent rehearsal; and (3) ask for recall of the trigram. Methodologically, this procedure tends to separate and deconfound the registration, retention, and retrieval phases of memory processing, allowing separate manipulation by the experimenter of any of those phases. It is therefore a generally preferable procedure (Murdock, 1967; Wickelgren, 1970). Peterson and Peterson were interested in the nature of short-term forgetting during intervals of a few seconds. They systematically varied the length of the retention interval from 3 to 18 sec and measured performance at retrieval. They produced a basic empirical decay function in which performance dropped off rapidly in the early seconds of a retention interval and thereafter somewhat more slowly, until at 18 sec performance asymptotes were close to zero. An exponential curve seemed to fit the data well.

What is the effect of the distractor task? Explanations tend to group themselves into two classes: decay and interference. Of the decay explanations, the simplest, no doubt, is the proposal by Brown (1958) that information spontaneously decays when rehearsal is prevented, and that rehearsal only prevents the onset of this decay, which will then proceed at an unvarying rate. By itself, this view is untenable, since many variables have a pronounced effect on the shape of the empirical decay function. These include repetition of the item at registration (Peterson & Peterson, 1959; Hellyer, 1962; Liu & Ma, 1970), proactive interference (Keppel & Underwood, 1962), and number of chunks in the to-be-remembered stimulus (Melton, 1963). Such interactions suggest that an unmitigated theory of autonomous decay is not tenable.

Other proposals that are operationally similar to the decay notion include the multiple trace decay theory of Wickelgren (1968) and the stimulus sampling view of Estes (1955), endorsed by Peterson and Peterson (1959). Such notions generally must be qualified to accommodate the effects of the variables known to have an impact on the shape of decay function, especially when that impact distorts the shape toward sigmoid (Bjork, 1970). These qualifications often diminish the simplifying power of the theories.

The classic alternative to time-dependent decay has been interference. By this notion, the effects of retention time are entirely due to the nature of the events that occur in that time. These events will mask, disrupt, recondition, or otherwise disturb the registered items, and the disturbing effect will be in proportion to the similarity of these events to the registered items and also to the number of such events. Thus, the retention period contains events that operate by the familiar retroactive interference paradigm to weaken the memories established at registration. Accordingly, the basic demonstration experiments have sought to detach these interference effects from the effects of time alone, either by varying the number of interpolated items in the distractor task or by varying the similarity of the distractor task to the learned item. In either case, retention time is held constant. Thus, Waugh and Norman (1965) showed faster forgetting with increased rates of interpolation, and Baddeley (1966) and Baddeley and Dale (1966) have shown that increasing acoustic or semantic similarity between the to-be-remembered items and the distractor task results in greater forgetting, holding time constant.

Another approach to the demonstration of interference effects in the retention phase comes from the literature on directed forgetting in short-term memory. Such studies have utilized a forget instruction to minimize proactive interference (e.g., Bjork, LaBerge, & Legrand, 1968; Elmes, 1969; Turvey & Wittlinger, 1969; Block, 1971) or retroactive interference (Reed, 1970).

We learn from Reed (1970) that interference due to subsequent learning is under the control of the subject's own strategy for allocating his short-term memory capacity. The mere fact that a second item has been registered and learned does not irreversibly guarantee that it will have an interfering effect on the first item. The subject can eliminate or minimize the interference by his compliance with the instructions to forget it. (Note that the forget instruction does not cause the item to be lost from memory. In this experiment and in Block's (1971) experiment, the "forgotten" items are equal to the nonforgotten ones in their availability for long-term recognition or relearning.) Block (1971) has successfully argued that the effect of the forget instruction is to differentiate the to-be-forgotten item from the to-be-remembered item, much in the same way that a class shift obtains release from proactive inhibition.

All this means that the classic retroactive interference due to competing item learning is probably not the correct explanation for the effect of the distractor task, because the subject doubtless does not hold the distractor material as an item in storage alongside the to-be-remembered item. He needs no forget instruction, since he has not sought to memorize the distractor material in the first place. Moreover, the distractor task is usually quite different from learning the to-be-remembered item, and there is accordingly little likelihood of confusing them as to-be-remembered items in memory.

If not competing item learning, what other explanation is possible for the effect of the distractor task? A common, almost standard, proposal has been that the distractor task prevents the rehearsal that is necessary to prevent spontaneous decay out of short-term storage. We have already criticized the inadequacy of spontaneous decay notions, as well as explanations based on a structural distinction between long- and short-term memory. Let us consider, however, an experiment that purported to explain the effect of the distractor task in terms of rehearsal prevention. Dillon and Reid (1969) varied the difficulty of the distractor task and showed that difficult material early in the retention period was far more disruptive than difficult material later in the period. A 15-sec retention period in which the first 5 sec were difficult and the last 10 sec easy was as disruptive of performance as if all 15 sec were difficult. A subsequent experiment reduced this critical period to the first 3 sec. The authors also showed that the difficulty in changing tasks from difficult to easy itself added a disruptive effect.

These authors concluded that the amount of information processing early in the retention interval was the critical variable, and that it operated by preventing rehearsal. Since such prevention of rehearsal accomplished almost all of its disruptive effects in the first 3 sec, the authors claimed that the short-term, decayable component of the memory was being quickly lost due to lack of rehearsal. The remaining asymptotic performance, from about 3 sec forward, was considered to exhibit the stable, nondecaying, long-term component of the memory.

Dillon and Reid's interpretation is compelling, at least according to their evidence. Could anything other than rehearsal prevention result from increasing the difficulty of the task? By their own assumption, task difficulty is equivalent to amount of information processing per unit time. If this increased amount of information is itself interfering, then we cannot distinguish the rehearsal-preventing properties of information processing and its interfering properties.

Fortunately, the experiments necessary to untangle this confusion have now been done. Deutsch (1970) showed that memory for the pitch of a tone is severely disrupted by the interpolation of further tones during the retention interval, even though these tones can be ignored. In contrast, the interpolation of a sequence of spoken digits produces only minimal disruption in pitch recognition, even when recall of these digits is required. Furthermore, the requirement to remember the tone does not result in decreased digit recall. Reitman (1971) gave two tasks that could be experimentally equated in terms of their effectiveness in preventing rehearsal. Both tasks were difficult and highly effective in preventing rehearsal. One task was a tonal detection task, the other a syllabic detection task. Presumably, the former was nonverbal, the latter verbal. The results were clear-cut: no loss in performance occurred across a 15-sec retention period occupied with the tonal task; the usual substantial loss occurred during the same period if it was occupied with the syllabic task. The result has been replicated by Schiffrin (1973). So we must reject rehearsal prevention as an explanation for the effects of time on memory and consider more carefully just what kind of interference or other process may be operating to depress performance over time.

The Dillon and Reid (1969) results do require that any interference theory of short-term forgetting explain why interference occurring earlier in the retention period is more disruptive than the same interference occurring later in the period. One possibility for the differential impact of early and late disruptions is that the disruptions act in a way similar to interpolated learning in the RI paradigm. In that case, early disruptions set up interference close in time to the to-be-remembered item, rendering the item less temporally discriminable from the interference than would be the case if the disruptions came later, thus farther away in time from the to-be-remembered item. If this possibility is to be adopted, we require some explanation of how a distractor task like digit addition, which is quite dissimilar to the target item, can be temporally confused with it.

Since we have already rejected the possibility that the distractor task represents an item that competes with the target item by retroaction, we are forced to the possibility that the distractor task records some set of features similar to features of the target item that thus would compete with them. Such competition would reduce or eliminate the effectiveness of those particular features in aiding retrieval of the item. All features of the target item would not be lost, but in the case where the target item has relatively few semantic features (as in the low-association CCCs in the Dillon and Reid study), a numeric distractor task, competing with the target for many of its acoustic features, might well set up substantial interference with the target item. This interpretation yields a simple prediction: a numerical distractor task would be considerably less disruptive if the to-be-remembered items were word triads (which would presumably have semantic features resistant to acoustic interference by the distractor task).

The interference being proposed here is not independent of time because the proximity in time between target and interference increases the disruptive effect. That could imply that some sort of time tagging or attribution (Yntema & Trask, 1963; Underwood, 1969) occurs, not only for the target item, but also for the interfering task. The interfering features of the distractor task will be disruptive only to the extent that they bear time tags similar to those borne by the same features of the target item. The principal alternative to a time-tagged interference would be a notion of the early distractor task as disrupting consolidation. Consolidation disruption as an explanatory principle has been fully critiqued elsewhere (Miller & Springer, 1973). For our purposes, it is sufficient to note that there is a simple operational test of the consolidation hypothesis. If the Dillon and Reid (1969) results are assumed, then the consolidation phase for short-term memory lasts no more than 3 sec. Distraction after 3 sec should therefore not have any disruptive effect. The entire weight of the STM literature indicates, however, that disruptions accumulate in their impact long after 3 sec, even if earlier distractions are generally more disruptive than later ones. If consolidation is to be retained as an explanation in such cases, its duration must be considerably extended; in other words, consolidation time must vary identically with the time required for the empirical STM decay curves to reach asymptote. This makes consolidation time dependent on a great many other variables and deprives it of its intended simplifying power. In fact, if consolidation time is so widely variable, then some basic defining characteristics of the notion itself are probably contradicted.

If increasing retention time degrades memory because of the interfering events that occur in that time, the difficulty does not show up until retrieval time, of course, which implies that the interference causes some features of the target item to lose their distinctiveness and thus their power to help distinguish the item from its surround. (This surround can be considered either as noise or as earlier competing items or as both.)

No doubt retention time itself has another deleterious effect on memory: it changes the circumstances of retrieval from what they were at acquisition. If successful retrieval requires that cues presented at registration again be presented at retrieval time (*e.g.,* Thomson & Tulving, 1970), then time itself would inevitably degrade performance by changing at least some of the retrieval cues, be they in the organism or outside.

In this connection, the distractor task can be considered as a set of new stimulus cues that were not conditioned at registration and therefore must now dilute the set of retrieval cues still operating at retrieval time. More simply, the distractor task changes the stimulus field at retrieval, and performance suffers from stimulus generalization decrement. The preceding analysis has been subjected to experimental test by Falkenberg (1972), who has shown that the extent to which the distractor task is presented before registration as well as after registration is the extent to which performance at retrieval is improved. Falkenberg termed this stimulus change a change in context. As expected, the effect statistically interacts with the length of the retention interval, indicating that the stimulus change resulting from the distractor task is increased as the distractor period is lengthened. On the other hand, this effect is independent of the amount of proactive inhibition. In fact, the stimulus change resulting from the distractor period selectively increases the number of intra-item or extra-experimental intrusion errors (perhaps due to guessing), leaving prior trial intrusions at the same level (Wood, 1971). The context change caused by the distractor task deprives the target item of some specifying features, compared to the surrounding noise or to a set of guessable alternatives, but it does not impair the discriminability of the target item from previous items. Here is some additional evidence, then, for the specificity of some of the features of a target item and their selective vulnerability to disruption. This view gains generality from the Murray and Newman (1973) result, showing that the nominal and positional features of a visual display can be selectively eroded by verbal or spatial distraction, respectively.

If retrieval is thus conceived as a process of using cues to the stored features of the target item to discriminate it from incorrect items or noise, then there looms the possibility of explaining the supposed distinction between short-term and long-term storage in terms of the use of different retrieval cues. In that regard, a helpful experiment has been reported by Tulving and Patterson (1968). Serial lists were learned that had four highly related words in the middle of the list, at the end, or not in the list at all. When in the middle, the related words were better recalled than control middle words, but little difference existed at the end of the list. More importantly, the total number of words recalled from a list with related middle words exceeded the number of words recalled from a control list by almost exactly the number of related words that were recalled. Thus, if the related words in the middle of the list could be considered a single functional unit, performance in terms of functional units was the same for both lists (with and without related middle words). Tulving and Patterson thus spoke of a "unitization" of the related words in memory. The most important result, however, was that such unitization did not occur when the related words were presented at the end of the list. If retrieval of the end of the list (most recent items) was considered as retrieval from primary memory (Waugh & Norman, 1965), then unitization did not occur in primary memory. Rather than speculate as to how the related words organized themselves into a unit in secondary memory (middle list items), Tulving and Patterson preferred to speak of two different kinds of retrieval mechanisms rather than two types of memory store. They suggested that the subjects used temporal cues for retrieval from the end of the list and hierarchical or organizational cues (Mandler, 1967) for the middle words.

The analysis offered by Tulving and Patterson stops short of specifying why a certain type of retrieval cue is used in a certain situation. Perhaps it is because those cues that give the maximum discriminative information about the item are used. Cue selection is a strategy decision made by the subject against the background of the memory discrimination problem he faces. Words at the end of the list, less subject to the interfering effects of time than are the middle words, are the best candidates for a successful retrieval in the first place. Accordingly, when the subject begins to retrieve these words, his problem is simply to discriminate them from each other. Obviously, common cues (when they are four related words) do nothing to assist this process and are therefore not used. Retrieval from the middle of the list, however, is a different problem. Here the words have already suffered the ravages of time and are less retrievable in the first place. The subject accordingly looks for and selects any cues that may assist him in distinguishing some words from the general background of hard-to-remember words. In this case, the relatedness of the words (which the subject has duly noticed and recorded at acquisition time) now becomes a helpful cue. (That the related words operate [in terms of the fixed capacity of the system] as a single functional unit or "chunk" need not imply that such a unit takes up as much memory or output channel capacity as a single unrelated word. It could as well imply that the discriminative power of the relatedness cue embraces more than one word, whereas the discriminative power of the cues used to retrieve other individual words is limited to those words themselves. The fixed capacity may be the number of discriminations that can be made, not the number of items that can be handled. There need not be a chunk as such.)

This analysis can also be applied to the often-observed saliency of acoustic cues in short-term memory versus semantic cues in long-term memory. After a short retention time, an item stands a relatively good chance of being retrieved. The retrieval cues used, therefore, need convey relatively little information about the item in order to render it distinct from other potential items or from noise. Acoustic cues, therefore, will be the efficient choice for the subject. When items have been in memory for a longer time, are less probably retrievable by that fact alone, and are thus more confusable with other items, semantic cues are the more efficient because of their greater discriminative power.

This review of evidence in the Peterson and Peterson paradigm has suggested the following sort of model. Registration involves encoding the item along many different dimensions and storing those encoded features as a complex representing the item. Ensuing time may degrade the item to some extent by storing features similar to those of the target item, thus rendering the target features less informative for discriminating the target from noise or other items. Time may also inevitably change some features of the stimulus situation at retrieval time, and these changes will be deleterious to the extent that they lessen the subject's ability to discriminate the item from noise or other items. Retrieval involves the use of cues that match some of the stored features of the item. Generally, the more cues that can be supplied at retrieval the better performance will be, but to be effective, these cues must help in discriminating the item from noise or other items and must actually have been recorded at registration.

The empirical decay curves generated by the Peterson paradigm are referable to the model suggested here. Thus, variables such as proactive interference, number of repetitions of the item at registration, and number of chunks in the to-be-remembered item can all be understood to modify the amount of interference (respectively, Keppel & Underwood, 1962; Bjork, 1970; and Melton, 1963). Consequently, they all interact with the length of the distractor period to produce diverging empirical decay curves for different levels of the variable in question. That implies that such variables multiply the interfering effects of the distractor period; their impact accumulates during the period of distraction, while the to-be-remembered item is held in storage. On the other hand, some variables, notably exposure time of the to-be-remembered item (Liu & Ma, 1970; Samuels, Butters, & Cermak, 1973) do not interact with the length of the distractor period: parallel empirical decay curves are generated for different levels of the variable. It can be assumed, therefore, that such a variable operates in a different manner from interference: instead of operating during the distractor period to multiply the interference, a noninteracting variable would be assumed to operate in a once-for-all fashion, independent of the length of the retention interval. In the case of exposure time, the effect is presumably felt at registration in the form of different extents of encoding of the to-be-remembered item—an effect whose consequences are the same in terms of absolute loss of memory performance regardless of the duration of the forthcoming distractor period.

This analysis suggests that one of the first facts we require is the effect of the amnesic syndrome on the shape of the Peterson decay curves. If amnesic decay curves are different at all from those of normals in the Peterson and Peterson situation, then we must know whether the curves diverge or are parallel. If they diverge, so that the impact of amnesia is greater the longer the distractor period, then we will be able to conclude that amnesia, like proactive interference, changes the amount of interference operating in the situation by multiplying the interfering effects of the distractor task. If, on the other hand, the curves are parallel, then we will be entitled to the conclusion that the amnesic syndrome affects either the registration process or the retrieval process, or both, but not the process by which the to-be-remembered item is held in storage. In the latter case, the question would then become whether the defect can be more specifically located at registration or at retrieval. By the model adopted above, registration defects would generally be understood to impair the encoding of the to-be-remembered item. A retrieval deficit, on the other hand, would suggest an impairment in the availability or usability of retrieval cues. (In these terms, a purely retrieval deficit would not be understood as a consequence of too much interference, proactive or otherwise, since that would predict diverging decay curves.)

III. EXPERIMENTAL EVIDENCE FOR THE NATURE OF THE AMNESIC MEMORY DEFECT

A. Retrieval Deficit in Peterson Short-Term Memory

The trend of present evidence tends to support the following conclusions: (1) Short-term memory performance, as measured in the Peterson paradigm, is impaired in the amnesic syndrome. (2) This impairment does not interact with the length of the retention interval (that is, amnesic and normal forgetting curves are parallel across the usually tested range of retention intervals). (3) Amnesia operates selectively to impair retrieval in short-term memory.

Butters and Cermak and their associates have consistently found a short-term memory deficit in many unpublished as well as published studies (e.g., Cermak, Butters, & Moreines, in press). This result, of course, must not be confused with the often-reported fact that amnesics have a normal immediate memory span. That may very well be true, but it is a fact independent of the sort of short-term forgetting over a period of several seconds that is measured by the Peterson paradigm. Immediate memory span relates to material held within the focus of conscious awareness —the primary memory of Waugh and Norman (1965). Short-term memory deals with the re-entry into awareness of material that was previously displaced from primary memory. We have ourselves replicated the finding of impaired performance by amnesics in the Peterson paradigm (Wood & Kinsbourne, 1974). Our results showed, moreover, that across a range from 3 to 18 sec, the amnesics' forgetting curve, though lower than that of normals (indicating less remembering), was parallel to it: there was no interaction between the groups (amnesics vs. controls) and the length of the retention interval. Recently, Milner (1974) has reported the same parallelity of Peterson decay curves for patients with differing extents of hippocampal excision.

In the literature, the main apparent contradiction to these results is the Baddeley and Warrington (1970) study, which presents identical forgetting curves across the period of 3–18 sec for amnesics and controls. Certain methodological issues, however, weaken the impact of this study as a counterexample to the above results. Specifically, Baddeley and Warrington did two things that might compromise their results: first, they used a 4-sec exposure period, which is rather longer than usual and which is known to increase performance substantially (Cermak & Levine, 1971); second, they made the distractor task easier for amnesics (counting backward by twos) than for normals (counting backward by threes). (This second aspect of their method is not without justification; amnesics do not, in fact, count backward by threes as fluently as normals, and it is fair to say that for them it is a more difficult task. It is appropriate therefore to make their distractor task somewhat easier, but the question remains how the distractor tasks can be equated for difficulty across the two populations. Baddeley and Warrington reported that the rate of counting backward was the same when normals did it by threes and amnesics did it by twos. It is not self-evident, however, that tasks that are executed at the same rate are necessarily equally difficult. A more satisfactory measure on which to equate the two tasks might be the number of errors made in counting backward.) More importantly, the long exposure period may have generated a ceiling effect. This is not at all fanciful, since Baddeley and Warrington themselves reported that the performance of both groups was better than might have been expected. If there were in fact a ceiling effect that prevented controls from showing as much improvement with prolonged exposure as amnesics, then an additional important observation is relevant. The effect of exposure time as an independent variable does not interact with the length of the retention interval (Liu & Ma, 1970;

Samuels, Butters, & Cermak, 1973). If a ceiling effect has obscured an underlying superiority of controls over amnesics in the Baddeley and Warrington study, the forgetting curve for controls should be higher than that for amnesics but both curves should be parallel, thus confirming our own results, reported above (Wood & Kinsbourne, 1974). It is a fair conclusion, therefore, that the trend of the evidence shows amnesics to be impaired in short-term memory performance in the Peterson paradigm.

It has been argued that amnesics have steeper decay functions over time in the Peterson paradigm than do normals (Cermak, Butters, & Goodglass, 1971). This argument, however, relied principally on the fact that amnesics and controls did equally well at a 0-sec retention interval. But this immediate repetition with no distractor task is not conceptually the same as memory performance after distraction. It has long been known that distraction is needed to elicit the amnesic memory defect. When performance across the range from 3 to 18 sec distraction is measured, there is little suggestion of interaction when trigrams are the to-be-remembered items, and the curves are strikingly parallel when words are the to-be-remembered items (as they were in the Wood and Kinsbourne, 1974, and the Milner, 1974, studies). Certainly if the null hypothesis is that there is no interaction, then it must be concluded that significant evidence against it is lacking.

There are theoretical consequences of the fact that the amnesics' forgetting curve is parallel to that of normals. Most variables affecting short-term forgetting do interact with the retention interval (Wood, 1973). One of the most important of these is proactive interference (Keppel & Underwood, 1962). Thus, proactive interference and amnesia operate on short-term forgetting in two different ways. This independence of amnesia and proactive interference is confirmed in the Wood and Kinsbourne (1974) study already cited above. Proactive interference was also manipulated in that study by the use of both 5-sec and 30-sec intertrial intervals for both groups (Peterson & Gentile, 1965; Cermak, 1970). Increased proactive interference (5-sec intertrial rest period) steepened the forgetting curve of both normals and amnesics, but both amnesic curves (high PI and low PI) were parallel to their respective counterparts for normals. Amnesia, in other words, subtracts a constant amount from performance, whatever the extent of proactive interference (5-sec intertrial rest vs. 30-sec intertrial rest), and whatever the length of the retention interval across the range of 3–18 sec. It can be concluded, therefore, that amnesia, at least in short-term memory, cannot be explained as an increased sensitivity to proactive interference as suggested in Warrington and Weiskrantz (1971).

That conclusion seems to contradict Cermak and Butters (1972, Experiments 1 and 2) who varied intertrial rest intervals for amnesics and normals and claimed to show that amnesics suffered more from short inter-trial rest intervals than normals did. But they used a proportional measure which somewhat obscures the absolute amounts of performance loss sustained by both amnesics and controls under the conditions of short intertrial rest periods. Again, there was only a mild suggestion of interaction when trigrams were the to-be-remembered item: normals lost 21% on the absolute scale; amnesics, approximately 32%. And again, when word triads were the to-be-remembered items, amnesic and normal losses due to the short retention interval were essentially equal (approximately 45% and 50%, respectively). The authors also showed that amesics were, like normals, likely to do worse on a given trial if the to-be-remembered item (word triad) on one trial is of the same class as the to-be-remembered item on the previous trial. Their justification for concluding that amnesics were more impaired by this condition than were normals, however, was based upon the same proportional calculation as before. No straightforward inter-action in terms of absolute performance was reported.

Amnesia is therefore to be classed in that limited group of variables that do not interact with the length of the retention interval. Note that any variable, such as proactive interference, which does interact with the length of the retention interval, must by virtue of that fact operate by augmenting the interfering or distracting nature of events that occur during the retention interval. Likewise, a variable that brings about a constant difference in performance, no matter how long the retention interval, must be presumed to operate in some other way, either by introducing a constant difference at registration time or a constant difference at retrieval time or both. Probably the only noninteracting variable that has been studied in any detail is the variable of exposure time of the to-be-remembered stimuli (Liu & Ma, 1970; Samuels, Butters, & Cermak, 1973; Cermak & Levine, 1971). It is noteworthy that the Samuels, Butters, and Cermak (1973) study, which varied exposure time between 150 msec and 1 sec, showed parallel forgetting curves for these two conditions, starting at 0-sec retention interval. That is, even at 0 sec (which constitutes simply a straightforward repetition of the to-be-remembered item), performance at 150 msec was diminished by the same amount as if the to-be-remembered item had been held in storage during a retention period of 18 sec. It can, of course, be seriously doubted whether such an increment in relation to increased exposure time at a 0-sec retention interval would occur throughout the range of possible exposure times, if for no other reason than that ceiling effects would obviously occur whenever exposure time was long enough to enable the subject to perceive the stimulus thoroughly in the first place. Liu and Ma (1970) showed parallel forgetting curves across the range of 3–27 sec, generated by exposures of 1, 2, and 4 sec.

The general case, then, appears to be that the additive or subtractive effects of the exposure time manipulation show up as constant differences in performance across a wide range of retention interval durations whenever there is any distractor period at all. (Simply repeating a to-be-remembered item does not qualify for inclusion in this general case, because there is no distractor period anyway, and performance falls within the range of immediate experience—the immediate or primary memory of James, 1890, and Waugh & Norman, 1965.) It is reasonable to suppose that the exposure time variable operates at the time of registration by determining the extent to which or the strength with which the to-be-remembered item is registered into memory, thus affecting retrieval performance by a constant amount regardless of the length of the retention interval.

Restriction on exposure time is, then, a candidate for simulating the amnesic defect. Amnesia could do the same things (less encoding or registration) that shortened exposure time does. A retrieval variable, however, could also subtract a constant amount from performance. So the question is whether the evidence on amnesia itself allows us to distinguish between these two possibilities, an encoding-registration deficit or a purely retrieval deficit.

The research of Cermak and Butters and their associates has concentrated on the possibility of a registration (encoding) difficulty. Does their evidence rule out a retrieval deficit and necessarily implicate an encoding deficit? We shall have to consider their experiments in some detail in order to answer this question. In several experiments, they have used serial list learning or paired associate paradigms (Cermak & Butters, 1972, Experiment 3; Cermak, Butters, & Gerrein, 1973, Experiments 1, 2, and 3). In all these experiments, some type of cueing was presented to the subjects to find out whether such cueing (category, synonym, homonym, etc.) could aid the subjects and thus imply that the to-be-remembered items were themselves encoded in ways suggested by the cues. The simple fact, however, is that in all these experiments the cues were provided at least at retrieval time; consequently, we are unable to discriminate between retrieval and encoding explanations for whatever differences appeared between amnesics and normals. The fourth experiment in Cermak, Butters, and Gerrein (1973) is of special interest. Subjects were presented a long list of words and were to respond whenever a word was repeated (had occurred earlier in the list). Some words in the list were in fact exact repetitions of earlier words. Others, however, were homonyms, normative associations, and synonyms. This is, of course, once again a retrieval cueing procedure and does not distinguish between retrieval and encoding processes. But notice the result: amnesics made more false recognitions to homonyms and associations than normals did, but they did not make significantly more synonym recognition errors. It is therefore not strictly the case that amnesics were deficient in semantic encoding or retrieval, although that is the interpretation given by the authors. An alternative interpretation is that the amnesics had laxer criteria for retrieval, based on acoustic or associative qualities. Amnesics, in other words, made overgeneral (nondiscriminating) retrievals when the retrieval cues were acoustic or associative, but were more discriminating (and like normals) when the retrieval was based on a semantic cue (synonym). What the authors interpreted as a semantic encoding deficiency may instead have been an acoustic and associative retrieval deficiency.

A second type of evidence for a verbal-semantic encoding deficit in amnesics consists in showing that, in the Peterson and Peterson paradigm, nonverbal materials (random shapes, piano notes, or unfamiliar tactile shapes) were remembered as well by amnesics as by controls, whereas verbal materials (written or spoken trigrams or tactile letters) were remembered less well by amnesics than by normals (Butters, Lewis, Cermak, & Goodglass, in press). The serious difficulty here is that for all types of to-be-remembered items, the distractor task was the same, counting backward. It is now apparent, however, (Reitman, 1971; Schiffrin, 1973; and Rowe, Philipchalk, & Cake, 1973) that verbal and nonverbal tasks do not interfere with each other as target item versus distractor task in the Peterson and Peterson paradigm. This independence of musical and other nonverbal items from verbal distraction may have an underlying basis in the fact that verbal and nonverbal processes are represented in different cerebral hemispheres in right-handers. Wood and Quigley-Fernandez (1975) have shown that left-handers perform less well when the item is verbal and the distractor task musical, than does a group of right-handers under the same conditions, although the groups are equal in performance with verbal item and verbal distractor. This greater interference between disparate tasks may reflect greater overlap in cerebral representation of verbal and nonverbal processes in left-handers and greater variability in the degree of that overlap (Hecaen & Sauget, 1971). It is to be expected, therefore, that amnesics and normals would both show forgetting of nonverbal materials when a nonverbal distractor task is used, and such is, in fact, the case (Cermak, 1974).

The final class of evidence in favor of a selective verbal and semantic encoding difficulty for amnesics comes from the use of the Wickens (1970) technique, so-called "release from proactive interference" in the Peterson paradigm. In this procedure, after being presented during early trials (here, Trials 1–4) with to-be-remembered items from a particular class, subjects receive a to-be-remembered item from a different class on the next (fifth) trial. The amount of "PI release" is the increment in performance as compared to the condition in which on Trial 5 the to-be-remembered item is also drawn from the original class. Thus, for example, consonant trigrams are presented for the first four trials and a digit triad is presented on Trial 5. Both amnesics and normals show a gain in performance or release from proactive interference on Trial 5, but if the shift is from one taxonomic category of word triads (such as animals) on Trials 1–4 to another taxonomic category (such as vegetables) on Trial 5, then amnesics show no gain in performance on Trial 5, although normals do (Cermak, Butters, & Moreines, in press). The authors interpreted these results as showing that while amnesics could encode on the basis of gross features of the to-be-remembered item, and thus were able to distinguish consonant trigrams from digit triads and so gain release from proactive interference on the shifted trial, they could not encode semantically to a level sufficient to allow them to distinguish taxonomic categories in memory. Thus a shift in taxonomic categories would gain them no release from proactive interference. A retrieval process, however, could in fact be operating here. Suppose that on Trial 5, at retrieval time, the subject is inaccurate in discriminating in time between the Trial-4 and Trial-5 items as they appear in storage; that is, the subject's temporal resolving power, his acuity for time distinctions in memory, is more coarsely grained than that of normals. In this case, the subject would be forced to search for attributes of the target item that transcend the characteristics of any single trial. On Trial 5, the only intertrial common attribute is that which has occurred on Trials 1–4. Thus, because the subject has no other attributes to guide him, he retrieves from the class of items that was presented on Trials 1–4. This analysis need apply only when a more subtle semantic distinction between the Trial-4 and the Trial-5 item is required. Normal performance on a shift from trigrams to digit triads, therefore, could simply imply that under those conditions the subject's retrieval capacities, pathologically limited though they are, are not in this single case unduly taxed.

The foregoing analysis yields two predictions: first, when a shift in taxonomic categories of word triads is made on Trial 5, the subject not only shows no release from proactive interference but he gives responses on Trial 5 that come from the class established on Trials 1–4; second, if the items on subsequent trials (6, 7, and 8) continue to be from the new class as established on Trial 5, the subject should soon gain the ability to retrieve from that class and thus show a delayed release from proactive interference. Thus, for example, on Trial 6 at retrieval time, the subject now has two intertrial categories available to him, the one established on Trials 1–4 and the one established on Trials 5 and 6. The discrimination between these two categories and the correct choice of the more recent one is now easier and might now fall within the subject's retrospective temporal resolving power. Both predictions are confirmed. On the first shifted trial (Trial 5), the subject gives a triad composed of items that would have been appropriate on Trials 1–4. Furthermore, if the new category is continued on Trials 6 and 7, subjects show a delayed release from proactive interference (Wood & Kinsbourne, 1974). If subjects can show a delayed release from proactive interference, then it can be argued that they have successfully encoded the attributes of the shifted material but have on the first shifted trial been unable to retrieve successfully the correct item on the basis of that encoded attribute. One might reply that delayed release from proactive interference simply means that it takes more than one trial for the subjects to encode the relative semantic attributes of the new class of materials. What that reply really suggests, however, is that amnesics can retrieve on the basis of semantic information if that information is repeated, but that they cannot easily do so if that information occurs only at one time or on one trial. This leads to the question of what frequency, itself, does to an item or an attribute of an item and takes us somewhat away from the present discussion. The matter will be reopened when we discuss the difference in impact of amnesia on episodic and semantic memory. But here the point is that none of the above studies allows us to say that the amnesic deficit is an encoding deficit and not a retrieval deficit, *vice versa,* or both (Talland, 1965).

We have experimentally tested the question of retrieval *vs.* registration difficulty by comparing pre-cueing *vs.* post-cueing in a modification of the Peterson and Peterson paradigm (Wood & Kinsbourne, 1974). Subjects received triads of words, each triad comprising a single category (*e.g.,* "oak, spruce, pine," or "red, blue, green"). Three such triads were separated from each other by 30 sec of digit distraction and were followed by 30 sec of such distraction. In the pre-cueing condition, subjects were told the category of the triad three times at registration time. In the post-cueing condition, the subjects were told at retrieval time (30 sec after the last triad) what the category was, and asked to name the triad. Post-cueing was equally beneficial regardless of whether there had been pre-cueing. But pre-cueing had no effect regardless of whether there was post-cueing. If it can be assumed that an encoding deficit could be at least partly overcome by category pre-cueing, which would aid the subject in encoding along the relevant category dimension (Cermak, Butters, & Gerrein, 1973), then performance at retrieval should be enhanced by such category pre-cueing regardless of the benefits of any category post-cueing procedure. This failure to find any benefits of pre-cueing, together with the finding of substantial benefits for post-cueing, suggests to us that a retrieval deficit is implicated. This result resembles that of Gardner, Boller, Moreines, & Butters

(1973), who likewise concluded, on the basis of pre- and post-cueing comparisons, that a retrieval deficit was at least part of the explanation for the amnesic memory loss.

It seems fair to conclude that the balance of the evidence favors a retrieval explanation of the amnesic defect in short-term memory as measured in the Peterson and Peterson paradigm.

B. Retrieval Deficit in Long-Term Memory

Another clear-cut demonstration that amnesics have a retrieval difficulty in spite of presumably normal encoding refers to the phenomenon of retrograde amnesia. It is to ask amnesics about events that we can assume were normally encoded; in other words, ask them about events that occurred before they sustained the damage that resulted in their memory defect. Thus, Sanders and Warrington (1971) asked amnesics about major events, some of which happened many years before the onset of their disorders, and showed deficits in such memory, when compared to normals.

Such retrograde amnesia (RA) regularly characterizes not only the amnesic syndrome proper, but also the traumatic amnesias (Russell & Nathan, 1946). The proceeds of clinical inquiry have led to the impression that the patients do not remember the circumstances that surround the onset of their disease, whether it was the Wernicke's encephalopathy that precedes Korsakoff's psychosis in alcoholics, or the brief and sudden impact on the skull that sets up traumatic amnesia. The patient almost invariably forgets the actual onset of the condition, and forgetting tends to be permanent. In the first 24 hours after a head injury patients are usually unable to give a coherent consecutive account of the events of the preceding day. Within a day or two this usually rapidly dissipates, leaving only a lacuna regarding the few seconds preceding the impact. But an appreciable number of patients have longer periods of RA, up to lengths of time measured in years, and in the amnesic syndrome RA of several or many years is frequent. In the traumatic cases this period of RA usually shrinks, often radically. In the amnesic syndrome shrinkage occasionally also occurs (Milner, 1970).

The fact of retrograde amnesia proves beyond question that defective registration (encoding) at input cannot account for the amnesia. Events obliterated by RA were registered long before memory processes became impaired. Shrinkage of RA shows that at least a substantial proportion of the forgotten material must have been maintained intact in some temporarily inaccessible store. An impairment in retrieval most comfortably accounts for the existence and shrinkage of RA. But this assumption seems to necessitate a curious proviso. The impairment in retrieval seems biased so as to bear with increased severity on memory for relatively recent events as compared to those more distant in time.

The phenomenon of RA has led theorists to propose a consolidation process prior to the more stable laying down of a memory. This hypothetical stage is supposed to be more vulnerable to interference, such as concussion or electroconvulsive shock, than the later stable state. Whatever the merits of this notion, it can hardly be applied to the longer RAs lasting months or even years. Nevertheless a similar principle has been applied to this situation by Wickelgren (1974), who proposed that the engram spontaneously gains over time in an attribute termed strength, which operationally is resistance to disruption. But is it necessary to make this additional assumption? It becomes less compelling when the phenomenology of RA is more closely examined.

Retrograde amnesia is typically incomplete. It is punctuated by "islands of remembering." Two events become condensed into one (Talland, 1965). The latter is disconnected out of context, and often mislocalized in time. As RA shrinks, it does not recede toward the time of onset of amnesia with any semblance of order. Rather, more "islands of remembering" sporadically appear, and only subsequently, as more gaps are filled, do the memories assume the continuity of a remembered chronological sequence. Williams and Zangwill (1952) have emphasized that it is primarily the temporal coherence of the memory train that is disturbed. When events are recalled, they are often displaced in time, and this occurrence particularly illustrates the pathologically coarsened grain of retrospective temporal discrimination by those patients.

We have used the procedure of Crovitz (1973) to ask amnesics to produce personal memories from some time in their lives in response to each word in a list of 20 high-imagery, high-frequency words. For example, if the word is "flag," the subject is to describe a personal memory that he has of flags or a flag. Normal subjects can do so for each of the 20 words and can confine that search to their childhood. Amnesics, by contrast, produce a very different type of response. With few exceptions, they do not retrieve individual events at all. They characteristically, instead, and contrary to instruction, retrieve categorical information about the appropriate use or general availability of the object represented by the stimulus word. For example, the subject says to the word "flag," "Of course I remember flags. Flags are for waving in parades, lots of times in parades." If the subject is pressed for a memory of any certain parade or any certain flag that he has ever seen, he continues to say that of course he has seen flags in parades because they are very common things in his life, but he is unable to remember any certain flag or any certain parade that he has ever seen. These results (Wood & Kinsbourne, 1974) are so clear-cut and dramatic as to leave little doubt: amnesics could retrieve from their childhood and also from some of the later years of their lives a considerable wealth of information, but on this task the information was entirely general and not bound to any single event. Memory for specific events in childhood is quite impoverished. The distinction we observe in the kinds of memories amnesics retrieve remands us of Tulving's (1972) distinction between episodic and semantic memory. It seems that the amnesics' responses are good examples of semantic memory (memory for meanings, rules, categories, *etc.*). The amnesics seem selectively deficient in retrievals from episodic memory (memory for discrete events, actual real-life occurrences, unique instances).

It is easy to understand why the temporal disorganization of retrieval from memory might mislead the cursory questioner into supposing that the patient is imaginatively living at some time in the past. Questions that call for a time-referenced choice of response from a set of possible alternatives might be met with a response that places the here-and-now many years back: "Who is the President?" "Eisenhower." But: "Name Republican Presidents." "Eisenhower, Nixon." (Dialogue with an amnesic in 1973.)

Premorbid memories may return sporadically. Perhaps for fortuitous reasons, if a closely related context presents itself, it may provide the retrieval process with the cues that it is itself not capable of evoking. A telling example is given by Russell and Nathan (1946) in a case of traumatic RA. A soldier who was concussed when his truck was wrecked could not remember this episode till he went to a war movie. A crash of gunfire brought back to him the crash of his truck in collision.

In this respect, RA could resemble the inaccessibility of early childhood memories. If episodic remembering necessitates an imaginative reconstruction of context, then, given the vastly different emotional climate of early childhood, it would be understandably difficult to reconstruct that early context. This difficulty might be lessened in certain stages of psychotherapy or hypnosis.

It follows from the above discussion that retrograde amnesia cannot validly be used as evidence in support of a strength theory of memory storage (Wickelgren, 1970) or of multistage theories of secondary memory.

The reason for the ostensibly greater effect of RA on relatively recent memory now becomes clear. It is that one customarily asks different kinds of questions about the recent and about the more distant past. Temporal cohension of memories is not expected for events that occurred long ago. So the questions asked about the very long term refer to discrete and salient events, mostly ones that might well have in the interim been much rehearsed by frequent recall in memory. This is particularly likely to be a source of confusion when patients are asked for free recall of unspecified prior events. They may then come up with some minutely described specific events that greatly impressed them in their youth. But once the experimenter begins to specify the kind of memory that is called for, as in Crovitz's paradigm, the poverty of these patients' recollection of old memories becomes painfully apparent. Questioning about recent events typically takes a different form, and relates to everyday rather than outstandingly impressive events. These are highly context-bound memories, and thus most vulnerable to defects in episodic retrieval. So it is not surprising that when Sanders and Warrington (1971) held question type constant, they found no selective sparing of very old memories, but rather a forgetting that was more severe the more time had passed.

C. Selective Episodic Memory Deficit, with Relative Sparing of Semantic Memory

Tulving has classified memory into two types, episodic and semantic. Episodic memory relates to the remembering of specific incidents or episodes in the subject's personal experience. It is basically biographical and typically relates to unique rather than repeated events. These memories are elicited by questions (cues) of the where, when, who type that specify context. In contrast, semantic memory is context-free. It consists of rules, skills, associations, and relations that are overlearned—all that we "know" in principle, irrespective of the circumstances under which this knowledge was acquired. We have already discussed the striking dissociation in the content of amnesics' long-term memory as measured in the Crovitz (1973) paradigm. Amnesics are seriously deficient in retrieving information about specific events from any time in their lives. Yet, categorical information, information about the appropriate use of objects and other such information, which is not tied to any specific instance, is relatively accessible to long-term retrieval.

Amnesics have repeatedly been reported to have acquired information or a skill while forgetting when or how they learned it. An example from Wood and Kinsbourne (1974) relates to the Fibonacci rule (start with two 1-digit numbers in immediately ascending sequence, e.g., 3, 4; the next number is the sum of the previous two, or 7; the next is the sum of the previous two, or 11; etc.). It was possible to teach amnesics the Fibonacci rule. On retest one day and again four months later, there was on each occasion substantial saving on relearning, but at four months no subject could remember ever doing the task before. The Fibonacci rule was successfully entered into semantic memory, but the teaching episodes could not be retrieved.

All instances of amnesic forgetting can fit into the category of episodic memory. But amnesics are able to learn some motor skills—mirror drawing (Milner, 1970), pursuit rotor (Corkin, 1968), perceptual closure—identification of incomplete figures, and cue-depleted words (Warrington & Weiskrantz, 1970b). Certainly they do not forget the vocabulary and syntax of the language, the social amenities, or other much rehearsed skills. All of these can be considered semantic memories and are relatively spared.

An essential ingredient of entry into semantic (as opposed to episodic) memory is repetition. This is indispensable in perceptual, language, and motor learning. With enough repetition (e.g., spontaneous mental rehearsal) even certain episodes may enter into semantic memory. Typically an amnesic can trot out one or two long-past episodic memories of a very salient and probably much rehearsed type (though even here it is necessary to check on the validity of the memory before accepting it as genuine). One consequence of the relative preservation of learning by repetition is the perseveration of response so often noted when amnesics are set memory tasks. In retrieving, the amnesic hits upon a recently repeated item or category, rather than on the single specific one asked for. Thus in our proactive inhibition release experiment, the patients on the category shift trial tended to respond not with the new but with the previously repeated old category. But after one or two more trials with the new category, release from proactive inhibition did occur with the repetition. The new category was now able to affect the retrieval process.

If the amnesic syndrome is due to a selective impairment of the ability to retrieve episodic memories, are there among neuropsychological syndromes also examples of selective impairment of semantic memory? Pribram (1969) has drawn attention to what he termed cortical amnesias and described as forgetting of context-free material (in contrast to the "contextual" amnesia due to "frontolimbic" disease). Barbizet (1970) has made a similar distinction, between specific (cortical) and general amnesias. Let us consider aphasic forgetting as an example of a material-specific deficit in semantic remembering.

It is general knowledge that whereas only the most severely affected receptive aphasics fail to understand individual words, many if not most aphasics show a varying degree of difficulty in comprehending sentences that consist of words that are individually well within their grasp. Brief consideration of what normally happens when we listen to speech will help clarify the mechanism of this disability.

As has been pointed out, the number of items of information that can be concurrently held in the focus of immediate experience is strictly limited. In normal conversation, it often takes many more words than this to make a point. The listener has to hold earlier words in mind while listening to later ones while he cumulatively grasps the meaning of the proposition. If he held discrete words in primary memory he would find his primary memory taxed beyond its limits, and words and their meanings would be lost. In fact, the listener uses the redundancy of the language to chunk, group, or unitize word groups and thus relieve the burden on primary memory without loss of comprehension (though perhaps with less ability to repeat verbatim).

Kinsbourne (1972) presented subjects with spoken letter sequences for immediate recall. The sequences varied in the extent to which they conformed to the transitional probabilities of English spelling (Miller, Bruner, & Postman, 1964). Young subjects had an increasingly longer immediate memory span, the more the sequences conformed to English spelling. Old subjects had lower scores under all conditions, but their performance also showed a monotonic increment with increasing approximation to English. But an aphasic group totally failed to show any such relationship. Their span was no greater with the most structured lists than with the ones that were quite random.

The young and old normal subjects were able to use the higher levels of approximation to group or unitize subsets of letter names and thus to minimize the burden on immediate memory capacity. Aphasics were unable to make such use of the proffered structure. Their impaired memory span was due to failure to recruit semantic (*i.e.,* overlearned) information to the task. If this result represents what happens when aphasics listen to sequences of words in conversation, then the comprehension difficulty could simply be explained as due to failure to unitize word groups, thus overloading and therefore losing crucial information from primary memory.

Aphasic word-finding difficulty and rarer aphasic variants such as color agnosia similarly represent categorically delimited forms of semantic memory difficulty. In the nonverbal sphere, disorders such as prosopagnosia (impaired memory for faces) might similarly be explained, if the patient, who is known to be able to identify constituent features of facial configurations, cannot grasp them in terms of their oft-experienced relationships, and thus is overburdened with fragmentary visual detail.

A crucial ingredient of a semantic memory deficit is that the forgetting is not limited to a particular response mode. Thus the word repetition defect of conduction aphasia, presented by Warrington and Shallice (1969) as a selective loss of short-term memory with sparing of long-term memory, is found only when subjects orally or in writing repeat the stimulus words. It is not found when they match successive sets of stimulus words (Kinsbourne, 1972; Strub & Gardner, 1974). Thus this deficit is not one of short-term or any other form of memory but instead represents a "disconnection" of verbal reponse from auditory (not visual) verbal input.

The distinction between episodic and semantic memory has a possible neural–anatomical correlate in the distinction between cortical and limbic amnesia, as we have seen (Pribram, 1969). The functional characteristics of episodic and semantic memory may also correlate well with different models of neural functioning. Thus, nerve net models in the tradition of Hebb (1949) depend on incremental changes in synaptic efficiency and seem well suited to semantic learning—that is, learning to attach a certain response to a certain stimulus or group of stimuli by dint of frequent repetition. Certainly, such models are capable of impressive feats of discrimination learning and pattern recognition. For example, PERCEPTRON (Rosenblatt, 1958) can learn to recognize the letters of the alphabet simply by repeated learning trials that alter the efficiencies of pathways between sensory, associator, and response units. It is the essence of such a system that it learns only what is constant across many trials. It is therefore resistant to individual instances of trainer error, precisely because it does not record individual events, but only their cumulative effect.

The other tradition is due to Lashley (1929) and uses the language of wave-front reconstruction. It is most extensively represented today by the various holographic theorists (Longuet-Higgins, 1968; Gabor, 1968; Barrett, 1969; Baron, 1970). It is the characteristic of such models that they can record individual events in great contextual richness; also they can play back the entire event when only part of the event and its context is presented. Such models, however, do not characteristically provide for the summation of a large number of events and the construction of context-free rules or attributes. It is possible to model holographic (Baron, 1970) or other wave-storage processes (Spinelli, 1970) with nerve nets consisting of mathematically characterized neurons or populations of neurons. When this is done, the distinction between an episodic and a semantic remembering mechanism becomes reducible to differing sensitivities of synapses due to changes resulting from one pass through the system. In Spinelli's OCCAM model (1970), for example, the net can be made to store a wave on a single presentation or it can require repeated presentations, depending solely on the parameters assumed for synaptic thresholds.

Despite this ability of some models to store either event or rule information, depending on parameter adjustment, the question is still open whether a full simulation of the semantic–episodic distinction is better accomplished by one flexible system or by two more specialized systems. As we have argued, the amnesic syndrome suggests a functional dissociability of the two kinds of remembering. Furthermore, a consideration of phylogeny as well as human ontogeny does suggest that if the underlying memory system is a unitary one, its capability for episodic remembering represents a more advanced state of the system than does its capability for semantic remembering. Developmentally, we learn some word meanings and other such semantic information before there is any evidence of episodic remembering.

D. Status of the Question of Different Types of Amnesia

As has already been mentioned, the amnesic syndrome results from damage to a range of structures in the brain. It is obviously at least theoretically possible that these different structures contribute differently to remembering. If so, there should be more than one type of amnesic syndrome; the nature of the memory deficit should in some way be determined by the locus of the lesion.

This proposal arises from the view that the structures involved in remembering are organized to some extent as parallel processes. Alternatively, they are arranged in series, in which case it would be quite feasible to obtain the same behavioral result from interruption of such a system at quite different neuro-anatomical locations.

No statistically adequate group comparisons exist that validate the notion of different types of amnesic syndromes. On the anecdotal basis, the most nearly convincing dichotomy relates to the incidence of confabulation in this syndrome.

Incorrect remembering is a dramatic feature of Korsakov's psychosis. It has been regarded as a hallmark of the syndrome (Bonhoeffer, 1904). It is called confabulation, implying that the patient either deliberately or subconsciously seeks to close the gaps in his memory with plausible inventions. But confabulation seems to coincide only with the early confusional stage of the amnesic syndrome and is not characteristic of the chronic syndrome (Talland, 1965). Also, nonalcoholic cases of amnesic syndrome do not confabulate. Either these are two variants of the syndrome, confabulatory and nonconfabulatory, respectively, or confabulation represents the response of persons of a particular personality type to a particular predicament. The facile, plausible, and suggestible alcoholic might voice some hazy recollection while mildly confused and confronted by clinicians with insistent claims on his memory, at least until he became negatively reinforced by social disapproval of his facile "remembering." At present there is as yet no reason to discard this economical account of confabulation. Confabulation cannot be accepted as defining a distinct variant of the basic amnesic disorder.

What form would convincing evidence of multiple amnesic syndromes have to take? Suppose that an amnesic patient differed from those reported in most studies in having little or no Peterson decrement. Before such a case be accepted as differing fundamentally from the rest, it must be clear that he is well matched to the sample. For instance, suppose that a design is one in which there is a relatively long initial inspection period for to-be-remembered material. If the patient is of above-average intelligence, he might use that time better than other amnesics and better also than controls, to encode the stimulus with all possible richness. This could well take substantial strain off his pathologically impaired retrieval mechanisms and result in tolerable performance after Peterson distraction.

E. Conclusion

We conclude that the amnesic syndrome illuminates normal short-term memory processing in two ways. First, by implicating retrieval mechanisms (and perhaps only retrieval mechanisms), it directs theoretical attention to such mechanisms in normal short-term memory. Secondly, it offers some behavioral and anatomical validation of Tulving's episodic versus semantic memory distinction.

BIBLIOGRAPHY

Adey, W. R. Investigation of hippocampal activity during conditioning. In E. Sokolov (Ed.), *Orienting reflex and problems of perception.* Moscow and New York: Macmillan, 1964.

Atkinson, R., & Schiffrin, R. Human memory: A proposed system and its control processes. In K. Spence & J. Spence (Eds.), *Advances in the psychology of learning and motivation research and theory,* Vol. 2. New York: Academic Press, 1968.

Baddeley, A. Short-term memory for word sequences as a function of acoustic, semantic, and formal similarity in short-term memory. *Psychonomic Science,* 1966, **5,** 233–234.

Baddeley, A. D., & Dale, H. C. A. The effect of semantic similarity on retroactive interference in long- and short-term memory. *Journal of Verbal Learning and Verbal Behavior,* 1966, **5,** 417–420.

Baddeley, A. D., & Warrington, E. K. Amnesia and the distinction between long- and short-term memory. *Journal of Verbal Learning and Verbal Behavior,* 1970, **9,** 176–189.

Barbizet, J. *Human memory and its pathology.* San Francisco: Freeman, 1970.

Barbizet, J., & Cany, E. A psychometric study of various memory deficits associated with cerebral lesions. In G. Talland & N. Waugh (Eds.), *The pathology of memory.* New York: Academic Press, 1969.

Baron, R. A model for cortical memory. *Journal of Mathematical Psychology,* 1970, **7,** 37–59.

Barrett, R. The cortex as interferometer: The transmission of amplitude, frequency, and phase in cortical structures. *Neuropsychologia,* 1969, **7,** 135–148.

Bernbach, H. A multiple-copy model for postperceptual memory. In D. Norman (Ed.), *Models of human memory*. New York: Academic Press, 1970.

Bickford, R., Mulder, D., Dodge, H., Svien, H., & Rome, H. Changes in memory function produced by electrical stimulation of the temporal lobe in man. *Research Publications of the Association for Nervous and Mental Diseases*, 1958, **36**, 227–243.

Bjork, R. Repetition and rehearsal mechanisms in models for short-term memory. In D. Norman (Ed.), *Models of human memory*. New York: Academic Press, 1970.

Bjork, R., & Allen, T. The spacing effect: Consolidation or retrieval encoding? *Journal of Verbal Learning and Verbal Behavior*, 1970, **9**, 562–572.

Bjork, R., LaBerge, D., & Legrand, R. The modification of short-term memory through instructions to forget. *Psychonomic Science*, 1968, **10**, 55–56.

Block, R. Effects of instructions to forget in short-term memory. *Journal of Experimental Psychology*, 1971, **89**, 1–9.

Bonhoeffer, K. Der Korsakowsche Symptomenkomplex in seiner komplex Beziehungen zu der verscheidenen Krankheitformen. *Allgemeine Zeitschrift für Psychiatrie*, 1904, **161**, 744.

Brown, J. Some tests of the decay theory of immediate memory. *Quarterly Journal of Experimental Psychology*, 1958, **10**, 12–21.

Butters, N., Lewis, R., Cermak, L., & Goodglass, H. Material-specific memory deficits in alcoholic Korsakoff patients. *Neuropsychologia*, in press.

Cermak, L. S. Repetition and encoding in short-term memory. *Journal of Experimental Psychology*, 1969, **28**, 321–326.

Cermak, L. S. Decay of interference as a function of the intertrial interval in short-term memory. *Journal of Experimental Psychology*, 1970, **84** (3), 499–501.

Cermak, L. Paper in symposium on pathological forgetting. International Neuropsychology Society, Boston, February 1974.

Cermak, L., & Butters, N. The role of interference and encoding in the short-term memory deficits of Korsakoff patients. *Neuropsychologia*, 1972, **10**, 89–95.

Cermak, L. S., Butters, N., & Gerrein, J. The extent of the verbal encoding ability of Korsakoff patients. *Neuropsychologia*, 1973, **11**, 85–94.

Cermak, L., Butters, N., & Goodglass, H. The extent of memory loss in Korsakoff patients. *Neuropsychologia*, 1971, **9**, 307–315.

Cermak, L., Butters, N., & Moreines, J. Some analyses of the verbal encoding deficit in alcoholic Korsakoff patients. *Brain and Language*, 1974, in press.

Cermak, L., & Levine, R. Encoding as a function of the presentation-rehearsal interval in short-term memory. *Psychonomic Science*, 1971, **23** (6), 423–424.

Chapman, L. F., Walter, R. D., Markham, C. H., Rand, R. W., & Crandall, P. M. Memory changes induced by stimulation of hippocampus or amygdala in epilepsy patients with implanted electrodes. *Transactions of the American Neurological Association*, 1967, **92**, 50–56.

Cohen, B. H. An investigation of recoding in free recall. *Journal of Experimental Psychology*, 1963, **65**, 368–376.

Cohen, B. H. Recall of categorized word lists. *Journal of Experimental Psychology*, 1963, **66**, 227–234.

Cooper, E., & Pantle, A. The total time hypothesis in verbal learning. *Psychological Bulletin*, 1967, **68**, 221–234.

Conrad, R. An association between memory errors and errors due to acoustic masking of speech. *Nature*, 1962, **193**, 1314–1315.

Conrad, R. Acoustic confusions in recent memory. *British Journal of Psychology,* 1964, **55,** 75–84.

Corkin, S. Acquisition of motor skill after bilateral medial temporal lobe excision. *Neuropsychologia,* 1968, **6,** 225–265.

Craik, F., & Lockhart, R. Levels of processing: A framework for memory research. *Journal of Verbal Learning and Verbal Behavior,* 1972, **11,** 671–684.

Crovitz, H. Unconstrained search in long-term memory. Paper presented at Psychonomic Society, St. Louis, October 1973.

Deutsch, D. Tones & numbers: Specificity of interference in short-term memory. *Science,* 1970, **168,** 1604–1605.

Dillon, R., & Reid, L. S. Short-term memory as a function of information processing during the retention interval. *Journal of Experimental Psychology,* 1969, **81,** 261–269.

Eimas, P. D., & Calitt, J. D. Selective adaptation of linguistic feature detectors. *Cognitive Psychology,* 1973, **4,** 99–109.

Elias, C. S., & Perfetti, C. A. Encoding task and recognition memory: The importance of semantic encoding. *Journal of Experimental Psychology,* 1973, **99** (2), 151–156.

Elmes, D. Role of prior recalls and storage load in short-term memory. *Journal of Experimental Psychology,* 1969, **79,** 468–472.

Estes, W. K. Statistical theory of spontaneous recovery and regression. *Psychological Review,* 1955, **62,** 145–154.

Falkenberg, P. Recall improves in short-term memory the more recall context resembles learning context. *Journal of Experimental Psychology,* 1972, **95** (1), 39–47.

Gabor, D. Improved holographic model of temporal recall. *Nature,* 1968, **217,** 104.

Gardiner, J. M., Craik, F. I. M., & Birtwistle, J. Retrieval cues and release from proactive inhibition. *Journal of Verbal Learning and Verbal Behavior,* 1972, **11,** 778–783.

Gardner, H., Boller, F., Moreines, J., & Butters, N. Retrieving information from Korsakoff patients: Effects of categorized cues and references to the task. *Cortex,* 1973, **9,** 165–175.

Gorfein, D. S., & Jacobson, D. E. Proactive effects in short-term recognition memory. *Journal of Experimental Psychology,* 1972, **95** (1), 211–214.

Grossman, L., & Eagle, M. Synonymity, antonymity, and association in false recognition responses. *Journal of Experimental Psychology,* 1970, **83,** 244–248.

Hebb, D. *The organization of behavior.* New York: Wiley, 1949.

Hecaen, H., & Sauget, J. Cerebral dominance in left-handed subjects. *Cortex,* 1971, **7,** 19–48.

Hellyer, S. Frequency of stimulus presentation and short-term decrement in recall. *Journal of Experimental Psychology,* 1962, **64** (6), 650.

Hick, W. On the rate of gain of information. *Quarterly Journal of Experimental Psychology,* 1952, **4,** 11–26.

Hofer, R. Intertrial proactive inhibition in short-term memory. *Psychological Reprints,* 1965, **17,** 755–760.

Houston, J. P. Short-term retention of verbal units with equated degrees of learning. *Journal of Experimental Psychology,* 1965, **70** (1), 75–58.

Hubel, D., & Wiesel, T. Receptive fields, binocular interaction, and functional architecture in the cat's visual cortex. *Journal of Physiology,* 1962, **160,** 106–154.

Hull, C. *Principles of behavior.* New York: Appleton-Century-Crofts, 1943.

James, W. *Principles of psychology.* New York: Holt, Rinehart & Winston, 1890.

Jarho, L. Korsakoff-like amnesic syndrome in penetrating brain injury. *Acta Neurologica Scandinavica, Supplementum 54,* 1973, **49,** entire issue.

John, E. *Mechanisms of memory.* New York: Academic Press, 1967.

Keppel, G., & Underwood, B. J. Proactive inhibition in short-term retention of single items. *Journal of Verbal Learning and Verbal Behavior,* 1962, **1,** 153–161.

Kinsbourne, M. Behavioral analysis of the repetition deficit in conduction aphasia. *Neurology,* 1972, **22,** 1126–1132.

Lashley, K. *Brain mechanisms and intelligence.* Chicago: University of Chicago Press, 1929.

Laughery, K., & Pinkus, A. Short-term memory: Effects of acoustic similarity, presentation rate, and presentation mode. *Psychoneurological Science,* 1966, **6,** 285–286.

Levy, C. M., & Jowaisas, D. Short-term memory: Storage interference and storage decay. *Journal of Experimental Psychology,* 88, **2,** 189–195.

Liu, I.-M., & Ma, H.-H. On the nature of a training trial in verbal learning. *Journal of Experimental Psychology,* 1970, **86** (1), 126–127.

Loess, H. Proactive inhibition in short-term memory. *Journal of Verbal Learning and Verbal Behavior,* 1964, **3,** 362–368.

Loess, H., & Waugh, N. Short-term memory and intertrial interval. *Journal of Verbal Behavior,* 1967, **4,** 455–460.

Longuet-Higgins, H. Holographic model of temporal recall. *Nature,* 1968, **217,** 104.

Mandler, G. Organization and memory. In K. Spence & J. Spence (Eds.), *Advances in the psychology of learning and motivation: Research and theory,* Vol. 1. New York: Academic Press, 1967.

Meissner, W. W. Learning and memory in the Korsakoff syndrome. *International Journal of Neuropsychiatry,* 1966, **4,** 6–20.

Melton, A. W., Implications of short-term memory for a general theory of memory. *Journal of Verbal Learning and Verbal Behavior,* 1963, **2,** 1–21.

Melton, A. W. The situation with respect to the spacing of repetitions and memory. *Journal of Verbal Learning and Verbal Behavior,* 1970, **9,** 596–606.

Miller, G. A. The magical number seven, plus or minus two: some limits on our capacity for processing information. *Psychological Review,* 1956, **63,** 81–96.

Miller, L. The effect of duration of item exposure on recall in a short-term memory paradigm. *Psychonomic Science,* 1970, **21,** 123–124.

Miller, G., Bruner, J. & Postman, L. Familiarity of letter sequences and tachistoscopic identification. *Journal of General Psychology,* 1964, **50,** 129–139.

Miller, R., & Springer, A. Amnesia, consolidation, and retrieval. *Psychological Review,* 1973, **80** (1), 69–77.

Milner, B. Amnesia following operation on the temporal lobes. In C. W. M. Whitty & O. L. Zangwill (Eds.), *Amnesia.* London: Butterworths, 1966.

Milner, B. Disorders of memory after brain lesions in man. *Neuropsychologia,* 1968, **6,** 175–179.

Milner, B. Residual intellectual and memory deficits after head injury. In A. Walker, W. Caveness, & McD. Critchley (Eds.), *The late effects of head injury.* Springfield, Ill.: Charles C. Thomas, 1969.

Milner, B. Memory and the medial temporal regions of the brain. In K. Pribram & D. Broadbent (Eds.), *Biology of memory.* New York: Academic Press, 1970.

Milner, B. Paper in symposium on pathological forgetting. International Neuropsychology Society, Boston, Mass., February 8, 1974.

Murdock, B. B., Jr. The retention of individual items. *Journal of Experimental Psychology*, 1961, **62**, 618–625.

Murdock, B. B., Jr. Distractor and probe techniques in short-term memory. *Canadian Journal of Psychology*, 1967, **21**, 25–36.

Murdock, B. B., Jr. Decoding as a function of the number of bits per chunk. *Journal of Experimental Psychology*, 1968, **78** (1), 1–7.

Murdock, B. B., Jr. & vom Saal, W. Transpositions in short-term memory. *Journal of Experimental Psychology*, 1967, 137–142.

Murray, D., & Newman, F. Visual and verbal coding in short-term memory. *Journal of Experimental Psychology*, 1973, **100** (1), 58–62.

Neisser, U. *Cognitive psychology*. New York: Appleton-Century-Crofts, 1967.

Oscar-Berman, M. Hypothesis testing and focusing behavior during concept formation by amnesic Korsakoff patients. *Neuropsychologia*, 1973, **11**, 191–198.

Patten, B. Modality specific memory disorders in man. *Acta Neurologica Scandinavica*, 1972, **48**, 69–86.

Peterson, L. R. Immediate memory: Data and theory. In C. Cofer, & Musgrave B. S. (Eds.), *Verbal behavior and learning: Problems and processes*. New York: McGraw-Hill, 1963.

Peterson, L. & Gentile, A. Proactive interference as a function of time between tests. *Journal of Experimental Psychology*, 1965, **70**, 473–478.

Peterson, L. R., & Peterson, M. J. Short-term retention of individual verbal items. *Journal of Experimental Psychology*, 1959, **58**, 193–198.

Pollatsek, A. Rehearsal, interference, and spacing of practice in short-term memory: Technical report. Ann Arbor: University of Michigan, Human Performance Center, 1969.

Pollack, I. Interference, rehearsal, and short-term retention of digits. *Canadian Journal of Psychology*, 1963, **17**, 380–392.

Pribram, K. The amnesic syndromes: Disturbances in coding? In G. Talland & N. Waugh (Eds.), *The pathology of memory*. New York: Academic Press, 1969.

Reed, H. Studies of the interference process in short-term memory. *Journal of Experimental Psychology*, 1970, **84** (3), 452–457.

Reitman, J. Mechanisms of forgetting in short-term memory. *Cognitive Psychology*, 1971, **2**, 185–195.

Rosenblatt, F. The perceptron: A probabilistic model for information storage and organization in man. *Psychological Review*, 1958, **65** (6), 386–408.

Rowe, E., Philipchalk, R., & Cake, L. Short-term memory for sounds and words. Paper presented at Psychonomic Society, St. Louis, November 1, 1973.

Russell, W. R., & Nathan, P. W. Traumatic amnesia. *Brain*, 1946, **69**, 280–300.

Samuels, I., Butters, N., & Cermak, L. Short-term visual memory: Effects of visual field, serial position, and exposure duration. *Perceptual and Motor Skills*, 1973, **36**, 115–121.

Sanders, H., & Warrington, E. Memory for remote events in amnesic patients. *Brain*, 1971, **94**, 661–668.

Scheirer, C. J. Effect of cueing, modality, and effective contiguous time on response latencies in short-term memory. *Journal of Experimental Psychology*, 1971, **88** (3), 429–432.

Schiffrin, R. Information persistence in short-term memory. *Journal of Experimental Psychology*, 1973, **100** (1), 39–49.

Scoville, W., & Milner, B. Loss of recent memory after bilateral lesions in the hippocampal lesions. *Journal of Neurology, Neurosurgery, and Psychiatry,* 1957, **20,** 11–21.

Spence, K. *Behavior theory and conditioning.* New Haven: Yale University Press, 1956.

Sperling, G. A model for visual memory tasks. *Human Factors,* 1963, **5,** 19–31.

Sperling, G. Successive approximations to a model for short-term memory. *Acta Psychologica,* 1967, **27,** 285–292.

Spinelli, D. N. OCCAM; A computer model for a content addressable memory in the central nevous system. In K. Pribram & D. Broadbent (Eds.), *Biology of memory.* New York: Academic Press, 1970.

Strub, R., & Gardner, H. The repetition defect in conduction aphasia: Mnestic or linguistic? *Brain and Language,* in press.

Talland, G. *Deranged memory: A psychonomic study of the amnesic syndrome.* New York: Academic Press, 1965.

Talland, G. *Disorders of memory and learning.* London: Penguin, 1968.

Thomson, D., & Tulving, E. Associative encoding and retrieval: Weak and strong cues. *Journal of Experimental Psychology,* 1970, **86** (2), 255–262.

Tulving, E. Episodic and semantic memory. In E. Tulving & W. Donaldson (Eds.), *Organization of memory.* New York: Academic Press, 1972.

Tulving, E., & Osler, S. Effectiveness of retrieval cues in memory for words. *Journal of Experimental Psychology,* 1968, **77,** 593–601.

Tulving, E., & Patkau, J. Concurrent effects of contextual similarity and word frequency on immediate recall and learning of verbal material. *Canadian Journal of Psychology,* 1962, **16,** 83–95.

Tulving, E., & Patterson, R. D. Functional units and retrieval processes in free recall. *Journal of Experimental Psychology,* 1968, **77** (2), 239–248.

Turvey, M., & Egan, J. Contextual change and release from proactive inhibition. *Journal of Experimental Psychology,* 1969, **81,** 396–397.

Turvey, M. T., & Wittlinger, R. P. Attenuation of proactive interference in short-term memory as a function of cueing to forget. *Journal of Experimental Psychology,* 1969, **80,** 295–298.

Tzeng, O. J. L. Stimulus meaningfulness, encoding variability, and the spacing effect. *Journal of Experimental Psychology,* 1973, **99** (2), 162–166.

Underwood, B. J. Attributes of memory. *Psychological Review,* 1969, **76,** 559–573.

Victor, M. The amnesic syndrome and its anatomical basis. *Canadian Medical Association Journal,* 1969, **100,** 1115–1125.

Victor, M., Adams, R. D., & Collins, G. H. *Wernicke-Korsakoff syndrome: A clinical and pathological study of 245 patients, 82 with post-mortem examinations.* Philadelphia: Davis, 1971.

Vinogrodova, O. Memory and the limbic system. In G. Horn & R. Hinde (Eds.), *Short-term changes in neural activity and behavior.* Cambridge: University Press, 1970.

Walley, R., & Weiden, T. Lateral inhibition and cognitive masking: A neuropsychological theory of attention. *Psychological Review,* 1973, **80** (4), 284–302.

Warrington, E., & Shallice, T. Selective impairment of auditory–verbal short-term memory. *Brain,* 1969, **92,** 885–896.

Warrington, E., & Weiskrantz, L. Amnesic syndrome: Consolidation or retrieval? *Nature,* 1970, **228,** 628–630. (a)

Warrington, E., & Weiskrantz, L. Verbal learning and retention by amnesic patients using partial information. *Psychonomic Science,* 1970, **20,** 210–211. (b)

Warrington, E. K., & Weiskrantz, L. Organizational aspects of memory in amnesic patients. *Neuropsychologia*, 1971, **9**, 67–73.

Waugh, N., & Norman, D. Primary memory. *Psychological Review*, 1965, **72**, 89–104.

Wickens, D. Encoding categories of words: An empirical approach to memory. *Psychological Review*, 1970, **77** (1), 1–15.

Wickens, D., Born, D., & Allen, C. Proactive inhibition and item similarity in short-term memory. *Journal of Verbal Learning and Verbal Behavior*, 1963, **2**, 440–445.

Wickens, D., Clark, S., Hill, F., & Wittlinger, R. Grammatical class as an encoding category in short-term memory. *Journal of Experimental Psychology*, 1968, **78**, 599–604.

Wickelgren, W. A. Acoustic similarity and intrusion errors in short-term memory. *Journal of Experimental Psychology*, 1965, **70**, 102–108.

Wickelgren, W. Sparing of short-term memory in an amnesic patient: Implications for a strength theory of memory. *Neuropsychologia*, 1968, **6**, 235–244.

Wickelgren, W. A. Multitrace strength theory. In D. Norman (Ed.), *Models of human memory*. New York: Academic Press, 1970.

Wickelgren, W. Memory: *The long and short of it. Psychological Bulletin*, 1974, **81** (1), 1–11.

Wickelgren, W., & Norman, D. Strength models and serial position in short-term recognition. *Journal of Mathematical Psychology*, 1966, **3**, 316–347.

Williams, M., & Zangwill, O. L. Memory defects after head injury. *Journal of Neurology, Neurosurgery and Psychiatry*, 1952, **15**, 54.

Wood, F. Proactive inhibition and context effects in short-term memory. Unpublished master's thesis, Wake Forest University, 1971.

Wood, F. Short-term memory processes. 1973. Unpublished manuscript.

Wood, F., & Quigley-Fernandez, B. Effects of handedness on short term verbal memory with musical distraction. Paper in symposium on cerebral laterality. International Neuropsychology Society, February 7, 1975, Tampa, Fla.

Wood, F., & Kinsbourne, M. Paper in symposium on pathological forgetting. International Neuropsychology Society, February 8, 1974, Boston, Mass.

Wood, F., & Stephens, J. Short-term memory loss in an amnesic syndrome: A case study. Unpublished manuscript, 1973.

Wright, J. H. Effects of formal interitem similarity and length of retention interval on proactive inhibition of short-term memory. *Journal of Experimental Psychology*, 1967, **75**, 386–395.

Yntema, D. B., & Trask, F. P. Recall as a search process. *Journal of Verbal Learning and Verbal Behavior*, 1963, **2**, 65–74.

CHAPTER

11

COMPARATIVE ASPECTS OF SHORT-TERM MEMORY MECHANISMS[1]

R. K. NAKAMURA
AND
M. S. GAZZANIGA

[1] This research was aided by USPHS Grant No. MH 17883-04 awarded to M. S. Gazzaniga.

Studies on cognitive processes in the subhuman primate may provide information for a model of cognitive mechanisms in man. In particular, it has long been hoped that controlled investigation of cognitive processes in the monkey with the available techniques of physiological manipulation would lead to important data applicable to humans. This chapter presents the broad outlines of what is at present known about short-term memory (STM) in humans, followed by a comparison of these results with data from the monkey. These comparisons will then be amplified with data arising out of our research on STM processes in the split brain monkey.

I. HUMAN STUDIES

There are a variety of STM tasks used with humans. One of the earliest (see Jacobs, 1887) examined memory span. In this task, subjects are given a list of items once and are immediately instructed to recall the items as presented. The list length is varied to determine the maximum number of items that can be recalled correctly. In a host of experiments the memory span has been shown to equal seven "items," plus or minus two (Miller, 1956).

Another technique, introduced by Peterson and Peterson (1959), tests recall when rehearsal is prevented by the subject's involvement in an intervening task. Thus, trigrams, though well within the memory span, were forgotten rapidly and recall approached zero with a delay of 18 sec.. This task has also been used to show that repetition (Peterson & Peterson, 1959) and greater meaningfulness (Peterson, Peterson, & Miller, 1961) of the item to be remembered improve performance.

A third line of research examines the nature of organization in STM. Here, for example, the subject may be asked to rehearse between one and three nonsense syllables. Subsequently, reaction time is measured for recognition of any one element in the set. It has been shown that reaction time increases as a function of the number of elements in the originally presented set. This was given as evidence that items in STM can be serially processed (Sternberg, 1966).

In general then, tasks for investigating human STM use various strategies that reduce the possibility of rehearsal, and tend to be recall rather than recognition tasks. Results from such studies show STM to be characterized by rapid forgetting, high liability to factors such as interference, salience, and meaningfulness, and limited to a number of storable items.

II. PRIMATE STUDIES

Early investigators of STM in the primate made extensive use of the delayed response (DR) task. Unfortunately the memory aspects of this task were contaminated with spatial orientation. Today, though it is sometimes thought of as involving "spatial STM," it is not used to study STM *per se*.

The delayed matching-to-sample task (DMTS) is at present the basic paradigm for the study of STM because it eliminates spatial orientation as a source of artifact. Its introduction predates the DR task (see Weinstein, 1941), but only in the last decade has it become the method of choice in studying primate STM.

A. Delayed Matching to Sample

In the delayed matching to sample task, a color or pattern sample is shown to the animal. The sample is then removed and a delay period ensues. Next, two comparison or matching stimuli are presented in random spatial sequence and the animal must choose the one last seen. Usually there are only two possible samples and these also serve as the matching stimuli.

More recently, D'Amato and Worsham (1974) have modified the DMTS task so that the monkey is forced more nearly to recall the correct sample than simply to recognize it. In one, the animal sees the sample figure and after a delay sees one comparison light. The animal must indicate that the comparison is either the same as or different from the sample. In the other task, the comparison stimuli bear only symbolic relationship to the sample. The animal must recall the sample seen and choose the stimulus that has come to represent the sample. D'Amato refers to this as a conditional match-to-sample.

Other modifications of the DMTS are possible. Jarrard and Moise (1971) have added multiple responding to neutral stimuli during the delay interval to simulate the backward counting distraction task of Peterson and Peterson (1959). We have used a multiple DMTS (MDMTS), which randomly intermixes different delays (see Glick, Goldfarb, & Jarvik, 1969).

Using simultaneous mutliple samples is another possibility that we have just begun to study.

Using the DMTS, then, makes a variety of methods available for the investigation of STM. Results based on these tasks can be divided into those manipulating the sample and those manipulating the delay.

B. Manipulation of the Sample

In general, manipulation that increased the salience or distinctiveness of the sample improved accuracy. Thus Jarrard and Moise (1971) found that repeating the sample before the delay improved performance, while using patterns that were more difficult to discriminate caused performance decrement. D'Amato and Worsham (1972), on the other hand, found no significant effects due to manipulating sample duration. It was interpreted here that the animal made a single observing response and the rest of sample duration simply contributed to the delay, unlike the Jarrard and Moise (1971) study, in which the monkey was forced to make repeated observing responses. Etkin and D'Amato (1969) increased the set of possible samples and did not affect performance.

C. Manipulation of the Delay

The universal finding is that of decreased performance with increased delay. More interesting, however, is that the monkey can retain high levels of accuracy with delays of over 3 min if they are trained with slowly increasing delays (Mello, 1971; D'Amato, 1973).

Filling the delay interval with various distractions or interferences reduces DMTS performance. Forcing the monkey to respond to irrelevant visual stimuli caused reduced levels of accuracy (Moise, 1970), though the temporal location of such interference in the delay does not appear to be important (Jarvik, Goldfarb, & Carley, 1969; Jarrard & Moise, 1971). A reduction of general luminance in the delay period increases performance (Etkin, 1970, 1972), whereas white noise (Worsham & D'Amato, 1973) and the amount of free movement (Jarrard & Moise, 1970) made by the animals does not affect it. This pattern of interference makes it appear to be largely modality specific; that is, visual stimuli interfere with visual tasks.

Increasing the ITI (intertrial interval) delay, which would presumably reduce the intertrial interference, does cause better performance according to Jarrard and Moise (1971).

D. Other Manipulations

D'Amato (1973) has shown that his monkeys could be trained to perform the yes–no task readily and the conditional matching task with much patience. Performance levels approximated those of normal DMTS tasks with differences that could be attributed to the difference in information about the sample available from the matching lights.

E. Another Task

Up to now no one has dealt with the chunk or channel capacity for the monkey other than Gazzaniga and Young (1967), who were concerned with another aspect of the situation. They found that a normal monkey could identify the lights that were on in a two-by-four grid but not do well on a three-by-four grid. The split-brain monkey performed this task with ease.

F. Possible Discontinuities between Monkey and Man

Two major distinctions between animal and human STM tasks are the differences between recall and recognition and the problem of the duration of animal STM. As far as is presently known, monkeys do not have a large symbolic store or response range, thus limiting primate investigations of STM to recognition tasks.

The importance of this difference between the human and primate tasks is still unclear. If it is true that a qualitative difference exists between recall and recognition (see Kintsch, 1970) this may indicate a discontinuity in human memory processes that cannot be examined in the monkey. Others argue (see for example Davis, Sutherland, & Judd, 1961) that recognition and recall are on a continuum of a unitary process. D'Amato (1973) identified the lack of cues of the sample at the matching stage as a crucial difference between recognition and recall. As mentioned earlier, he reduced these cues for the monkey and found only slight declines in performance, thus supporting the unitary process concept of recognition and recall. This is evidence that a significant distinction between monkey and human memory need not be made on this basis.

With respect to the duration of STM, Peterson and Peterson (1959) determined that in man STM decayed to near chance within 18 sec; Mello (1971) found that monkeys could perform well above chance at delays of up to 3 min. D'Amato (1973) found that his monkeys could perform above 90% correct at intervals beyond 2 min. Unless we assume that

STM in the monkey is radically different from human STM, this discrepancy can be reasonably explained only by postulating a rehearsal loop to refresh primate STM. This notion received support when Jarrard and Moise (1971) forced monkeys to respond to neutral lights for varying intervals of the delay period and found that accuracy depression was related to amount of interpolated responding, although accuracy remained well above chance even at 60 sec. D'Amato (1973) agreed that rehearsal accounts for the monkeys' STM performance after eliminating superior consolidation, visual after-images, and the difference between recognition and recall as possible sources.

G. Summary

The foregoing studies indicate that STM in the monkey is in almost every significant way similar to that of human STM. It decays with increasing delay and decays faster when interpolated responding is required, implying a rehearsal loop. It is manipulated by interfering stimuli or increases in salience of the item to be remembered, and it shows signs of limited chunk capacity. The main areas yet to be examined are memory of multiple lists and the recognition–recall distinction.

III. SPLIT-BRAIN RESEARCH

Our current interest in problems of memory in the monkey stems from the analysis of cognitive functions in the split-brain animal. This well-known preparation (Sperry, 1961; Gazzaniga, 1970) divides the cortices of the cerebral hemispheres through section of the corpus callosum and anterior commissure. Using this technique, aspects of the contribution of the forebrain commissures to cognitive processes, the differences between hemispheres in animals, and the quality of cognitive functions in a single hemisphere can be examined. In what follows, we will review some of the major findings on the functions of the forebrain commissures in relation to cognitive functions and then discuss some recent research on STM and the split brain.

A. Cognitive Functions of the Separated versus Whole Brain

A number of studies on cats (Sechzer, 1970; Meikle, 1964; Voneida & Robinson, 1970) and dogs (Mosidze, Rizhinashvili, Totibadze, Kevanishvili, & Akbardia, 1971) report that spilt-brain mammals show cognitive deficits compared to normals. In most cases these authors do not control for sources of artifact such as surgical trauma and sensory damage. Also, in contrast are three studies on discrimination learning in monkeys documenting learning times, which reveal no differences between splits and normals (Hamilton & Gazzaniga, 1964; Myers, 1965; and Gazzaniga, 1966).

In humans with commisurotomy, early studies suggested there were no major cognitive deficits resulting from hemisphere disconnection (Gazzaniga, Bogen, and Sperry, 1965). On the other hand, STM studies suggested each hemisphere was below normal in its information-handling capacity (Gazzaniga, 1968). Yet, when both hemispheres were working together, the scores fell into the normal range. Recently, Milner and Taylor (1972), studying the same series of patients, reported evidence that the split-brain patient is not as good as normal or brain-damaged cases in carrying out a spatial STM task.

Since previous work has not clearly resolved these questions and the more general question of the callosal contribution to intellectual function we have begun a series of experiments on monkeys to clarify the effects of commissurotomy on learning and memory. The following study examines the effects of commissurotomy on STM using a MDMTS.

B. Short-Term Memory and Multiple Delayed Matching to Sample

The subjects were five young rhesus monkeys, 6–10 lb. One had undergone section of the anterior commissure, corpus callosum, hippocampal commissure, and optic chiasm prior to testing. The other five began as normals, two of which were split in the course of the study. The surgical procedure accomplished via section has been described in detail previously (Sperry, 1968, Gazzaniga, 1970).

The animals were tested in a soundproof booth, with their heads inside a head restrainer that allowed the experimenter to close off visual stimulation to either eye. The animal faced a black plexiglass panel with three translucent screens. An IEE projector behind each screen turned them red or green, and the animals could respond to the lights by pressing the screens, which closed a microswitch. The screens therefore both presented the stimulus and received the animal's response. A water reward was delivered in a tube directly to the mouth. All animals were deprived of water for 22 hr, tested, and then allowed free access to water for one hour.

At the beginning of training, all monkeys were conditioned to perform a single color matching task with no delay. A red or green light would appear on the top screen until it was turned off by the monkey's pressing on the screen. Immediately the red and green choice colors would appear at the bottom screens. A press on the screen of the color matching the earlier presentation would be rewarded with 0.5 cc of water and a simultaneous clearing of the lights. An incorrect response cleared the colors with no reward. After four seconds a new trial would begin.

Subsequently, a delay period was introduced between the initial response of the monkey and the projection of the choice colors. As the animals met criterion performances, the delay was increased. Finally, after the animal could perform at delays up to 20 sec, four different delays of 0, 2, 6, and 18 sec were intermixed in a modified random sequence in the same session.

All animals were run for 160 trials daily. The tasks were presented and results recorded on a PDP-8I computer. On the initial condition, both eyes were open and the monkeys were tested on the delayed matching task until average weekly performance peaked. Animals CH and PR were normal controls throughout the testing. MR and BT were tested both before and after the split-brain operation. These animals required complete retraining after being split. SC was used in this study only post-operatively.

Four of the monkeys, MR, PR, CH, and SC, were tested on a lengthy series in which right-eye-open, left-eye-open and both-eyes-open sessions were in random sequence.

Figs. 11–1a and 11-1b show the averaged data comparisons for splits vs. normals. Each of the points to the left showing total percent correct for each animal is the result of at least 800 trials, and the points of the various delays denote in turn at least 200 trials. Fig. 11-1a shows best performance for each animal with both eyes open, averaged over 1 week. Fig. 11-1b shows the best performance for each animal with his best eye open, also averaged over 1 week. Combined, the splits do better than normals (Figs. 11-2a and 11-2b) under both conditions and at all delays, though this difference is not significant. There was also no significant interaction between operative condition and delay. Thus, split brain animals are not worse than normals at any delay.

Figs. 11-3a, 11-3b, and 11-3c show the data from a left-eye-open, right-eye-open, and both-eyes-open randomization series for three normal monkeys. Each eye condition was tested for a total of 10 days. In all cases, the curves show a high degree of overlap with the total accuracies within 1.5% of each other. The differences between conditions were highly insignificant.

Figs. 11-4a and 11-4b show the data for two split monkeys run on the same schedule as the above normals. In both cases there is a large difference between the right-eye-open and left-eye-open conditions. This difference is significant for both monkeys. In addition, the curves cannot be

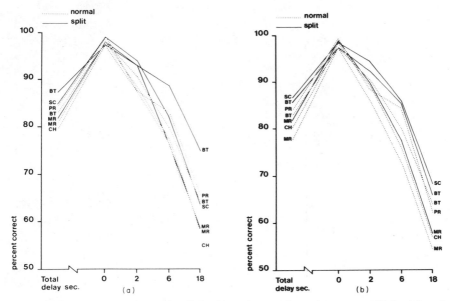

Fig. 11-1. Comparison of split brain and normal monkeys on multiple delayed matching task with both eyes open (a) and one eye open (b).

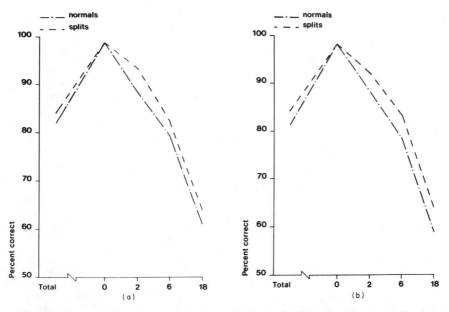

Fig. 11-2. Averaged comparisons between split brain and normal monkeys on multiple delayed matching task, again with both eyes open (a) and one eye open (b). While the split brain monkeys do better, the differences do not reach significance.

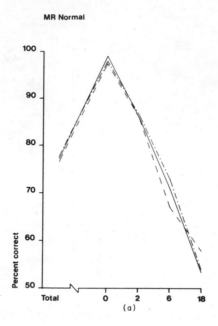

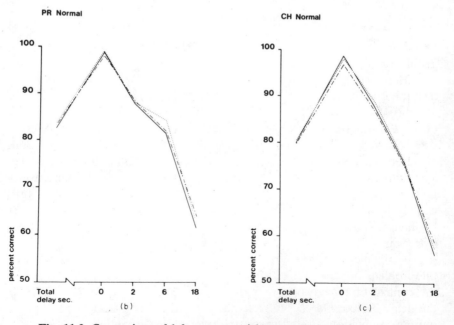

Fig. 11-3. Comparison of left-eye-open, right-eye-open conditions on three normal monkeys (a,b,c).

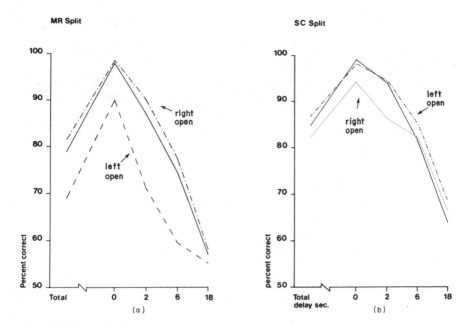

Fig. 11-4. Comparison of left-eye-open, right-eye-open, and both-eyes-open conditions on two split-brain monkeys (a,b). Note the great difference between the left-eye-open and right-eye-open conditions.

superimposed with good fit, as is the case with the normals, though this distinction does not reach significance.

Here we have been testing monkeys on a multiple DMTS; that is, we have randomly intermixed DMTS trials with delays of 0, 2, 6, and 18 sec. On this task, our animals dropped to near chance levels at the 18-sec delay. Clearly something has happened to the memory trace during the delay. If we test the animals exclusively at the longer delay, as was done on initial training, the monkeys will show accuracies of 90% or better. The difference in accuracy between this and the intermixed condition suggests that monkeys must supply an active process to operate successfully at long delays, and this may be rehearsal. An implication of this is that by intermixing delays, one may get a decay curve relatively unconfounded by rehearsal.

A significant sidelight of this study is a suggestion for the solution to the problem of rehearsal control in the monkey. The classic approach to the control of rehearsal is to place other tasks (similar or different) in the delay period. On the other hand, if rehearsal is an active process requiring motivation and effort on the part of the organism, then another method of controlling rehearsal is to control motivation.

C. Serial Processing Capacities in the Separated Hemispheres

In this preliminary study, one split-brain monkey was trained on a task similar to the Sternberg (1966) STM paradigm for humans.

First, a letter, either A or B, appeared on a panel (Fig. 11-5). The monkey was required to push the panel, which in turn illuminated the top

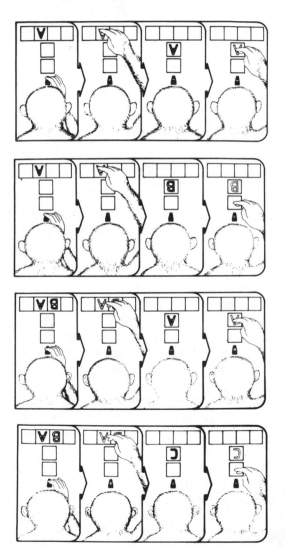

Fig. 11-5. Shows training procedure for testing memory set size in monkeys. First a letter appears and the animal hits the button that terminates its presentation and initiates the probe. If the probe was a member of the set, the monkey hits the top button; if different, the monkey hits the bottom unilluminated button.

one of two other panels, placed one on top of the other, with either an A or a B. The top panel was to be pushed if the two letters were the same and the bottom if they were different. Thus, the monkey was given a memory set size of 1 and subsequently, probed with a letter asking if that was a member of the set or not. When the monkey achieved good performance, the memory set was increased to 2. Another letter, C, was added to the stimulus letters and the monkey was shown two of the three letters. After responding to these, the animal was shown A, B, or C and had to indicate if it had been part of the 2-letter memory set.

Using this technique, animal HRY had no difficulty learning the problem, and when reaction times were compared, it consistently took longer (approximately 35 msec) when the memory set size was 2 versus 1.

D. Discussion

We have used the delayed matching task to examine the monkeys' ability to store one bit of information for a variable period of time in one hemisphere or a whole brain. The serial processing tasks also examined the STM capacity of a half brain. The data clearly support the conclusion that separation of hemispheres by cutting the forebrain commissures does not impair the monkey in comparison with his preoperative state and that the monkey has STM process reminiscent of those seen in man. Thus, it appears unlikely that forebrain commissurotomy *per se* will cause a deficit in STM. One hemisphere does not depend on the other for adequate STM operation.

At the same time, in comparing the performances of each hemisphere in our split-brain animals on the DMTS, a strong differences from the normal state became apparent. Whereas the normal animal shows virtually identical performances on any eye condition, the split-brain monkey yields very dissimilar curves, with one hemisphere showing definite superiority over the other. This is a striking example of the ability of forebrain commissurotomy to result in distinct cognitive systems.

This finding is consistent with the results of Gibson and Gazzaniga (1971) and Gibson (1973), which indicated the possibility that the separation of hemispheres may create two systems with differentiable motivational states. Thus, what appears to be dominance of one hemisphere on DMTS may reflect more a differential in motivational states, with the dominant half-brain having a greater probability of responding to the particular reward than the opposite hemisphere.

The results of these studies make it clear that a complete memory system exists in each hemisphere, suggesting that a single hemisphere in the monkey is, with respect to performance, the functional equivalent of the whole brain. Of course, the cautionary note must be added that the general cognitive capacity and learning rates of the single hemisphere may be impaired when compared to commissure-intact controls. Indeed, preliminary results indicate that split brain monkeys are impaired compared to normals in ability to perform a task that requires simultaneous storage of two items of information in one hemisphere (Nakamura & Gazzaniga, 1974).

E. Visual-Motor Mechanisms in STM Processes

Recently we have been investigating an interference phenomenon that appears to arise from the split-brain preparation (Gazzaniga & Hillyard, 1973; Nakamura & Gazzaniga, 1973).

One split brain, one partially split brain (anterior commissure intact), and two normal control monkeys were trained on a color-matching task with the right eye and a pattern matching task with the left eye. The tasks

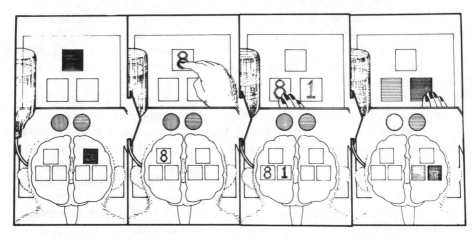

Fig. 11-6. Illustration of sequencing in the nested matching tasks. At first a color comes on at the top projector and polarized filters direct this to the right hemisphere in the split-brain, split-chiasm monkey. Then, a number comes on that is directed to the left hemisphere. Next, two numbers come on at the bottom, and the monkey gets a water reward for hitting the one previously seen. Finally, two colors come on and again the monkey gets a water reward for hitting the one previously seen.

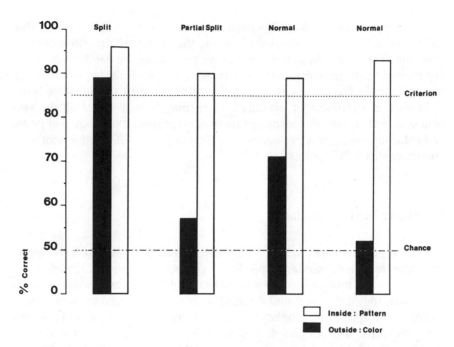

Fig. 11-7. Illustrates the performance of each monkey on the "nested" matching tasks during the week in which the animals performance peaked. Only the split-brain monkey could surpass criterion on both tests.

were then intermixed such that one task (color) was started before and completed after the other task (pattern), thus nesting one task inside the other. Fig. 11-6 illustrates the sequence of the task. The separation of each task to the appropriate eye was maintained with the use of polarizing filters. Both hands were free, but all animals used one hand exclusively in all conditions (split brain used left hand, all others right hand).

Initially, all monkeys were able to do the inside task at or near pre-intermixing levels, while the outside task performance fell to near chance levels. Extensive training improved all animals slightly, but only the fully split-brain animal was able eventually to do both tasks at 85% levels (Fig. 11-7). Clearly, the forebrain commissures are active in the normal interference processes that limit the STM system.

The transitory interference shown by the split-brain monkey cannot be attributed to aspects of the visual input because these were carefully separated. Direct interhemispheric interference at the cortical level can also be ruled out because the forebrain commissures were cut.

One possibility is that the interference or forgetting seen here in this STM task is effected subcortically and is the result of the efferent programming emanating from the hemisphere processing the inside task. With the intercortical inhibitory pathways sectioned, the hemisphere processing the inside tasks cannot readily relinquish motor control to the other hemisphere. The improvement eventually seen may be the result of the two hemispheres learning to coordinate their efforts through cross-cueing strategies. In any case, these results suggest that it is the activated motor system that limits STM processes.

F. Sensory-Motor Coupling

In a related experiment, we sought to determine the role of intra-hemisphere sensory-motor couplings as compared to those involving inter-hemispheric integration through subcallosal midbrain mechanisms. In particular, four different visual discriminations were trained to each hemisphere of two split-brain monkeys. In all training and testing, reaction times were measured and tabulated. When each animal with each hemisphere could easily perform all problems separately or randomly intermixed at a moderate response time of approximately 2 sec, special training commenced with one eye and one hand. Here, the time allowed for response to a problem was gradually reduced till the stimulus was presented for only 500 msec. As can be seen from Figs. 11-8a and 11-8b, the animals gradually became quite proficient until their scores dropped to approximately 350 msec.

At this point, animal HRY was forced to use the opposite un-supertrained eye. The results show that there was essentially no disruption of efficiency of performance when using an eye-hand combination that had never before performed at this level of efficiency.

This result is consistent with the view that sensory-motor mechanisms involve motor systems that are equally accessed by the two separated hemispheres. The actual site of this coupling is not known. Moreover, the results show that sensory-motor coupling developed in one hemisphere during the course of the high efficiency training is not a specific process peculiar to that hemisphere. Since the untrained hemisphere immediately performs at a high level using a sensory system with no prior experience at this rate of efficiency, it would suggest such sensory-motor couplings involve common-motor systems exclusively.

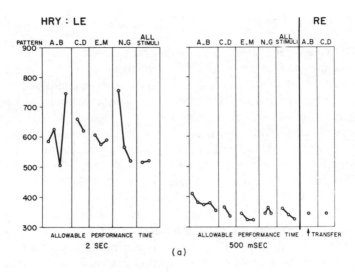

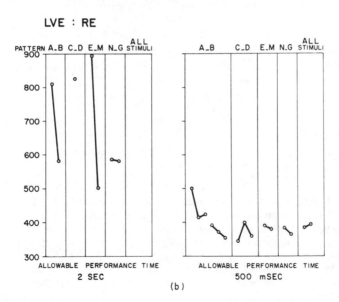

Fig. 11-8 (a,b). Split-brain monkeys were trained four different visual discriminations. When working at 90% accuracy or better, their performance time was perfected by allowing only 500 msec to respond. Both animals were able to perform as well when all four discriminations were intermixed as when one was presented alone. In addition HRY, who had learned the discriminations with the opposite hemisphere prior to the efficiency training, immediately was able to perform the task at the fast speed with this eye.

IV. SUMMARY

The STM task carried out in the split-brain monkey make it clear that a single hemisphere contains all the mechanisms necessary to store and retrieve a single bit of information with no decrement compared to a normal animal. In addition, information-retrieval time appears to be an increasing function of the number of stored bits, which is consistent with Sternberg's findings with humans. This apparent identity of the single hemisphere with the whole brain must be viewed with caution since some new evidence points to certain load limits of the half brain. At the same time, it is becoming clear that examination of STM in the single hemisphere can yield models of memory applicable to man.

Finally, we have been investigating the role of the motor output component of STM processing. There, interference phenomenon seen in split-brain monkeys trying to solve a problem requiring bihemispheric attention would appear to be a problem of competing responses at the motor output. It is the motor system that is the first stage of linkage between STM processes in the separated hemispheres. This link has been demonstrated in the foregoing study, in which motor-response times associated with one hemisphere in a split brain monkey instantly transferred to the other. We thus propose that a normal and major function of the forebrain commissures is the suppression of competing motor responses. These responses may in turn be a major source of the interference seen in a variety of memory tasks.

REFERENCES

D'Amato, M. R. Delayed matching and short-term memory in monkeys. In G. H. Bower (Ed.), *The psychology of learning and motivation. Advances in research and theory*, Vol. 7. New York: Academic Press, 1973, pp. 227–269.

D'Amato, M. R., & Worsham, R. W. Delayed matching in the capuchin monkey with brief sample durations. *Learning and Motivation*, 1972, **3**, 304–312.

D'Amato, M. R., & Worsham, R. W. Retrieval cues and short-term memory in capuchin monkeys. *Journal of Comparative and Physiological Psychology*, 1974, **86**, 274–282.

Davis, R., Sutherland, N. S., & Judd, B. R. Information content in recognition and recall. *Journal of Experimental Psychology*, 1961, **61**, 422–429.

Etkin, M. W. *Ambient light-produced interference in a delayed matching task with capuchin monkeys*. Unpublished doctoral dissertation, Rutgers University, 1970.

Etkin, M. W. Light-produced interference in a delayed matching task with capuchin monkeys. *Learning and Motivation*, 1972, **3**, 313–324.

Etkin, M. W., & D'Amato, M. R. Delayed matching-to-sample and short-term memory in the capuchin monkey. *Journal of Comparative and Physiological Psychology,* 1969, **69,** 544–549.

Gazzaniga, M. S. Interhemispheric communication of visual learning. *Neuropsychologia,* 1966, **4,** 261–262.

Gazzaniga, M. S. Short-term memory and brain bisected man. *Psychonomic Science,* 1968, **12,** 161–162.

Gazzaniga, M. S. *The bisected brain.* New York: Appleton-Century-Crofts, 1970.

Gazzaniga, M. S., Bogen, J. E., and Sperry, R. W. Observations on visual perception after disconnection of the cerebral hemispheres in man. *Brain,* 1965, **88,** 221.

Gazzaniga, M. S., & Hillyard, S. A. Attention mechanisms following brain bisection. In S. Kornblum (Ed.), *Attention and performance.* New York: Academic Press, 1973.

Gazzaniga, M. S., & Sperry, R. W. Language after section of the cerebral commissures. *Brain,* 1967, **90,** 131–148.

Gazzaniga, M. S., & Sperry, R. W. Simultaneous double discrimination response following brain bisection. *Psychonomic Science,* 1966, **4,** 261–262.

Gazzaniga, M. S., & Young, E. D. Effects of commissurotomy on the processing of increasing visual information. *Experimental Brain Research,* 1967, **3,** 368–71.

Gibson, A. R. *Independence of cortico-hypothalamic feeding mechanisms in brain bisected monkeys.* Unpublished doctoral dissertation, New York University, 1973.

Gibson, A. R., & Gazzaniga, M. S. Hemisphere differences in eating behavior in split-brain monkeys. *Physiologist,* 1971, **14,** 150.

Glick, S. D., Goldfarb, T. L., & Jarvik, M. E. Recovery of delayed matching performance following lateral frontal lesions in monkeys. *Communications in Behavioral Biology,* 1969, **3,** 299–303.

Hamilton, C. R., & Gazzaniga, M. S. Lateralization of learning of color and brightness discrimination following brain bisection. *Nature,* 1964, **201,** 220.

Jacobs, J. Experiments on "prehension." *Mind,* 1887, **12,** 75–79.

Jarrard, L. E., & Moise, S. L. Short-term memory in the stumptail (*M. speciosa*): Effect of physical restraint of behavior on performance. *Learning and Motivation,* 1970, **1,** 267–275.

Jarrard, L. E., & Moise, S. L. Short-term memory in the monkey. In L. E. Jarrard (Ed.), *Cognitive processes of nonhuman primates.* New York: Academic Press, 1971.

Jarvik, M. E., Goldfarb, T. L., & Carley, J. L. Influence of interference on delayed matching in monkeys. *Journal of Experimental Psychology,* 1969, **81,** 1–6.

Kintsch, W. *Learning, memory and conceptual processes.* New York: Wiley, 1970.

Meikle, T. H., Jr. Failures of interocular transfer of brightness discrimination. *Nature,* 1964, **202,** 1243–1244.

Mello, N. Alcohol effects on delayed matching to sample performance by rhesus monkeys. *Physiology and Behavior,* 1971, **7,** 77–101.

Miller, G. A. The magic number seven, plus or minus two: Some limits on our capacity for processing information. *Psychological Reviews,* 1956, **63,** 81–97.

Milner, B., & Taylor, L. Right hemisphere superiority in tactile pattern recognition after cerebral commissurotomy: Evidence for nonverbal memory. *Neuropsychologia,* 1972, **10,** 1–16.

Moise, S. L. Short-term retention in Macaca Speciosa following interpolated activity during delayed matching from sample. *Journal of Comparative and Physiological Psychology,* 1970, **73,** 506–514.

Mosidze, V. M., Rizhinashvili, N. K., Totibadze, N. K., Kevanishvili, Z., & Akbardia, K. K. Some results of studies on split brain. *Physiology and Behavior*, 1971, **7**, 763–772.

Myers, R. E. The neocortical commissures and the interhemispheric transmission of information. In E. G. Ettlinger (Ed.), *Functions of the corpus callosum*. London: Churchill, 1965.

Nakamura, R. K., & Gazzaniga, M. S. Interhemispheric interference in split-brain monkeys. *Federation Proceedings*, 1973, **32**, 367a.

Nakamura, R. K., & Gazzaniga, M. S. Reduced information processing capabilities following commissurotomy in the monkey. *Physiologist*, 1974, **17**, 294.

Peterson, L. R., & Peterson, M. J. Short-term retention of individual verbal items. *Journal of Experimental Psychology*, 1959, **58**, 193–198.

Peterson, L. R., Peterson, M. J.,& Miller,GA.Short-term retention and meaningfulness. *Canadian Journal of Psychology*, 1961, **15**, 143–147.

Sechzer, J. A. Prolonged memory and split-brain cats. *Science*, 1970, **169**, 889–892.

Sperry, R. W. Cerebral organization and behavior. *Science*, 1961, **133**, 1749.

Sperry, R. W. Mental unity following surgical disconnection of the cerebral hemispheres. *The Harvey Lecture Series*, 1968, **62**, 293–323.

Sternberg, S. High speed scanning in human memory. *Science*, 1966, **153**, 652–654.

Voneida, T. J., & Robinson, J. S. Effect of brain bisection on capacity for cross comparison of patterned visual input. *Experimental Neurology*, 1970, **26**, 60–71.

Weinstein, B. Matching-from-sample by rhesus monkeys and by children. *Journal of Comparative Psychology*, 1941, **31**, 195–213.

Worsham, R. W., & D'Amato, M. R. Ambient light, white noise, and monkey vocalization as sources of interference in visual short-term memory of monkeys. *Journal of Experimental Psychology*, 1973, **99**, 99–105.

CHAPTER
12

MEMORY PROCESSES AND
THE HIPPOCAMPUS[1]

ROBERT L. ISAACSON

For the past 20 years, more or less, the hippocampus has been associated with "recent memory." This association is based upon descriptive

[1] The work described in this paper and performed in my laboratory is supported by Grant NIMH-MH-16384-04 from the National Institute for Mental Health. I would like to express my appreciation to the following people for their generous advice on the ideas in this manuscript: Dr. Carol Van Hartesveldt, Mr. Michael L. Woodruff, and Ms. Barbara Schneiderman. I would also like to thank Mrs. Virginia Walker for her help in efficiently completing the several drafts of this paper and the final copy.

and experimental reports of relatively few patients suffering from temporal lobe epilepsy with surgical brain damage to mesial aspects of the temporal lobe. The surgery was undertaken for the relief of the epileptic disorder. The general conclusion from the evaluation and study of these patients has been that a functional bilateral lesion of the hippocampus was necessary for a disturbance of recent memory. In principle, this could be produced either by a bilateral surgical procedure or a unilateral temporal lobe resection in the presence of a continuing disease process in the remaining temporal lobe. In passing, it should be noted that disturbances in memory are not limited to instances in which selective damage to the temporal lobe systems is established or even suspected. Such disturbances can be found after damage to diecephalic systems (*e.g.*, Whitty & Zangwill, 1966; Victor, Adams, & Collins, 1971). Nevertheless, the main emphasis has remained centered upon the mesial temporal lobe structures and upon the hippocampus in particular. In a recent article I reviewed much of the literature on the effects of hippocampal damage on memory in human patients and suggested that the disease processes leading to, or remaining after surgery may be related to the memory disorders found after temporal lobe surgery (Isaacson, 1972a).

The recent memory deficits found in the patients reported by Scoville (1954), Milner (1959), Scoville and Milner (1957), and Penfield and Milner (1958) may be considered in relation to the terms and ideas commonly used by students of verbal learning and memory. In this literature, short-term memory is often considered to be related to the retention of information beyond the immediate span of attention and covering a period of minutes. It is thought to be of limited capacity since only a limited number of "chunks" of information can be processed at any moment in time. Furthermore, information in short-term memory is thought to be rapidly forgotten unless there is rehearsal to strengthen its traces. Short-term memories are disrupted by the presentation of materials that sound like or look like the to-be-stored information. In contrast, when information is held in long-term memory, the greatest confusion occurs when items that have meanings similar to the stored information are given to the subjects. Therefore, the transition from short-term to long-term memory may involve the translation of information into meaningful verbal units. Short-term memory is often thought of as a temporary state in which image quality—whether it be visual, acoustic, or tactual—of the to-be-remembered-stimulus is preserved.

It must be stressed that these distinctions between long- and short-term memory are not absolute. Materials are altered in short-term memory; indeed, constructive changes can be found in the recollection of verbal materials after a very brief period of time (Zangwill, 1956). Abstraction and reorganization along lines of meaningfulness can occur even when the information falls within the span of attention.

It must also be pointed out that it is not fair to assume that the various stages of memory represent a progression. It need not be the case that material is first represented in short-term memory and either passed into long-term storage or forgotten. It is possible that there is parallel and simultaneous processing of information in both long-term and short-term systems.

Despite the observation that brain-damaged patients have some difficulty in the formation of habits, that is, responses used to deal with relatively unchanging aspects of the environment, there are reasons to consider habits and memories as distinctive systems. Aphasic patients have more difficulty in learning verbal materials by heart than in recalling the learned information in their own ways with their own reconstruction of the material (see Zangwill, 1972). This suggests that the comparison of retention in the animal and the human must be made with great care to distinguish among tasks requiring the learning and retention of habits as opposed to the learning and retention of information presumed to be of a more transient nature.

The memory deficits reported for patients with presumptive bilateral hippocampal damage do not seem to be an impairment in the transition of memories from the immediate span of attention to short-term memory; instead, they seem to be indicative of a disturbance related in some way to the long-term memory of events occurring after surgery. Therefore, the deficit as it is described in the literature is one involved with long-term storage or retrieval of information that has become available for accumulation after the surgery. The patients remember things as long as their attention continues to be directed upon them but quickly forget them when their attention is diverted. This suggests that they have an intact short-term memory but the deficit could arise in the transition to longer-term mechanism storage. In fact, this is the position advocated by Milner (1972).

A different point of view has been presented by Warrington and Weiskrantz (1972). These authors suggest that information does achieve the status of long-term storage in amnesic patients, but they have difficulty in its retrieval. By using testing techniques that prevent the intrusion of previously acquired materials, they were able to show that patients with recent memory disorders were able to demonstrate their retention of material learned in the past. With the usual testing tchniques, this material would have been beyond recall and presumed lost. If a person is tested for the retention of verbal materials by repeatedly presenting sets of similar verbal materials, intrusion errors occur when a response appropriate to an early set inappropriately occurs in a later set. These intrusions represent a carry-over from the past into the present. They interfere with the memory of the task at hand. It is one source of the proactive interference effect described by Underwood and Postman (1960). Experienced subjects who are tested repeatedly for retention of verbal materials come to learn new lists increasingly quickly, but they also forget the lists previously learned increasingly rapidly. The rapid forgetting of previously studied materials leads to the more rapid acquisition of the new. To the extent that the old materials are not forgotten, acquisition of the new and its subsequent retention will be impaired. The Warrington–Weiskrantz view would lead us to expect that the patients with temporal lobe damage would have difficulty retaining new information because of an excessive retention of previously learned materials.

In general, studies of the effects of bilateral hippocampal damage in animals have not revealed any deficits that seem related to either short-term or long-term memory (see Isaacson, 1974 and reviews by Douglas, 1967; Kimble, 1968). Animals with surgically induced damage to the hippocampus learn both many kinds of appetitive and aversive tasks as quickly as normal animals. There is no forgetting of the task between one day and the next, as might be expected on the basis of the human literature. Often their learning of simple behavioral problems is more rapid and enduring than that of normal animals.

In my opinion there are now two ways the differences between the animal and human data can be reconciled. I have already suggested the first (Isaacson, 1972a): there is something about the combination of the epileptic processes and the surgically induced brain damage that interacts to produce the memory disorder. The second is related to the possibility that hippocampal damage allows too much from the past to be remembered, and this interferes with the retrieval of the stored information—*i.e.,* the hypothesis put forward by Weiskrantz and Warrington.

I. EPILEPTOGENIC LESIONS AS A BASIS OF MEMORY FAILURE

When studies of the effects of epileptogenic lesions of the hippocampus on behavior were first undertaken in my laboratory, we elected to use the two-way active avoidance response as the first behavioral task to be studied. We did so because in this task animals with radical bilateral hippocampal lesions excel over normal animals and the control animals with destruction limited to the posterolateral neocortex (Isaacson, Douglas, & Moore, 1961). To produce the epileptiform activity in the hippocampus, we injected liquid or crystalline penicillin. In many of its forms, this antibiotic produces a reliable focus of epileptiform activities although little is known about the duration of such foci in chronic preparations.

Our initial results were encouraging. Both Schmaltz (1971) and Olton (1970) found that rats with penicillin injected into the hippocampus acquired the two-way active avoidance response only with great difficulty. Furthermore, there was a great amount of forgetting from one training day to the next. This, we felt, was an especially favorable result. The animals showed some learning of the problem within a day (when their attention was presumably continually focused on the task) but seemed to forget it by the following day. The effect was most prominent in animals with one hippocampus removed surgically and the other injected with penicillin.

These studies demonstrated that bilateral surgical destruction of the hippocampus produced a much different behavioral effect than did the introduction of an epileptogenic agent into one hippocampus when the other was removed or the introduction of the epileptogenic agent into both hippocampi.

Incidentally, the introduction of penicillin into the hippocampus often (but not always) produced long-lasting changes in the electrical activity recorded from the hippocampus. Months after a single injection of the antibiotic, spike and wave discharges can be found in the hippocampus of some animals. In other animals, abnormal slow-wave activity can be seen. In still others, the EEG activity in the hippocampus is essentially normal. To date we have not been able to establish a firm correlation between the type of chronic change produced in the EEG by the penicillin and the behavioral effects observed.

It was natural for us to examine the effects of epileptogenic agents placed into the hippocampus on appetitive tasks. Woodruff and Isaacson (1972) did this using a simple operant visual discrimination task. The results were clear-cut: the rats with penicillin implanted into the hippocampus were not different from normal animals in the learning of the task. In contrast, the animals with bilateral surgical lesions of the hippocampus were impaired. These results are shown in the first three figures. In Fig. 12-1, the performance of the normal animals is shown. These results are described in terms of an analysis of three types of errors that can be made in the training situation. The animals had to learn to press the lever over which a small light bulb was illuminated. Two levers and two light bulbs were provided the animals in the conditioning chamber. A correct response produced a food pellet. An incorrect response produced a brief "time out" period. The "correct" lever was randomly selected by our computer after every correct response, but after an error had been made, the "correct"

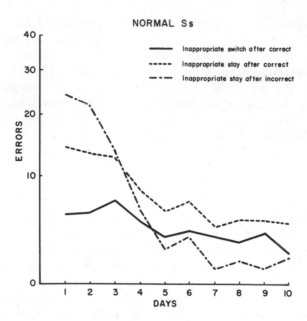

Fig. 12-1. Analysis of the three types of errors made by normal animals over the course of training in the visual discrimination described in the text. Data from Woodruff and Isaacson (1972).

lever was always the one other than that on which the erroneous response had been made. We did this to minimize perseverative errors made on the same lever. Therefore, three kinds of errors can be made that are related to the animal behavior toward the two levers from trial to trial. (1) The animal can fail to change to the other lever after an error. (2) After a correct response, the animal can fail to change to the other bar on the next trial when the other lever is indicated as "correct" by the light above it. (3) After a correct response, the animal can fail to stay with the same lever on the next trial when it is indicated as "correct" by the light above it.

Only the last two types of errors give us any information about the animals learning the relationship between the position of the light and the lever on which a response should be made. The first type of error can be reduced by switching levers after an error without regard for the light. As shown in Fig. 12-1, all three types of errors are reduced by the normal animals over the course of training. In Fig. 12-2, the same pattern of error reduction is found in animals with penicillin implanted into the hippocampus. However, in Fig. 12-3, the behavior of the animals with bilateral hippocampal damage shows that only one type of error was reduced over

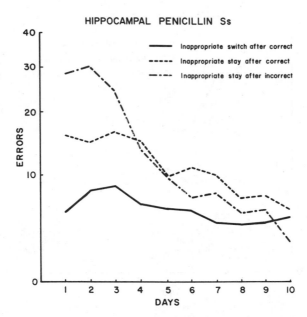

Fig. 12-2. Analysis of the three types of errors made by animals with penicillin injected into the hippocampus over the course of training in the visual discrimination task. Data from Woodruff and Isaacson (1972).

training: the switching of levers after errors. No reduction in the two forms of errors that could be made after correct responses was observed. Since these errors are the only ones indicative of learning the discrimination *per se,* it could be presumed that those animals with the bilateral surgical lesions of the hippocampus failed to acquire the discrimination while the animals with epileptogenic lesions of the hippocampus did so in essentially the same fashion as normal animals. A similar failure of penicillin implanted into the hippocampus to disrupt a discrimination task has been found by Schmaltz, Wolf, and Trejo (1973), although they used an auditory discrimination task.

In a subsequent experiment (Woodruff, Van Hartesveldt, & Isaacson, in preparation) animals with penicillin implanted into the hippocampus were tested in the DRL-20 operant task. The DRL-20 task was selected because performance on it is especially sensitive to bilateral hippocampal destruction (Clark & Isaacson, 1965). The usual impairment was found in animals with bilateral surgical destruction of the hippocampus. These animals performed inefficiently after the surgery and had a very high rate of response.

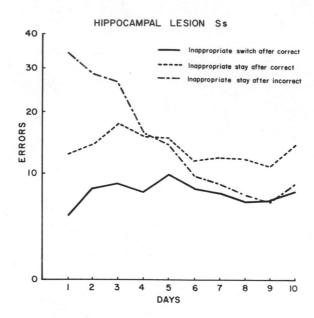

Fig. 12-3. Analysis of the three types of errors made by animals with large, bilateral hippocampal lesions over the course of training in the visual discrimination task. Data from Woodruff and Isaacson (1972).

Animals with penicillin introducted into the hippocampus, however, did not show the substantial reduction in the efficiency of performance. They continued at approximately their preoperative levels of efficiency. They maintained this level throughout the remainder of the experiment, even though the normal animals (and other control groups) improved in their performance. This would indicate that the animals with penicillin implanted into the hippocampus were not affected in the same way as those with the surgically induced lesions on the schedule, but that they were affected: their efficiency of performance did not improve over the course of postoperative training. These results are illustrated in Fig. 12-4. The performance level attained before surgery was maintained but no further improvement in performance was found.

Dr. Michael Woodruff, who is now completing his dissertation in my laboratory, thought that the failure to obtain deficits in these studies of animals in which penicillin had been introduced into the hippocampus may have been due to the failure of the drug to produce a sufficiently active focus of abnormal activity. Therefore, in conjunction with Woodruff and Kearley (Woodruff, Kearley, & Isaacson, in press) a study was undertaken in which small amounts of penicillin were injected daily into the

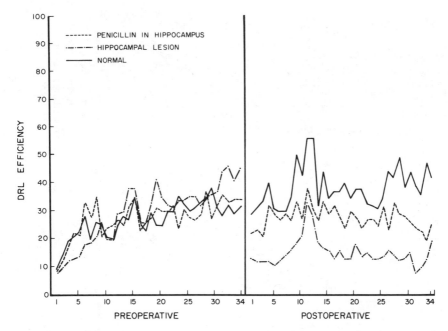

Fig. 12-4. Preoperative and postoperative efficiences of performance on the DRL-20 schedule of normal animals, animals with large bilateral hippocampal lesions, and animals with penicillin implanted into the hippocampus. Data from Woodruff, Van Hartesveldt, and Isaacson (in preparation).

hippocampus or into the posterior neocortex (visual neocortical areas) in rats. Electrical recordings were made before and after the microinjection of the drug and before and after learning. Each day the animals were behaviorally evaluated on the visual discrimination task described above (Woodruff & Isaacson, 1972). A complete description of the results obtained by Woodruff, Kearley, and Isaacson must await publication of the article because several aspects of the training and evaluation procedures demand special consideration, but several facts are clear: injection of the antibiotic into the visual areas of neocortex produces a continuing deficit in the task, but bilateral injection of the drug into the hippocampus produces only a small and transient effect (see Fig. 12-5c).

The effects of the penicillin placed in the visual areas are remarkable and not susceptible to easy interpretation. Fig. 12-5a shows the performance of the normal animals in this study. Fig. 12-5b shows the performance of animals receiving daily injections of penicillin into the posterior neocortex on the first 10 training days. Little or no improvement of performance on

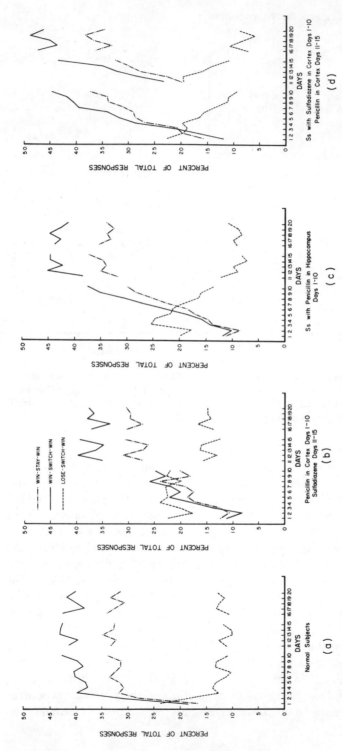

Fig. 12-5. Percent of total responses made in accordance with three strategies by four groups of animals: (a) normal animals; (b) animals with penicillin injected into posterior neocortex on days 1–10, sodium sulfadiazene injected into the same region on days 11–15, and no injections made on days 16–20; (c) animals with penicillin injected into hippocampus on days 1–10, sodium sulfadiazene injected into the same area on days 11–15, and no injections made on days 16–20; and (d) animals with sodium sulfadiazene injected into posterior neocortex on days 1–10, penicillin injected into the same area on days 11–15, and no injections made on days 16–20. Data from Woodruff, Kearley, and Isaacson (in press).

the task is observed. On the other hand, as soon as sodium sulfadiazene is injected instead of penicillin (Day 11) the performance of these animals immediately reaches levels comparable with those of control animals.[2] This suggests that the behavioral deficit produced by the penicillin is one not attributable to the animals failing to acquire and to store the appropriate information. Adequate performance on the task is impossible. When the neocortical perturbations are removed, i.e., when the penicillin injections are stopped, the material that has been learned and stored can be expressed in behavior. Yet, in this experiment we also found that the behavioral deficits produced by penicillin application can be mitigated by previous injections of sodium sulfadiazene into the visual cortex during the course of initial training. One group of animals had this other antibiotic injected into the visual cortices over the first 10 days of training. Beginning on Day 11 of training, daily penicillin injections were made in the same brain areas through the same cannulae: an immediate depression of behavior was noticed, but in this group of animals improvements in performance did occur. This is shown in Fig. 12-5d. Over the course of the next 4 days, levels of performance were attained comparable to those of animals in which only the sodium sulfadiazene had been injected. This differential effect of the penicillin on performance, depending upon the prior training and/or prior injection of sodium sulfadiazene remains to be explained.

These results are similar to those reported by Kraft, Obrist, and Pribram (1960) in that animals with discharging epileptogenic foci produced by alumina cream application in the occipital cortex are impaired animals in visual discriminations. However, it was not possible for them to determine if relief from the epileptic activity would have resulted in an immediate enhancement of performance. Kraft et al. also demonstrated the specificity of the effects produced by application of alumina cream on the occipital cortex: performance on visually mediated tasks was affected, a spatial alternation task was not.

The differential effects of the penicillin upon behaviors indicative of retention and those indicative of learning have been noted previously. Alumina cream applications to either the striate (Henry & Pribram, 1954) or the prestriate (Chow & Obrist, 1954) produce animals in which the performance of previously established visual discriminations are relatively unaffected. Kraft et al. properly called attention to the differences between

---

[2] Sodium sulfadiazene is an antibiotic often used as a control substance in studies in my laboratory since it is much less epileptogenic than most forms of penicillin.

the performance of animals with epileptogenic foci in acquisition and retention testing. Our recent results would suggest that neither acquisition nor
retention is affected by the epileptogenic foci but that performance during
acquisition is severely disturbed while performance during retention is not.

But in contrast to the prodigious effects produced by injection of penicillin into the visual cortex, injections of the drug into the hippocampus
produces only a transient impairment in the task. Over the course of 4 or
5 days, the animals come to exhibit reasonably high levels of performance.
It is as if other animals with hippocampal injections come to tolerate the
abnormal conditions produced by the hippocampal focus of epileptiform
discharges.

The animals in this experiment were prepared with chronic recording
electrodes bilaterally placed in the posterior neocortex, in the hippocampus, and in the mesencephalic reticular formation, regardless of where the
penicillin was to be introduced. In all animals the prolonged, daily administration of the antibiotic led to the spread of epileptiform discharges from
the site of application to the other recording sites. When the primary focus
was produced in the visual neocortex, secondary epileptiform activity could
be recorded from the hippocampus, for example. When the focus was established in the hippocampus, epileptiform activity could be recorded from
the visual cortices. This means that it is the site of the drug application that
is critical for the behavioral changes, since both hippocampus and posterior
neocortex showed pronounced and correlated epileptiform discharges regardless of the site of penicillin application.

Even though the recording of abnormal electrical activities is not
predictive of a behavioral deficit whereas the location of the actual site
of injection is, the amount of epileptiform activity induced by the drug
is related to the degree of impairment. Nakajima (1972) has found that
injections of various antibiotics into the limbic system produce behavioral changes more related to the electrographic abnormalities obtained
than to the extent protein synthesis is inhibited. We also have found a
relation between the degree of epileptiform activity and the behavioral impairment. The greater the frequency of induced spike discharges, the greater
the behavioral impairment (Woodruff, Kearley, & Isaacson, in press).
Apparently the ability to produce electrographic abnormalities is a
crucial event for the disruption of learning, but the electrical discharges
themselves are not disruptive. The ability to produce disruptive reactions in
brain tissue is related to changes going on at the cellular boundaries of the
damaged tissue, but perhaps our attention has been centererd too greatly
upon the electrical events, themselves.

Because the initiation of epileptiform activities in the hippocampus
fails to produce behavioral changes commensurate with memory deficit in

all appetitive tasks, an overall memory impairment hypothesis seems untenable. If epileptiform activity in the hippocampus does affect memory, it affects memories for specific types of abilities in specific situations. The best known are those required in the two-way active avoidance paradigm. Because of the limited amount of data available, it is not even possible to know if other types of avoidance behaviors would also be affected.

If epileptogenic foci in the hippocampus influence only memories of specific kinds, then the question of specific neural systems for memory of certain types of tasks must be re-examined. Thompson, Baumeister, and Rich (1962) have argued for separate subsystems responsible for the retention and postoperative relearning of simultaneous and successive discrimination problems. In particular, these authors believe that when a spatial component is introduced into a visual discrimination task, the system involving the visual cortex, posterior thalamus, lateral hypothalamus, and habenulopeduncular tract has to be supplemented by an "anterior" system involving the anterior neocortex, globus pallidus, and anterior thalamic nuclei. Other work from Thompson's laboratories has tried to relate visual discriminations with the types of motives and incentives used to induce performance (e.g., Thompson, Rich & Langer, 1964; Thompson, 1963).

The possibility that the hippocampus may play a special role in the mediation of painful stimulation was advanced by Delgado (1955) on the basis of the effects produced by electrical stimulation of the structure. Even though it is clear that hippocampal stimulation and lesions can produce behavioral effects in tasks performed to obtain many types of rewards, a special contribution of the hippocampus to tasks learned under penalty of aversive stimulation cannot be rejected.

II. PROACTIVE INTERFERENCE

Since Warrington and Weiskrantz believe that unforgotten verbal associations from the past adversely influence the retrieval of new information in patients with amnesic disorders, it might be expected that animals with hippocampal damage also carry forward too much of the past into the present. Weiskrantz (1971) had already suggested that this type of explanation could serve as the basis for reconciling the differences between the memory deficits described in patients with temporal lobe damage and the failure to find such deficits in nonhuman primates. Accordingly, the behavioral effects produced by hippocampal lesions in rats and other nonprimates were re-examined to determine if the approach could be useful at the nonprimate level. One of the first indications that this might be so came from the experiment of Schmaltz and Isaacson (1966). We found that animals with bilateral hippocampal damage were impaired on a DRL-20 task only if they had been exposed to a schedule of continuous reinforcement (CRF) sometime earlier, either immediately before the transition to the DRL-20 task or before the operation that produced the hippocampal destruction. One interpretation is that the earlier training on CRF had established an expectation for certain reinforcement contingencies that was difficult for the lesioned animals to overcome.

The general argument is that animals with hippocampal damage come to develop expectations about their worlds that in some way become dominant in their effects upon behavior. The past no longer provides a normal basis for the future: it provides an abnormal and inappropriate base.

Kimble and I (Isaacson & Kimble, 1972) recently attempted to define these effects more precisely. It had been established before that animals with hippocampal lesion learn many tasks more readily than do normal animals. These include some avoidance tasks, some operant tasks, and some discrimination tasks. On the other hand, if the animals are trained in the same apparatus using a different set of reinforcement contingencies, they often are substantially impaired. The surprising fact is that this "second-learned task," the one on which they are impaired, can be one they would have learned quite readily if they had been trained on it as the first problem to be learned.

Let us consider what happens when animals with hippocampal destruction attempt to learn a simultaneous discrimination problem. In this case, animals are placed in a T-maze. They are hungry. At the end of one arm of the maze there is food while the food box at the other end is empty. The signal for the correct response is the color of the two cross arms of the T-maze. One cross arm is black, the other white. The spatial locations of the black and white arms are randomly determined. Some animals were trained to go to the black arm of the maze, others to the white. All animals, including those with neocortical or hippocampal lesions, learn the problem quickly and learn to approach food in the black arm more quickly than they learn to approach food in the white arm. This is probably due to the effect of a species-characteristic tendency to approach the darker areas of the maze. In any case, the animal does learn to approach the white arm of the maze easily, and by inference, to overcome this species-characteristic behavioral tendency. I think the best way to describe this tendency to approach the black arm of the maze is in terms of the ease or likelihood that an hypothesis will be entertained. Rats are more likely, it seems, to test the hypothesis "follow the black road" than "follow the white road," even when they have had surgical brain damage. Two points must be made, however: (1) the view that rats tend to approach black more readily than white is a statistical concept. There are some animals, albeit only a few, that begin by testing "follow the white road," and (2) that rats with hippocampal damage can readily change the hypothesis being tested on the basis of the feedback from their responses when they are experimentally naïve. They become reluctant to change only when the "well has been poisoned" by their past experiences.

The recognition that animals entering a training situation test a number of hypotheses during initial training and that the sequences of hypotheses tested are not identical goes a long way in explaining the variability often found in the results of many experiments. Indeed, some animals begin testing the correct hypothesis almost immediately. Such animals can "learn" the problem without any error trials. They begin with the correct idea and stay with it. If this, too, is inappropriate, they try again. The problems exhibited by animals with hippocampal damage are reflected in the carry-over of information and strategies from the past into the present, and this must be explained on the basis of their use of hypotheses. Even in experimentally naïve animals with hippocampal lesions, there is some evidence for a *general* lack of flexibility of hypotheses; they seem to have some resistance to giving up an hypothesis. Our analysis (Isaacson & Kimble, 1972) showed that even the acquisition of a simple simultaneous discrimination problem, in which animals were trained to approach an illuminated arm of a T-maze for a water reward, the animals with hippocampal damage tended to test fewer hypotheses before settling on the correct solution. In an earlier report, Kimble and Kimble (1970) found that the lesioned animals tended to hold "position hypotheses" longer than control animals but that this did not affect the rate at which the problem was acquired. The length of time the lesioned animals held a brightness hypotheses was not different from that of normal animals. The learning of the problem by the animals with hippocampal lesions was at least as proficient as that of normal animals.

In the analysis presented in our report (Isaacson & Kimble, 1972), only two hypotheses were evaluated in the maze discrimination task: a hypothesis about the place the rewards were located and a hypothesis about the brightness cues of the maze. Animals with hippocampal lesions held one of these hypotheses on 81% of their training trials, while normal animals held one of the two hypotheses on 54% of their trials. This means that the normal animals may hold different, perhaps more complex, hypotheses or they behave without guidance of an hypothesis on about half of the pre-solution training trials. Both lesioned and intact animals can entertain more complicated hypotheses (*e.g.*, alternation of responses), but these were not evaluated in the learning of the discrimination task. In either case, the animals with hippocampal lesions were less flexible, *i.e.*, they held detectable, simple hypotheses on the majority of their training trials while the normal animals did so on about half of their training trials.

After learning this brightness discrimination problem the animals were subjected to an extinction procedure. Rewards were not given after any response. Most of the normal and control-lesion animals quickly stopped running the maze, while most of the animals with hippocampal lesions kept running. The normal animals became "more flexible" during extinction. They kept with a particular hypothesis (spatial or brightness) for only a few trials and then went on to test the other hypothesis for a few more trials. Then, they just stopped running in the maze entirely. In contrast, the animals with hippocampal lesions tended to exhibit long strings of responses in accord with some hypothesis. Usually this hypothesis was the brightness hypothesis on which they had been trained. Some animals continued to respond on a brightness hypothesis but the one diametrically opposed to the one on which they had been trained. These animals might begin to respond consistently toward the white arm even though they had been rewarded in the past for approaching the black arm. Other animals began testing a spatial hypothesis once again—e.g., "go right," "go left"— even though this hypothesis had never been rewarded and had been abandoned early in acquisition training.

The point to be emphasized is that when placed on an extinction regime, the response of an animal with limbic system damage is not merely the perseveration of the response previously rewarded. It exhibits a reaction that goes beyond such a simple form of behavior: (1) behavior is "energized" and "activated," and (2) old, formerly rejected, hypotheses are brought back into play. Both of these effects combine to produce the behavioral deficits found when the lesioned animals are taught to modify their behavior. They are proactive in the sense that the conditions that lead to the behavioral disruptions appear when the resources of the past no longer serve the present and are not seen when the animal is trained de novo. Furthermore, the conditions under which the animals fail to perform adequately are those in which the environment has been unreliable. Changes in the external world have forced the animal to exhibit a flexibility that is no longer available to him.

The interfering effects of the past in the lesioned animals depend upon the type of past experiences and the requirements of the new situation. Winocur and Salzen (1968) demonstrated that animals with dorsal hippocampal lesions could exhibit good postoperative retention of a simple visual discrimination based upon the size of a black circle on a white background. However, when these animals were tested postoperatively under any of four "transfer conditions" in which the test stimuli were different from those used in preoperative training, the animals with hippocampal damage were severely impaired. These authors showed that the results were not predictable on the basis of a perseveration of errors to specific stimuli or of a perseveration of responses. The animals were deficient in the transfer test, but not because of "perseverative behaviors" defined on the basis of overt responses. The lesioned animals became impaired, however, when the environment was uncertain.

In a subsequent study, Winocur and Mills (1970) found that a negative transfer is found in the behavior of normal animals when they are trained on a brightness discrimination task preoperatively and a pattern discrimination problem postoperatively. This interference is considerably exaggerated in animals with hippocampal destruction. These authors also investigated the question of the generality of the interference produced by training in several tasks. To do so, they tested animals in an operant task (CRF), an active avoidance task (one-way), and a simultaneous brightness discrimination task, using different orders of the tasks for different groups of animals. All testing was done postoperatively for the brain lesioned animals. They found that the animals with hippocampal damage acquired the tasks at the same rates regardless of the order in which they were experienced. This implies that the transfer impairments found in animals with hippocampal damage are restricted to tasks similar to ones experienced in the past and yet that have some new uncertainty introduced in them.

While the negative transfer effects produced by hippocampal destruction are real, their magnitude depends upon the extent to which a particular mode of responding is "favored" by the subjects. Riddell, Malinchoc, and Reimers (1971) reported the effects of training animals in three problems in an operant situation. The animals were trained to make a lever press response at one end of the box which then allowed the animals to make responses on two pigeon keys at the other end of the box. All animals were first trained to make a brightness discrimination and then a position discrimination to criterion performance on the pigeon keys. Finally, they were given training in a response alternation task. All training was given postoperatively for the lesioned animals.

The animals with hippocampal lesions were impaired in learning the alternation response but not in learning the other two problems. Since others (e.g., Means, Walker, & Isaacson, 1970; Jackson & Strong, 1969) have shown that animals with hippocampal damage are not impaired in learning an alternation problem in an operant setting, there is presumptive evidence that the prior experiences had negatively affected performance in this problem. It could well be asked why the training in the brightness discrimination had not affected performance in the position problem. Perhaps the "place hypothesis" is very prominent in rats and they readily fall back on it under conditions of uncertainty, especially those with hippocampal destruction.

III. REPRISE

From consideration of the history of research on the relationship between memory and limbic system activity in animals, it has become clear to me that a giant obstacle has been blocking progress: the naïveté of many investigators, including myself, about the nature of memory and its converse, forgetting. Many of us were looking for a key to memory, which we considered to be some unitary entity, some global capacity of the organism. Of course, we were studying forgetting and should have realized that the rules governing forgetting may well be different for different kinds of materials or for information arriving over different sensory modalities. Forgetting is a phenotypic response of the organism, defined in a particular experimental situation, and there can be many genotypic causes. When a system is disrupted by penicillin, electrical, or chemical stimulation, the effect can be one in which information cannot be stored or processed relative to those modalities influenced by that particular system, but the effects may also be upon the expression of that which has been learned and stored —as demonstrated in our animals with penicillin placed daily into the visual cortex.

It is clear that both lesions of the hippocampus and disturbances produced by penicillin affect active avoidance behavior but in different directions. This would associate the hippocampus with aversively motivated tasks. Therefore, I would propose that the biochemical and electrical changes induced by penicillin injection into the hippocampus especially influence performance on avoidance tasks, and in a more general sense I would assume that epileptiform pertubations affect learning and memory only when induced in systems that are closely or essentially involved in the performance of a particular type of task. Epileptiform disturbances of the hippocampus do not disturb the storage or retrieval of information about some appetitive tasks.

On the other hand, surgically induced damage to the hippocampus produces an animal that learns quickly and an animal in which this information carries over into the future in an unusually imperative fashion. This makes it difficult for these animals to adopt new ways of responding in situations where a previously established way of responding must be altered. These proactive effects can produce behavioral changes that are easily interpreted as memory deficits in certain circumstances.

IV. THE LIMBIC SYSTEM:
A PERSPECTIVE

The mechanisms whereby the hippocampus and other limbic structures modify strategies, hypotheses, and retrieval are largely unknown, yet there are some hints now available as to the limbic system and its general role in the regulation of behavior. In many ways these are speculations that go beyond available data, and yet they are preliminary first steps toward a more adequate formalization of the relationship between the limbic system and the other portions of the brain.

Perhaps the easiest perspective is that provided by MacLean (1970). He suggested that advanced brains can be considered to be a composite of three types of systems: (a) reptilian brain, (b) a protomammalian brain, and (c) a neomammalian brain. The reptile brain includes portions of the basal ganglia, the diencephalon, and midbrain and brainstem mechanisms. Upon this "fundamental core" of all brains is imposed the protomammalian brain—the limbic system. Lastly the neocortical mantle emerges as the newest neural system.

In some ways, the last two "brains" must be considered luxuries. Animals with little more than reptilian brains eat, sleep, love, fight, learn, and remember. They learn quickly and remember indefinitely. They are perfectly suited for the formation of habits that relate them to an invariant environment. Sharks need to learn but a few things and to remember them well, since the sea provides relatively constant conditions for their survival. Changes in the sea leads to changes in the populations of animals that survive. Some genetic variants are more adequately suited to the new conditions than others. The species changes and survives as a result of changes in the gene pool but the individual may not. To the shark, blood means eat. It is a rule for the shark to live by and it does so effectively.

On land, conditions and climates change more rapidly. Adjustments in behavior must be made more quickly and these adjustments require ways in which to terminate established behavior and form new behavior. It is especially interesting that we must stop old ways of behaving before beginning new ones. My suggestion is that this is precisely the role played by the limbic system.

The limbic system is a system only because each of its components has relatively direct connections with the hypothalamus. Different parts of each limbic system structure exert facilitatory and inhibitory influences upon the several parts of the hypothalamus and the systems that run through it. These systems energize and regulate the organized patterns of behavior and thought. At least certain portions of each limbic system structure influence the hypothalamus, which, when activated, causes the suppression of on-going behaviors. Other portions of the limbic system structures facilitate ongoing behaviors.

The various structures of the limbic system regulate regions of the posterior hypothalamus, which itself is dualistic: there is a lateral portion that can be considered responsible for the activation and maintenance of behavior sequences, and a medial portion that produces the cessation of behavior. Since I have suggested that all structures of the limbic system act to regulate the lateral and medial portions of the hypothalamus, the question can be raised as to why there are so many different types of components of the system. If they all act to achieve the same end results, why are they so different? The answer, I believe, is that each of the limbic system structures is especially "tuned" to specific events of the external or internal worlds. The amygdala could be responsive to changing conditions of hunger, sex, and aggression; the septal area to thirst and some emotional reactions; and the hippocampus to neocortical activities, especially those related to the relationship of the present circumstances to what had been anticipated. Thus, each structure could be tuned to specific types of activity of the individual and his world. The behavioral effects produced by lesions or electrical stimulation of a structure would be quite different depending on the region of that structure influenced, the susceptibility of that area to the specific parameters of stimulation, and the circumstances in which the stimulation occurs.

The effects of hippocampal destruction upon the hypothesis behavior of animals during acquisition and extinction resemble the effects obtained when electrical stimulation is applied to the lateral hypothalamus. For example, such stimulation can increase an animal's resistance to extinction (Deutsch, Howarth, Ball, & Deutsch, 1962) and activate responses that have been previously extinguished. It can facilitate the acquisition and performance of animals on certain behavioral schedules (Huston, 1971). It also fits into the view I have proposed (Isaacson, 1972b) on the basis of many types of evidence that the effects of hippocampal destruction in animals produce an overall ergotropic balance (in terms of Hess, 1949, and Gellhorn, 1970), although the main change toward an ergotropic state is found under conditions of environmental uncertainty as was originally suggested by Klüver (1965).

I believe that inhibitory controls exerted by the hippocampus are of two kinds. The first has to do with the regulation of "arousal" or "activation" of the nervous system and the second has to do with the regulation of the ways in which the animal has learned to respond in the training situation. The first aspect is that discussed above and is related to the tendencies toward an ergotropic balance in the lesioned animals. It must be assumed that under conditions of environmental uncertainty, there are mechanisms (probably associated with diencephalic or brainstem systems) that produce a state of increased arousal and activation. These, in turn, are normally suppressed by the hippocampus. Failing such suppression because of surgical or accidental damage, the responses to environmental uncertainty are exaggerated. The second aspect of hippocampal suppression relates to an inhibition of neural systems responsible for the patterns of on-going behaviors. These are the neural systems responsible for the behaviors acquired in the past in any particular set of circumstances.

My suggestion is that the neural systems affected by hippocampal activity related to arousal and to the energizing of specific, acquired patterns of behavior will be found in the hypothalamus. Whether they will turn out to be identical diencephalic systems is problematic at the present time.

There is still considerable controversy concerning the presence of separate "drive" and "reinforcement" systems of the hypothalamus (see Deutsch & Howarth, 1963; Gallistel, Rolls, & Greene, 1969; Panksepp, Gandelman, & Trowill, 1969). The theory being advocated here would support a dualistic system, although the term "reinforcement" does not quite describe the system underlying previously learned behaviors accurately.

If the effects of hippocampal activation are to suppress the activity of lateral hypothalamic systems when conditions of uncertainty arise, the on-going behaviors suppressed are those representing the older, long-term memories. This suppression allows new actions to be taken, new memories to be formed. With practice, this suppression of the past can become more or less habitual and perhaps even conditioned. Subjects entering the psychological laboratories to learn new lists of nonsense syllables day after day may well come to anticipate the suppressive effects of the previously acquired lists that will be necessary. In any case, the effect will be to interrupt older memories. Accordingly, it could be that the short-term memory system(s) is relatively unaffected by the descending hippocampal influences. This would suggest that tasks in which behavior can be effectively governed by short-term memories will be relatively unaffected by hippocampal destruction. This would, in turn, lead to the anticipation that the intertrial intervals used in the training of animals would be of considerable importance. A deficient long-term memory storage or retrieval could transform an easy, stable training situation into one in which the contingencies of behavior are uncertain. This would, in accordance with the proposed model, produce a condition in which perseveration of prior ways of responding are continued and in which there is also an excessive behavioral activation. Tasks with intertrial intervals such that information can be held in a short-term memory storage system between trials might be capable of solution by the animals with hippocampal lesions whereas those that depend more upon some form of long-term storage might be overwhelming for the lesioned animals.

Such results have been reported. Animals with hippocampal damage show perseveration of an approach response in a straight runway during extinction conditions if there are 10 min between trials but not if there are 10 sec between trials (Jarrard, Isaacson, & Wickelgren, 1964; Jarrard & Isaacson, 1965). Animals with similar lesions are dramatically impaired in the acquisition of a spatial discrimination in a T-maze when trained with 24 hours between trials (Means, Woodruff, & Isaacson, 1972), a deficit not observed if the trials are given under more usual training conditions. Nevertheless, the fact is that in many training conditions animals that have been subjected to hippocampal destruction do remember what has been learned on one day and carry it over as a basis of performance on subsequent days. This means that any simple model based on a long-term storage or retrieval dysfunction must be incorrect.

In fact, the failure of a simple dysfunction model is easily demonstrated in the runway experiment performed by Jarrard, Isaacson, and Wickelgren (1964). In the original acquisition of the runway task, animals with hippocampal lesions acquired the problem as rapidly as did the control animals at either a 10 min or 10 sec intertrial interval. The intertrial interval effect was observed only when circumstances changed—i.e., when the animals no longer found food at the end of the runway during extinction. In the study by Means et al. (1972) the animals had experience in exploring the maze with food in the food cups and during spontaneous alternation testing with no food available in maze before the actual discrimination training was begun. Therefore it is likely that the lesion-produced effects related to the time between trials is found only when the animals are called upon to change their behavior after having prior experiences with the training situation—another example of the excessive proactive effects produced by the lesions.

However, the analysis of the situation is still not complete, because the lesioned animals that do learn to withhold the runway response during extinction when tested with the 10-sec intertrial interval continue to do so when tested on subsequent days. They "retain" and "retrieve" over this 24-hour period. This distinction between what is retained and what is not after an environmental change can be interpreted using a hypothesis framework. If the animals "solve the problem"—i.e., confirm the correct hypothesis—this will be transferred from one day to the next. What is not transferred over a matter of seconds is the "information" derived from the preceding response. For the lesioned animals, this information dissipates rapidly and is soon lost. This may be due to the perseveration of hypotheses-testing behavior after the change in the environment.

I hold the view that one of the fundamental roles played by the limbic system is the suppression of established ways of responding—i.e., memories, under specified changes in the environment. For the hippocampus, this includes environmental uncertainties. With hippocampal damage, this lack of suppression causes perseverative activities, both cognitive and behavioral, based on the animals' past experiences and their own species-characteristic tendencies. This produces a tendency toward impaired retrieval of newly stored information relative to the older, more established patterns of behavior and consequently to greater proactive interference effects. This enhanced interference makes the animal less able to cope with the environment and actually produces a positive feedback condition, a "vicious circle" of effects that tend to augment the observable deficits.

REFERENCES

Chow, K. L., & Obrist, W. D. EEG and behavioral changes on application of AL(OH)₃ cream on preoccipital cortex of monkeys. *AMA Archives of Neurology and Psychiatry*, 1954, **72**, 80–87.

Clark, C. V., & Isaacson, R. L. Effect of bilateral hippocampal ablation on DRL performance. *Journal of Comparative and Physiological Psychology*, 1965, **59**, 137–140.

Delgado, J. M. R. Cerebral structures involved in transmission and elaboration of noxious stimulation. *Journal of Neurophysiology*, 1955, **18**, 261–275.

Deutsch, J. A., & Howarth, C. I. Some tests of a theory of intracranial self-stimulation. *Psychological Review*, 1963, **70**, 444–460.

Deutsch, J. A., Howarth, C. I., Ball, G. C., & Deutsch, D. Threshold differentiation of drive and reward in the Olds effect. *Nature*, 1962, **196**, 699–700.

Douglas, R. J. The hippocampus and behavior. *Psychological Bulletin*, 1967, **67**, 416–422.

Gallistel, C. R., Rolls, E., & Greene, D. Neuron function inferred from behavioral and electrophysiological estimates of refractory period. *Science*, 1969, **166**, 1028–1029.

Gellhorn, E. The emotions and the ergotropic and trophotropic systems. *Psychologische Forschung*, 1970, **34**, 48–94.

Henry, C. E., & Pribram, K. H. Effect of aluminum hydroxide implantation on cortex of monkey on EEG and behavior performance. *Electroencephalography and Clinical Neurophysiology*, 1954, **6**, 693–694.

Hess, W. R. *Das Zwischenhirn*. Basel: Schwabe, 1949.

Huston, J. P. Relationship between motivating and rewarding stimulation of the lateral hypothalamus. *Physiology and Behavior*, 1971, **6**, 711–716.

Isaacson, R. L. Hippocampal destruction in man and other animals. *Neuropsychologia*, 1972, **10**, 47–64. (a)

Isaacson, R. L. Neural systems of the limbic brain and behavioral inhibition. In

J. Halliday & R. Boakes (Eds.), *Inhibition and learning.* New York: Academic Press, 1972. (b)

Isaacson, R. L. *The Limbic System.* New York: Plenum Press, 1974.

Isaacson, R. L., Douglas, R. J., & Moore, R. Y. The effects of radical hippocampal ablation on acquisition of avoidance responses. *Journal of Comparative and Physiological Psychology,* 1961, **54,** 625–628.

Isaacson, R. L., & Kimble, D. P. Lesions of the limbic system: Their effects upon hypotheses and frustration. *Behavioral Biology,* 1972, **7,** 767–793.

Jackson, W. S., & Strong, P. M., Jr. Differential effects of hippocampal lesions upon sequential tasks and maze learning in the rat. *Journal of Comparative and Physiological Psychology,* 1969, **68,** 442–450.

Jarrard, L. E., & Isaacson, R. L. Hippocampal ablation in rats: Effects of intertrial interval. *Nature,* 1965, **207,** 109–110.

Jarrard, L. E., Isaacson, R. L., & Wickelgren, W. A. Effects of hippocampal ablation and intertrial interval on runway acquisition and extinction. *Journal of Comparative and Physiological Psychology,* 1964, **57,** 3, 442–444.

Kimble, D. P. Hippocampus and internal inhibition. *Psychological Bulletin,* 1968, **70,** 285–295.

Kimble, D. P., & Kimble, R. J. The effect of hippocampal lesions on extinction and "hypothesis" behavior in rats. *Physiology and Behavior,* 1970, **5,** 735–738.

Klüver, H. Neurology of normal and abnormal perception. In P. H. Hoch & J. Zubin (Eds.), *Psychopathology of perception.* New York: Grune & Stratton, 1965.

Kraft, M. S., Obrist, W. D., & Pribram, K H. The effect of irritative lesions of the striate cortex on learning of visual discriminations in monkeys. *Journal of Comparative and Physiological Psychology,* 1960, **53,** 17–22.

MacLean, P. D. The triune brain, emotion, and scientific bias. In F. O. Schmidt (Ed.), *The neurosciences, second study program.* New York: Rockefeller University Press, 1970.

Means, L. W., Walker, D. W., & Isaacson, R. L. Facilitated single alternation go, no-go performance following hippocampectomy in the rat. *Journal of Comparative and Physiological Psychology,* 1970, **72,** 278–285.

Means, L. W., Woodruff, M. L., & Isaacson, R. L. The effect of a 24-hour intertrial interval on the acquisition of a spatial discrimination by hippocampally damaged rats. *Physiology and Behavior,* 1972, **8,** 451–462.

Milner, B. The memory defect in bilateral hippocampal lesions. *Psychiatric Research Reports,* 1959, **11,** 43–52.

Milner, B. Disorders of learning and memory after temporal lobe lesions in man. *Clinical Neurosurgery,* 1972, **19,** 421–446.

Nakajima, S. Interference with relearning in the rat after hippocampal injection of Actinomysin-D. *Journal of Comparative and Physiological Psychology,* 1969, **67,** 457–461.

Nakajima, S. Biochemical disruption of memory: Reexaminations. Paper presented at 20th International Congress of Psychology, Tokyo, 1972.

Olton, D. S. Specific deficits in active avoidance behavior following penicillin injection into the hippocampus. *Physiology and Behavior,* 1970, **5,** 957–963.

Panskepp, J., Gandelman, R., & Trowill, J. A. A reply to Gallistel. *Psychonomic Science,* 1969, **16,** 26–27.

Penfield, W., & Milner, B. Memory deficit produced by bilateral lesions in the hippocampal zone, *AMA Archives of Neurology and Psychology,* 1958, **79,** 475–497.

Riddell, W. I., Malinchoc, M., & Reimers, R. Shift and retention deficits in hippocampectomized and neodecorticate rats. Unpublished manuscript, 1971.

Schmaltz, L. W. Deficit in active avoidance learning in rats following penicillin injection into hippocampus. *Physiology and Behavior,* 1971, **6**, 667–674.

Schmaltz, L. W., & Isaacson, R. L. The effects of preliminary training conditions upon DRL-20 performance in the hippocampectomized rat. *Physiology and Behavior,* 1966, **1**, 175–182.

Schmaltz, L. W., Wolf, B. P., & Trejo, W. R. FR, DRL, and discrimination learning in rats following aspiration lesions and penicillin injection into hippocampus. *Physiology and Behavior,* 1973, in press.

Schneider, G. E. Two visual systems. *Science,* 1969, **163**, 895–902.

Scoville, W. B. The limbic love in man. *Journal of Neurosurgery,* 1954, **11**, 64–66.

Scoville, W. B., & Milner, B. Loss of recent memory after bilateral hippocampal lesions. *Journal of Neurology, Neurosurgery and Psychiatry,* 1957, **20**, 11–21.

Thompson, R. Thalamic structures critical for retention of an avoidance conditioned response in rats. *Journal of Comparative and Physiological Psychology,* 1963, **56**, 261–267.

Thompson, R., Baumeister, A. A., & Rich, I. Subcortical mechanisms in a successive brightness discrimination habit in the rat. *Journal of Comparative and Physiological Psychology,* 1962, **55**, 487–491.

Thompson, R., Rich, I., & Langer, S. K. Lesion studies on the functional significance of the posterior thalamomesencephalic tract. *Journal of Comparative Neurology,* 1964, **123**, 29–44.

Underwood, B. J., & Postman, L. Extraexperimental sources of interference in forgetting. *Psychological Review,* 1960, **67**, 73–95.

Victor, M., Adams, R. D., & Collins, G. H. *The Wernicke–Korsakoff syndrome.* Oxford: Blackwell, 1971.

Warrinton, E. K., & Weiskrantz, L. An analysis of short-term and long-term memory defects in man. In J. A. Deutsch (Ed.), *The physiological basis of memory.* New York: Academic Press, 1972.

Weiskrantz, L. Comparison of amnesic states in monkey and man. In L. Jarrard (Ed.), *Cognitive processes in non-human primates.* New York: Academic Press, 1971.

Whitty, C. W. M., & Zangwill, O. L. (Eds.), *Amnesia.* London: Butterworths, 1966.

Winocur, G., & Mills, J. A. Transfer between related and unrelated problems following hippocampal lesions in rats. *Journal of Comparative and Physiological Psychology,* 1970, **73**, 162–169.

Winocur, G., & Salzen, E. A. Hippocampal lesions and transfer behavior in the rat. *Journal of Comparative and Physiological Psychology,* 1968, **65**, 303–310.

Woodruff, M. L., & Isaacson, R. L. Discrimination learning in animals with lesions of hippocampus. *Behavioral Biology,* 1972, **7**, 489–501.

Woodruff, M. L., Kearley, R., & Isaacson, R. L. Deficient brightness discrimination produced by daily intracranial injections of penicillin in rats. *Behavioral Biology,* in press.

Woodruff, M. L., Van Hartesveldt, C., & Isaacson, R. L. Performance on DRL-20 task by animal with aspiration and epileptogenic lesions of hippocampus, 1973, in preparation.

Zangwill, O. L. A note on immediate memory. *Quarterly Journal of Experimental Psychology,* 1956, **8**, 140–143.

Zangwill, O. L. Remembering revisited. *Quarterly Journal of Experimental Psychology,* 1972, **24**, 123–138.

CHAPTER

13

TWO FACES OF MEMORY CONSOLIDATION: STORAGE OF INSTRUMENTAL AND CLASSICAL CONDITIONING[1]

ALLEN M. SCHNEIDER

[1] The research from our laboratory reported here was supported by NSF Grant GB 35205 to Swarthmore College. The secretarial skills of Mrs. Peggy Long and the critical comments of Linda Stanton and Jonathan Tyler added immeasurably to the preparation of this chapter.

It was recognized as early as the turn of the century that the enduring property of learning, the part commonly referred to as memory storage, must involve a structural change in the nervous system. Seventy years later, the neural repository of storage (the engram, as it has been called) remains an enigma. Some have sought its anatomical locus, others have worried about its form, and both endeavors have been complicated by the possibility that the engram changes with age.

I. THE AGING OF MEMORY

It is generally acknowledged that memory storage, as a physical residue of learning, depends on neural activity during learning for its formation; but once formed, storage remains apart from ongoing neural activity, lying in a dormant state ready to be reactivated or recalled at a later date. Questions have been raised regarding the time that it takes ongoing neural activity to transform into its enduring structural counterpart. Although it is tempting to assume that the transition is immediate, that the time for transition coincides with the duration of the training trial, there is a plethora of evidence indicating the contrary. Transition continues after the termination of the training trial, and memory is gradually fixated by a process known as memory consolidation.

The consolidation notion was first proposed at the turn of the century by Mueller and Pilzecker (1900). They found that human subjects, given two lists of words to learn, had difficulty in recalling material from the first list after learning the second. The learning of recent items interfered with the recall of older ones. To explain the results, Mueller and Pilzecker postulated a process, called memory consolidation, that ensues immediately after training to transform fragile short-term memory into durable long-term memory. In the same spirit, but much more recently, Tulving (1969) found that subjects asked to concentrate on proper names in a list of words, tended on subsequent recall tests to forget the items immediately preceding the proper names. Apparently the act of concentrating on the names interfered with consolidation of the preceding items.

The notion of memory consolidation was further buttressed by detailed clinical reports of traumatic amnesia recounted by Russell and Nathan (1946). For example, a person receiving a blow to the head who has difficulty in recalling the events that immediately preceded the trauma has no or less difficulty in recalling events that occurred earlier in time. In most cases, however, the lost memories recover. Immediately after the concussion the person may not recall anything that occurred that day, but a month later he may recall most things that occurred the day of the trauma except the events that immediately preceded the trauma; memory of these events is often permanently lost.

In addition to accounting for the selective loss of short-term memory following head trauma, the distinction between fragile short-term memory and durable long-term memory accounts for obvious imperfections in normal memory. For example, a phone number is remembered until dialed and then lost and must be looked up again before redialing. According to the consolidation theory, the neural activity initially triggered by the number is sufficient for us to recall it temporarily (short-term memory) but is not sufficient to cause a permanent impression on the nervous system representing long-term memory. In summary, the consolidation concept of memory storage postulates that there are two storage codes, one dynamic and short-term in span, one static and long-term in span, and a fixating process that mediates the transformation from one (the short-term memory) to the other (long-term memory).

It remained for Hebb (1949) to reify the notion of consolidation by postulating that short-term memory is represented by a transient electrical code that is vulnerable to interference and long-term memory is represented by a durable chemical code that is resistant to interference. Specifically, Hebb postulated that the ongoing neural activity caused by the learning experience does not stop with termination of the training trial; instead, the neural impulses continue for a time after the trial as short-term memory and, if persistent, transform into durable long-term memory.

II. EXPERIMENTAL ANALYSIS OF THE CONSOLIDATION PROCESS

If we could observe memory storage directly, our problem of analysis would be simplified, but unfortunately we cannot. Instead, we are forced to infer storage from overt behavior. This inference puts us on delicate ground because there is not a one-to-one relation between storage and its expres-

sion. For example, ablation of frontal lobes in monkeys appeared to interfere with short-term memory (Jacobsen, Wolfe, & Jackson, 1935). Animals had difficulty in remembering under which cup a reward was placed
if a brief interval was interpolated between the time they observed the
placement and the time they were allowed to respond (a delayed-response
procedure). They behaved as if they could not store the learned information for more than a few minutes. The data were initially taken as evidence
for disruption of short-term memory. Subsequently, however, it was found
that frontal animals are highly distractable, raising the possibility that the
impaired retention following the short delays was related to attentional
rather than storage processes. More refined analysis has revealed that if the
distractions are minimized during the delay, the impaired retention tends
to decline (Malmo, 1942).

One solution to separating storage from performance processes is an
experimental paradigm known as the *retrograde design*. Traditionally, experimental analysis of memory storage has consisted of three procedural
steps. The first is training, which requires that the organism receive stimuli,
execute responses, and associate the two in some relatively permanent
storage form. The second procedural step is the training-test interval, which
requires that the organism maintain storage of the stimulus–response association over time. The third and final step is testing, which requires that the
organism perceive the conditioned stimulus, thereby activating the stored
association, and execute the response. Within this framework it is assumed
that storage is expressed in one form or another in each of the three stages.
In the training and testing stage, isolation of storage is complicated by performance processes, but during the training-test interval, storage operates
in the absence of performance processes. On the basis of these assumptions,
it appears that what is needed to study storage independent of performance
processes is a retrograde-type design. In such a design the neural or biochemical effects of reversible amnesic agents such as electroconvulsive
shock (ECS) are both confined to the training-test interval, thereby eliminating performance effects, and triggered at varied but precise intervals
after training, thereby tracing possible changes in short- and long-term
storage.

III. DEFINING THE TIME SPAN
OF CONSOLIDATION

If, according to Hebb, short-term memory exists in an electrical form,
reverberates, and eventually results in long-term memory, one should be
able to mark the point of transition from short- to long-term memory by

scrambling the electrical properties of the system at different times after learning. When memory is in its short-term electrical form, the scrambling should result in amnesia. When memory is transformed into its long-term chemical form, the scrambling should cease to have amnesic effects. The point in time at which the scrambling ceases to produce amnesia marks the length of the consolidation period.

As a prototype for this kind of analysis, let us consider an experiment conducted by Chorover and Schiller (1965). Two groups of rats were trained, were given ECS either 0.5 or 30 sec after training, and were tested 24 hr later; the 0.5-sec group showed amnesia, the 30-sec group showed retention. These data depict the type of time-dependent effects that are tempting to equate with changes in storage; the 0.5-sec old memory is encoded in a vulnerable state, the 30-sec-old memory is encoded in a resistant state, and the transition from the vulnerable to the resistant state, commonly referred to as consolidation, occurred within the first 30 sec after training.

IV. CHALLENGING THE NOTION OF MEMORY CONSOLIDATION

The notion of memory consolidation has been undermined by a simple but perplexing observation. If consolidation thinking is correct and memory storage consists of a chain of events (beginning with learning, passing through transient short-term memory, and ending with enduring long-term memory), then disruption during short-term memory should abort the chain and result in permanent amnesia. But it does not! Amnesia is not permanent: animals given ECS shortly after training may indeed be amnesic the next day and even for several days, but eventually the amnesia dissipates and memory recovers.

Recently Quartermain, McEwen, and Azmitia (1972) defined some of the boundary conditions necessary to restore retention following ECS-induced amnesia. Rats were trained in a one-trial passive-avoidance procedure and were convulsed 1 sec later. Training consisted of delivering a punishing footshock for stepping from a small to large compartment. Quartermain *et al.* found that the amnesic effects of ECS were temporary. In fact, they discovered that retention could be restored in two different ways: by repeated test trials, or by a single test trial and a reminder shock.

In the repeated test trial procedure, after receiving training and convulsion, the rats were given one test trial per day for 3 days. For the first 2 days, the rats were allowed to step from the small to the large compartment without punishing footshock. On the third day, the animals tended to avoid stepping through, thus showing recovery of retention. Further analysis indicates that the test trial procedure itself was critical in restoring retention. Control animals, not given the test trials but simply left in their home cages for several days, showed no recovery when finally tested.

The reminder-shock procedure was more involved but equally compelling. Rats given ECS 1 sec after training showed amnesia on two subsequent retention tests, the first given 24 hr and the second given 48 hr after training. If, however, following the first retention test, the rats were given a reminder shock (*i.e.,* footshock outside the training apparatus), the animals showed retention on the second test trial. With further analysis, it became apparent that it was not the reminder shock *per se* that restored retention. Instead, and equally important, was the first test trial and the interval between that trial and the reminder shock. If the first test trial were omitted and only the reminder shock given or if the first test trial were followed 23 hr later by reminder shock, retention was not restored. If, on the other hand, the first test trial was followed 1 hr later by reminder shock, retention was restored.

With closer analysis it is apparent that the interval variable is double-edged: one interval lies between the first test trial (Test 1) and the reminder shock, a second interval lies between the reminder shock and the second test trial (Test 2). Variations in one coincide with variations in the other: the 1-hr and 23-hr interval between Test 1 and reminder shock correspond, respectively, with the 23-hr and 1-hr interval between reminder shock and Test 2. Quartermain et al. ignored the confounding and centered their attention on the interval between the first test trial and reminder shock. Schneider, Geller, Moskowitz, and Weinberg (1972), on the other hand, unraveled the confounding and obtained data indicating that the second interval, not the first, was critical for recovery (*i.e.,* the time between the reminder shock and the second test trial was critical for recovery). They found that if reminder shock were given 1 hr before the second test it produced amnesia, and if reminder shock were given 23 hr before the second test, retention resulted independent of the length of the first interval (i.e., the time between the first test trial and the reminder shock). Apparently the reminder shock, in addition to restoring retention, exerts a proactive effect on performance during the second retention test blocking performance 1 hr but not 23 hr later.

That recovery occurs is clear; the reason it occurs is enigmatic. To maintain a theory of memory consolidation in the face of these data, new assumptions must be made and old assumptions must be changed. No longer can the assumption be that ECS completely destroys memory; instead, the assumption must be one of partial destruction (McGaugh & Herz, 1972). No longer can the assumption be that ECS prevents consolidation; instead, the assumption must be that the consolidation rate is suppressed by ECS (Cherkin, 1969) and is accelerated by reminder shock. In light of these complications one wonders if consolidation theory has not overextended its theoretical bounds and worked itself into an untestable state by incorporating assumptions to account for every nuance of the data. What is needed is a theory that accounts for the retrograde amnesia gradient and recovery from amnesia and yet maintains some semblance of parsimony so that it can be tested.

The first problem is to account for the retrograde amnesia gradient. The interval between training and ECS is critical; for example, with a 1-sec interval between training and ECS, amnesia is produced the next day, with a 30-sec interval between training and ECS, retention results.

The second problem is to account for the unique conditions that produce recovery. Time alone, for example, does not produce recovery: simply returning animals to their home cages for several days after training and ECS does not restore retention. Instead, what is needed during the waiting period is a series of test trials, or a single test trial plus reminder shock.

V. THE AFTEREFFECTS THEORY: A FIRST ATTEMPT AT RESOLVING THE DILEMMA

It is worth elaborating on recovery from amnesia, for it has played a decisive role in guiding our theoretical posture. The first clear experimental demonstration of recovery from amnesia was reported by Zinkin and Miller (1967) and, although they used repeated test trials, because they made no note of their importance, it was generally assumed, at least by us, that time alone could also produce recovery. In light of the recovery data and our misimpression regarding the restoring conditions, we dismissed the consolidation notion. It was nonsense to think that memory could be destroyed by ECS and yet eventually recover. Accordingly, we proposed an aftereffects theory.

We assumed that ECS produces neural aftereffects that prevail for several days, thereby interfering with performance during the initial retention tests and resulting in amnesia. We further assumed that the aftereffects eventually subside, thereby permitting performance during later tests and resulting in recovery. If we stop here, however, one question remains: why the retrograde amnesia gradient? If amnesia is caused by aftereffects produced by ECS, then amnesia should not depend on the interval between training and ECS. Obviously it does. The assumption that had to be made was clear: ECS delivered 0.5 sec after training produced greater aftereffects and thereby more pronounced amnesia than ECS delivered 30 sec after training. The rationale for the assumption was also clear: the stress reactions accompanying punishing footshock during training are maximal immediately after training and decay 30 sec later, thereby providing a differential background for interacting with and potentiating the neural effects of ECS.

To engage in an exercise of logic, conjuring up assumptions to account for the data is a necessary first step; to have data supporting the assumptions is the crowning last step. Supportive data appeared on two fronts, neural and behavioral.

Neural support came largely from three studies. As a first approach, Nelson and Fleming (1968) examined whether the neurochemical effects of ECS could be modified by an antecedent footshock. Their analyses, which centered on brain catecholamines, revealed substantially elevated levels in animals receiving footshock followed by ECS compared with animals that received footshock alone or ECS alone. More recently, Chorover and DeLuca (1969) shifted the focus from neurochemical to neuroelectrical events accompanying ECS and refined the analysis to include variations in the footshock–ECS interval. Although comparison among groups indicated that convulsive activity increased in the cortex with increases in footshock–ECS interval, intragroup analysis revealed substantial individual differences. Normally variance of this type would be disconcerting, but, as Chorover and DeLuca point out, because the behavioral effects of ECS on retention are also characterized by variability, it is not surprising that the neural effects should also be characterized by individual differences, especially if they are related to the behavioral effects.

Prompted by the possibility of accounting for individual differences in retention following ECS, Schneider, Kapp, Sherman, and Schoenberger (1970) conducted an experiment in which, in addition to varying the training–ECS interval and monitoring cortical and hippocampal activity, they also monitored retention behavior. They found that relative to the 0.5-sec training–ECS group, the 30-sec training–ECS group tended to show shorter duration of hippocampal seizures and greater retention.

That there is evidence at the neural level for an interaction between stress and ECS is a necessary but not sufficient step to test the theory. What is needed is behavioral evidence: does the interaction between stress and ECS play a role in amnesia? The major evidence for stress playing a critical role in the behavioral effects of ECS comes from studies showing that ECS can be delivered virtually anytime after training and produce amnesia so long as the ECS is preceded by footshock (Schneider & Sherman, 1968). That the amnesic effects of ECS do not depend on its temporal relation with training, but rather with stress-related footshock, provided compelling support for the aftereffects theory. Although some (*e.g.,* Banker, Hunt, & Pagano, 1969) have had difficulty replicating these data, others have extended the analysis to show that potentiation is not limited to footshock but can be affected by such conditions as conditioned aversive stimuli (Misanin, Miller, & Lewis, 1968) or motivational state (Howard & Meyer, 1971). Furthermore, these latter results were not taken as evidence for potentiation but rather were taken to indicate that the conditioned aversive stimuli or motivational state reactivated old memories that were then destroyed by ECS.

The problem is that neither explanation, potentiation, or reactivation, account for the more recent data of Quartermain *et al.,* which clearly show that recovery from conventionally produced amnesia depends on repeated test trials or a single test trial plus reminder shock. This is not to say that the notions of potentiation and reactivation are not important, but it is possible that they simply add a new dimension to the consolidation process (*i.e.,* destruction of reactivated storage) rather than negate an old one.

VI. MEMORY CONSOLIDATION RECONSIDERED

Our aftereffects thinking apparently was an oversimplification and, accordingly, we formed a more complex theoretical base with a wary eye toward testability. Two assumptions were advanced. Neither assumption is new, but together they stand as a unique solution to resolving the disparity between the retrograde amnesia gradient and the recovery data. One assumption focuses on the conditioning processes that ensue during passive-avoidance training; the other assumption deals with the effects of ECS on the conditioning processes.

VII. ASSUMPTION 1: PASSIVE-AVOIDANCE TRAINING— A CASE OF BOTH INSTRUMENTAL AND CLASSICAL CONDITIONING

Recently, with few exceptions (*e.g.,* Tenen, 1965; Pinel, 1969; Herz, 1969), the training procedure used to study ECS-induced amnesia has taken some form of passive-avoidance training. Our attention centers on the stepthrough passive-avoidance procedure.

Animals that receive a single punishing footshock for stepping from a small to large compartment tend to refrain from making the stepthrough response on subsequent test trials. That there is a single training trial, however, does not mean that there is necessarily a single conditioning process. As a working assumption, suppose that there are two conditioning processes (*e.g.,* Church, Wooten, & Matthews, 1970) operating concurrently during passive-avoidance training to effect an increase in the response latency during the test. One process is instrumental avoidance conditioning produced by the *contingency* between the stepthrough response and footshock. The other process is classical fear conditioning produced by the *contiguity* between apparatus cues, particularly those in the large compartment, and the footshock.

It is further assumed that each conditioning process exerts its primary effect at different times during the course of retention testing. On the first test trial, the long-latency retention response is taken to reflect primarily instrumental avoidance: the animal refrains from emitting the response for which it was previously punished. On subsequent trials, the instrumental avoidance response extinguishes: the animal steps into the large compartment. It is at this time, once the stepthrough response occurs, that the classically conditioned fear response comes into play. The cues in the large compartment, the compartment that earlier contained footshock during training, elicit fear. The classically conditioned fear is conceived to operate as an aversive stimulus, re-establishing the instrumental avoidance by serving as a conditioned punisher for the stepthrough response. Specifically, the animal steps into the large compartment, comes into contact with cues that, when paired with footshock during training, became aversive in their own right. The cues in turn serve to punish the stepthrough response during testing in the same instrumental way as, but perhaps to a lesser extent than, footshock during training.

VIII. ASSUMPTION 2: THE EFFECTS OF ELECTROCONVULSIVE SHOCK

A. Destroying Storage of Instrumental but not Classical Conditioning

Suppose that ECS has a selective effect on the two conditioning processes; suppose that it destroys short-term memory of instrumentally conditioned responses but does not affect memory of clasically conditioned responses. This assumption marshals some support from data reported by Mendoza and Adams (1969) and, more recently, Hine and Paolino (1970). The data from both studies agree that the amnesic effects of ECS depend on the type of response used to measure retention: animals given

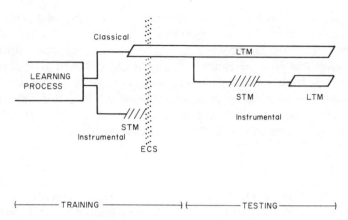

Fig. 13-1. A model of the effects of electroconvulsive shock (ECS) on classical and instrumental storage. Passive-avoidance training constitutes two conditioning processes, instrumental and classical. ECS destroys short-term instrumental memory (STM), but has no effect on classical memory. The classical long-term memory (LTM) serves as a conditioned punisher for reacquisition of the instrumental memory.

footshock for stepping from a small to large compartment and given immediate ECS, when tested the next day show no signs of behaviorally avoiding the large compartment yet do show signs of conditioned fear such as heart-rate suppression, urination, and defecation. Avoidance behavior, such as refraining from stepping into a previously shocked compartment, is usually taken as instrumentally conditioned. Autonomic behavior, such as heart-rate suppression, is usually taken as classically conditioned. In short, then, the data may be taken to indicate that ECS disrupts memories formed by instrumental but not classical conditioning (Fig. 13-1).

B. Accounting for the Retrograde Amnesia Gradient and Recovery of Retention

According to the theory, the retrograde amnesia gradient is produced because ECS destroys short-term but not long-term storage of instrumental avoidance. Further, it is assumed that the amnesia gradient will show on only the first few trials because it is on these initial trials that retention normally reflects the instrumental avoidance.

Recovery of retention, on the other hand, presumably occurs because classically conditioned fear is immune to the destructive effects of ECS and serves, during subsequent test trials, as a conditioned punisher for reconditioning the instrumental avoidance. Taken in this theoretical framework, the stages for recovery can be represented as follows: (1) amnesia or, equivalently, the short-latency response on the initial test trial is due to the destructive effects of ECS on instrumental avoidance; (2) retention or, equivalently, the gradual recovery of long-latency responses on subsequent trials is due to acquisition of the instrumental avoidance; (3) acquisition during the test trials is caused by the contingency between the stepthrough response and the conditioned punishing properties of the apparatus cues in the large compartment; (4) the punishing properties of the cues, because they are classically conditioned, survive the effects of ECS.

C. Testing the Theory

The crux of the argument, although it may seem contradictory, is that the test trial is a learning trial. The test trial serves not to revive memories suppressed by ECS, but to recondition memories destroyed by ECS. Reconditioning hangs on the delicate thread of classically conditioned fear. The reconditioning properties of the test trial, according to the theory, depend on the contingency between the stepthrough response and the conditioned fear properties of the test apparatus.

To clarify the rationale for testing the theory, it is worthwhile to contrast its view of recovery with the more traditional explanation. It is here that the two positions clearly differ. Traditionally, recovery has been taken to indicate the return of an avoidance response originally formed and stored during training. We disagree. According to our position, the avoidance response seen during recovery has no relation to the avoidance that is formed during training. For example, if we could tag the avoidance that is formed during training and follow its course after ECS, we would discover that it is permanently lost, despite the fact that an avoidance *behavior* recovers. At the risk of belaboring the point, recall that this prediction is based on two assumptions: first, the instrumental avoidance acquired during training is destroyed by ECS; second, the instrumental avoidance that we see during testing is a product of a totally new learning experience, one that ensues during testing and that depends on the classically conditioned residues of training.

To test the theory we separated the instrumental from the classical component within the passive-avoidance training and assessed the degree to which each contributes to recovery. Traditional thinking argues that acquisition of the instrumental avoidance is essential; our position maintains that acquisition of the clasically conditioned fear is essential.

As a first step in testing whether classical conditioning alone was sufficient to produce recovery, we searched for a way to eliminate the instrumental and retain the classical component of passive-avoidance training. We have interpreted passive-avoidance training to constitute both instrumental and classical conditioning. Instrumental conditioning depends on the contingency between response and punishment, whereas classical conditioning depends on the contiguity between apparatus cues and punishment. Accordingly, we modified the stepthrough training procedure. To eliminate instrumental conditioning, we dropped the contingency between stepthrough response and punishment; to retain classical conditioning, we placed the animals directly in the large, lighted compartment and gave them footshock. As a measure of effectiveness in eliminating instrumental and retaining classical conditioning, we gave the animals two retention tests, one 24 hr and the other 48 hr after the direct placement training. We expected weak retention initially, because presumably retention on the first test depends on instrumental avoidance, and stronger retention later, because presumably retention on the second test depends on the conditioning effects of the first test trial (*i.e.,* contingency between stepthrough and conditioned fear). The results were encouraging: on the first test trial, the animals showed weak retention and tended to step into the large compartment; on the second test, they did not.

With some confidence that the direct-placement procedure effectively isolated classical conditioning, we proceeded to the main purpose of the experiment. We sought to answer the following question: could retention of instrumental avoidance recover following ECS even though the training procedure was designed to prevent acquisition of the instrumental avoidance? Two groups were given the direct placement training (*i.e.,* placed in the large, lighted compartment and given footshock) and were convulsed 1 sec after termination of footshock. One group was tested the next day and was given reminder shock 1 hr after the test. The other group was not tested the next day but was given the reminder shock. Both groups were tested the following day. Consistent with Quartermain's data, we found that the test trial was indeed critical in restoring retention; the group receiving both the test trial and reminder shock showed recovery, the other group did not. Of course the important point is not that the test trial plus reminder shock produced recovery, but that they produced recovery of an avoidance response that could not have been acquired during training. On this basis we concluded that the test trial serves to produce new learning of the avoidance rather than revive an old memory.

That recovery does not depend on acquisition of the avoidance response during training is only part of the picture. The question remains, on what does recovery depend? We argue that the critical variable is the classically conditioned fear, presumably established by the contiguity between footshock and the apparatus cues and operating during the test trial as a conditioned punisher. To test this notion, we gave animals conventional training (*i.e.,* punishment for stepping from a small, dark to a large, lighted compartment) followed by ECS and the same reminder shock and test trial procedure used in the last experiment with one major exception: we altered the stimulus condition in the large compartment during the first test trial from light (which prevailed during training) to dark. Stimulus conditions during the second test trial were the same of those during training. Our reasoning was as follows: if recovery is due to the conditioned aversive properties of the apparatus cues during the first test trial, then altering those cues should reduce recovery even though the animals are trained conventionally and acquire the instrumental avoidance. Control animals received training plus convulsion and the test-reminder shock procedure, except the stimulus conditions during testing remained unaltered from those during training. Consistent with our prediction, animals given the modified test trial showed significantly less recovery on the second test trial than animals given conventional test trials in which stimuli remained unaltered. Recently we replicated this result using the repeated test trial procedure (Schneider, Tyler & Jinich, 1974).

IX. STORAGE OF INSTRUMENTALLY AND CLASSICALLY CONDITIONED BEHAVIOR: DO THEY DIFFER IN FORM OR PLACE?

The data are clear: Avoidance behavior recovers, even though it is not acquired during training, as long as the conditioned aversive properties of the test trial remain intact. We take these data to support two assumptions: first, the test trial induces recovery because it acts as a learning trial; second, ECS destroys short-term storage of the instrumentally conditioned avoidance but does not affect storage of the classically conditioned fear. A point must be belabored: that classically conditioned storage is not destroyed by ECS is no reason to conclude that it is indestructible. Classical storage, like instrumental storage, may be destructible and may consolidate but, unlike instrumental storage, it may be located in neural sites outside the influence of ECS. Indeed data indicate that the cortex contains circuitry for instrumental but not classical conditioning. Surgically removing the cortex in rats before training totally abolished instrumental conditioning but had no effect on classical conditioning (DiCara, Braun, & Pappas, 1970). Similarly, chemically inactivating the cortex with spreading depression immediately after training produced amnesia of instrumental but not classical conditioning, even after the depression wears off (Schneider, Kapp, & Rosenberg, 1971). On the other hand, the hippocampus may contain circuitry for classical but not instrumental conditioning. Chemically or electrically inactivating the hippocampus immediately after training inter-feres with retention of classically (Kapp & Schneider, 1971) but not in-strumentally conditioned responses (Kapp, 1973).

X. CONCLUSION

The data are encouraging. The theory has withstood its first test. Conceived from data indicating a dissociation between the amnesic effects of ECS on autonomic (*i.e.,* heart rate suppression) and skeletal (*i.e.,* avoidance of stepthrough response) memory, the theory accounts for the single most perplexing result to the consolidation position. It explains re-covery from amnesia without resorting to any device other than basic learning principles. Any definitive conclusions regarding the theory must be held in abeyance until more data become available. It is hoped, how-ever, that the theory we propose here will, at the very least, serve as a working hypothesis for generating new ideas and experiments.

REFERENCES

Banker, G., Hunt, E. B., & Pagano, R. Evidence supporting the memory disruption hypothesis of electroconvulsive shock action. *Physiology and Behavior,* 1969, **4,** 895–899.

Cherkin, A. Kinetics of memory consolidation: Role of amnesic treatment parameters. *Proceedings of National Academy of Sciences,* 1969, **63,** 1094–1101.

Chorover, S. L., & DeLuca, A. M. Transient change in electrocorticographic reaction to ECS in the rat following footshock. *Journal of Comparative and Physiological Psychology,* 1969, **69,** 141–149.

Chorover, S. L., & Schiller, P. H. Short-term retrograde amnesia in rats. *Journal of Comparative and Physiological Psychology,* 1965, **59,** 73–78.

Church, R. M., Wooten, C. L., & Matthews, T. J. Contingency between a response and an aversive event in the rat. *Journal of Comparative and Physiological Psychology,* 1970, **72,** 476–486.

DiCara, L., Braun, J., & Pappas, B. Classical conditioning and instrumental learning of cardiac and gastrointestinal responses following removal of neocortex in the rat. *Journal of Comparative and Physiological Psychology,* 1970, **73,** 208–216.

Hebb, D. O. *The organization of behavior.* New York: Wiley, 1949.

Herz, M. J. Interference with one-trial appetitive and aversive learning by ether and ECS. *Journal of Neurobiology,* 1969, **1,** 111–122.

Hine, B., & Paolino, R. M. Retrograde amnesia: Production of skeletal but not cardiac response gradients by electroconvulsive shock. *Science,* 1970, **169,** 1224–1226.

Howard, R. L., & Meyer, D. R. Motivational control of retrograde amnesia in rats: A replication and extension. *Journal of Comparative and Physiological Psychology,* 1971, **74,** 37–40.

Jacobsen, C. F., Wolfe, J. B., & Jackson, T. An experimental analysis of the functions of the frontal association area in primates. *Journal of Nervous and Mental Disorders,* 1935, **82** 1–14.

Kapp, B. S. Personal communication, 1973.

Kapp, B. S., & Schneider, A. M. Selective recovery from retrograde amnesia produced by hippocampal spreading depression. *Science,* 1971, **173,** 1149–1151.

Malmo, R. B. Interference factors in delayed response in monkeys after removal of frontal lobes. *Journal of Neurophysiology,* 1942, **5,** 295–308.

McGaugh, J. L., & Herz, M. *Memory consolidation.* San Francisco: Albion, 1972.

Mendoza, J. E., & Adams, H. E. Does electroconvulsive shock produce retrograde amnesia? *Physiology and Behavior,* 1969, **4,** 307–309.

Misanin, J. R., Miller, R. R., & Lewis, D. J. Retrograde amnesia produced by electroconvulsive shock after reactivation of a consolidated memory trace. *Science,* 1968, **160,** 554–555.

Muller, G. E., & Pilzecker, A. Experimentelle Beiträge zum Lehre vom Gedaechtniss. *Zeitschrift für Psychologie und Physiologie Ergänzungsband,* 1900, **1,** 1–300.

Nelson, H. C., & Fleming, R. M. Effects of electroconvulsive shock and prior stress in brain amine levels. *Experimental Neurology,* 1968, **20,** 21–30.

Pinel, J. P. J. A short gradient of ECS-produced amnesia in a one-trial appetitive learning situation. *Journal of Comparative and Physiological Psychology,* 1969, **68,** 650–655.

Quartermain, D., McEwen, B., & Azmitia, E. Recovery of memory following amnesia in the rat and mouse. *Journal of Comparative and Physiological Psychology,* 1972, **79,** 360–370.

Russell, W. R., & Nathan, P. W. Traumatic amnesia. *Brain,* 1946, **69,** 280–300.

Schneider, A. M., Geller, E., Moskowitz, D., & Weinberg, J. Recovery from ECS-induced amnesia: A reminder-shock analysis. Paper presented at the meeting of the Eastern Psychological Association, Boston, 1972.

Schneider, A. M., Kapp, B., & Rosenberg, S. Temporary amnesia produced by pre-training hippocampal potassium chloride: A strength of conditioning effect. Paper presented at the meeting of the Psychonomic Society, St. Louis, 1971.

Schneider, A. M., Kapp, B., Sherman, W., & Schoenberger, G. Neural seizure patterns and ECS-induced amnesia. Paper presented at the meeting of the Eastern Psychological Association, Atlantic City, 1970.

Schneider, A. M., & Sherman, W. Amnesia: A function of the temporal relation of footshock to electroconvulsive shock. *Science,* 1968, **159,** 219–221.

Schneider, A. M., Tyler, J., & Jinich, D. Recovery from retrograde amnesia: A learning process. *Science,* 1974, **184,** 87–88.

Tenen, S. S. Retrograde amnesia from electroconvulsive shock in a one-trial appetitive learning task. *Science,* 1965, **148,** 1248–1250.

Tulving, E. Retrograde amnesia in free recall. *Science,* 1969, **164,** 88–90.

Zinkin, S., & Miller, A. J. Recovery of memory after amnesia induced by electroconvulsive shock. *Science,* 1967, **155,** 102–104.

CHAPTER

14

A SINGLE-TRACE, TWO-PROCESS VIEW OF MEMORY STORAGE PROCESSES[1]

PAUL E. GOLD
AND
JAMES L. McGAUGH

[1] This work was supported by Research Grant MH 12526 from the National Institute of Mental Health, United States Public Health Service.

I. INTRODUCTION

There is extensive evidence that a variety of treatments administered to animals shortly after training can either facilitate or impair the memory of the training experience (Glickman, 1961; McGaugh, 1966; Jarvik, 1972; McGaugh & Herz, 1972; McGaugh, Zornetzer, Gold, & Landfield, 1972; McGaugh, 1973). The basic finding of studies of the post-training treatments on memory is that the effects are time dependent: the effect of the treatment on memory decreases as the interval between the training and the treatment is increased. These findings have been interpreted as indicating that the fixation or consolidation of a durable memory trace involves processes that continue for some period of time following the training experience. Yet, it is clear from our experiences as well as from experimental findings that retention of a new experience can be measured almost immediately after the experience. These observations fit well with the dual-trace view of memory proposed by Hebb (1949) and Gerard (1949, 1955) a quarter century ago. According to this view, an experience produces a labile short-term memory (STM) process that promotes the retention of recent experiences and initiates the development of a more slowly developed long-term memory (LTM) trace. A sequential dual-trace hypothesis thus provides a theoretical framework that explains how an organism can show good retention at both short and long intervals after training and, at the same time, explains why the effect of a treatment on memory diminishes with time after training.

However, as discussed below in detail, more recent evidence that is inconsistent with a sequential dual-trace model led to the formulation of an alternative hypothesis, a parallel dual-trace model. According to this hypothesis, both STM and LTM processes are initiated immediately after training. The STM trace grows rapidly and then decays in a matter of hours; the LTM trace grows more slowly and is relatively permanent (McGaugh, 1969; Barondes, 1970). In these models, the longest retrograde amnesia (RA) gradient that can be obtained in a particular behavioral task indicates the time after training prior to the formation of LTM.

Both types of dual-trace models are based on the assumption that memory storage takes time because of biological constraints on the time required for permanent memory fixation—that is, the time necessary for the neurobiological coding of an experience to be completed. However, there is another way to view the same information. Is it possible that there is some advantage in taking time before committing any information to permanent storage? It is clearly not beneficial to store all experiences permanently. Nor is it always useful or possible to evaluate the significance of an experience until information about the benefits or detriments of that experience is available to the organism. Such considerations led us to consider the possibility that time-dependency may reflect the time during which an organism selects from all experiences those that should be committed to permanent storage. Before presenting a model of memory storage that deals with time-dependent memory processes in this way, we will explain how the previous dual-trace models of memory storage account for available data and point out some limitations of these theories.

A. Gradients of Retrograde Amnesia

It was in the context of dual-trace models that the length of a RA gradient became an important issue. According to either the sequential or parallel dual-trace hypotheses outlined above, the RA gradient provides a measure of time necessary for the formation of long-term memory, a time-constant that would be of critical importance to neurobiologists interested in memory processes. Unfortunately, the hypothetical time constant has turned out to be anything but constant. The length of RA gradients ranges from seconds to days—possibly even years (Squire, in preparation). Although the length of an RA gradient was a source of confusion and controversy for many years (cf. McGaugh & Herz, 1972), it was not until recently that the variability in RA length was systematically related to variations in the expected conditions used in such studies. There is now a large body of evidence indicating that the length of a RA gradient varies directly with the severity of the amnesic treatment (Alpern & McGaugh, 1968; Miller, 1968; Cherkin, 1969; Gold, Macri, & McGaugh, 1973; Gold, McDonald, & McGaugh, 1974; Haycock & McGaugh, 1973). For example, using direct cortical stimulation, Gold et al. (1973) found that the length of an RA gradient varied from 5 sec to 4 hr with stimulation of frontal or posterior cortex at intensities ranging from 2 to 8 mA. These results, presented in Fig. 14-1, provide direct evidence for the view that the post-training period is a time during which the susceptibility of memory to disruption gradually decreases. The same data can be replotted to describe a time-dependent increase in the threshold intensity that will produce RA (Fig. 14-2).

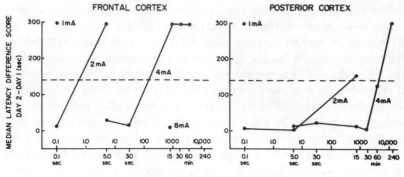

Fig. 14-1. Effect of direct cortical stimulation on retention. Animals were trained on a one-trial inhibitory (passive) avoidance task. After training, direct stimulation (1–8 mA) was administered to either frontal or posterior cortex. Nonstimulated control animals show good (300 sec) retention. Note that the training–treatment interval during which cortical stimulation produced RA varied directly with the stimulation intensity.

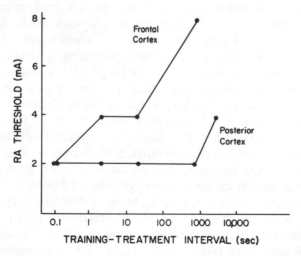

Fig. 14-2. Change with time in threshold intensity necessary to produce RA. The results of the experiment described in Fig. 14-1 can be represented more simply as an increase with time in the minimal intensity necessary to produce RA. These results are consistent with the view that a single memory trace increases in resistance to brain stimulation with time after training. In addition, the results suggest that memory storage may never become completely resistant to amnesic treatments.

Such results suggest the possibility that memories may never be fully consolidated but, instead, simply become decreasingly susceptible to disruption with time after training. Even if the hypothesis of continued gradual consolidation proves to be incorrect, it is very difficult to reconcile results of the RA gradient studies cited above with the traditional sequential processes dual-trace model. It is clear that RA gradients cannot provide direct information about the duration of a STM process if the gradient is influenced by the treatment intensity. However, on logical grounds alone it is possible to conclude that RA gradients need not reflect the time course of a memory process. RA gradients directly reflect only the time-course of the susceptibility of a memory trace to disruptive influences; any statements about underlying memory storage processes based on such evidence are inferential (Weiskrantz, 1966; McGaugh & Dawson, 1971; Dawson, 1971). It is, therefore, apparent that a particular RA gradient reveals neither the time-course of STM nor the time necessary for growth of a LTM trace.

B. Delayed Onset of Amnesia

The sequential dual-trace model of memory also has difficulty handling the results of several studies that suggest that amnesia develops over time after training (Albert, 1966; Agranoff, 1971; Barondes & Cohen, 1967, 1968; Geller & Jarvik, 1968; Squire & Barondes, 1972; McGaugh & Landfield, 1970; Zerbolio, 1971; Kesner & Conner, 1972). In these studies, animals are first trained and then receive an amnesia treatment. In most amnesia studies, retention tests are delayed by 24 hr or more. However, if retention tests are administered at shorter intervals, animals perform well for some time—usually up to several hours—after the treatment. One interpretation of these results is that amnesic treatments disrupt LTM but not STM; therefore, the retention performance reveals the decay of a STM process—a decay that is usually masked by the development of LTM. According to this view, a sequential dual-trace model is therefore ruled out. One way to explain the rapid forgetting curves is with a parallel dual-trace model in which STM and LTM are both initiated soon after an experience (Barondes & Cohen, 1968; McGaugh & Landfield, 1970; Zerbolio, 1971; Kesner & Conner, 1972). According to this interpretation, the rapid forgetting observed after amnesia treatments may reveal the time course of a STM process—information that RA gradients cannot provide. In most of these studies, the decline in retention performance occurs over a 3–6 hr period. If this were the extent of variability, one could assume that procedural differences (e.g., task, motivational level) account for the differences in STM. However, in some cases the time course of forgetting is much more rapid; in other cases the time course is considerably longer. For example, McGaugh and Landfield (1970), Miller and Springer (1971), Zerbolio (1971), and Watts and Mark (1972) found that decay occurred in less than 1 hr. On the other hand, Agranoff (1971) observed accelerated memory decay over a period of several days; Hughes, Barrett, and Ray (1970a, 1970b) found that forgetting was accelerated over a period of several weeks.

More importantly, if the forgetting rate actually indicates the decay of a STM trace, the rate should not be affected by such variables as the training-treatment interval or the intensity of the amnesic treatment. It is therefore of interest to note that McGaugh and Landfield (1970) found that if ECS was administered 8 sec after training, the retention deficit was complete when first tested 1 hr later. However, when the ECS was administered 20 sec after training, retention was still evident 1 hr after training. Results obtained by Hughes et al. (1970a) are even more damaging to the STM decay interpretation. In this study, not only did the forgetting curve vary with the training-treatment interval, but the forgetting rate varied directly with the intensity of the ECS. Forgetting occurred over a period of weeks in this experiment. Therefore, one must either assume: (1) that both STM and LTM are susceptible to disruption with amnesic treatments, in which case forgetting curves do not directly reflect the time course of STM, though they still may indicate the presence of STM (McGaugh & Dawson, 1971), or (2) accelerated forgetting curves need not provide direct support for a dual-process memory theory (Deutsch, 1973; Hughes et al., 1970a).

We have now described two types of results that seem to argue clearly against a sequential dual-trace model. In order to handle these data, the parallel dual-trace models necessarily become rather complex. For example, McGaugh and Dawson (1971) suggest that STM and LTM overlap for some time after training and, in addition, suggest that LTM formation is dependent on the short-term processes (Fig. 14-3). According to this view, amnesic treatments act indirectly on LTM by accelerating the decay of STM. The amount of long-term retention is determined by the duration of STM survival, a rate that varies with the treatment intensity. This model requires a major addition to the assumptions underlying the ancestral sequential dual-trace hypothesis. The model postulates not only STM and LTM processes in parallel, but also that these processes are interrelated in that the strength of the final LTM trace is determined by the duration of the STM trace. Nonetheless, although the model has become somewhat more complex, it does handle the results of most memory disruption and

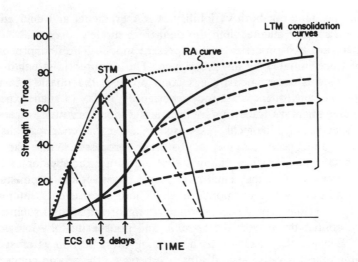

Fig. 14-3. Possible relationship between STM, LTM, and RA gradients. According to this dual-trace model, STM and LTM are in parallel shortly after training. In addition, the duration of STM determines the extent of growth of LTM. Amnesic treatments may then act by accelerating the decay of STM. The decay of STM is shown in this figure by thin dashed lines that descend from the STM curve at the point at which ECS is administered. The accelerated decay of STM results in a decrease in the asymptotic strength of LTM (heavy dashed lines). (From McGaugh & Dawson, 1971.)

facilitation studies and provides an explanation for the delayed onset of amnesia following an amnesia treatment.

II. A SINGLE-TRACE, TWO-PROCESS MODEL

In the previous section we discussed two types of results that add considerable complexity to dual-trace models of memory storage processes—variability in RA gradients and accelerated forgetting after an amnesic treatment. Barondes (1970) noted that although the data obtained in studies of RA gradients are consistent with a single-trace model of memory storage processes, the studies that find a delayed onset of RA seem to suggest a dual-trace model. Similar considerations led us to believe that single- and dual-trace models might both be correct in a sense. In the present model we propose that a single memory trace is modulated by a second nonspecific process. This model attempts to provide a theoretical framework that accounts for both variability of RA gradients and delayed onset of RA in a simpler manner than the dual-trace models.

There are two processes in the present model. The first process is a memory trace initiated by an experience. The asymptotic strength of the memory trace is determined by a second process, the phasic nonspecific physiological consequences of the experience. Thus, (1) an experience establishes a memory trace that is transient (soon forgotten) unless (2) the nonspecific physiological response to an experience establishes a brain state that promotes memory storage processes. Any experience causes specific physiological changes that constitute the memory trace; in addition, an experience may elicit nonspecific physiological responses, such as changes in arousal or hormonal levels. These latter events continue for some time after the experience. Normally, reinforcing stimuli such as food or shock contribute to both the specific and nonspecific physiological responses. Because the mechanisms underlying these responses must differ, we assume that it is possible to distinguish between them both conceptually and experimentally.[2]

According to the single-trace, dual-process model, later retention of an experience is modulated by somewhat delayed nonspecific physiological consequences of the original experience that determine the efficiency of memory storage processing. The mechanism by which nonspecific responses modulate memory storage processes may include any of a variety of influences on the brain such as changes in arousal level or release of hormones. It is also possible that the influence of nonspecific responses is mediated by peripheral events monitored directly by the brain, such as heart rate, blood pressure, a food-satiety mechanism, etc.

Fig. 14-4 depicts how, according to this hypothesis, the strength of a memory trace is influenced by nonspecific consequences of stimulation. The strength of the memory trace is shown as a solid line (left ordinate); the strength of a nonspecific process is shown as a dotted line (right ordinate). The dashed line is a minimal (threshold) strength of the trace needed for behavioral expression (Cherkin, 1972).

In Fig. 14-4a, the curves describe a case in which an event of little consequence to the organism (as defined by the lack of a significant nonspecific response) produces only a transient memory trace. In this case, the transient memory is comparable to a STM trace of other models. In Fig. 14-4b, we see that with a stronger motivational intensity, there is a greater nonspecific response, resulting in enhanced strength of the memory

---

[2] Of course, at a reductionistic level, both of the processes described here may involve very specific biological mechanisms. The relative specifiicity of the two processes is in terms of the information coded for the experience.

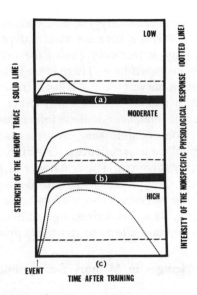

Fig. 14-4. Relationship between a single memory trace and the nonspecific physiological consequences of an experience. The solid line indicates the strength of the memory trace, the dotted line the strength of the nonspecific physiological consequences of training, and the dashed line indicates a minimal memory trace strength necessary for behavioral expression. (a) with low motivational intensity, a memory trace is initiated. However, the nonspecific physiological response is weak and therefore does not promote LTM storage. (b) With moderate motivational level, a sufficient nonspecific physiological response is established to promote some permanent storage. (c) In this case, a strong motivational level produces a high nonspecific physiological response level that promotes optimal memory storage.

trace and prolonged retention. According to this view, both the decrease in strength and the prolonged retention are the direct result of the somewhat delayed nonspecific physiological consequences of training, which are postulated to establish a brain state that promotes efficient memory storage. The intensity of the nonspecific responses will, of course, vary with motivational intensity along a continuum. In Fig. 14-4c, we see that a more intense motivational stimulus will exaggerate the feedback, allowing still greater strength of the memory trace. We assume that an increase in the strength of the memory trace results in greater durability of the trace over long retention intervals: the stronger the trace, the slower the forgetting.

To summarize this hypothesis, then, there are two processes involved in memory storage. The first process is the memory trace. The stability of the memory trace is regulated by a second process—the modulating influence provided by the nonspecific physiological consequences of the experience. The principal difference between this and previous dual-process models of memory storage is that only one of the processes is a memory trace in the hypothesis proposed here. There is no independent STM trace in this model. A retention curve (see Fig. 14-4a) revealing what has been termed STM is simply a special case in which either the experience produces minimal nonspecific influences or these influences are blocked. Thus, this model of memory consolidation suggests a mechanism that selectively promotes storage of significant experiences. Trivial events are stored temporarily and then quickly forgotten. The remainder of this paper illustrates the way the single-trace, dual-process theory of memory storage processes accounts for much of the evidence previously gathered in support of dual-trace models. In addition, we will describe some additional predictions from the model and our preliminary efforts to test these predictions.

A. Time-Dependent Changes in Memory Susceptibility to Modification

Possible alterations in the strength of a memory trace may continue for long periods of time after training. For example, retention performance in rats may improve for hours (McGaugh, 1966; Jaffard, Destrade, Soumireu-Mourat, & Cardo, 1974) or even a week or more after training (Huppert & Deutsch, 1969; cf. Deutsch, 1973). Recent evidence suggests that under special conditions, amnesia or facilitation can also be obtained days after training (Flexner, Flexner, & Stellar, 1963; Cherkin, 1969; Jamieson, 1972; Alpern & Crabbe, 1972; Lewis, Bregman, & Mahan, 1972). In addition, human amnesias often extend weeks (Barbizet, 1970), or possibly years (Squire, 1974), back in time.

We have already described the logic and the extensive evidence that support the belief that the results of RA gradient studies define neither the time course of a STM process nor the time necessary for the formation of a LTM process. It seems clear that the threshold treatment intensity necessary to produce RA increases gradually with time after training (Fig. 14-2). These results indicate that a memory trace becomes less and less susceptible to disruption with time after training. In addition, the results are consistent with the view that the gradual decrease in susceptibility may reflect quantitative changes in a single memory trace rather than a qualitative change from STM to LTM. According to this view, the increasing resistance to disruption may reflect a gradual increase in the neural representation of the engram. Possible mechanisms, for example, include changes in synaptic efficiency of a particular set of cells or an increase in the number of cells involved. As the neural representation of an experience becomes more pronounced, or perhaps more widespread in the brain, a mild amnesic treatment is less likely to modify the engram than is a more intense treatment. Whatever the neural mechanism, the principal point here is that the data obtained in amnesia studies suggest that the susceptibility of a memory trace to disruption changes in a quantitative fashion with time after training. Thus, the model explains: (1) the variability in RA gradients and (2) the gradual increases with time after training in the treatment intensity necessary to disrupt memory.

Thus far, we have discussed memory disruption in terms of a treatment acting directly on the memory trace itself, disrupting the neural representative of an experience before it has sufficient quantitative strength to resist the particular treatment used. However, a second possible disruptive mechanism is also predicted by the model. This mechanism involves interference with the nonspecific physiological consequences of the experience; that is, by eliminating the nonspecific response, a treatment might cause the events to be quickly forgotten, as if they were trivial. This mechanism of action would be particularly useful in accounting for RA gradients of several hours or less, since this time-course would seem to be a likely duration of the nonspecific processes.

At the present time, the mechanisms of disruption by which different treatments act on memory is not clear. However, the model predicts that under some conditions it may be possible to compensate experimentally for the effects of an amnesic treatment on the nonspecific process. Of particular interest here is a study by Barondes and Cohen (1968). In this experiment, animals received either ECS or cycloheximide shortly after training. Forgetting occurred over a 4-hr period. However, footshock or injections of amphetamine or corticosteroids prevented amnesia if the drug was injected shortly after training and amnesic treatment. At longer intervals after the training–amnesic treatment sequence, the compensatory treatments were ineffective. Barondes and Cohen interpreted these data as suggesting that (1) the gradual onset of RA reflected STM decay, and (2) arousal (reinstated by the compensatory treatments) was important for the conversion of STM to a LTM trace. Alternatively, we suggest that the compensatory treatments may replace the disrupted nonspecific mechanisms initiated by training, thus allowing the memory trace to continue its growth in strength as if the amnesic treatment had not been administered. Results similar to those obtained by Barondes and Cohen (1968) have also been obtained using another stimulant. Strychnine administered shortly after an ECS treatment blocks the production of RA in mice (McGaugh, 1966; Duncan & Hunt, 1972). In addition, several studies indicate that stimulation of the midbrain reticular formation compensates for the amnesia produced by fluothane anesthesia (Bloch, Deweer, & Hennevin, 1970;

Deweer, 1970; cf. Bloch, 1970). It is important to note that in all of these cases, the effectiveness of the treatment in reducing amnesia diminished with time after training.

B. Delayed Onset of Amnesia

We have seen that the delayed onset of RA after an amnesic treatment varies with the treatment intensity. In addition, the accelerated forgetting may take place over a period of minutes (McGaugh & Landfield, 1970; Miller & Springer, 1971; Watts & Mark, 1972) or forgetting may occur over a period of days or weeks (Agranoff, 1971; Hughes et al., 1970a, 1970b). According to the present hypothesis, one possible explanation of these results is that the accelerated forgetting occurs because of a direct effect of an amnesic treatment on the memory trace. A memory trace weakened by such a treatment might be expected to decay more rapidly than a trace that is not impaired. Alternatively, a second interpretation of the time-dependent decrease in retention is that the decay curves simply represent accelerated forgetting, which occurs as the result of interference with nonspecific physiological consequences of training. When the feedback is eliminated, very rapid forgetting would occur, as in a case of an experience that is without motivation. Thus, the behavioral results might appear similar to those described in Fig. 14-3a. However, the rate of forgetting will clearly vary directly with the intensity of the nonspecific response to an experience. The extent to which amnesic treatments disrupt the nonspecific events will vary with the intensity of the treatment or the training–treatment interval; we have described several studies that indicate that both intensity or training–treatment interval influence forgetting rates. It is therefore consistent with the present hypothesis that the particular forgetting rates obtained under different conditions may be quite disparate.

Thus, the present hypothesis can account for the same RA data as dual-trace hypotheses. In addition, it accounts more simply for the variability in RA gradients, drug compensation for amnesia treatments, and the variable rate of memory decay after an amnesic treatment.

C. Memory Facilitation

In addition to explaining the results of RA studies, the present hypothesis accounts well for the findings of studies of facilitation of learning with drugs and electrical stimulation of the brain. In agreement with previous models (e.g., McGaugh & Dawson, 1971), one explanation is that facilitating treatments directly influence memory storage processes. However, the present model presents an equally plausible alternative to this view. A major implication of the present model is that if it were possible to impose the nonspecific aftereffects of strong reinforcement on an organism after training with weak reinforcement, that animal's retention performance should be improved. A relatively high arousal level is common to most, if not all, learning situations. It is, therefore, important to note that increasing an animal's arousal level shortly after training may improve later retention performance. For example, direct stimulation of the midbrain reticular formation facilitates retention in many situations (Denti, McGaugh, Landfield, & Shinkman, 1970; Bloch, 1970). Post-trial hippocampal stimulation also facilitates retention in many situations (Erickson & Patel, 1969; Landfield, Tusa, & McGaugh, 1973; Destrade, Soumireu-Mourat, & Cardo, 1973). Furthermore, these effects are time-dependent; *i.e.,* the stimulation is ineffective if delayed after training. In addition, many studies now show that post-trial administration of several drugs will facilitate memory for a wide variety of tasks (McGaugh, 1973). All effective drugs are known to increase arousal level. With all drugs tested, there is an inverted-U dose–response curve for memory facilitation. The dose–response curve for a particular drug on different tasks is not constant. In different tasks, or with different motivational levels, the peak dose for memory facilitation shifts. Our hypothesis predicts that the most effective dose is one that maximizes the nonspecific physiological consequences of training; the most common general mechanism may be arousal level. Traditional behavioral studies suggest that the influence of arousal level itself on learned performance follows an inverted-U function (Malmo, 1967). Thus, high doses of memory facilitation treatments may be disruptive because the arousal level is so high that appropriate memory storage processes are blocked. Alternatively, high doses of these drugs may produce additional alterations in neural activity, such as brain seizures, which disrupt memory storage processes. Low doses, of course, are ineffective simply because they do not add sufficiently to the arousal processes.

This general interpretation is supported by recent findings. For example, Krivanek (1971) pointed out that memory facilitation with pentylenetetrazol is often weak in avoidance tasks (*e.g.,* Bovet, McGaugh, & Oliverio, 1966; Irwin & Benuazizi, 1966; Pearl & McKean, 1967). On the other hand, similar doses of pentylenetetrazol are very effective in facilitating memory when appetitive tasks are used (Krivanek & Hunt, 1967; Krivanek & McGaugh, 1968). Since avoidance tasks are presumably more stressful, the animals' arousal levels are undoubtedly very high—probably higher than in appetitively motivated tasks. According to our hypothesis, these findings suggest that if the task is highly arousing to the organism, the addition of a stimulant (via drug injections) should be of little benefit to the organism, and in fact, may place the arousal level on the falling phase of the inverted-U function. Krivanek (1971) obtained data that directly support this view. She trained animals on an avoidance task using either high or low footshock levels. At high footshock levels, the degree of memory facilitation was smaller and the maximally effective dose of pentylenetetrazol was lower than that found when low footshock was used. It therefore seems that the organism's feedback level after training interacts with the drug injection. Similar results are apparently obtained using post-trial stimulation of the midbrain reticular formation to facilitate memory (cf. Bloch, 1970). Such results are perhaps not surprising, but the inverted-U hypothesis helps clarify the nature of the interaction between the animal's arousal level as produced by training and imposed by the experimental treatment.

General central nervous system arousal level is, of course, not the only consequence of training. Since most of the work being discussed here involves avoidance training, let us consider physiological effects of the footshock other than general arousal level. The primary effects seem to be hormonally mediated. Adrenocorticotropic hormone (ACTH), vasopressin, thyroid hormone, peripheral epinephrine, and gonadotrophic hormones are all released following footshock (Mangili, Motta, & Martini, 1966). We suggest that these peripheral mechanisms may also influence memory storage processes, either via direct or indirect central nervous system action. The prediction is that post-trial injections of some of these hormones will facilitate memory. As is described below, preliminary evidence supports this view. In a sense, these studies simply suggest that drugs other than central nervous system stimulants may facilitate memory. However, these data gain importance because an animal subjected to training will itself release hormones at levels directly proportional to the motivational level used (footshock intensity, in the case being considered here). We suggest that the hormonal levels secreted in response to the footshock modulate the degree to which the preceding information will be stored. At low levels, the events will soon be forgotten as trivial. At higher levels, a brain state is established which maximizes the efficiency of memory storage processes. At very high levels, increased efficiency is overridden by the disruptive effects of the treatments through mechanisms that are not understood.

We will now describe some of our preliminary attempts to examine this general hypothesis. Recently, we developed a one-trial inhibitory (passive) avoidance task that is suitable for studies of memory facilitation. In this task, animals are pretrained to lick from a water spout at the end of a long alley. The task is very sensitive to footshock level, allowing us to set the motivational intensity at low levels without greatly increasing behavioral variability. Retention is measured the day after training as latency to lick from the water spout. We have tested three hormones thus far: epi-

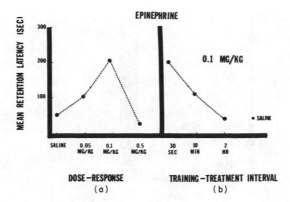

Fig. 14-5. Effect of post-trial epinephrine injections on retention. Animals were trained on a one-trial inhibitory (passive) avoidance task with a weak footshock. Retention latencies of control animals that receive only saline are quite low. Retention latencies of animals that received appropriate post-trial epinephrine injections were significantly higher. (a) Immediately after training, animals received epinephrine injections at different doses. The most effective dose was 0.1 mg/kg, which significantly facilitated retention performance ($p < .001$). (b) As the injections of the best dose (0.1 mg/kg) were delayed after training, the effect on memory decreased. Again, immediate post-trial injections facilitated retention ($p < .001$); in the 10-min and 2-hr delay condition, the injections were ineffective ($p < 0.1$ and $p > 0.2$, respectively).

nephrine, ACTH, and vasopressin. Most of the data we have obtained thus far are based on experiments in which epinephrine injections are administered after training. There is little doubt that an aversive stimulus causes the release of this hormone. The results of immediate (20–30 sec) and delayed post-trial subcutaneous injections of epinephrine are shown in Fig. 14-5. In this experiment, a low footshock level (0.7 mA, 0.35 sec) was used. Saline controls had a low retention latency (*i.e.,* approximately 50 sec latency to lick) as measured 24 hr after training. However, rats that received 0.1 mg/kg epinephrine 20–30 sec after training had retention latencies of approximately 200 sec. Delayed injections were ineffective. As can be seen, the effectiveness of the drug follows the inverted-U pattern. At doses above 0.1 mg/kg, epinephrine appears to disrupt retention performance, although the effect is masked by the low retention performance in the control group. Further, as Fig. 14-5 shows, the same dose (0.1 mg/kg) that produced the greatest facilitation of retention when low footshock was used is disruptive when administered after high footshock (Fig. 14-6). This suggests that the injections of epinephrine have effects that add to the physiological responses initiated by the footshock. The interaction between footshock level and epinephrine injection dose was as predicted by an inverted-U model.

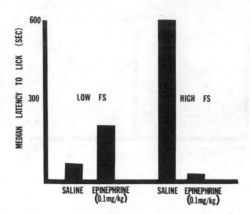

Fig. 14-6. Interaction of motivational intensity and effect of epinephrine on retention. Animals were trained on an inhibitory avoidance task using either a weak (0.7 mA, 0.35 sec) or strong 2 mA, 1 sec) footshock. Immediately after training, epinephrine injections were administered. Under the low footshock conditions, epinephrine facilitated retention ($p > .01$). Under the high footshock condition, the same dose of epinephrine disrupted retention ($p < .01$).

We have obtained similar results with vasopressin and ACTH. When rats were given a moderate level of footshock (2 mA, 0.4 sec), approximately half the animals were facilitated by post-trial injections of a low dose of vasopressin or ACTH. The others were disrupted. Furthermore, the degree of disruption increased as the dose increased. In addition, we found that the effect of ACTH on memory varies with the motivational intensity. In this study post-trial injections of a single dose of ACTH (6 I.U.) facilitated retention when low footshock was used during training and disrupted retention of strong footshock.

Although these findings are preliminary, they suggest that memory facilitation may involve processes that exaggerate the physiological consequences of training. Viewed from this perspective, the importance of an event is defined for the organism by the nonspecific consequences of the experience. The mechanism underlying the modulation of the memory trace by nonspecific physiological processes is as yet unclear. However, in terms of the present model, the important point is that it seems likely that the facilitation may be mediated by mechanisms normally available to an untreated animal under conditions of higher motivation.

D. Behavioral Evidence for Time-Dependent Memory Storage Processes

Thus far, we have described a model that appears to satisfy much of the data obtained in studies designed to modify memory storage processes.

Of course, many behavioral studies may be viewed as supporting dual- or multi-trace models of memory storage processing. This section will review these studies and describe the manner in which the single trace, dual-process hypothesis also handles most of the results with relative ease.

1. Massed vs. Spaced Trials

There is an extensive literature that shows that training administered with brief intertrial intervals is less efficient than training with longer intertrial intervals (cf. Munn, 1950). The optimal intertrial interval varies in different situations but is generally several minutes long. According to dual-trace hypotheses, these results suggest that time is required for the memory trace to attain long-term status. If trials are given too rapidly, all are in a short-term memory system at the same time. Consequently, during the transfer to long-term memory, the value of additional massed trials is diminished. The single-trace, dual-process model explains the same results somewhat differently (Fig. 14-7). After each trial, time is required for the growth in intensity of the nonspecific peripheral processes that are initiated by the trial (Fig. 14-7a). If training is administered with brief intertrial intervals, the nonspecific processes initiated by each trial cannot summate over the first few trials (Fig. 14-7b). An animal still learns reasonably well under these conditions, of course. The value of each trial under massed training will gradually increase since an animal will receive later trials after the nonspecific physiological response to earlier trials has been established. However, spaced trials will be more efficient. Thus, if the intertrial interval is longer, the intensity of the nonspecific response produced by the preceding trial is large at the time of the next trial (Fig. 14-7c). Therefore, the memory of the previous trial has already grown in strength and, in addition, the processes initiated by the new trial produce a continual and increased nonspecific response. Still longer intertrial intervals should be slightly less efficient because of forgetting occurring between trials or because of dissipation of the nonspecific response (Fig. 14-7d). In this way then, the effects of intertrial interval on acquisition rate are predicted by the hypothesis proposed here.

2. Retention Curves

Cherkin (1971) examined the retention performance of chicks at various times after training with a one-trial inhibitory avoidance task. In these studies, the animals received no post-trial treatment. When the motivational level was set carefully, the retention curves showed an increase in retention at very short post-trial intervals. This initial rise was followed by a decrease and finally by another increase in avoidance performance. Cherkin (1971) interpreted these results as indicating that a STM proc-

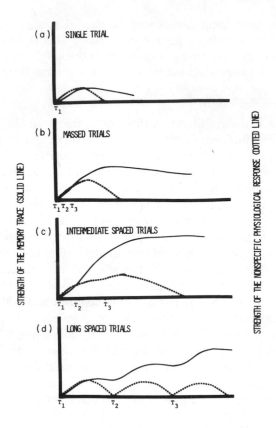

Fig. 14-7. Effects of intertrial interval on acquisition. Strength of the memory trace is designated with solid lines; the dotted lines indicate the level of the nonspecific physiological consequences of training. T_n = Trial Number. (a) Single trial: the weak nonspecific physiological response produced by training does little to promote the development of the memory trace, which then decays rapidly. (b) Massed trials: because the intertrial interval is short, the nonspecific physiological consequences of any one trial add to the relatively low nonspecific state reached after the previous trial. Therefore, although learning certainly takes place under these conditions, acquisition is less efficient than with the spaced trials below. (c) Intermediate spaced trials: this is the most efficient training situation. In this case, the intertrial interval is adjusted so that the nonspecific consequences of each trial add to the maximal response of the previous trial. Thus, acquisition is very efficient. (d) Long spaced trials: only slightly less efficient than (c), long spaced trials occur after the nonspecific consequences of the previous trial have terminated. However, the memory trace has a full chance to develop for each trial; therefore, each new trial adds to the near-maximum memory trace, with very little decay occurring between trials.

ess undergoes initial growth followed by decay. During decay of STM, a long-term process increases in strength, controlling behavior and revealing a second increase in retention performance. Thus, the retention curves were interpreted as indicating that two memory processes control behavior at different times after training. The first is a transient process—STM—which soon decays. However, a long-term process then increases in strength to restore a high performance level. It is important to note that this type of retention curve is seen only under conditions of weak motivational intensity.

The single-trace, dual-process model explains these data in the following way. The memory trace begins its growth immediately after training. The growth can be seen in the results of very short training-test intervals. However, the immediate nonspecific consequences—perhaps central arousal level—of the experience are weak because of the weak motivation. Other nonspecific responses, such as hormonal changes, may require several minutes before the hormone levels are significantly altered. Thus, the trace is established but begins to decay. At a later time, nonspecific peripheral mechanisms (perhaps hormone levels) reach a maximum, causing the now weakened memory trace to resume growth and decay much more slowly (forgetting). Thus, the retention curve may indicate fluctuations in the strength of a memory trace that reveal the modulating influences of the nonspecific process.

In active avoidance tasks, retention curves as measured at different times after training typically are characterized by an inverted-U; this phenomenon is the Kamin effect (Kamin, 1963). In these studies, rats show poorer retention when tested at intermediate intervals after training (usually 1–6 hr) than when tested before or after this time. One interpretation of these results is that the curve indicates a period between the decay of STM and the growth of LTM (Cherkin, 1969; Zerbolio, 1969). According to the model being presented here, the results may reflect the modulating influences of hormones on the strength of the memory trace, as discussed just above.

However, in explaining the delayed dip in retention performance, other interpretations must also be considered. For example, Brush and Levine (1966) showed a correlation between corticosteroid levels and performance at different intervals after training. They suggested that the poor performance seen 1–4 hr after training reflects a temporary deficit in the pituitary-adrenal response to stress. They assume that when an animal's stress response is poor, the animal does not perform adequately in avoidance situations. Thus, the Kamin effect may reflect a time at which performance, not memory storage, is poor because of low pituitary-adrenal activity (cf. Brush, 1971). There are, of course, other alternative explanations of the time-dependent changes in performance (*cf*. Spear, 1971; Barrett, Leithe, & Ray, 1971; Pinel & Mucha, 1974).

More recent evidence also suggests that the Kamin effect may reflect a performance deficit rather than a memory storage deficit. Holloway and Wansley (1973) reported that the retention deficit occurs not only at 6 hr after training but also 30, 54, and 72 hr after training. These results are very difficult to interpret although the possible entrainment of performance to a circadian rhythm is very intriguing. For the purpose of the present paper, however, the results obtained with the Kamin effect seem to reflect a state of the organism during which there is poor retrieval. Nonetheless, it should be observed that these results—with the exception of the Holloway and Wansley (1973) results—can readily be incorporated into the single-trace, dual-process model of memory storage processes.

3. Physiological Correlates of Short-Term Memory

There are many transient neural events that follow training (*e.g.*, Sheer, 1970; Verzeano, Laufer, Spear, & McDonald, 1970; Stamm & Rosen, 1972; Fuster & Alexander, 1971; Fuster, 1973; Olds, Disterholft, Segal, Kornblith, & Hirsch, 1972). These events may be interpreted as correlates of a STM process. However, the physiological correlates of STM cannot themselves define a STM process. At the time of training, the neural output to the periphery and feedback from it are both transient events. Any neural correlate of STM can equally well be described as a correlate of the physiological events outside of the central nervous system or the nonspecific central physiology and consequence of training. As emphasized in the present hypothesis, the nonspecific central and peripheral changes may be a part of memory processing and, therefore, deserve more attention than they presently receive.

III. CONCLUSIONS

The theoretical position taken in this paper is that: (1) A single-memory-trace hypothesis handles available evidence about memory processes at least as well as dual- or multi-trace models. (2) In addition, a second factor is important—feedback about the consequences of the experience. In terms of parsimony, then, we have gained little in comparison to previous dual-trace models. At least two processes are still necessary, but one process is not a memory trace in the usual sense. (3) As usually demonstrated experimentally, STM is a special case of the single-trace hypothesis. We wish to emphasize that it is not time to discard the notion of a STM process. The results obtained do not in any way require the rejection of models that include STM processes. Instead, we simply attempted to describe a model in which it is not necessary to postulate a STM process to account for available data.

A major prediction of the present hypothesis is that post-trial treatments that mimic the consequences of training will under some conditions facilitate retention of that training experience. Although the results are still preliminary, studies of hormonal modulation of memory storage processes provide encouraging support for the hypothesis. Perhaps the best feature of the model is that it relates these physiological consequences of training to memory storage processing by mechanisms that are normally available to an animal. It seems reasonable to us that the nonspecific physiological consequences of an experience gained evolutionary significance in terms of short-term survival. For long-term use of these experiences, it seems likely that the available consequences of experiences began to provide a brain state that determined long-term memory storage.[3] If the physiological consequences of an experience are considerable, the organism would best retain that experience for long periods of time. If the consequences are trivial, the experience is best forgotten quickly. Thus, time-dependent memory processes may be the result of the development of a mechanism with which organisms select from recent experiences those that should be permanently stored.

REFERENCES

Agranoff, B. W. Effects of antibiotics on long-term memory formation in the goldfish. In W. K. Honig & P. H. R. James (Eds.), *Animal memory*. New York. Academic Press, 1971.

Albert, D. J. The effect of spreading depression on the consolidation of learning. *Neuropsychologia*, 1966, **4**, 49–64.

Alpern, H. P., & Crabbe, J. C. Facilitation of the long-term store of memory with strychnine. *Science*, 1972, **177**, 722–724.

Alpern, H. P., & McGaugh, J. L. Retrograde amnesia as a function of duration of electroshock stimulation. *Journal of Comparative and Physiological Psychology*, 1968, **65**, 265–269.

Barbizet, J. *Human memory and its pathology*. San Francisco: W. H. Freeman, 1970.

Barondes, S. H. Multiple steps in the biology of memory. In F. O. Schmitt (Ed.), *The neurosciences: A second study program*. New York: Rockefeller Press, 1970.

Barondes, S. H., & Cohen, H. D. Delayed and sustained effect of acetoxycycloheximide on memory of mice. *Proceedings of the National Academy of Science, U.S.A.*, 1967, **58**, 157–164.

Barondes, S. H., & Cohen, H. D. Arousal and the conversion of "short-term" to "long-term" memory. *Proceedings of the National Academy of Science, U.S.A.*, 1968, **61**, 923–929.

[3] See Kety (1970) for a similar discussion of the evolution of a role for central nervous system biogenic amines in memory storage.

Barrett, R. J., Leith, N. J., & Ray, O. S. The effects of pituitary–adrenal manipulations on time-dependent processes in avoidance learning. *Physiology and Behavior,* 1971, **7,** 663–665.

Bloch, V. Facts and hypotheses concerning memory consolidation. *Brain Research,* 1970, **24,** 561–575.

Bloch, V., Deweer, B., & Hennevin, E. Suppression de l'amnesie retrograde et consolidation d'un apprentissage a essai unique par stimulation reticulaire. *Physiology and Behavior,* 1970, **5,** 1235–1241.

Bovet, D., McGaugh, J. L., & Oliverio, A. Effects of posttrial administration of drugs on avoidance learning of mice. *Life Sciences,* 1966, **5,** 1309–1315.

Brush, F. R. Retention of aversively motivated behavior. In F. R. Brush (Ed.), *Aversive conditioning and learning.* New York: Academic Press, 1971.

Brush, F. R., & Levine, S. Adrenocortical activity and avoidance learning as a function of time after fear conditioning. *Physiology and Behavior,* 1966, **1,** 309–311.

Cherkin, A. Kinetics of memory consolidation: Role of amnesic treatment parameters. *Proceedings of the National Academy of Sciences, U.S.A.,* 1969, **63,** 1094–1101.

Cherkin, A. Biphasic time course of performance after one-trial avoidance training in the chick. *Communications in Behavioral Biology,* 1971, **5,** 379–381.

Cherkin, A. Retrograde amnesia in the chick: Resistance to the reminder effect. *Physiology and Behavior,* 1972, **8,** 949–956.

Dawson, R. G. Retrograde amnesia and conditioned emotional response incubation reexamined. *Psychological Bulletin,* 1971, **75,** 278–285.

Denti, A., McGaugh, J. L., Landfield, P., & Shinkman, P. G. Facilitation of learning with posttrial stimulation of the reticular formation. *Physiology and Behavior,* 1970, **5,** 659–662.

Destrade, C., Soumireu-Mourat, B., & Cardo, B. Effects of posttrial hippocampal stimulation on acquisition of operant behavior in the mouse. *Behavioral Biology,* 1973, **8,** 713–724.

Deutsch, J. A. The cholinergic synapse and the site of memory. In J. A. Deutsch (Ed.), *The physiological basis of memory.* New York: Academic Press, 1973.

Deweer, B. Acceleration de l'extinction d'un conditionnement par stimulation reticulaire chez le rat. *Journal of Physiology,* 1970, **62,** 270.

Duncan, N., & Hunt, E. B. Reduction of ECS produced retrograde amnesia by posttrial introduction of strychnine. *Physiology and Behavior,* 1972, **9,** 295–300.

Erickson, C., & Patel, J. B. Facilitation of avoidance learning by posttrial hippocampal stimulation. *Journal of Comparative and Physiological Psychology,* 1969, **68,** 400–406.

Flexner, J. B., Flexner, L. B., & Stellar, E. Memory in mice as affected by intracerebral puromycin. *Science,* 1963, **141,** 57–59.

Fuster, J. M. Unit activity in prefrontal cortex during delayed-response performance: Neuronal correlates of transient memory. *Journal of Neurophysiology,* 1973, **36,** 61–78.

Fuster, J. M., & Alexander, G. E. Neuron activity related to short-term memory. *Science,* 1971, **173,** 652–654.

Geller, A., & Jarvik, M. E. The time relations of ECS-induced amnesia. *Psychonomic Science,* 1968, **12,** 169–170.

Gerard, R. W. Physiology and psychiatry. *American Journal of Psychiatry,* 1949, **106,** 161–173.

Gerard, R. W. Biological roots of psychiatry. *Science,* 1955, **122,** 225–230.

Glickman, S. E. Perseverative neural processes and consolidation of the memory trace. *Psychological Bulletin,* 1961, **58,** 218–233.

Gold, P. E., Macri, J., & McGaugh, J. L. Retrograde amnesia gradients: Effects of direct cortical stimulation. *Science,* 1973, **179,** 1343–1345.

Gold, P. E., McDonald, R., & McGaugh, J. L. Direct cortical stimulation: A further study of treatment intensity effects on retrograde amnesia gradients. *Behavioral Biology,* 1974, **10,** 485–490.

Haycock, J. W., & McGaugh, J. L. Retrograde amnesia gradients as a function of ECS-intensity. *Behavioral Biology,* 1973, **9,** 123–127.

Hebb, D. O. *The organization of behavior.* New York: Wiley, 1949.

Holloway, F., & Wansley, R. Multiphasic retention deficits at periodic intervals after passive-avoidance learning. *Science,* 1973, **180,** 208–210.

Hughes, R. A., Barrett, R. J., & Ray, O. S. Retrograde amnesia in rats increases as a function of ECS-test interval and ECS intensity. *Physiology and Behavior,* 1970, **5,** 27–30. (a)

Hughes, R. A., Barrett, R. J., & Ray, O. S. Training to test interval as a determinant of a temporally graded ECS-produced response decrement in rats. *Journal of Comparative and Physiological Psychology,* 1970, **71,** 318–324. (b)

Huppert, F. A., & Deutsch, J. A. Improvement of memory with time. *Quarterly Journal of Experimental Psychology,* 1969, **21,** 267–271.

Irwin, S., & Benuazizi, A. Pentylenetetrazol enhances memory function. *Science,* 1966, **152,** 100–102.

Jaffard, R., Destrade, C., Soumireu-Mourat, B., & Cardo, B. Retention on appetitive tasks as a function of the amount of original learning and acquisition-retention interval in mice. *Behavioral Biology,* 1974, **11,** 89–100.

Jamieson, J. L. Temporal patternings of electroshock and retrograde amnesia. Unpublished doctoral dissertation, University of British Columbia, 1972.

Jarvik, M. E. Effects of chemical and physical treatments on learning and memory. *Annual Review of Psychology,* 1972, **23,** 457–486.

Kamin, L. J. Retention of an incompletely learned avoidance response. *Journal of Comparative and Physiological Psychology,* 1963, **56,** 713–718.

Kesner, R. P., & Connor, H. S. Independence of short- and long-term memory: A neural systems approach. *Science,* 1972, **176,** 432–434.

Krivanek, J. Facilitation of avoidance learning by pentylenetetrazol as a function of task difficulty, deprivation and shock level. *Psychopharmacologia,* 1971, **20,** 213–229.

Krivanek, J., & Hunt, E. B. The effects of posttrial injections of pentylenetetrazol, strychnine and mephenisin on discrimination learning. *Psychopharmacologia,* 1967, **10,** 189–195.

Krivanek, J., & McGaugh, J. L. Effects of pentylenetetrazol on memory storage in mice. *Psychopharmacologia,* 1968, **12,** 303–321.

Landfield, P. W., Tusa, R. J., & McGaugh, J. L. Effects of posttrial hippocampal stimulation on memory storage and EEG activity. *Behavioral Biology,* 1973, **8,** 485–505.

Lewis, D. J., Bregman, N. J., & Mahan, J. J. Cue-dependent amnesia in rats. *Journal of Comparative and Physiological Psychology,* 1972, **81,** 243–247.

Malmo, R. B. Motivation. In A. M. Freedman & H. I. Kaplan (Eds.), *Comprehensive textbook of psychiatry.* Baltimore: Williams & Wilkins, 1967.

Mangili, G., Motta, M., & Martini, L. Control of adrenocorticotrophic hormone. In L. Martini & W. Ganong (Eds.), *Neuroendocrinology,* Vol. 1. New York: Academic Press, 1966.

McGaugh, J. L. Time-dependent processes in memory storage. *Science,* 1966, **153,** 1351–1358.

McGaugh, J. L. Facilitation of memory storage processes. In S. Bogoch (Ed.), *The future of the brain sciences.* New York: Plenum Press, 1969.

McGaugh, J. L. Drug facilitation of learning and memory. *Annual Review of Pharmacology,* 1973, **13,** 229–241.

McGaugh, J. L., & Dawson, R. G. Modification of memory storage processes. *Behavioral Science,* 1971, **16,** 45–63.

McGaugh, J. L., & Herz, M. J. *Memory consolidation.* San Francisco: Albion, 1972.

McGaugh, J. L., & Landfield, P. W. Delayed development of amnesia following electroconvulsive shock. *Physiology and Behavior,* 1970, **5,** 1109–1113.

McGaugh, J. L., Zornetzer, S. F., Gold, P. E., & Landfield, P. W. Modification of memory systems: Some neurobiological aspects. *Quarterly Review of Biophysiology,* 1972, **5,** 163–186.

Miller, A. J. Variations in retrograde amnesia parameters of electroconvulsive shock and time of testing. *Journal of Comparative and Physiological Psychology,* 1968, **66,** 40–47.

Miller, R. R., & Springer, A. D. Temporal courses of amnesia in rats after electroconvulsive shock. *Physiology and Behavior,* 1971, **6,** 229–233.

Munn, N. L. *Handbook of psychobiological research on the rat.* Boston: Houghton, Mifflin, 1950.

Olds, J., Disterhoft, J. F., Segal, M., Kornblith, C., & Hirsh, R. Learning centers of rat brain mapped by measuring latencies of conditioned unit responses. *Journal of Neurophysiology,* 1972, **35,** 202–219.

Pearl, S., & McKean, D. B. Pentylenetetrazol: Faliure to improve memory in mice. *Science,* 1967, **157,** 220.

Pinel, J. P. J., & Mucha, R. F. Role of footshock-produced activity and reactivity functions in the production of incubation and Kamin gradients. *Behavioral Biology,* 1974, **11,** 353–363.

Sheer, D. E. Electrophysiological correlates of memory consolidation. In J. L. McGaugh & M. J. Herz, *Molecular Mechanisms in Memory and Learning.* New York: Plenum Press, 1970.

Spear, N. E. Forgetting as retrieval failure. In W. K. Honig & P. H. R. James (Eds.), *Animal memory.* New York: Academic Press, 1971.

Squire, L. R. Amnesia for remote events following electroconvulsive therapy. *Behavioral Biology,* 1974, **12,** 119–125.

Squire, L. R., & Barondes, S. H. Variable decay of memory and its recovery in cycloheximide-treated mice. *Proceedings of the National Academy of Science, U.S.A.,* 1972, **69,** 1416–1420.

Stamm, J. S., & Rosen, S. C. Cortical steady potential shifts and anodal polarization during delayed response performance. *Acta Neurobiologia Experimentalis,* 1972, **32,** 193–209.

Verzeano, M., Laufer, M., Spear, P., & McDonald, S. The activity of neuronal networks in the thalamus of the monkey. In K. Pribram & D. E. Broadbent (Eds.), *Biology of memory.* New York: Academic Press, 1970.

Watts, M. E., & Mark, R. F. Drug inhibition of memory formation in chickens. II. Short-term memory. *Proceedings of the Royal Society of London,* 1972, **178,** 455–464.

Weiskrantz, L. Experimental studies of amnesia. In C. W. M. Whitty & A. L. Zangwill (Eds.), *Amnesia.* London: Butterworths, 1966.

Zerbolio, D. J. Memory storage: The first posttrial hour. *Psychonomic Science,* 1969, **15,** 57–58.

Zerbolio, D. J. Retrograde amnesia: The first post-trial hour. *Communications in Behavioral Biology,* 1971, **6,** 25–30.

CHAPTER

15

PROTEIN-SYNTHESIS
DEPENDENT AND PROTEIN-
SYNTHESIS INDEPENDENT
MEMORY STORAGE
PROCESSES[1]

SAMUEL H. BARONDES

[1] Supported by grants from The Alfred P. Sloan Foundation and The National Institute of Mental Health (MH 18282).

Although memory storage is measured by psychological techniques, everyone agrees that it is mediated by an alteration in functional intercellular relationships in the brain. There are two major questions in contemporary research on memory in experimental animals: (1) how many processes are involved in memory storage, and (2) what biological reactions are responsible? Tentative answers to these questions have been presented (for example, see Barondes, 1965, 1970; Roberts & Flexner, 1969; Agranoff, 1972). The purpose of this chapter is to consider a series of proposals about the mechanisms of memory storage in light of: (1) continuing experimental studies of the effects of inhibitors of cerebral protein synthesis on learning and memory in mice and (2) contemporary knowledge of cellular regulatory processes.

I. STUDIES WITH INHIBITORS OF CEREBRAL PROTEIN SYNTHESIS

A. The Basic Phenomenon

In these experiments on memory, a potent inhibitor of cerebral protein synthesis, usually cycloheximide or acetoxycycloheximide is injected (subcutaneously, intracranially, or intracerebrally) before or shortly after training. Acquisition curves of drug-injected and control mice are compared, and groups of experimental and control mice are tested for retention at one of a number of times after training. If extensive (usually about 95%) inhibition of cerebral protein synthesis is established before and during brief training, the following results are observed: (1) learning curves of drug-treated and experimental mice are identical (Cohen & Barondes, 1968); (2) retention measured minutes to hours after training is normal (Barondes & Cohen, 1967), although the duration of the normal retention varies with the experimental situation (Squire & Barondes, 1972); (3) retention measured hours to days after training is markedly impaired (Barondes & Cohen, 1967, 1968a), although recovery is sometimes observed thereafter (Flexner, Flexner, & Roberts, 1966; Quartermain & McEwen, 1970; Daniels, 1971; Serota, 1971; Squire & Barondes, 1972); (4) in some situations in which the drug is given after training, amnesia develops (Barondes & Cohen, 1968a), although it may not be as profound as is observed when the drug is given before training. The potency of the post-trial injections of the drug is reduced the longer after training the drug is given (Geller, Robustelli, Barondes, Cohen, & Jarvik, 1969).

The simplest interpretation of these results is that cerebral protein synthesis is not required for learning or memory for minutes or hours after training but is required thereafter. However there are a number of objections to this interpretation, which will be considered next.

B. Some Problems in Interpretation

1. Problem of Side Effects Unrelated to Inhibition of Protein Synthesis

It is commonly known that the effects of a drug on a process may be due to some unknown primary action rather than to the action for which the drug is being used. This is not an idle objection because all the cerebral protein-synthesis inhibitors that have been used for studies of this type have detectable side effects that appear to be unrelated to inhibition of cerebral protein synthesis. In mice, the following observations have been made:

1. Puromycin, a potent protein-synthesis inhibitor that produces permanent amnesia if given before training (Barondes & Cohen, 1966) also produces disturbances in hippocampal electrical activity (Cohen, Ervin, & Barondes, 1966) and lowers the threshold to pentylenetetrazol-induced seizures (Cohen & Barondes, 1967).

2. Cycloheximide, another potent cerebral protein-synthesis inhibitor that produces amnesia (Cohen & Barondes, 1967), has no detectable effect on hippocampal activity (Cohen, Ervin, & Barondes, 1966), and does not lower the seizure threshold (Cohen & Barondes, 1967).

3. Cycloheximide affects the spontaneous locomotor activity of mice (Segal, Squire, & Barondes, 1971; Squire, Geller, & Jarvik, 1970).

4. Isocycloheximide, a stereoisomer that has no effect on cerebral protein synthesis and no amnesic effect, shares the activity effect of cycloheximide (Squire & Barondes, 1973; Segal et al., 1971).

5. Anisomycin, a member of a third class of protein-synthesis inhibitors that produce amnesia (Flood, Rosenzweig, Bennett, & Orne, 1973; Squire & Barondes, 1974), produces slight effects on spontaneous locomotor activity of mice (Squire & Barondes, 1974).

6. An analogue of anisomycin that has far less effect on cerebral protein synthesis and no amnesic effect shares this effect on activity (Squire & Barondes, 1974).

These studies indicate that all the protein-synthesis inhibitors thus far studied have side effects that may be unrelated to inhibition of cerebral protein synthesis. Undoubtedly, other side effects would be found if appropriate assays were used. Yet the known side effects are either unique to one particular drug or are shared by structurally related compounds that have neither an amnesic effect nor a substantial effect on cerebral protein synthesis. When added to the finding that three structurally unrelated classes of drugs—puromycin, cycloheximide, and anisomycin—have similar effects on learning and memory, this is strong evidence that the amnesic action of these drugs is due to their shared property of inhibiting cerebral protein synthesis.

2. Problem of Side Effects Caused by Inhibition of Protein Synthesis

Since all these active drugs impair cerebral protein synthesis, it remains possible that they act by producing some nonspecific effect on memory due to protein-synthesis inhibition rather than by inhibiting the synthesis of protein specifically required for memory storage. This could come about in two ways. First, the drugs might make the animal sick by turning off protein synthesis. Fortunately, sickness does not appear until several hours after the drugs are given and disappears within a day. The animals can therefore be tested for retention long after sickness has abated. Yet having been sick sometime after training could be responsible for the amnesia observed later. This is unlikely because administration of the drug to mice 30 min after training in a discrimination task has no amnesic effect (Barondes & Cohen, 1968a, Squire & Barondes, 1972) either when the animals are tested at a time when they are sick or a day later when they have recovered.

Another possibility is that turning off protein synthesis 30 min before training leads to an abnormal brain state at the time of training. This could occur in two ways. For example, inhibition of cerebral protein synthesis might deplete the levels of a protein with a short half-life by preventing its replacement. Were precise levels of this protein required for normal brain function, an abnormal brain state might develop. Inhibition of protein synthesis might also lead to accumulation of a metabolite, such as an amino acid neurotransmitter, whose levels rise because amino acid is not being used up in the course of protein synthesis.

These possibilities are unlikely because of the results of studies on the comparative effectiveness of establishing different levels of protein-synthesis inhibition at different times before training. If inhibition of 95% of cerebral protein synthesis was established only 5 min before training, there was marked impairment of long-term memory (Barondes & Cohen, 1968a). However, if inhibition of slightly less than 90% of cerebral protein synthesis was established for several hours before training and was maintained during training, no amnesia was found (Barondes & Cohen, 1967). Yet prolonged inhibition of close to 90% of cerebral protein synthesis for hours before training should lead to more extensive depletion of rapidly turning over brain proteins (*e.g.* with half-lives of 10 min, the shortest known) and to more extensive accumulation of metabolites than would be the case when slightly higher inhibition was established only 5 min before training was begun. The fact that the latter treatment had a far more potent amnesic effect strongly suggests that the level of inhibition of cerebral protein synthesis during or shortly after training is the critical variable for production of amnesia. This is presumably because the inhibitor must block the synthesis of protein specifically required for memory; the precise level of inhibition during or shortly after training will determine how effectively this result is produced.

3. Lack of Amnesic Action of Cerebral Protein-Synthesis Inhibitors in Certain Situations

Another reason to question a requirement for cerebral protein synthesis for long-term memory is that inhibition of cerebral protein synthesis produces amnesia only under carefully controlled conditions. Extensive experimentation has shown that: (1) amnesia is observable only if brief training is given; with extensive training, normal memory is observed even if 95% of cerebral protein synthesis is inhibited (Barondes & Cohen, 1967; Cohen & Barondes, 1968; Squire & Barondes, 1972); (2) no amnesia is observed if the dose of the drug is reduced so that inhibition is less than 95% in some situations (Squire & Barondes, 1973) or less than 90% in others (Barondes & Cohen, 1967); and (3) in some cases where brief training is given and more than 95% of cerebral protein synthesis is inhibited, only transient amnesia is observed. Memory is impaired 1 day after training, but may be improved or normal when tested 7 days after training (Flexner *et al.*, 1966; Quartermain & McEwen, 1970; Serota, 1971; Daniels, 1971; Squire & Barondes, 1972).

These findings in no way contradict an absolute requirement for cerebral protein synthesis for long-term memory storage. Two alternative explanations may be considered: (1) the protein-synthesis dependent process is induced so strongly by normal training that interference can be observed only under conditions of weak training and almost total inhibition of cerebral protein synthesis; (2) the protein-synthesis independent process may persist for many hours after training and initiate the protein-synthesis dependent process when the effect of the inhibitor has declined.

The first of these explanations underscores the difference between measurement of a biological regulatory response like memory storage and a more directly measurable biological regulatory response, like increased synthesis of an enzyme in response to a perturbation. In the latter case, direct measurement of the enzyme level is possible by homogenizing the tissue and performing an enzymatic assay. Within limits, it is found that: (1) the greater the perturbation, the greater the increase in enzyme; (2) the greater the inhibition of protein synthesis, the smaller the increase in the enzyme level in response to the perturbation. In contrast, memory storage is assayed by the behavior of the animal and probably does not vary linearly with the underlying biological regulatory response. For example, a small degree of training might produce no measurable effect on the behavior of the animal although a significant biological alteration may have been produced in the brain. On the other hand, substantial memory might become measurable only when an extensive response is produced; small increments in training might magnify this response in a nonlinear fashion. These arguments may be restated as follows: (1) the underlying biological mechanism in memory must be measured indirectly; (2) its strength is probably an exponential function of training that may continue to grow while detectable memory has reached an asymptote; (3) the process may be quite redundant. Given these arguments, it is easy to see how brief training and extensive inhibition of cerebral protein synthesis may both be required to observe an amnesic effect.

Another feature of the memory storage process might be inferred from its refractoriness to inhibition of cerebral protein synthesis in certain situations. This finding suggests the operation of a persistent protein-synthesis independent process that may be converted to a protein-synthesis dependent memory storage process over long periods of time. Prolonged training might make this process last longer so that it would be still operative after cerebral protein synthesis had recovered. Long-term memory might, therefore, result. Support for this comes from studies that relate the duration of inhibition after (varying degrees of) training with the degree of amnesia produced (Flood *et al.,* 1972, 1973).

The existence of a protein-synthesis independent process in mice that lasts for many hours is also directly suggested by the finding that memory may be detectable for many hours after training (Barondes & Cohen, 1967; Squire & Barondes, 1972), even with brief training and very extensive inhibition of cerebral protein synthesis. Whereas it might be argued that this memory is due to the very small amount of protein-synthesizing capacity that escapes inhibition by these drugs, a protein-synthesis independent process that lasts for this period of time could certainly be responsible.

There is also support for the possibility that the protein-synthesis independent process can trigger a protein-synthesis dependent process when inhibition of cerebral protein synthesis has waned. For example, it has been shown that in mice trained after injection of cycloheximide, injection of amphetamine 3 hr after training, a time when cerebral protein-synthesizing capacity had substantially recovered, led to the development of permanent memory (Barondes & Cohen, 1968b). This has been interpreted as indicating a conversion of a short-term memory storage process to a long-term memory storage process by an "arousal-producing" effect of amphetamine. If inhibition of cerebral protein synthesis was re-established before injections of amphetamine, the development of long-term memory was blocked (Barondes & Cohen, 1968b).

In light of these findings, it seems possible that protein-synthesis independent memory may last for hours after training and that its duration may be a function of the degree of training. With prolonged training, amnesia may not develop because the short-term process can induce protein-synthesis dependent memory storage when the effects of inhibition are gone. Transient amnesia followed by recovery of memory could also be explained in these terms. Thus it might be argued that the protein-synthesis independent process is no longer capable of mediating measurable memory one day after training but is still capable of inducing the long-term response that develops over days. Other arguments that could explain the recovery of memory and that are consistent with a requirement for cerebral protein synthesis for long-term memory have been presented previously (Barondes & Squire, 1972).

From this discussion it may be concluded that: (1) the failure of inhibitors of cerebral protein synthesis to impair long-term memory if prolonged training is given or if some cerebral protein synthesizing capacity escapes inhibition does not exclude an absolute requirement for cerebral protein synthesis for long-term memory; (2) a durable protein synthesis independent memory storage process that is usually operative for hours but could even be operative for days might be inferred.

II. DURATION OF SHORT-TERM AND LONG-TERM PROCESSES

The outstanding characteristic of memory storage is its rapid onset with training and its continuous persistence for weeks, months, or years. The purpose of this section is to consider: (1) the nature and degree of persistence of the protein-synthesis independent process presumably required for short-term memory, and (2) the probable mechanism for maintaining long-term memory storage for very long periods of time.

A. Nature and Persistence of the Protein-Synthesis Independent Process

A number of biological regulatory mechanisms are independent of cerebral protein synthesis and provide examples of the types of mechanisms that could be used in short-term memory storage. One particularly relevant set of examples involves structural changes in proteins. For the purposes of this discussion, these can be divided into the relatively evanescent allosteric changes and the more stable changes based on the addition or removal of a residue covalently bound to the protein. The former involves a change in the folding of a protein molecule through its association with a regulatory molecule. The change in configuration of the protein alters its function. An example of such a response is the allosteric regulation of the enzyme tyrosine hydroxylase by norepinephrine (Weiner, 1970). Combination with this neurotransmitter reduces the activity of the enzyme. Since the norepinephrine molecule is freely dissociable from the enzyme, this is a very rapidly reversible response, and refolding and resumption of normal enzyme activity occurs promptly upon the dissociation. This might occur within milliseconds but could last considerably longer if high levels of the regulatory molecule were maintained.

A more long lasting configurational change in a protein occurs by covalent addition of a residue to the protein. For example, some proteins can be phosphorylated and thereby activated. There are well-known examples of protein kinases that are activated by cyclic AMP and phosphorylate other proteins (Segal, 1973). Phosphorylation alters the function of the protein; this change persists as long as the phosphate group remains attached. To restore the phosphorylated protein to its previous level of enzymatic activity requires the action of another enzyme, a phosphatase. The duration of such a covalent structural change differs strikingly from that of an allosteric change, although it too may be established within milliseconds of a perturbation. The covalent structural change could last for very long periods of time (hours or days) if not reversed either by a specific enzymatic step or by degradation of the entire modified protein.

There is indeed some evidence that a reaction of this type may occur at synapses. Thus it has been shown that subcellular fractions of brain enriched in synaptic fragments contain a specific membrane protein that is phosphorylated *in vitro* in the presence of cyclic AMP (Ueda, Maeno, & Greengard, 1973). Although it is not known whether or not this protein is associated with a synapse, and whether or not it has any effect on synaptic efficacy, it is an example of the type of reaction under discussion. Recent studies with intact *Aplysia* ganglia maintained in culture indicate that amines or dibutyryl cyclic AMP mediate increased phosphorylation of a specific phosphoprotein (Levitan and Barondes, 1974). The change in phosphorylation persists for hours after removal of the amine, indicating that a change based on phosphorylation may be quite persistent. This is an example of the type of process that could mediate short-term memory for hours in the absence of protein synthesis.

On the basis of present information it is not possible to decide whether or not the protein-synthesis independent short-term memory storage process is mediated by an allosteric change or one dependent on alteration in protein structure by addition or removal of a covalently linked residue. The arguments above, which suggested that the protein-synthesis independent process may persist for hours or even days, certainly favor the more durable covalent process.

There is also a practical reason which makes the covalent alternative more attractive. This is because covalent processes would be far easier to detect than allosteric processes. It might be very difficult to detect a relatively transient allosteric process in an intact synapse because of the limited contemporary technology for such work. Biochemical techniques that require disruption of tissue would probably separate the regulatory molecule from the protein. In contrast, a durable covalent process might be sought by the incubation in the presence of a radioactive residue suspected of being covalently linked to produce the configurational change. For example, search for a relative increase in radioactive phosphate incorporation into a synaptic component in response to repetitive neuronal stimulation is feasible and potentially productive.

B. The Problem of Maintenance

If one accepts that long-term memory is due to synthesis of protein, it is not readily apparent how this change can persist for months or years. This is because proteins in the brain tend to have half-lives in the range of days or weeks (Barondes & Dutton, 1972), which means that normal degradative processes have reduced the newly synthesized protein to half its initial value within this period of time. Because of this it is difficult to conceive of memory storage based on protein synthesis surviving for months or years without either postulating: (1) an unusually long half-life for the proteins that mediate memory storage or (2) the existence of an "autocatalytic" process in memory storage.

There are indeed proteins that have very long half-lives. An example is collagen, the protein in connective tissue. The rarity of such durable proteins make them unattractive candidates for prolonged maintenance of memory, but a protein of this nature cannot be dismissed. It also seems reasonable to consider that the changes that mediate long-term memory storage may set in motion an "autocatalytic" process that leads to maintenance of the altered state produced by this protein. Because of the existence of considerable base-line synaptic activity in the nervous system, this seems an attractive possibility. In this view, the proteins involved in memory storage facilitate a synaptic relationship so that basal release of a neurotransmitter into the synapse now has a higher probability of activating it than in the pre-learning stage. This basal activity and the resultant re-activation might be sufficient to act as a form of "rehearsal" of the memory. It could thereby maintain the molecular change by continuously inducing the synthesis of the proteins that mediate long-term memory storage. On the many proposals about "autocatalytic" processes in the biological literature, the reader might wish to consult one specifically directed to the problem of memory storage (Bass & Moore, 1971).

III. SUMMARY

On the basis of the arguments presented early in this essay, it seems likely that long-term memory storage depends on cerebral protein synthesis, but that short-term memory does not. On the basis of this and the arguments presented in the latter part of the essay, the following series of working hypotheses appear reasonable: (1) memory storage is mediated by at least two processes (Processes I and II); (2) both processes alter the threshold of one or a number of synapses in the nervous system; (3) Process I begins immediately (with no detectable lag) upon training and may last in a detectable form for hours thereafter; (4) Process I is mediated either by a configurational change in a protein or by a reaction that involves the formation or breaking of a covalent bond; (5) Process II begins within minutes after training and augments for hours or longer; (6) Process II is mediated by the synthesis of protein; (7) the protein(s) that mediate Process II have half lives similar to usual brain proteins (days to weeks) but they could be far more durable; (8) if the protein(s) that mediate Process II are not particularly durable, the change in the synaptic relationship produced by Process II could be "autocatalytic."

REFERENCES

Agranoff, B. W. Learning and memory: Approach to correlating behavioral and biochemical events. In R. W. Albers, G. J. Siegel, R. Katzman, & B. W. Agranoff (Eds.), *Basic neurochemistry*. Boston: Little, Brown, 1972.
Barondes, S. H. Relationship of biological regulatory mechanisms to learning and memory. *Nature*, 1965, **205**, 18–21.
Barondes, S. H. Cerebral protein synthesis inhibitors block long-term memory. *International Review of Neurobiology*, 1970, **12**, 177–205.
Barondes, S. H., & Cohen, H. D. Puromycin effect on successive phases of memory storage. *Science*, 1966, **15**, 595–597.

Barondes, S. H., & Cohen, H. D. Delayed and sustained effect of acetoxycycloheximide on memory in mice. *Proceedings of the National Academy of Science, U.S.A.*, 1967, **58**, 157–164.

Barondes, S. H., & Cohen, H. D. Memory impairment after subcutaneous injection of acetoxycycloheximide. *Science*, 1968, **160**, 556–557. (a)

Barondes, S., & Cohen, H. Arousal and the conversion of "short-term" to "long-term" memory. *Proceedings of the National Academy of Science, U.S.A.* 1968, **61**, 923–929. (b)

Barondes, S. H., & Dutton, G. R. Protein Metabolism in the Nervous System. In R. W. Albers *et al.* (Eds.), *Basic neurochemistry*. Boston: Little, Brown, 1972.

Barondes, S. H., & Squire, L. R. Slow biological processes in memory storage and "recovery" of memory. In J. L. McGaugh (Ed.), *The chemistry of mood, motivation and memory*. New York: Plenum Press, 1972.

Bass, L., & Moore, W. J. A proteolytic memory element based on the integrating function of the neuron. *Brain Research*, 1971, **33**, 451–462.

Cohen, H. D., & Barondes, S. H. Puromycin effect on memory may be due to occult seizures. *Science*, 1967, **157**, 333–334.

Cohen, H. D., & Barondes, S. H. Acetoxycycloheximide effect on learning and memory of a light–dark discrimination. *Nature*, 1968, **218**, 271–273.

Cohen, H. D., Ervin, F., & Barondes, S. H. Puromycin and cycloheximide: Different effects on hippocampal electrical activity. *Science*, 1966, **154**, 1557–1558.

Daniels, D. Aquisition, storage and recall of memory for brightness discrimination by rats following intracerebral infusion of acetoxycycloheximide. *Journal of Comparative Physiology*, 1971, **76**, 110–118.

Flexner, L. B., Flexner, J. B., & Roberts, R. B. Stages of memory in mice treated with acetoxycycloheximide before or immediately after learning. *Proceedings of the Academy of Science, U.S.A.*, 1966, **56**, 730–735.

Flood, J. L., Rosenzweig, M. R., Bennett, E. C., & Orne, A. E. Influence of training strength on amnesia induced by pretraining injections of cycloheximide. *Physiology and Behavior*, 1972, **9**, 589–600.

Flood, J. L., Rosenzweig, M. R., Bennett, E. C., & Orne, A. E. The influence of duration of protein synthesis on memory. *Physiology and Behavior*, 1973, **10**, 555–562.

Geller, A., Robustelli, F., Barondes, S. H., Cohen, H. D., & Jarvik, M. E. Impaired performance by post-trial injections of cycloheximide in a passive-avoidance task. *Psychopharmacologia*, 1969, **14**, 371.

Levitan, I. B., & Barondes, S. H. Octopamine- and serotonin-stimulated phosphorylation of specific protein in the abdominal ganglion of *Aplysia californica*. *Proceedings of the National Academy of Science, U.S.A.*, 1974, **71**, 1145–1148.

Quartermain, D., & McEwen, B. S. Temporal characteristics of amnesia induced by protein synthesis inhibitor: Determination by shock level. *Nature*, 1970, **228**, 677–678.

Roberts, R. B., & Flexner, L. B. The biochemical basis of long-term memory. *Quarterly Review of Biophysiology*, 1969, **2**, 135–173.

Segal, D., Squire, L. R. & Barondes, S. H. Cycloheximide: Its effects on activity are dissociable from its effect on memory. *Science*, 1971, **172**, 82–84.

Segal, H. L. Enzymatic interconversion of active and inactive forms of enzymes, *Science*, 1973, **180**, 25–32.

Serota, R. G. Acetoxycycloheximide and transient amnesia in the rat. *Proceedings of the National Academy of Science, U.S.A.*, 1971, **68**, 1249–1250.

Squire, L. R., & Barondes, S. H. Variable decay of memory and its recovery in cycloheximide-treated mice. *Proceedings of the National Academy of Science, U.S.A.,*
1972, **69,** 1416–1421.

Squire, L. R., & Barondes, S. H. Memory impairment during prolonged training in
mice given inhibitors of cerebral protein synthesis. *Brain Research,* 1973, **56,** 215–
225.

Squire, L. R., & Barondes, S. H. Anisomycin, like other inhibitors of cerebral protein
synthesis, impairs "long-term" memory of a discrimination task. *Brain Research,*
1974, **66,** 301–308.

Squire, L. R., Geller, A., & Jarvik, M. E. Habituation and activity as affected by
cycloheximide. *Communications in Behavioral Biology,* 1970, **5A,** 249.

Ueda, T., Maeno, H., & Greengard, P. Regulation of endogenous phosphorylation of specific protein in synaptic membrane fractions from rat brain by adenosine
3′:5′ monophosphate. *Journal of Biological Chemistry,* 1973, **248,** 8295–8305.

Weiner, N. Regulation of norepinephrine biosynthesis. *Annual Review of Pharmacology,* 1970, **10,** 273–290.

AUTHOR INDEX

Numbers in italics refer to the pages on which the complete references are listed.

SUBJECT INDEX

A

Abnormal forgetting, short-term memory and, 6
Acetoxycycloheximide, 11, 381
Acoustic memory, 107–151
  acoustic properties of speech and, 109
  compared to visual, 108–111
  duration of, 108–111
Acoustic similarity, *see* Similarity, acoustic
Actinomycin-D, 4
Active memory, 172–176
Adrenocorticotropic hormone (ACTH), 17, 368–370
Aftereffects theory and electroconvulsive shock, 345–347
Amnesia, *see also* Retrograde amnesia; Amnestic syndrome
  delayed onset, 359–361, 366
  different types of, 284–285
  electroconvulsive shock and, 3–6, 11, 30–31, 349–350, 357–366
  long-acquisition, 59, 70–71

macromolecular synthesis and, 11, 17–18, 379–390
protein synthesis and, 11, 13, 17–18, 379–390
Amnestic syndrome, *see also* Amnesia
  manifestations of, 258
  registration versus retrieval, 259, 276–277
  semantic memory and, 274
  short-term memory versus long-term memory and, 258–259
  short-term memory processes and, 257–291
  theories of short-term memory and, 258–261
Amphetamine, 384–385
Anatomical substrates of memory, 13–14, *see also* Brain damage and memory; Split brain
  amnestic syndrome and, 260–261
  verbal versus musical, 114–115
Anisomycin, 381–382
Antibiotics, *see* Protein-synthesis independent processes; Protein-synthesis inhibitors

403

E

Electroconvulsive shock
  aftereffects theory, 345–347
  amphetamine and, 365
  consolidation theory and, 343–345
  cycloheximide and, 365
  effects of, 348–352
  memory strength and vulnerability, 3–6
  recovery of retention, 343–345, 349–350
  retrograde amnesia and, 3–6, 11, 30–31, 343–345
  stress and, 346–347
  strychnine and, 365
  theory of effect, 350–353
Epileptogenic lesions, 316–325
Episodic memory deficit, 280–284
Exhaustive search model
  long-term memory and, 221–224
  memory scanning and, 198–202
  parallel comparisons and, 213–215
  trace-strength discrimination and, 211–213

F

Facilitation, heterosynaptic, 21, 22, 24
Facilitation of memory
  drugs and, 366–370
  electrical stimulation and, 366–370
Forgetting
  abnormally rapid, 6
  amnestics versus normals, 270–272
  curves, 7–8
  electroconvulsive shock and, 4–5
  experimental amnesia and, 359–361, 366
  long-term retention and, 44
  memory processes and, 330
  resistance to, 42
  short-term retention and, 44

H

Habituation, 32
  cellular analysis, 23
  low-frequency depression and, 22

protein synthesis and, 32
Handedness, pitch localization and, 116–122
Hemispheric specialization, 114–115, 117–122, 274
Heterosynaptic facilitation, 21, 22, 24
Hippocampus
  difference between human and animal memory defects, 316
  long-term storage, 315
  memory processes and, 313–337
  proactive interference and, 315–316, 325–330
  retrieval and, 315
Human short-term memory, 294–295
  compared to monkey, 297–298
  hippocampus and, 313–337

I

Iconic memory, 182, 192
  duration of, 184–187, 192
  Sperling's model, 108, 154
  transfer to short-term memory, 187–188
Ilusion, auditory, 115–119
Imagery, long-trace memory and, 50
Immediate memory span, amnestics versus normals, 269–270
Information processing, visual paradigm, 182–183
Inhibition, presynaptic, 21
Instrumental conditioning
  consolidation and, 339–354
  electroconvulsive shock and, 348–349
  passive–avoidance training and, 347–348
Interference
  distractor task and, 261–273
  interpolated, 49, 112–113
  proactive, 175–176, 259, 274–276, 316, 325
  retrieval and, 247–253
  storage, 69
  theory, 66–71
Interpolated
  interference, 49
  learning, 69–70
  tones and pitch memory, 112–113

A 5
B 6
C 7
D 8
E 9
F 0
G 1
H 2
I 3
J 4